P9-DHC-947

HOW TO STUDY
IN COLLEGE

Third Edition

HOW TO STUDY
IN COLLEGE

Walter Pauk

Director, Reading Research Center
Cornell University

CARNEGIE LIBRARY
LIVINGSTONE COLLEGE
SALISBURY, NC 28144

HOUGHTON MIFFLIN COMPANY • Boston
Dallas   Geneva, Illinois   Hopewell, New Jersey   Palo Alto

125179

Copyright © 1984 by Houghton Mifflin Company.

All Rights Reserved. No part of this work may be reproduced or transmitted in any form or by any means, electronic or mechanical, including photocopying and recording, or by any information storage or retrieval system, except as may be expressly permitted by the 1976 Copyright Act or in writing by the Publisher. Requests for permission should be addressed to Permissions, Houghton Mifflin Company, One Beacon Street, Boston, Massachusetts 02108.

Printed in the U.S.A.

Library of Congress Catalog Card Number: 83-80896

ISBN: 0-395-34250-3

Cover painting: Richard Anuskiewicz, Primary Contrast, 1965, The Currier Gallery of Art: Gift of the Saul O. Sidore Memorial Foundation.

EFGHIJ-BP-898765

Contents

5   YOUR VOCABULARY

7 SPECIAL SKILLS

Preface

TO THE THIRD EDITION

Over thirty years' experience with helping students develop better study skills has convinced me that any student who wants to be helped can be helped. Time and again students have told me that by learning a particular technique for taking notes, remembering what they read, reviewing for an examination, or attacking a difficult subject, they have achieved a major breakthrough. Moreover, it often happens that improvement in one or two study techniques helps a student to solve a range of other study problems.

The Approach of This Text

How to Study in College is based firmly on the belief that students are not primarily interested in theory, and most of them have little patience with solely inspirational talk. What they want is straightforward, practical instruction on how to tackle and overcome their special difficulties. They want something they can readily understand and apply, and something that works. This book stresses practical study techniques which, in my experience with thousands of students at universities and two-year colleges, have been found to work.

These techniques are the product of extensive trial and experiment based on accepted educational and learning theory. Theory is never presented, however, without specific instruction on how to apply it. After all, the person who needs penicillin is seldom cured by learning the history of antibiotics. The chief method of this book, then, is to translate theory and the findings of research into tools which students can grasp and use. In making the book concrete, I have relied heavily on visual examples. Students are shown economical ways of scheduling their time. They are shown facsimiles of lecture notes and the relative advantages and disadvantages of various methods of notetaking. They are shown how topic sentences and transitional expressions summarize an idea and relate the parts of a discussion. They are shown how and how not to mark the books they study, to take notes on their reading, and to answer questions on an examination. They thus learn by vivid example to apply the principles to which research in learning and education has led us.

It is crucial, of course, that students learn rather than merely memorize—that they retain their knowledge so that it provides a solid foundation for more. For this reason I am wholeheartedly against techniques designed solely to help students memorize information the night before a test. Such techniques can fill the mind with "knowledge" that melts away after an examination and leaves everything to be done over again. Real learning results from persistent, careful study, and real learning lasts.

Finally, no textbook, no matter how up-to-date, is truly useful if it is written in a style that is boring, confusing, or excessively difficult to read. I have therefore written and edited with the aim of achieving a conversational tone, to make reading seem like a person-to-person chat.

What's New in the Third Edition?

This third edition of *How To Study in College* is the product of extensive revision and updating. Research into how we learn continues to uncover fascinating new possibilities for enhancing the tasks of students and teachers alike. The results and implications of recent research are incorporated in every chapter of the third edition. Four new chapters on tests and examinations offer students concrete suggestions on how to prepare for and take six different types of tests. A new chapter covers an increasingly important facet of the educational process, "Understanding Visual Materials." I explore five different study systems designed to help students get the most out of their textbooks, and ten new systems for improving reading skills.

The third edition also explains mnemonic devices that can aid students in remembering important information. In addition, discussion of how to listen better was developed to help students get more out of lectures and class discussions.

Every chapter has been augmented by three valuable new features. First, each chapter begins with a list of objectives, so that students can see at the outset what skills and ideas the chapter will present. Second, chapter summaries, presented in a question-answer format, are an aid to reviewing. Third, further reinforcement of chapter material is provided by end-of-chapter quizzes entitled "Have You Missed Something?"

Acknowledgments

Warm and sincere words of thanks must go to those who are deeply and permanently linked to this book: Prof. Marvin D. Glock for giving me the opportunity to enter the field of reading and study skills as a graduate teaching assistant; Ian D. Elliot, now managing editor for a large publishing house, but then an editor for fraternity publications, who helped and advised me in transforming the original mimeographed version into a more readable first edition; and Dr. Nancy V. Wood, now Director of Study Skills and Tutorial Services, the University of Texas at El Paso, but then a graduate teaching assistant in the Cornell Reading and Study Skills Program, for certain materials she originally prepared for that program.

I recall with gratitude the late Henry F. Thoma, the Houghton Mifflin editor who first saw the tiny spark of possibility in the mimeographed version and who encouraged, advised, assisted, and guided me in developing the scope and format of the first edition. I am deeply grieved that during the preparation of this edition he passed away.

My sincere appreciation and thanks also go to those who contributed chapters to this and previous editions: Prof. Kenneth Greisen of Cornell University for his chapter on studying science; Prof. James A. Wood of the University of Texas at El Paso for his chapter on speaking effectively; and Jane E. Hardy of Cornell University for her chapter on writing good papers. The material of these fine chapters has been updated and reworked in the third edition.

I am deeply indebted to two old standbys whose chapters are now included in the Instructor's Manual: Prof. William G. Moulton of Princeton University for his chapter on studying a foreign language; and Prof. Harrison A. Geiselmann of Cornell University for his chapter on studying mathematics.

The latest addition to the acknowledgment list is Ross James Quirie Owens, whose experience as a writer, director, and cinematographer prepared him to put some final touches on the manuscript, but especially on the mini-overviews that precede each chapter and the quizzes that end each chapter. I'm grateful to him for his expertise and friendship.

I must also thank the following reviewers of the text and manuscript for their many fine suggestions:

William J. Bean, *Daytona Beach Community College*

James Blake, *Manhattan Community College*

Sallie Ann Brown, *El Camino College*

David E. Butt, *Pennsylvania State University*

Barbara Clennon, *North Hennepin Community College*

Nannette Commander, *Georgia State University*

Paul Dudenhefer, *State Technical Institute of Memphis*

Marilyn G. Eanet, *Rhode Island College*

John Elder, *Sinclair Community College*

Sarah D. Fine, *Enterprise Junior College*

Pauline B. Griskey, *University of Wisconsin*

Woodrow L. Holbein, *Citadel Military College*

James F. Mullen, *Bloomsburg State College*

George A. Simmons, *Lorain County Community College*

Laurence Welch, *Peninsula College*

James W. Wiley, *Baylor University*

Carolyn Wilkie, *Indiana University of Pennsylvania*

John Zehnder, *Modesto Junior College*

Finally, I am eternally grateful to my many students, who have taught me much so that I may pass on a little to others.

W.P.

To the Student

No two students study exactly alike. A technique that fits your style of learning may not fit your friend's. Just as your personality differs from your friend's, so do your individual strengths and weaknesses.

In this serious business of studying and learning, you have to observe yourself as you study to notice what you do best and when. Such information about yourself is essential if you are to use your time and energies wisely.

What's Your Style?

Here are some examples of what I mean by styles of studying and learning.

Reading, listening, and doing

Some students learn best by *reading*, others by *listening*, and still others by *doing* things. Of course, you must do all three to learn in college, but each individual does one more effectively than the others.

If *doing* things is your strong suit, then you should know that a warm-up period is generally needed before you really get into your subject. But once you get going and concentration is high, you can keep studying for a long stretch without a break. So, when you schedule a long assignment, allot yourself a big block of time to take advantage of your momentum.

The physically active student

If you find it hard to study sitting inactively most of the time, especially when reading a textbook, then try pacing back and forth in your room, stopping only to underline and make notes. During your restless periods, do things that demand activity, such as filling gaps in your lecture notes, looking up definitions of words you've written down, working mathematical problems, filling in the cue column in your lecture notes, underlining textbooks, and so forth.

"I work well under pressure."

What this probably means is that you somehow get the job done; that is, you grind out a paper or pass an exam by working far into the night. The chances are great, however, that the quality of learning will be poor, and what you learn will be forgotten rapidly. There's also the danger of creating a health problem. Working under pressure pushes up your blood pressure, and if blood pressure is pushed up too often, *it will stay there.*

"I work poorly under pressure."

If you do, simply recognize that that's the way you are, and plan so that you avoid pressure. An early start on all your assignments will result in quality learning and in more permanent retention. Those are great rewards.

Sprinters

If you are a sprinter, you can get a lot of

studying done in a few hours of intense work; but after those few hours, the amount of work accomplished drops off. So plan to first study the subjects that require high concentration and comprehension, and leave active work, such as doing math problems, for last.

Long-distance runners

If you are a marathon runner, you can work at a steady pace over many hours and still be productive. Nevertheless, you should do the hardest subjects first, because you too are bound to show some signs of slowing down as you continue to work hour after hour. Save the easiest for last.

The efficient, effective student (and others)

Alex Main of the University of Strathclyde, Scotland, noted that the effective student

Has a regular study schedule
Works to a timetable
Usually works at the same times each day
Works mostly in a regular study place
Works for short periods with frequent rest breaks
Reviews notes soon after a lecture
Does not leave work to the last minute
Does not get easily distracted
Does not need exams for motivation[1]

However, by questioning new undergraduate students, Main found the following:

1. One-third of all students tend to put off work and leave too much for the last minute.
2. Almost half of them get easily distracted when studying.
3. A similar proportion lose interest when things get too difficult.
4. More than a third need exams to make them study.
5. Forty percent of all students have no regular work schedule.[2]

---

[1]Alex Main, *Encouraging Effective Learning* (Edinburgh: Scottish Academic Press, 1980), p. 2.

[2]Main, *Encouraging Effective Learning*, p. 2.

Make Your Own Study-Skills Packet

In this book you will find many ideas, tips, and systems for becoming a better learner, but no one should try to follow them all. Instead, select and try those you believe will do you the most good. To make a wise selection, follow this procedure. First, make sure that you not only comprehend the idea, but also see the reason or principle behind the idea. Second, consider how the idea would fit in with the way you do things. Third, give each promising idea a try to see if it works before adopting it. In other words, look upon this book as a kit from which you can select the pieces and make your own individual study-skills packet, to fit your particular needs and personality. But realize that, to make a new packet, you must discard some of your present ways of doing things. Discarding is hard, so you might want to remember the following epigram by Kirk M. Sorensen: "When the horse is dead, get off."

References to Research

There are a number of references to research in this book. They should not, however, lead you to conclude that the writing is cold and scientific; nor should you conclude that the ideas are written in hard-to-read scientific language. As you will find, the writing is informal, instructional, and as straightforward as possible. There are, however, two reasons why I included references in this book: First, to give credit to the people who originally put forth the data and ideas; and second, to lend scientific authority to some of the statements that I make.

Let me briefly expand on this second reason. We sometimes get tired of hearing the freely given advice of parents and teachers—much of which we assume was okay twenty years ago but doesn't apply now. Since I didn't want my ideas placed in that category, I dug deeply into research to back up my claims. For example, I believe so strongly in the value of a good breakfast to start each day that I sought out the most reputable reference I could find, the U.S. Department of Agriculture. You will notice that brand names of foods are not mentioned in my discussion of nutrition; nor are the researchers part of any commercial corporation. Consequently, the research results that I cite can be taken at face value.

Reading the Chapters

On the title page of each chapter, you'll find a mini-overview, almost like a menu. Read it through, before you read the chapter, to whet your appetite for the content of the chapter. Then read the chapter straight through thoughtfully, and read the chapter summary carefully. Now, with the understanding you've gained from the summary, go back and re-read any part of the chapter that you're especially interested in. Make notes on any techniques or ideas that you would like to try or remember.

End-of-Chapter Questions

These questions were designed to *teach*, not to *test;* you'll find no trick questions and no traps to lead you to an incorrect answer. Take each question at its face value, and answer it to the best of your ability.

Look upon each incorrect answer as a suggestion that you re-read the pertinent portion of the chapter. By re-reading and then rethinking the question and answer, you will greatly strengthen your understanding of the entire concept—which, after all, is the reason you are reading this book or taking the course in which this book is used.

A Final Word

To state in one sentence what I've tried to do in this book, I'll rely on the words of Ralph Waldo Emerson: "The best service one person can render another person, is to help him help himself."

PART I

YOUR GOALS

Many persons have a wrong idea of what constitutes true happiness. It's not attained through self-gratification, but through fidelity to a worthy purpose.

—HELEN KELLER

1
Mastering Study Skills

"Why am I here?" Some of history's greatest philosophers have posed this question about their presence in the universe. As a student, you may have asked the same question about your presence in the classroom. This chapter explains how study skills can help you find and reach your goal. In it, we discuss . . .

- The will to learn
- The power of study skills
- Flexibility
- The secret of mastery
- "The great equalizer"
- Independent learning

and finally

- What this book can do for you

3

*E*DUCATION IS THE GREAT EQUALIZER. Or is it? You may feel that it's really designed to separate geniuses from dunces—and that you come close to fitting in the latter category! College is a big new experience, and for many students it is bewildering.

Consider Joe, a well-meaning guy sitting on a stone bench outside the student union. It is twenty minutes until his first class in freshman English, and he's worried that he won't find the time to do all the assignments. The teacher has a fierce reputation. And two other courses—introduction to electronics and the math survey—sound hard, too. Maybe the course in modern American society won't be too hard. And his last course, small ensembles, should be fun because he has been playing the trumpet since he was thirteen. But, all in all, he has three tough courses and he doesn't know how he will get through them.

Besides, there are a lot of other things on Joe's mind. His morning ride gets him to the campus half an hour too late for his first class, and he'll have to find other transportation. And if he stays after 4:30 in the afternoon to use the library or the gym, he won't have a ride home. He's met a great girl named Jill that he'd like to take to a movie, but he isn't sure how much homework he'll have to do—and then there's the transport problem again. Besides, he still has to break up with his girl at home, and he doesn't know how to do it without hurting her feelings. Maybe he should get a part-time job, so he can buy a car.

His course schedule is a hodgepodge, he knows that. But although he has good SAT scores in math, he isn't sure what he ought to be studying. His adviser told him he would have to decide on a major by the end of the semester, and that's just one more worry. He's taking the electronics and math courses just in case he decides to major in something technical. On the other hand, even though he's good at math, he also enjoys theatre, music, and reading a good book if he doesn't have to hurry through it.

What's wrong with Joe? Not much, really. He is intelligent (you have to be intelligent to get into college these days), he has an amiable personality, and he thinks college is where he wants to be. But he doesn't have a clear idea of what he wants to get out of college, and he has a lot of other things on his mind besides studying. He is temporarily at sea because he lacks a sense of purpose and doesn't know which of his many problems to tackle first. Happily, he soon gets his priorities straightened out as he proceeds through this book.

Contrast Joe with Linda, a sophomore who is intent on becoming an elementary school teacher. She has a special interest in teaching children with dyslexia. She knows her major career goal, and she wants to know everything she can about children and about teaching. In addition, she wants to learn as much about Western culture as her schedule of education courses will permit. So she has planned to take a number of courses in history, literature, and art.

However, Linda has trouble concentrating on her studies, even though she tries. For instance, when she discovered that her new dorm roommate *must* play the radio during study hours, Linda began to do her studying in the library. That was a good move, but it didn't solve all her problems. Her boyfriend has just transferred to another college two thousand miles away, and she misses him. For two weeks now she has been moping around, but she knows that she'd better start working hard on her course in educational psychology. She realizes that she must subordinate other interests and problems to her primary goal of becoming a good teacher.

Now let's sum up. Here are four distinguishing characteristics of the successful college student:

1. The successful student has a clear educational goal (try writing yours down on paper).
2. The successful student recognizes that the college years offer a unique opportunity for intellectual development, and is willing to subordinate other concerns to take advantage of that opportunity.
3. The successful student has good study skills.
4. The successful student has the will to succeed.

"All right," you may say, "that's fine for someone who knows where he's going, but I'm here because everyone else is. I just hope I can decide on a major before it's too late. How can I acquire a clear educational goal, anyway? How can I achieve academic success when I don't know how? How can I compete with the geniuses?"

These are all good questions. And you, yourself, will be able to answer them soon.

THE WILL TO LEARN

The will to learn can count more than all the techniques this book can teach you. Abraham Lincoln walked twenty miles to borrow a book. Booker T. Washington, born in slavery, walked five hundred miles to go to a high school that would give him the education he craved. But what if you don't already have this strong drive to learn all you can? What if you don't have the "passion for learning" that has been attributed to Michael Faraday, who, entirely self-educated, became England's foremost scientist? You ask yourself, "Can I succeed when I don't have the tremendous drive that Faraday, Lincoln, and Booker T. Washington had?"

The answer is yes. Because success, even a small success, strengthens the will. And the strengthened will provides us with additional power to work even harder. This in turn helps ensure more success, and so the upward spiral begins and accelerates.

It doesn't matter which comes first, will or success. In some people, a strong natural curiosity and love of learning lead to academic success. In others, academic success brings a natural interest in the things that one is doing well.

The will to succeed can provide you with the power to get up in the morning, attend classes, study assignments, rewrite a paper, hold out for long-range goals, and do many other things. But if the will is to keep on providing the power, it must be recharged from time to time by the source of all this energy. The source is *success*.

This book can show you the techniques of academic success. It moves from very basic matters like maintaining your emotional balance and organizing your time to such specifics as the best way to organize a research paper and how to study science. We assume that you already have the desire to learn as much as you can. But even if you lack this desire now, a little success based on these techniques will help you acquire it. And if you already know what you want out of college, this book can help you achieve it in the most direct and most effective way.

THE POWER OF STUDY SKILLS

Don't underestimate the importance and power of study skills. Study skills are efficient ways for using your time and mind.

In a survey at a large university, the students were asked about the reasons for their success or lack of success. The two items that were mentioned most frequently are study habits and interest (Table 1.1). To successful students, study skills seem even more important than their interest in a subject. And that's not just my opinion: It's the opinion of people who have first-hand knowledge of the power of study skills.

Students usually recognize the value of study skills, but they are often slow to adopt them. This hesitancy to change old ways is a common human trait. The recommended procedure is to try either one study

Table 1.1 Successful and Unsuccessful Students Rate the Effect of Study Habits and Interest

Reasons Given by **Successful** Students for Their Success		Reasons Given by **Unsuccessful** Students for Their Lack of Success	
Good study habits	33%	Lack of study habits	25%
Interest	25%	Lack of interest	35%

Source: Data from Henry Clay Lindgren, *The Psychology of College Success* (New York: Wiley, 1969), p. 49.

technique or an entire system for only a few weeks, to experience at first hand how these skills work. However, it takes a flexible mind to begin the process.

ARE YOU FLEXIBLE?

Some students continue to use homemade study methods that have, again and again, proved unsuccessful. This may be a sign of inflexibility. To test your flexibility, try to solve the problem shown in Figure 1.1.

Without fully realizing it, we all have enough creativity to get out of the rut. But to get the process of creativity started, we often need some pump-priming. This book shows you how to adapt methods, systems, and techniques of study to suit your unique needs.

The purpose of the nine-dot exercise was to make you realize how difficult it is to break out of old grooves of thinking. Once we see the solution, we think, "How easy! Why didn't I see it myself?" You'll find that this is also true for study techniques. People keep on using their old hit-or-miss techniques when methods are available to help everyone study more constructively and more efficiently.

Effective study methods can be learned and made habitual. One's college life should be run systematically, just as any job or profession is run. Many people have voluntarily reported that they became successful students only when they scheduled their time realistically and used systematic study procedures.

THE SECRET OF MASTERY

With almost no formal schooling, Michael Faraday became Britain's leading scientist. How did he do it?

Figure 1.1 The Nine-Dot Problem. Try to connect these dots by drawing four straight lines without taking your pencil from the paper and without retracing any lines. The solution appears on page 9.

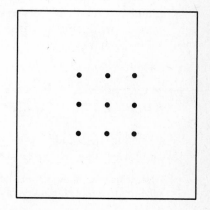

In his carefully kept diary, he tells how he mastered the material given in a public lecture by Sir Humphry Davy, the renowned chemist:

> *On leaving the lecture room I proceeded immediately homewards and in that and the next night had generally drawn up a second set of notes from the first. These second notes were more copious, more connected and more legible than the first.*[1]

Later, Faraday showed his notes to Sir Humphry and inquired whether he had understood the lecture correctly. Davy was so impressed by the young man's industry and intelligence that he offered Faraday a post as his laboratory assistant.

I am *not* advocating the rewriting of classroom notes; rather, I want to point out that the secret of Faraday's thorough learning and remembering of information was his *mastering of the information through overlearning.* Notice that, in the same night, he reworked the notes and amplified them in his own words. To do so he had to rethink the entire lecture, probably reciting it aloud as he rewrote it. This technique of learning and overlearning is the secret of mastery.

To make progress in any subject or field, you must master its basic facts or principles as soon as possible. It doesn't matter whether the subject is accounting, philosophy, or welding. You must master the basics; otherwise you will have nothing on which to build. You will merely be going through the motions of getting an education. You will be putting in time without having anything to show for it.

Mastery converts ideas and principles into "magnets." These magnets then draw the supporting facts and details around themselves naturally, like iron filings. And the greater the mastery, the greater is the magnetic field. This means that you will not only remember the material more accurately and longer, but you will also have established a magnetic center to which you can continue adding facts and details as you encounter them in the days, weeks, months, or years to come.

The real reward for mastering our material is that mastery frees us to *think* with the material. We no longer need to expend our energies merely to retain it. Mastery converts us from filing cabinets into computers with brains. But learning and mastery are personal. No one can do for you what only you are able to do.

STUDY SKILLS: THE GREAT EQUALIZER

By using the study skills explained and illustrated in this book, you should be able to master any assignment at the level of even the most

[1]Reproduced with the permission of the Royal Institute from Faraday's manuscript notes on a lecture on geology delivered by Mr. Tatum, February 17, 1811.

Figure 1.2 Answer to Problem in Figure 1.1. Begin at the top left corner and follow the arrows.

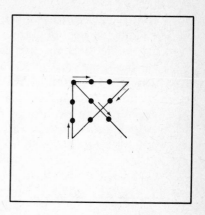

brilliant student. After all, there is just so much to know about an assignment. Once you have mastered it, you have reached the theoretical 100 percent mark. The brilliant student can't do any more than that. He or she may, however, master the assignment in half the time. Some people have, through training, run the mile in four minutes, whereas others run the mile in eight minutes; both, however, run the same distance. This book will help you run the distance. And, if you keep practicing, you will also reduce the time it now takes you. In other words, if you are willing to put in sufficient time and effort, and use the study techniques presented in this book, you should be able to master your assignments along with the best of them. These techniques are designed to help you do the very best you can with the abilities you have.

INDEPENDENT LEARNING: THE GOAL OF STUDY SKILLS

"No one can teach you, but you may learn." Though we may hear or read the greatest words of wisdom, they will remain mere words unless we *internalize* them. We may remember the names of the courses we have taken over the years: algebra, history, geology, French, and so forth. But unless we have internalized the subject matter or have studied it very recently, we will not recall what we have "learned."

With good study skills, you will not only learn material more thoroughly and permanently, but you will also be less dependent on your teachers. As long as you look to someone else for an "interpretation" or "explanation," you will not be a free person intellectually.

To become an independent studier, you must have the desire and courage to open a textbook, read it, study it, and ponder it. Then you must be able to get up in class the next day, or write on paper a week or so later, saying, "As I interpret the author, he says . . . ."

Eddie Rickenbacker, auto racer, ace fighter pilot in World War I, and businessman, had to leave school when he was only twelve years old. Later in life, he fully realized the need for further education. To keep working, earning, and learning all at the same time, Rickenbacker decided to take a course by correspondence. This experience, as he relates it, is a prime example of a person becoming an *independent studier* and a self-learner. Here is his story:

Then I heard of the International Correspondence School in Scranton, Pennsylvania. I wrote, and the answer came back promptly. Even then, in 1905, the ICS had exactly what I wanted, a course in mechanical engineering, complete with a special section on the automobile and internal-combustion engines.

The first lesson, I do not mind admitting, nearly finished my correspondence-school education before it began. It was tough, and I was a little rusty when it came to formal education. I had to teach myself to study all over again, and, furthermore, I had to teach myself to think. I did not realize then, as I laboriously worked away at the lessons all alone, that I was receiving a greater benefit from them than I would have received from the same courses in a classroom. As there was no teacher of whom I could ask an explanation, I had to work out the answers myself. Once I reached the answer through my own individual reasoning, my understanding was permanent and unforgettable.

From the book Rickenbacker *by Edward V. Rickenbacker (Englewood Cliffs, N.J.: Prentice-Hall, 1967), pp. 31–32.*

You may wonder at this point, Why go to college in the first place? or What are teachers for? Well, it is very true that you could study on your own, but you would probably do so inefficiently. Since you do not know the subject, you do not know where to start, how much of a bite to take, and so forth.

College courses are set up on the basis of years of experience. The purpose of the course is to guide you through the various steps efficiently. The teacher is there to explain and amplify your textbook; to direct your research in the library, the laboratory, and the field; to encourage and supervise your self-learning by setting limited as well as long-range goals; to stimulate thinking through classroom discussions; to measure your progress through quizzes, research papers, and examinations.

But only you can educate yourself.

WHAT THIS BOOK CAN DO FOR YOU

C. D. Spielberger, a noted psychologist, found that more highly anxious students not only received poorer grades than less anxious students, but also dropped out of college because of academic failure.[2] Other researchers strongly suggest that students overcome anxiety by using systematic procedures for taking notes, organizing ideas, encoding verbal information, remembering, and so forth.

We all experience some anxiety, and if anxiety can be overcome through good study systems and techniques, then this book might be your answer. Here, you'll find systems and techniques that will not only fit your needs but also blend with your personality. And when study systems blend with your needs and personality, you'll experience success. It all adds up to this: There's no better way to overcome anxiety than with the self-confidence that comes from academic success.

SUMMARY

What's the best way to get ahead in life?	The best way is through education. Some, like Faraday, can make it through self-study, but even Faraday had the guidance of Sir Humphry Davy.
Why is a goal so important?	Everyone needs a target to shoot at; otherwise, time and energy will be scattered. And a goal keeps you going when times are rough.
The Will to Succeed: What is it?	It is the deep-seated blind faith in yourself and in your plan that makes you keep trying (not quitting) even when everything seems to be going against you.
Why do study skills help you to learn quicker and better?	Researchers have found out a great deal about how a person learns. Hard work is necessary, of course, but it is not enough. The hard work must be directed where it will do the most good, by using proven techniques.
What does flexibility have to do with changing habits?	It takes a flexible mind to see the value in a new system, and self-discipline to adopt it.

[2]C. D. Spielberger, "The Effects of Manifest Anxiety on the Academic Achievement of College Students," *Mental Hygiene* 46 (1962), 420–426.

Overlearning: What is it? Why overlearn?

With fifteen minutes of study, you could list the names and dates of fifteen famous battles. But, a day later, you'd find that you'd forgotten 75 percent of them. The only way to remember more is by overlearning. For example, if, after the original fifteen minutes of study, you had spent an *additional* fifteen minutes practicing, you would forget only 50 percent of them. That's still quite a loss, but it's also quite an improvement. The more you overlearn, the more you will remember.

What is self-learning?

Each individual must *personally* think and rethink, in his or her mind, the words of a lecturer or author until they are truly understood. Eddie Rickenbacker said it well: "Once I reached the answer through my own individual reasoning, my understanding was permanent and unforgettable." In other words, *you have to do it for yourself and usually by yourself.*

What's an independent studier?

An independent studier is someone who is willing to spend time alone with nothing but the materials and study techniques that he or she needs to begin and continue the process of self-learning. The independent studier, in the process of self-learning, must be truly free and self-sufficient both physically and intellectually.

HAVE YOU MISSED SOMETHING?

At the end of each chapter, you will find questions similar to the ones that follow. Answering these questions will give you practice in taking tests. Also, if you find you've made errors when you check your answers against those given at the back of the book, these errors can point to chapter topics that you need to review.

1. SENTENCE-COMPLETION. Complete the following sentences with one of the three words listed below each sentence.

   a. More than anything, changing your study habits requires _____.

   intelligence   flexibility   interest

b. Anxiety can be overcome _____.

occasionally   masterfully   systematically

2. **MATCHING.** In each blank space in the left column, write the number preceding the phrase in the right column that matches the left item best.

_____ a. Overlearning	1. Can block acquiring good study habits
_____ b. Study habits	2. Turns ideas into magnets
_____ c. Inflexibility	3. Depends on the will to learn
_____ d. "Hard work"	4. Results in mastery
_____ e. Mastery	5. Often is effort without efficiency
_____ f. Academic success	6. Can be made habitual

3. **TRUE-FALSE.** Write *T* beside the *true* statements and *F* beside the *false* statements that follow.

_____ a. Overlearning should be avoided if possible.

_____ b. The nine-dot puzzle is one test of flexibility.

_____ c. Not all fields require mastery.

_____ d. Self-study can be efficient.

4. **MULTIPLE-CHOICE.** Choose the phrase that completes the following sentence most accurately, and circle the letter that precedes it.

This book will

a. add to your anxiety.
b. eliminate the need for teachers.
c. teach you techniques of academic success.
d. point you toward the right career.

*A man too busy to take care of his health is like
a mechanic too busy to take care of his tools.*
—SPANISH PROVERB

2

Understanding Your Emotional and Physical Needs

Sound mind, sound body. It's tough to have one without the other. A world champion chessplayer trains like a title-seeking boxer. And any boxer would be a cinch to beat if tension and worry took the power out of his punch. This chapter includes pointers on good mental and physical health for boxers, chessplayers, and students alike . . .

- Coping with stress
- Eleven tension releasers
- Tension and physical health
- The danger of being Type A
- Counteracting the artery busters
- Relaxing and how to do it

and
- Seven health habits

plus
- Social behavior
  and academic studies

E VERY STAGE OF YOUR LIFE involves growth and change and decision-making and adjustment, sometimes pleasant, sometimes painful. The college years are unique because they offer the opportunity to devote your time and energy to becoming the person you want to be. A sense of balance and order in living—a healthy emotional and physical climate—is essential for success in college. And it is through living each day realistically that you can best maintain your emotional and physical health.

Most of us worry too much, criticize too much, get angry too often, and become too tense. When we mix such a variety of emotions with studying, we become inefficient. This inefficiency then triggers a cycle of emotions: We begin to worry about low grades and about all the work yet to be done, and we spend so much time worrying that we don't get the work done, which triggers still more worry.

STRESS AND TENSION

Stress is not the same thing as worry or tension. Dr. Hans Selye of the University of Toronto has studied stress since 1936. He says:

> *What is stress? It's the spice of life or the kiss of death—depending on how we cope with it. Stress gives us the means to express our talents and energies and pursue happiness; it can also cause exhaustion and illness, nervous breakdowns, heart attacks, accidents. Strictly speaking, stress is simply the body's non-specific response to any demand made on it, and is not necessarily synonymous with nervous tension or anxiety. . . .*
>
> *Fundamentally, it is not the quality or intensity of the events that counts. What matters is not what happens to us, but the way we take it. That is why I recommend that, in everyday life, you judge how you are taking the stress of your life at any particular moment; if there are too many signs of distress in your feelings and behavior, there are various little tricks to minimize these.*[1]

In other words, stress is the body's response to a demand placed on it—and tension is the wrong response.

Tension can wear out our bodies through high blood pressure, heart attacks, stomach ulcers, and raw nerves. Dr. Selye recommends the use of *deviation* to combat worry. This is the turning aside of a worry by, for example, concentrating on another thought, or involving oneself in some physical activity.

Here are some ways to combat tension before it starts:

First, stay away from situations that you know will produce tension.

Second, be *overprepared* for examinations, discussions in class, and

[1]Reprinted from Hans Selye, M.D., "How to Master Stress," *Parents* 52 (November 1977).

speeches. You'll still feel anxious, but once you concentrate on what you're saying or writing, anxiety and tension will disappear. If you're not overprepared, you'll probably become tense.

Third, if you feel guilty and tense for taking the time to relax—to play, to see a movie, or just to rest, then do this: Before taking time off, work hard at your assignments so that you'll feel you've earned the right for a rest or a change of pace.

Fourth, I am certain that the greatest producer of tension is plain procrastination; that is, not doing those things that we should have done. No pill will cure this one. But the ingredients for curing even an advanced case of procrastination are already in your hands and they are sure and certain: The ingredients are self-discipline and self-organization. Remember, you can take charge of your own life. Henry Ford said, "If a person thinks he *can* do a thing, he's right, but if he thinks he *cannot* do the same thing, he's still right."

Here's how to take control of your life: Before going to bed every night, list on a 3×5 card, in the order of importance or order of execution, the "things to do tomorrow." Then tomorrow, as you do them, say to yourself "First things first," and cross off each completed task. This system will let you sleep soundly every night.

ELEVEN TENSION RELEASERS

Getting rid of tensions can help you maintain and improve both your emotional health and your physical state. (And keeping physically fit will have a positive effect on your emotional state.) The National Association for Mental Health recommends these eleven tension releasers.[2]

1. Talk It Out

When you are worried, it is a good idea to talk things over with someone. It is foolish to bottle up your worries; instead talk with some level-headed person you can trust.

In school you can talk to a good friend or your faculty adviser. Other sources of help include professional counseling services, which are provided by most colleges. If you are worried primarily about your grades, the teacher of reading and study skills can help you. Or you might go to

[2]This material on the "eleven things you can do" is adapted from *How to Deal with Your Tensions*. Copyright © National Association for Mental Health. Used by permission.

the dean of students, who is sure to have information on where you can get friendly help.

Other people to talk to include the clergy, people where you work (including your boss), and members of your family or family friends.

Above all, *talk to somebody.* Talking things out helps relieve strain, helps you see your worry in a clearer light, and often helps you see what you can do about it.

2. Escape for a While

When things go wrong, it is often helpful to get away from the problem for a while, to lose yourself in some kind of activity. In school, walk over to the gym to shoot some baskets, go see a movie, or read an interesting magazine. If it is evening, take a shower and go to bed early to rest a weary body and mind.

If you cannot physically get away from your problem, try an *imaginary* escape to a quiet book-lined study, a small lake high in the mountains, or whatever place you find especially peaceful. Even a few moments in your imaginary retreat can refresh you.

Another way to escape is to decide that you will not face a certain problem until a specified time. "Tomorrow at nine-thirty I will consider topics for my research paper." Then you are completely free of that problem until nine-thirty tomorrow.

Making yourself stand there and suffer can be a form of self-punishment, not a way to solve a problem. It is perfectly realistic to escape long enough to recover your perspective and renew your strength. That way, you can come back and deal with your difficulty when you are in better condition emotionally and mentally.

3. Channel Your Anger

If you find that you're "blowing your top" pretty regularly, remember that this action may give you a *temporary* sense of righteousness or power, but it will probably leave you feeling foolish and sorry in the end. If you feel like lashing out at someone, try holding off for awhile until you can put your emotional energy to some good use. A good way to hold off is to hum a tune—any old tune—to yourself. Or inwardly recite some poem you learned long ago, or visualize last summer's vacation trip. Do anything to put your mental and emotional energies on another track. Whatever you do, do it calmly, because you will then have a powerful principle of psychology working for you: If you act with outward calmness, the chances are great that you will gain genuine inward calmness.

Some people control themselves in this way: They hold their tongues, but mentally rehearse how they will "tell the person off" tomorrow. Then they seldom find any need to do so actually. Frequently, the next day, they have a sheepish smile for the other person who, in turn, responds with a smile. Other people control their anger by playing a hard game of tennis or working extra hard on a tough assignment. The important principle here is to channel your "angry" energy constructively.

Furthermore, as a student, you should know this: Anger destroys thought. Have you ever tried to think rationally when angry? It can't be done. So learn to keep anger out.

Sometimes a real problem has caused the anger. In that case, waiting a day or two will leave you much better prepared to handle the problem intelligently.

4. Give in Occasionally

If you find yourself getting into frequent quarrels, try standing your ground only on what you sincerely believe is right. But then do so calmly, and make allowance for the fact that you *could* be wrong. Even if you're dead right, it's easier on your system to give in once in a while on matters that are not fundamentally important. If you yield some ground, you'll usually find that others will too. The result will be a relief from tension, possibly a practical solution, and a satisfying sense of having achieved control over your emotions.

A practical way to avoid arguments is this. No matter how sure you are of a fact or idea, put yourself in a neutral corner by starting with a tentative remark like "I may be wrong, but as I see it . . ." or "Don't you think that . . . ?" Notice the difference. If you had instead said, "I believe that . . . ," you would have put yourself into a tight corner. Then if your listener confronted you by saying, "I don't agree with you," you would have had to come out fighting.

5. Do Something for Others

If you worry about *yourself* all the time, try doing something for *somebody else*. This technique will take the steam out of your own worries and—even better—give you a fine feeling of having done something worthwhile.

If you know someone who is heavy with worries, here are two things you can do to help. First, let the person know that you're interested, that you care. A person who's "fighting the whole world" will be relieved to know someone wants to be on his or her side. Your friendly attitude can help this person to calm down and adopt a more relaxed attitude toward life.

Second, be a good listener. People with worries need someone with whom they can share their troubles. Make yourself available, and when the person starts talking, listen quietly with little interruption. You don't need to criticize or give advice; just listen and show that you care.

6. Take One Thing at a Time

For people under tension, an ordinary work load can seem unbearable. Remember that this is a temporary condition. You can work your way out of it. How? By tackling a few of the most urgent tasks one at a time. Once you take care of the first few items, you'll see that the rest can also be done.

Sometimes a person's obligations really do outrun the time available for them. In that case, the least important things must be left undone, however painful that may be. Certainly it is less painful than collapsing from overwork. However, most people who feel that they are under too much pressure are suffering more from the *feeling* than from actual overwork.

There's great practical value in dealing with your worries and cares one at a time. Consider this story of a father, in Italy, who tied a bundle of small sticks together with a strand of twine. Handing the bundle to his son, he said, "Here, break these sticks in half."

Using his hands, knees, and feet, and try as he might, the son could not snap a single stick. Tired and sad, the boy said, "Father, take back the bundle, I cannot break it." Without a word, the father untied the twine and, using only his fingers, snapped each stick, one by one.

The lesson is clear: Unbundle your cares and worries, and solve them one by one.

7. Don't Be Too Hard on Yourself

Some people expect too much from themselves and are in a constant state of worry and anxiety because they think they are not achieving as much as they should. They try for perfection in everything. Admirable as this ideal is, it is an invitation to failure, for no one can be perfect in everything. Decide which things you do well (usually they are the things you like to do best, the things that are most important to you), and put your major effort into these. As for the things you can't do so well, give them an honest effort, but don't take yourself to task if you can't achieve top honors or break records.

Don't belittle your accomplishments by comparing them with stories you hear about the accomplishments of others. Remember, you hear only about the successes, not the many failures. The other person is just as fallible as you are.

Finally, do *not* go to bed with thoughts of failure in your head. End up your study by reading a short story or essay on your favorite subject. Keep a special book handy for this. I often turn to Washington Irving's *Sketch Book* and go to bed smiling at the thought of Ichabod Crane; or, I leaf through an outdoor-products catalog and go to bed thinking about next summer's canoe trip.

8. Go Easy with Your Criticism

Some people expect too much of others and feel frustrated, even betrayed, when another person does not measure up to those expectations. Each person has his or her own virtues, shortcomings, values, and right to develop as an individual. We are unfair to others when we try to fit them into our pattern. If you find a lot to criticize in other people, perhaps you are holding them to a standard that you would like to attain yourself. Instead of being critical of others, search out and encourage their good qualities. You and they will feel better for it.

One way to keep a rational perspective is to remember these words of the great German writer and thinker, Goethe: "I see no fault committed by others that I have not committed myself."

9. Give the Other Person a Break

When you are under emotional tension, you may feel that you have to "get there first"—to edge out the other person, even if the goal is as trivial as getting ahead in a cafeteria line. Everything becomes a contest, and somebody is bound to get hurt, either physically, as on the highway, or emotionally and mentally in the endeavor to lead a full life. It need not be this way; competition is contagious, but so is cooperation. When you give the other person a break, you often make things easier for yourself. When people no longer feel that you are a threat to them, they stop being a threat to you.

10. Make Yourself Available

Many of us have the feeling that we are being left out, neglected, rejected. Often we just imagine that others are slighting us, when in reality they are eager for us to make the first move. Instead of shrinking away and withdrawing, it is healthier and more practical to keep yourself available and to make some of the overtures instead of always waiting to be asked. Of course, it is equally a mistake to push yourself forward on every occasion. Doing so is often misinterpreted, and it may lead to real rejection. There is a middle ground between withdrawing and pushing. *Try it.*

11. Take Time out for Recreation

Many people drive themselves so hard that they allow themselves too little time for recreation. And recreation is essential for good physical, mental, and emotional health. People who find it hard to take time out should schedule definite hours for some form of recreation—tennis, squash, jogging, or just plain walking. Almost everyone feels refreshed after working for an hour or so on a hobby or other absorbing interest. And almost everyone benefits from a change of pace from the usual work or study.

Exercise is an especially good form of recreation because it permits you to "blow off steam" in a way that is good for you and good for your friends. Not only is it good for you emotionally, but it keeps you in good physical condition as well. Moreover, recent biochemical research indicates that regular exercise increases the level of endorphins (chemicals) in the brain. These chemicals affect one's sense of well-being. The more endorphins, the better you feel and the better your outlook on life.

TENSION AND HEART ATTACKS

Tension can become a habit—a part of a person's behavior pattern. And an unhealthy behavior pattern can lead to heart attack at a relatively early age, according to Dr. Meyer Friedman and Dr. Ray Rosenman.[3] These two researchers identified the well-known Type A (unhealthy) and Type B (healthy) behavior patterns. In the United States, about 50 percent of the population exhibit Type A behavior, about 40 percent exhibit Type B, and about 10 percent exhibit a combination of the two.

Type A (High Risk) Behavior

Here's the behavior pattern that destroys the heart's arteries:

1. Excessive competitiveness (always out to beat everyone)
2. Constant impatience (always complaining while standing in line)

[3]Rosenman, R. H., et al., "Coronary Heart Disease in the Western Collaborative Group Study," *Journal of the American Medical Association*, 233, No. 8 (1975), 872–877.

3. Struggle with time (always rushing to do just one more thing)
4. Insecurity (always talking of past achievements)
5. Aggressiveness (always physically edging out both people and cars)
6. Free-floating hostility (always having someone to dislike)
7. Concern about numbers (always counting possessions or accomplishments)

The behavior pattern you develop in college will continue right on into your business, professional, and personal life. The chances are that if you're Type A in college, you'll probably be a super–Type A in the business world. The saving grace is that you can be whatever you want to be. If you judge that you now have some Type A habits, begin *right now* to redirect yourself toward a healthy personality with a life-saving behavior pattern. Here are some things you can do. The eleven tension releasers will also help, and so will the health habits discussed later in this chapter.

How to Counteract the Seven Artery Busters

1. EXCESSIVE COMPETITIVENESS.   Take every opportunity to be magnanimous (genuinely unselfish). The mellow, righteous, comforting feeling will add years to your life.

2. CONSTANT IMPATIENCE.   Fuming, while standing in line, will change stress into distress. To convert "waiting in line" into a pleasant experience, whip out your pocket dictionary and *read* it. Open it to any page, and just read definitions. There's adventure, wonder, and knowledge in every entry.

3. STRUGGLE WITH TIME.   The solution is going to bed an hour earlier and getting up an hour sooner, to get a head start on the day. And a leisurely breakfast will set a positive tone for the rest of the day.

4. INSECURITY.   Don't talk about your past successes. Your accomplishments will be discovered naturally in conversation. Then, people will have a high regard for you because you didn't brag about them.

5. AGGRESSIVENESS.   Have you ever been caught in the wrong line of traffic and had to move over into another lane? Remember how grateful you were when some considerate soul let you move in? Well, when you let someone else move in in front of you, in a similar situation, that feeling will be even better.

6. FREE-FLOATING HOSTILITY.   Of the seven behaviors on this list, I believe this is the most corrosive. It involves an unusually strong and secretive dislike for one or more people. Whenever an opportunity arises, unfavorable comments are made. The hostile person tries to "look good" by making others "look bad." To regain your perspective, help others in little ways, such as by holding a door open for someone, or even by smiling more and saying more thoughtful and sincere "good mornings."

7. CONCERN ABOUT NUMBERS.   The root of this behavior is one's desire to gain friends and be recognized and praised by them. The idea is that possessions and accomplishments will attract the praise of smiling friends. There are, however, at least two flaws in behavior of this sort: First, there will never be *enough*; and second, that's no way to gain friends. So work hard, but don't make possessions and accomplishments your life's only goals. Also, don't boast about them, and keep them in proper perspective.

RELAXING YOUR TENSIONS AWAY

Whether you're playing golf or baseball, singing or dancing, studying or reciting, every good teacher will tell you to do so in a relaxed way. Yes, work hard—but never under tension, and do not strain.

Relaxation not only makes you feel better and thus work better, but it affects your memory as well. Memory doesn't work well under tension and strain. You know how vexing it is when you have a name on the tip of your tongue, but the name just won't come forth. Then, when you stop straining and begin talking about something else in a relaxed and normal way, the name comes bobbing up like a cork.

Your memory will work best when your mind is not under tension and when you are not straining. This is important to know because hours of studying will be useless if you can't remember what you've learned. But suppose you're using the eleven tension relievers and working on a healthy behavior pattern. You get plenty of sleep and eat reasonably. Yet ten minutes before an important exam you feel as tense as you've ever been. What can you do to relax? Plenty! Here are four sure-fire relaxation methods, followed by one tension preventer.

The Count-of-Three Method

Just before an exam, just before an interview, or just before seeing a dentist, your palms are sweating, your body is tense, and your breath is short and shallow. Here's what to do (count slowly and calmly through each step):

1. Through the nose, inhale slowly while silently counting to three.
2. Hold your breath for the count of three.
3. Through the nose, exhale slowly while silently counting to three.
4. With breath out, count to three.
5. Repeat the cycle (steps 1 to 4) several times. (Once you have the rhythm, you need not continue counting; but keep up the same timing and the same pauses.)

The Doctors' Method

Medical science has come up with an extremely practical breathing exercise to reduce blood pressure: Breathe in until the lungs can hold no more, and then take in a quick extra gasp of air, through the mouth. Breathe out slowly and evenly. Repeat this seven times. What works for high blood pressure also works for high exam anxiety. You can quietly practice this exercise while studying for your exams and during an exam.

The Palming Method

Here's another method that you can use easily, especially at your desk at home or in the library:

1. Close your eyes gently, and cover them with the palms of your hands.
2. Avoid any pressure upon the eyeballs by resting the lower part of the palms on the cheekbones, and the fingers on the forehead. The eyeballs should never be pressed, rubbed, massaged, or handled.
3. Now, the light is fully excluded from the eyes, even though the eyeballs remain untouched.
4. Mentally visualize some pleasant scene or incident. Move your eyes to different parts of the visualized picture. Don't stare at any one spot. For example, if you are seeing a lake, first look at the near shore, then at the far shore, then at the forests at both ends. Movement of the eyes is important in this method. In less than a minute, you'll feel relaxed again. Repeat this minute's worth of relaxation whenever you feel stress.

The Optimum-Rest Method

Five minutes in the position of optimum rest are equal to hours of sleep, says Professor Richard Parks, who has worked as a director with hundreds of students and actors.[4] So if you still have a lot of studying to do, but find yourself tense, tired, and tempted to take a nap, here's a better substitute:

1. Lie flat on your back on the floor (use a rug or pad).
2. Raise your knees, keeping your feet flat on the floor.
3. Separate your feet to about eighteen inches (about shoulder width).
4. Point your toes in and your heels out.
5. Allow your knees to come together in a relaxed way.
6. Cross your arms so that your hands hang limply alongside your neck.
7. Close your eyes, relax your mind, and imagine your favorite serene, quiet scene. You should look somewhat like Figure 2.1 on page 26.

The Believe-in-You Method

You can use the four methods above to treat actual tension. It is better, of course, to prevent or preclude tension before it starts. S. C. Kobasa, a psychologist, says that when you are facing a stressful situation, you can prevent overreaction and aggravation simply by *believing that you are in control and that you can find a solution to any problem or crisis.*[5] The secret is not to make negative self-statements. For example:

Negative (not this)	*Positive (think this)*
Three exams in two days is more than I can handle.	I've survived worse things than this. I'll just do the best I can.
This time there's no escape.	I'll just hang in there. There's always a way out.
Can't do these math problems.	I'll work them as far as I can, and then see the T.A. first thing in the morning.
Can't get started on this research paper. Never could write.	I'll make a list of ten titles or topics, then see the instructor in the morning for ideas.
Can't make heads or tails out of this chapter. I'll just forget it.	I'll go as far as I can, identify what it is I don't understand, and then see the T.A. or instructor immediately.

So use your head, not your emotions, when problems pop up in front of you like space invaders.

---

[4]Richard Parks, *How to Overcome Stage Fright* (Fremont, Calif.: F-P Press, 1979), p. 57. Our thanks to Professor Parks for the ideas for both the method and the figure.

[5]S. C. Kobasa, "Stressful Life Events, Personality, and Health: An Inquiry into Hardiness," *Journal of Personality and Social Psychology*, 37 (1979), 1–11.

Figure 2.1 Optimum Rest.

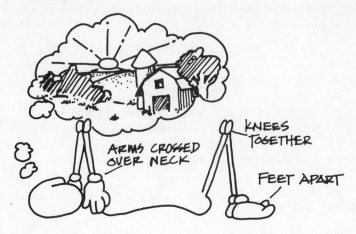

KEEPING AND IMPROVING
YOUR HEALTH

The health habits you form in college, for better or for worse, are likely to stick with you for the rest of your life. Habits are personal things, but each of us should form habits only when we know their implications.

The Seven Magic Habits
of Health

A study of seven important health habits was performed by the Human Population Laboratory of Alameda County, California. The subjects were 6,928 adults, who were chosen as a cross section of people and not for any special condition of health. The habits studied were these:

1. *Smoking:* Never smoke.
2. *Exercise:* Engage in some physical activity.
3. *Alcohol:* Use very moderately or not at all.
4. *Sleep:* Get seven to eight hours regularly.
5. *Weight:* Maintain the proper weight.
6. *Breakfast:* Always eat a balanced breakfast.
7. *Snacking:* Do not eat between meals.

Women who followed six to seven of these habits lived more than *seven years* longer than women who followed only zero to three of these habits. Men who followed six to seven of these habits lived more than *eleven years* longer than men who followed only zero to three of these habits. This longer life was due to good health habits and *not* to the initial condition of the subjects' health.

The seven habits listed above are actually very easy to follow. In light of the tremendous benefits they provide, one wonders who in the world would think so little of life as not to follow them. I do not think any person would trade a year of his or her life for any amount of money; yet, for no money at all, many people trade as many as *eleven* years of their lives. This may be due to ignorance, but most likely is due to the lack of personal discipline.

Habit Power

Habits—good ones or bad ones—are powerful things. William James had a few words to say about the power of habit:

> The hell to be endured hereafter, of which theology tells, is no worse than the hell we make for ourselves in this world by habitually fashioning our characters in the wrong way. . . . Every smallest stroke of virtue or of vice leaves its never-so-little scar. The drunken Rip Van Winkle, in Jefferson's play, excuses himself for every fresh dereliction by saying, "I won't count this time!" Well, he may not count it, and a kind Heaven may not count it; but it is being counted none the less. Down among his nerve-cells and fibres the molecules are counting it, registering and storing it up to be used against him when the next temptation comes. Nothing we ever do is, in strict scientific literalness, wiped out.[6]

Coffee and Cigarettes

"Do you drink coffee?"

Various studies have linked coffee to diabetes, heart attack, and cancer of the colon, urinary tract, and stomach. Now, as reported in *Time*, "Harvard University researchers announced a statistical link between coffee and cancer of the pancreas. . . . Pancreatic cancer claims 22,000 lives a year. It is the fifth largest cause of cancer death in the U.S., behind cancer of the lungs, colon, breast, and prostate. It is also virtually incurable; fewer than 2% of patients survive five years after diagnosis."[7]

[6]William James, *Psychology* (New York: Henry Holt, 1893), p. 150.
[7]*Time*, March 23, 1981, p. 73.

The researchers admit that the problem needs further study. But, the leader of the team, Dr. Brian MacMahon, who used to drink three cups a day, said, "But I will tell you that I myself have stopped drinking coffee."

"Do you smoke?"

The New England Medical Association released this report: Male cigarette smokers (those who continue to smoke) have a premature death rate 50% higher than *former* smokers (those who smoked, but quit). Furthermore, male cigarette smokers (those who continue to smoke) have a premature death rate 70% higher than that of men who have *never* smoked.

One California doctor, when asked how long it takes for a cigarette to harm you, answered, "About three seconds." Smoking starts your heart pounding an extra fifteen beats per minute and raises your blood pressure about twenty points. It leaves cancer-causing chemicals in your body and cuts your wind. It begins to neutralize the defenses of the lungs against other poisons being drawn in by affecting the cilia, which are tiny hairlike structures that line the airways to your lungs. These cilia normally beat back and forth as you swallow or breathe, cleaning the mucus in your throat of germs and foreign particles. In smokers, the cilia move hardly at all. In fact, the infamous "smoker's cough" is caused when cigarette smoke paralyzes the cilia and robs the lungs of their best defense against foreign substances.

Avoiding the Dragged-Out Feeling

In most cases, the causes of "that dragged-out feeling" are quite easily correctable. All you need to do is eat the proper food, get sufficient sleep, take time for daily exercise, and keep yourself under control emotionally. The dragged-out feeling often prevents you or excuses you from getting down to the hard, concentrated work which is necessary if something is to be accomplished. The really sad thing—the tragic thing—is that this condition can persist throughout life; then, as a result, at least part of a life has been wasted.

Contributing causes of the dragged-out feeling include television, which keeps the mind unchallenged; overeating, which contributes to coronary disease; and cars, which keep the body unexercised. But there's a bright side. You can do something about all these bad habits right now. Stay away from junk food, and don't buy even one can of sugar-loaded (and perhaps caffeine-loaded) soda from the "iron-master" dispensers that fill every nook and cranny in every building. Forget about the habit-forming television set, and get to bed earlier. Try jogging, which costs almost nothing, and jumping rope, which will keep you in shape when you can't get outside. Remember, the rest of your life is still before you.

SOCIAL BEHAVIOR
AND ACADEMIC STUDIES

Your social relationships will affect your academic performance either negatively or positively. Happy, positive relationships promote a general feeling of well-being and will surely carry over to your studies. Your concentration will be better, your energy boundless. You will learn and remember better. But, when social relationships are negative, your self-concept will be low, your concentration poor, energy will be lacking, and nothing will seem very worthwhile.

Over 200 years ago, Lord Chesterfield gave his son some advice. These are truly words of distilled wisdom, as valuable now as they were then. Follow this advice and you can avoid distraction, even heartache.

THE TWELVE DIAMONDS OF WISDOM

1. *Talk often, but never long. Don't bore your friends.*
2. *Tell stories or jokes seldom. If you do, be brief.*
3. *Never hold anybody against his will in order to be heard out.*
4. *In company of others, avoid whispering to your neighbor.*
5. *Avoid talking about yourself.*
6. *Have a frank and open manner, but always be reserved inside, for every unguarded expression will be used against you when it is to someone's advantage.*
7. *Always look people in the face when you speak to them, for then you can tell whether they are with you or against you.*
8. *Don't spread or receive gossip and scandal.*
9. *Don't mimic. The person mimicked is insulted, and an insult is never forgiven.*
10. *Never swear by way of emphasis. A poor impression is made, and furthermore, it is wicked.*
11. *Loud laughter is the mirth of the mob. A person of good sense is therefore only seen to smile, but never laugh.*
12. *Whatever you say, say it distinctly, gracefully, and with a pleasant smile.*

Paraphrased and heavily condensed from Letters to His Son by Philip Dormer Stanhope, 4th Earl of Chesterfield (London: Dent, 1945). First published in 1774.

SUMMARY

What is the single greatest cause of tension?

Worry is the greatest cause of tension, and the greatest cause of worry is procrastination—the things that we should have done but didn't do.

What is meant by deviation?

Deviation means putting a worry out of mind by concentrating on some pleasant thought, or by engaging yourself in some physical activity.

What is the one best way to fight tension?

To be prepared for any situation that may cause tension. In college, this means to be *overprepared* for exams, class discussions, and other stressful situations.

Can emotions affect learning?

Definitely yes! Emotions involve the whole body, thus affecting your ability to concentrate, think, remember, and learn.

How does talking your worries over with someone help?

When you put your worries into words, you see them more realistically; often, a solution occurs as you talk. Conversely, cooped up in your mind, the worries get bigger, stronger, and uglier.

Isn't escaping from a worry, even for a while, a bit cowardly?

No! Don't stand there and stew. Rather, take your mind off the worry by doing something else. You'll gain strength and perspective and come back to handle the worry more realistically.

Isn't telling someone off a good way to get anger out of your system?

No! It's the worst thing you could do, for two reasons: First, you'll regret each "telling-off" for the rest of your life; second, the adrenalin in your system won't let you sleep that night.

Isn't giving in a sign of weakness?

No! Rather, it's a sign of maturity. Let the other fellow expound while you sit there in wise, thoughtful silence. Furthermore, you won't learn anything new if you do all the talking and arguing.

How does doing something for others help oneself?

When you help someone, you experience the warm glow of humaneness. In other words, more is actually done for yourself than for the receiver of your good deed.

Aren't you being helpful when you criticize someone?

No! Remember, the other person is getting his or her share of hard knocks naturally. A smile and a good word are more helpful.

How does giving the other person a break help?

When you give someone a break, your self-image will rise like a rocket. Try it once and it will become a habit.

How can one take time out for recreation when there's so much to do?

As a slave to your studies, you'll drag through them wearily, taking longer and not getting much out of them. Reward yourself with some recreation. You'll get more done academically, physically, mentally, and emotionally. Recreation will help you make the time to relax.

We can't always be without tension, can we?

That's right. You can't be as limp as a wet dish cloth and still get things done. The secret is to relax after you finish a job. With relaxation, tension and blood pressure go back to normal.

What makes a Type A person especially prone to heart attacks?

Tension! Type A people keep themselves under constant pressure by being excessively competitive, impatient, insecure, aggressive, hostile, fighting time, and rushing to get just "one more thing done" even when mentally, physically, and emotionally exhausted.

What's the count-of-three method of relaxing?

This method deals with controlled breathing; that is, breathing in and out slowly, and holding to the count of three with air in and out. It relaxes you because you are concentrating on your breathing rather than on some tension-producing event.

What is the doctors' method for overcoming tension by promoting relaxation?

Breathe in until the lungs can hold no more, then take a sudden quick extra gulp of air through the mouth. Then breathe out slowly and evenly. Repeat this several times.

What's the palming method of relaxing?

In the palming method, you use the palms of your hands to cover your already closed eyes and thus block out all light. The absence of light puts you into a relaxed, quiet, dreamy mood.

What's the optimum-rest method of relaxing?

Optimum rest means you relax your whole body. You do so by lying on your back, flat on the floor, with hands limply draped over your neck, feet drawn up toward your body, and knees resting against each other. This relaxation is equal to hours of sleep.

What is the basis of the believe-in-you method of relaxation?	In this method, you simply believe in your ability to control, or find a solution to, any situation. You think positively about yourself and your actions in each situation.
What are the seven magic habits of health?	The four *dos* are exercise, sleep, weight control, and balanced breakfasts. The three *don'ts* are smoking, snacking, and drinking alcohol.
How do social relationships affect school work?	To begin with, social problems are personal problems. They hang onto you like barnacles, making *concentration* on academic subjects most difficult. On the other hand, positive social relationships can add enthusiasm to your academic life.

HAVE YOU MISSED SOMETHING?

1. **SENTENCE-COMPLETION.** Complete the following sentences with one of the three words listed below each sentence.

   a. The greatest producer of tension and worry is _____.

   procrastination   smoking   insomnia

   b. Anger is best handled when it is _____.

   channeled   released   forgotten

2. **MATCHING.** In each blank space in the left column, write the number preceding the phrase in the right column that matches the left item best.

   _____ a. Criticism

   _____ b. Counseling

   _____ c. Deviation

   _____ d. Failures

   _____ e. Worries

   _____ f. Endorphins

   _____ g. Optimum rest

   _____ h. Attitude

   _____ i. Smoking

   1. Redirects worrying
   2. Should be forgotten at bedtime
   3. Overused by most of us
   4. Change stress into distress
   5. Cuts your wind
   6. Takes the cork off bottled-up worries
   7. Can cause or cure tension
   8. Create a sense of well being
   9. Method of tension release

3. **TRUE-FALSE.** Write *T* beside the *true* statements and *F* beside the *false* statements that follow.

_____ a. Your lifelong behavior patterns are often established in college.

_____ b. A balanced breakfast may help prolong your life.

_____ c. When things go wrong it helps to get away for a while.

_____ d. You can stave off impatience by carrying pocket work.

_____ e. Tension can have an effect on memory.

4. **TENSION RELEASERS.** Write "Yes" beside the tension releasers only.

_____ a. Escape for a while.

_____ b. Tell someone off.

_____ c. Give in occasionally.

_____ d. Do several things at once.

_____ e. Offer criticism freely.

_____ f. Don't be too hard on yourself.

_____ g. Make yourself available.

5. **MULTIPLE-CHOICE.** Choose the phrase that completes the following sentence most accurately, and circle the letter that precedes it.

One way to avoid tension is to

a. begin procrastinating.
b. work hard without rest.
c. be overprepared for exams.
d. face tension situations.

One of the best lessons that anyone can learn in life is how to use time wisely.

—WILLIAM A. IRWIN

3

Controlling Your Time

Are we slaves to time? It almost seems as though we are. This chapter shows you how to make time work for you instead of the other way around. In it, you'll find out . . .

- How to manage time
- How to gain time
- How to use time-saving tips
- How to make a schedule
- How to fit work, school, and fun into one day

and

- How to get things done

Y OUR SUCCESS OR FAILURE in college depends directly upon your use of time. Use it wisely, and you'll prosper. Use it poorly, and you'll fail to do the job you came to do. I strongly believe that the management of time is the number one skill to master in college.

Because we don't pay for time in the way we pay for a loaf of bread, we forget that time has great value. To emphasize the value of time, at least partially, time is often equated with money. That is, a dollar value is put on each hour of time—like a pay rate. For example, if your time is worth $12 an hour, then a wasted minute means you lost 20 cents. But time is worth far more than money; time is *life itself*, and no price can be put on that.

If a doctor told you that you had but one year to live, would you just sit around waiting for the year to pass? No! You'd probably make a list titled, "Things I Want to Do Before I Die." Then you'd take determined and vigorous action. But action without planning wouldn't get you very far. You'd be like the fellow who jumped on a horse and rode off in all directions. As silly as this may sound, many people muddle through life hurrying in all directions at the same time.

TIME: WHO'S IN CONTROL?

If you want to be in control of your time and your life, you must believe in this one line from *Invictus*, a poem by William E. Henley: "I am the master of my fate: I am the captain of my soul." To be the master of your fate, to sit in the driver's seat, you must control time and not let time control you. To control time, you must have a *goal*, you must have a *plan*, and you must take *action*.

Importance of a Goal

A goal is a target toward which you can direct your efforts. Without a goal, you are bound to move off in the wrong direction, thus wasting time and effort. When asked how he was able to plow such a straight furrow across a long field, a farmer replied, "I always pick a target at the other end of the field, keep my eye on it, and plow plumb toward it."

So, whatever you want to become—a computer programmer, electronics technician, engineer, or medical doctor—you'd better choose your goal. Then, like the farmer, you will have a distant target to keep you on a straight path.

Your goal should be more specific and less general than simply getting a college education. You need to formulate a clear notion of not only *what* you want in college and life, but also *why* you want it.

There will be some very rough days in college when things seem to be falling apart. That's when you'll need a lifeline to hold onto. That's when a goal can provide the needed perspective and the power to keep you going, to hang in there. It's the goal that establishes the deep-seated, almost blind faith that if you keep going, things will work out all right.

Importance of a Plan

With a goal in mind, it is not too hard to make a plan for reaching that goal. For example, if your goal were to become a computer programmer, one part of your plan would have to deal with financing: Could your parents handle it, or would you work part time and go to school part time? Another part of your plan would deal with the courses you need to take—both over the long term and year by year. Still another part, with the way you would use your summers. And so on. Much of the planning seems to "fall into place" once your goal is set.

It is a good idea to take a clean sheet of paper and write on it (1) what type of job or profession you'd like, (2) how you plan to prepare for it, (3) what you have done and are doing presently, and (4) what you plan to do henceforth to progress toward your goal. Having written it, you will have *thought* through your goal and plan. It is private, but now you have something concrete to talk to your adviser about, to modify if necessary, and to direct your efforts so that they aren't haphazard and wasted.

Don't underestimate the value of thinking out and writing your goal and your plan. With such a document you greatly increase your chances for success.

Taking Action

This is the hard part, the weak link in the chain. When action is not taken, goals and plans become nothing. The saddest words in life, "It could have been," become reality.

In plain words, taking action boils down to *self-discipline*. Actually, it is easy to adapt oneself to military discipline, and it is not too hard to cope with the discipline imposed upon us as children. But the hardest type of discipline is the kind that we must impose upon ourselves. Yet this is the kind of discipline we must have if we are to take the action required to implement our plans.

I think Thomas Huxley said it best: "Perhaps the most valuable result of all education is the ability to make yourself do the thing you have to do, when it ought to be done, *whether you like it or not*." And Count

Leo Tolstoy, the Russian author of _War and Peace,_ wrote, "There never has been, and cannot be, a good life without self-control."

In the rest of this chapter, we apply these concepts—goals, planning, and action, control and self-control—to the effective use of your limited time.

PROGRAMMING TIME TO GAIN TIME

The way we use time—or waste it—is largely a matter of habit. It is not easy to change old habits. But if they are bad habits, they put a ceiling on achievement. For example, a baseball player with a poor batting stance can become quite a good hitter—up to a point. But unless he changes the poor stance, further progress is doubtful. To change and begin almost all over again—to break a bad habit and make a good one—takes determination and will. But the decision to change brings the chance for success. If you find that you need more time for all your studies and other activities, consider programming (or scheduling) your time. You are almost certain to "gain" extra time much sooner than you would think.

Where Does All the Time Go?

In an effort to find out specifically how he spent his time, a student kept a diary of his daily activities for one week. He found that his "ten-minute" coffee break was nearer forty minutes. Figure 3.1 (page 38) shows one page of his diary, with an analysis that demonstrated to the student how he could avoid dribbling away minutes and save hours for both recreation and study.

Reasons for Programming Time

How much spare time do you have every day? The student whose activities record appears in Figure 3.1 would probably answer: "None. There are not enough hours in a day for all the things I have to do." That's the way things may seem, but it's not necessarily the way they are. Table 3.1 (page 39) shows how students at one university spent time in four main activities, during a typical week. When we subtract the total from 168 (the number of hours in a week), we still have a balance of 69.5 hours unaccounted for—almost ten hours a day. But in spite of this wealth of time, college students never seem to have enough of it.

Figure 3.1 Record of One Day's Activities and Suggestions for Making Better Use of Time

Time Start	End	Time Used	Activity - Description	
7:45	8:15	:30	Dress	Paste 3 X 5 cards on mirror: laws of economics; psychological terms; statistical formulas. Study while brushing teeth, etc.
8:15	8:40	:25	Breakfast	
8:40	9:00	:20	Nothing	Look over textbook assignment and previous lecture notes to establish continuity for today's psychology lecture.
9:00	10:00	1:00	Psychology - Lecture	
10:00	10:40	:40	Coffee - Talking	Break too long and too soon after breakfast. Work on psychology notes just taken; also look over economics assignment.
10:40	11:00	:20	Nothing	
11:00	12:00	1:00	Economics - Lecture	
12:00	12:45	:45	Lunch	Rework the lecture notes on economics while still fresh in mind. Also, look over biology assignment to recall the objective of the coming lab.
12:45	2:00	1:15	Reading - Magazine	
2:00	4:00	2:00	Biology Lab	
4:00	5:30	1:30	Recreation - Volleyball	
5:30	6:00	:30	Nothing	Use this time to read a magazine or newspaper.
6:00	7:00	1:00	Dinner	
7:00	8:00	1:00	Nap	Not a good idea. Better finish work, then get a good night's sleep.
8:00	8:50	:50	Study - Statistics	
8:50	9:20	:30	Break	Break is too long.
9:20	10:00	:40	Study - Statistics	
10:00	10:50	:50	Chat with Bob	Good as a reward if basic work is done.
10:50	11:30	:40	Study - Accounting	Insufficient time allotted, but better than no time.
11:30	11:45	:15	Ready for bed	While brushing teeth, study the 3 X 5 cards. Replace cards that have been mastered with new ones.
11:45	7:45	8:00	Sleep.	

You can gain extra time in only two ways: first, by doing the job in less time than usual, and second, by using small blocks of time that you usually waste. The first way requires that you study more efficiently. This book provides a great many time-saving techniques. The second way requires that you schedule your time. This chapter offers a number of proven suggestions.

Table 3.1 Time Spent by Students in a Typical
Week

Activity	Hours Spent
Sleep	49.3
Study	19.8
Classes and Labs	18.7
Meals	10.7
Total	98.5

Source: Arthur A. Dole, "College Students Report on the
Use of Time," *The Personnel and Guidance Journal* 37
(May 1959), p. 635.

Some people feel that it's a waste of time to make a schedule. In fact,
planning *saves* time and energy. Sure, it takes time to program your time.
But the time you spend making a schedule is returned to you, several
fold, when you work—and relax—according to your schedule. Spending
a little time to make a schedule saves a lot of time that would otherwise
be wasted. And there's an unseen bonus: We all walk a bit lighter and
sleep a bit sounder when a well-planned job is done well.

Some people feel that keeping to a schedule makes robots or slaves
of them. But just the opposite is true. The people you see dashing madly
from class to library to gym, or eating a junk-food lunch on the run—
they are slaves to time because they are not in control of their time. The
student who schedules his or her time, who decides how it will be used,
is obviously the master of time rather than its slave.

Some people won't schedule their time because they want to be
"flexible." But the disorganized person wastes so much time that there
really isn't any time left to be flexible with. On the other hand, scheduling frees up time for a variety of activities. And flexibility can certainly
be built into a schedule.

So programming actually gives you more time, makes you the master
of your time, and provides the flexibility that *you* want. Here are some
additional benefits that you can derive from programming.

> *Gets you started.* We all know how hard it is to get started. Often a
> well-planned schedule can be the external force that gives us a
> needed shove.
> *Prevents avoidance of disliked subjects.* The mind can play tricks.
> Without actually deciding to do so, we can keep ourselves from
> doing something we don't like by occupying ourselves with favor-
> ite subjects.
> *Monitors the slackening-off process.* By apportioning time properly,
> we can keep ourselves from slackening as the semester wears on.

Eliminates the wrong type of cramming. If cramming just before exams is to be *effective*, the original studying and learning must take place day by day.

Makes studying enjoyable. When done without the pressure of time, studying and learning can be intensely interesting.

Promotes cumulative review. Sandwiching in short review periods is the best way to retain knowledge, as well as to prepare for future exams. It is less fatiguing and more effective to review a subject in four *distributed* thirty-minute sessions than in a single *massed* two-hour session.

Frees the mind. To keep from forgetting details, we may think them and rethink them. This often leads to a tense feeling of pressure and confusion. Putting things to do on paper takes them off the mental treadmill.

Controls the study break. Rewarding yourself with a ten-minute break when you finish a scheduled block of study helps minimize "clock watching." During short breaks, stand up, walk around, or just stare out the window—but keep in mind the subject you're studying. Then you won't need a warm-up period when you resume studying.

Keeps you from overlooking recreation. Physical and social activities are needed for a well-balanced personality, good health, and more efficient study sessions. On the other hand, allowing extracurricular activities to outweigh studies probably accounts for more failures in college than anything else.

Helps raise your recreational efficiency. One of the saddest wastes of time and pleasure is to intermix study time and recreation time— that is, when studying we keep thinking how nice it would be to be playing some game; and, when playing, we think about all the studying that needs to be done.

Regulates daily living. Without a plan to guide us, assignments are bound to pile up. When they do, we lose control, and our daily living is thrown into chaos. With a schedule, even weekends and holidays can be free from worry.

HOW TO MAKE A SCHEDULE

Scheduling Principles

Just as there are basic rules for driving a car, no matter how long or short a trip you are taking, so there are basic rules for making a study schedule.

The following list includes general principles that apply to all study schedules.

Eliminate dead hours. Make each block of one hour a productive unit. Some of the most important lessons of our lives are learned in less time.

Use daylight hours. Research shows that each hour used for study during the day is equal to one and a half hours at night.

Study before recitation-type classes. For a course in which you recite and discuss, it is an advantage to study just before class. The material will be fresh in your mind.

Study after lecture-type classes. For a lecture course, retention and understanding are aided by a review of your lecture notes immediately after class.

List according to priorities. By putting first things first, you are sure to get the most important things done on time.

Avoid too much detail. Packing a weekly schedule with too many details is a waste of time for two reasons: First, the time it takes to make such a schedule could be better used in studying a subject directly; second, the chances of following such a schedule are very, very slim.

Know your sleep pattern. We all have daily cycles of sleepiness and alertness. If your work, classes, and circumstances permit it, sleep when you're sleepy and study when you're naturally alert.

Discover how long to study. The rule of thumb that you should study two hours for every hour in class is a rough guide at best. The time required varies from student to student and from subject to subject. So start out allowing two hours of study for every hour in class, but adjust the hours according to your experience, as you find out how long it takes to master each assignment.

Plan blocks of time. Optimum efficiency is reached by planning in blocks of one hour: fifty minutes to study, and ten minutes for a break.

Allow time for sleep. The necessity for eight hours sleep every night is supported by medical evidence. We should make no mistake about it: The quality of one's education depends on sufficient sleep.

Eat well-balanced meals. Take time for good meals. Living on greasy foods or other low-protein diets most of the time is no way to treat the body and brain. Dietary deficiencies result in irritability, fatigue, and lack of pep.

Double your time estimates, and start long jobs ahead of time. Most people tend to underestimate time. To avoid discovering the hard way that you cannot bang out a 1500-word paper in three hours the evening before it is due, start ridiculously early, thus allowing more time.

Don't pack your schedule too tightly. Be precise, but leave room for the inevitable last-minute problems that require your time.

Make a plan for living, not merely for studying. After all, life, even in college, is many-sided, and its many sides must be recognized.

Types of Schedules

It is important for each individual to choose the type of schedule that fits his or her circumstances best. Some students work better with a detailed schedule, whereas others work better with a brief list of things to do. Circumstances also influence the type of schedule a student should make. There are on-campus students, commuting students, married students, employed students, night-class students, and part-time students, and each has different scheduling requirements. Every student should *adapt* the principles of schedule building to his or her personal circumstances, rather than *adopt* some ideal model which fits hardly anybody.

The schedule for *you* is the schedule that *works.* With time and experience, you can refine your schedule until it is an almost perfect fit for your situation.

THE MASTER SCHEDULE.   Any plan to schedule time and activities must have at its core a master schedule—that is, a fixed schedule of activities. A master schedule needs to be drawn up only once each semester, unless changes occur in the basic program. Figure 3.2 shows a useful form for making out a master schedule. First, fill in all required school activities, such as courses, classes, and laboratory periods. Second, add other regular activities, such as a part-time job, commuting time, sports, and regular meetings. Third, add housekeeping chores, sleeping, and eating. With fixed activities accounted for, the blank spaces on the chart are available for weekly or day-by-day planning. Such a master schedule, on a 5×8 card taped over your desk or carried in your notebook, unclutters your mind. More important, it enables you to visualize the blank boxes as actual blocks of time into which you may fit necessary activities.

With the master schedule as your base, you can devise any type of schedule that fits your unique combination of courses, your part-time or full-time job, and your personality.

Monday/Wednesday/Friday

9–10 A.M. Use the free period after history (a lecture course) to study lecture notes.

Figure 3.2 A Master Schedule

	Mon.	Tues.	Wed.	Thurs.	Fri.	Sat.	Sun.
7-8	← Dress and Breakfast →						
8-9	History		History		History	Dress + Breakfast	
9-10		Phy. Ed		Phy Ed.		Phy Ed.	Dress + Breakfast
10-11		Chem.		Chem.		Chem.	
11-12	French		French		French		
12-1	← Lunch →						
1-2	Math	Film making	Math	Film making	Math		
2-3				↑			
3-4				Chem. lab.			
4-5	English		English	↓	English		
5-6							
6-7	← Dinner →						
7-8							
8-9							
9-10							
10-11							
11-12	← Sleep →						

10–11   Since French (at 11) is a recitation course, prepare by studying during the free period that precedes class.

2– 3 P.M.   In math class (1–2) problems are usually discussed and worked out on the blackboard. Take very brief notes on both discussion and blackboard work. Then, because math problems can quickly become "cold," use the free period (2–3) to go over the work covered in class during the preceding hour.

3– 4	English (4–5) is often a discussion period. Use the free hour to study and warm up in advance.
7– 8	Evening study time begins. Start with English, your last class, so that any notes you have taken can be reviewed before forgetting takes place.
8– 9	Study French, giving priority to the notes and assignments of the day.

THE DETAILED WEEKLY SCHEDULE.   Some people work best when guided by a weekly schedule that is an expansion of the master schedule. If the demands on your time are both heavy and predictable, then you may need a detailed weekly schedule. This kind of schedule needs to be made out only once, early in the semester. A sample weekly schedule is shown in Figure 3.3; the list that follows indicates how the principles of scheduling were used to set it up.

Monday through Friday/Saturday

7– 8 A.M.	Avoid the frantic dash and the gobbled (or skipped) breakfast by getting up on time.
12– 1 P.M.	Take a full, leisurely hour for lunch.
5– 6	Relax before dinner—your reward for a day of conscientious work.
7– 9	Keep up with current notes and assignments by systematic studying.
9–10	To forestall cramming at quiz and examination times, give some time every day to a review of previous assignments and ground covered to date.
10	A "cease-study" time of ten P.M. is an incentive to work hard during the day and early evening.
10–12	You should devote some time every day to reading books that truly interest you. Recreational reading and conversation help you "unwind" for a good night's sleep.

Tuesday/Thursday/Saturday

8– 9 A.M.	Since chemistry (10–11) is your "hard" subject, build your morning study program around it. An hour's study before class will make the class period more meaningful.
11–12	Another hour's study immediately after chemistry class will help you remember the work covered in class and move more readily to the next assignment.

Special

Tuesday	2–5 P.M., library: theme
Sunday	7–9 P.M., English theme

Figure 3.3 A Detailed Weekly Schedule Based on a Master Schedule. Assume that this schedule is your own, and study it in the light of the analysis in the text.

Time	Mon.	Tues.	Wed.	Thurs.	Fri.	Sat.	Sun.
7–8	← — Dress and Breakfast — →						↑
8–9	History	Study Chem.	History	Study Chem.	History	Study Chem.	
9–10	Study History	Phy. Ed.	Study History	Phy. Ed.	Study History	Phy. Ed.	Church, Recreation, Conversation, Recreational Reading
10–11	Study French	Chem.	Study French	Chem.	Study French	Chem.	
11–12	French	Study Chem.	French	Study Chem.	French	Study Chem.	
12–1	← — Lunch — →						
1–2	Math	Film-making	Math	Film-making	Math	↑	
2–3	Study Math	Library: Theme	Study Math	↑	Study Math	Recreation, Special Projects, Extra Work on Difficult Subjects	
3–4	Study English	"	Study English	Chem. Lab.	Study English		
4–5	English	"	English	↓	English		
5–6	← — Recreation — →						
6–7	← — Dinner — →						
7–8	Study English	Study Math	Study English	Study Math	Study English	Recreation, Conversation, Reading; Extra Work on Thorough Review.	English Theme
8–9	Study French	Study History	Study French	Study History	Study French		English Theme
9–10	Review English	Review French	Review History	Review Math	Review Chem.		Study History
10–11	← — Recreational Reading — →						
11–12	← — Conversation, Sleep — →						↓

For some assignments you will need to schedule blocks of time, to do research or to develop and follow up ideas.

Saturday   From noon on, Saturday is left unscheduled—for recreation, for special projects to which you must devote a concentrated period of time, for extra work on difficult subjects, for thorough review.

Sunday   This is your day until evening. Study history before you
            go to bed, because it is the first class you'll have on
            Monday morning.

THE ASSIGNMENT-ORIENTED WEEKLY SCHEDULE.   Another type of weekly schedule is based primarily on assignments, rather than on available time. It is
a supplement to the master schedule and can be used whenever you face
unusual or long-term assignments. Since it schedules specific assignments, it covers only one specific week.

Figure 3.4 shows a weekly assignment schedule. The format is simple: Draw a horizontal line to divide a lined sheet of paper approximately
in half. Use the upper portion to list your subjects, assignments, esti-

Figure 3.4 A Weekly Schedule Based on Assignments. To provide a time dimension,
this schedule is being made out on Saturday, November 11, for the coming week.

Subject	Assignment	Estimated Time	Date Due	Time Due
Electronics	Chap. V - 32 pp. - Read	2 hr.	Mon. 13th	8:00
English	Paper to Write	18 hr.	Mon. 20th	9:00
Math	Problems on pp. 110-111	3 hr.	Tues. 14th	10:00
Industrial Safety	Make shop layouts	8 hr.	Fri. 17th	11:00
Graphics	Drawing of TV components	6 hr.	Fri. 17th	1:00
Electronics	Chap. VI - 40 pp. - Read	2½ hr.	Weds. 22nd	8:00

Day	Assignment	Morning	Afternoon	Evening
Sun.	Electronics - Read Chap. V English - Find a Topic			7:30 - 9:30 9:30 - 10:30
Mon.	English - Gather Notes Math - Problems		2:00 - 6:00	7:00 - 10:00
Tues.	English - Gather Notes Industrial Safety	8:00 - 10:00	3:00 - 6:00	7:00 - 10:00
Wed.	English - First Draft Graphics		2:00 - 6:00	7:00 - 10:00
Thurs.	Industrial Safety English - Paper Graphics	8:00 - 10:00	3:00 - 6:00	7:00 - 10:00
Fri.	English - Final Copy Electronics		2:00 - 6:00	7:00 - 9:30
Sat.				

mated study times, and due dates. Then, using the due dates and esti-mated times as control factors, check your master schedule for hours available. Choose enough hours to do each job, and write them on the appropriate line on the bottom portion of the weekly schedule sheet. *Then stick to your schedule.* Give study hours top priority. As long as you do, the remaining free hours will be really free.

THE DAILY SCHEDULE.   You will probably want to have a daily schedule that you can carry around with you. A 3×5 card is just the right size. It will fit perfectly into your shirt pocket or handbag so that it will be at hand when you need it.

Every evening before leaving your desk, look at your master schedule to determine your free hours and courses for the next day; then, on the card, jot down a plan for the next day: the subjects you plan to study, the errands, appointments, physical exercise, recreation, and any other activ-ities you want to do, with the time you allot for each. The five minutes so spent are vastly important for two reasons: First, you will have a writ-ten record to which you can refer, and this will unclutter your mind. Sec-ond, you will have mentally thought through your day, thus putting into action a psychological clock that will help keep you on schedule.

Notice in Figure 3.5 (page 48) that the daily schedule is organized on the basis of *blocks of time*, rather than fragments of time. By assigning a block of time to each topic or activity, you will ensure that you work at peak efficiency.

LONG-TERM ASSIGNMENTS.   Most assignments are not portioned out in bite-sized, day-by-day units. Some assignments span a week; some a month; and some, like research papers and projects, an entire semester. Though it pays to study every day, some long-term planning must also be done.

You are likely to have one or two long-term assignments at all times, and it is possible to get confused if you have too many separate schedules. It is best to keep a record of the full assignments and their due dates in your notebook for each subject. But get started on these assign-ments early by allotting some time to each of them on your daily sched-ules. If you still have trouble remembering to do them, you may need to make out a weekly assignment schedule like the one shown in Figure 3.4.

Students with Jobs

Students who hold full-time or part-time jobs usually have less time and less energy to use for studying than regular full-time students; conse-quently, they must use both time and energy very carefully. The main difference is that the full-time student can use big blocks of uninter-

Figure 3.5 A Daily Schedule

FOR MONDAY

8 - 9	Psychology - Review Chapter V and lecture notes
9 - 10	Psychology lecture
10 - 11	Economics lecture
11 - 12	Economics - fix up notes, begin Chapter VII
1 - 2	Campus store - Pick up paper and binder, pen, lead, calculator
2 - 5	Engineering - work on assignment
5 - 6	Exercise - Tennis court with Joan.
7 - 10	Accounting and Math

Review: Just before class is a good time to review the high points of chapters previously studied. Also review the previous lecture for continuity.

Fix up notes: The very best time to fix up lecture notes, and review them simultaneously, is immediately after the lecture.

After lunch: This is a good time to give yourself a semi-break from academic work and do some necessary errands.

2-5 block: This is a valuable block of time during which you should be able to read the assignment and work out the assigned problems without losing continuity.

Exercise: After an entire day with the books, some exercise and a shower will help to put an edge on your appetite, as well as making a definite break between study during the day and study during the evening.

After dinner: Both subjects need unbroken time for efficient production. Use the block of three hours to do a balanced amount of work for each, depending on the assignments.

Breaks: Breaks are not listed. You judge for yourself when a break is best for you. Also, the break should be taken when you arrive at a good stopping point.

rupted time for studying, whereas the job-holding student must devise ways for using scattered pieces of time.

For the working student, the daily study schedule should simply be a list of things to do, in the order of priority. Assigning specific times is likely to lead only to frustration. And study materials should be in a form that permits them to be carried about for use whenever there is some spare time.

LIST OF THINGS TO DO.   To be successful, you should have some sense of urgency about referring to your list and studying whenever an opportunity presents itself. Figure 3.6 shows a typical daily list for a working student.

PREPARING NOTES FOR STUDY ON THE RUN.   To take advantage of pieces of spare time, you must have study materials in a form that is readily available. One way to make materials available is to write or type notes on small cards; another way is to record notes on cassettes.

Figure 3.6 A Things-to-Do Schedule
for a Working Student

```
1. Basic Math
    - 5 problems to solve
2. Shorthand
    - Learn 50 characters
3. Accounting - definitions
_____
Bread - 2
Eggs - 1 doz.
Margarine - 1 lb.
```

After reading an assignment or attending a lecture, select from it only the information that you believe is important enough to master. Using your own words, write or type this information on 3×5 or 5×8 cards. The same notes, or a portion of them, can then be recorded on cassettes. If you have time for only one of these, I strongly suggest using the cards.

HOW TO STUDY ON THE RUN. Here are some ways to study during time periods that are ordinarily only half-used.

1. Paste or tack small metal or plastic clips near mirrors and on walls, at eye level. Place a note card in each clip. While shaving or combing your hair, or while washing dishes, for example, you can read the notes on the cards. Cards placed in clips can be easily changed, whereas pasting or taping them to walls is not so practical.
2. To vary the routine and to use the sense of hearing, listen to a cassette or two while going through your morning routine.
3. When you drive your car to work, listen to several cassettes, instead of music on the radio. Or, if you have only cards, recite aloud from memory (not verbatim) some of the ideas, formulas, or definitions that are on the cards. After you stop driving, read the cards to check your accuracy.
4. As you walk from the parking lot to your place of work, flip through several of your note cards, or listen to a cassette.
5. At lunch, while munching a sandwich in your place of work, do a problem or two in math; or, if you prefer, listen to a cassette.

Making good use of small pieces of time will enable you to devote more time to your family, job, and school without scrimping on sleep.

TIPS FOR SAVING TIME

You are given twenty-four hours of time every day. You get no more and no less, whether you're rich or poor, stingy or spendthrift, deserving or undeserving. You cannot buy more time or manufacture more time.

There are, however, three ways for accomplishing more within the hours given you: First, through study skills, you can become more efficient, thus accomplishing more within the allotted time; second, through the use of bits, pieces, and chunks of time that were once wasted or thought too insignificant, you can accomplish almost as much as if you had a second parallel life; and third, through self-discipline, you can form good habits and eliminate bad ones.

Old habits are difficult to break, and new ones are difficult to make when they don't "come naturally." But it can be done. Here are three cardinal rules to follow:

1. *Develop a strong determination.* To make or break a habit, your determination must be powerful enough to carry you over rough spots. Every day you succeed, the success of your plan is made more certain.
2. *Never, never make an exception.* Making an exception is like dropping a carefully wound ball of string. "A single slip undoes more than a great many turns will wind again," says William James.[1] You must be in constant command of yourself and your life. Never willingly lose a battle.
3. *Take every opportunity to put your good habit to work.* In other words, always practice what you want to come naturally.

These rules can help you turn the following time-saving tips into good study habits.

Carry pocket work. Never, never be without pocket work. Always carry something you can do while waiting in lines and in places (post offices, grocery stores, bus stations, and air terminals), when sitting down to rest, while eating alone, and so forth.

Guard against the power of Parkinson's law. When making a schedule or sitting down to do an assignment, make a hard estimate of the time needed to finish the assignment. Then try hard to finish it in that time. If you don't set a time limit, Parkinson's law will take over; that is, the assignment will stretch itself to fill whatever time you have available.

Set priorities realistically. Keep in mind the personal maxim, "First things first." Do the most important things first, and begin them immediately. Nothing will inspire you to do more work than having something already done and behind you.

Start writing that paper. Get that first sentence down. It doesn't matter whether it's good or poor. Getting started, getting to think and to concentrate—that's the thing.

---

[1] William James, *Psychology* (New York: Henry Holt, 1893), p. 145.

Never look back. Stop hacking up your self-image and filling your stomach with ulcer-producing acids through regrets and self-blame. Wipe your life's slate clean, and resolve to do a better job immediately by making no snap judgments or fast decisions. In sum, stop wasting time on the past.

Beware of the four great robbers of time. They are:

1. Laziness: "I just don't feel like doing it."
2. Sidetracks: "Oh, I better see Mike first."
3. Procrastination: "I'll do it later."
4. Day-dreaming: "Some day I'll amaze them all."

Have courage. It takes personal courage to follow a good time schedule because you'll be leaving average students behind, even those who are your friends. There is a loneliness when you do so, but you must march to the beat of your own drum.

Concentrate your time and efforts. Some students jump from subject to subject when studying, thus distributing and dissipating their time and efforts. In the end, many things are touched but none are finished. When you focus the sun's rays onto a piece of paper, they will burn a hole through it. But unfocused rays of light, like scattered time and effort, make no impression at all.

Use your subconscious mind. All of us have, at one time or another, awakened in the night or early morning with a bright idea or even a solution to a problem that we've been thinking about. Such ideas and solutions are often the work of the subconscious mind. It works while the conscious mind is resting or asleep. Upon awakening, if you want to capture such ideas or solutions, you had better write them down immediately; if you don't, they'll be lost. Many creative people know this; that's why they keep pad and pencil near their beds. Another good way to use your subconscious mind is to make out your 3×5 schedule card just before going to bed. The subconscious mind will work on the items all night while your conscious mind is asleep.

Beat the sleepy feeling. While studying, if you get sleepy before your scheduled sleep time, don't knuckle under by taking a nap. Instead, pick up your textbook, stand up, and pace the floor, reading aloud as you do. The sleepy feeling will pass, and you'll be a winner. You'll also sleep better that night.

Use your precious spare time to think. Here's one of the very best ways to save time, or to use time that is almost always wasted by the majority of students. While walking *from* a class, try to recall all the main points of the lecture you just heard. If you're walking *to* a class, try to recall the main points of the lecture given at the last meeting of the class. At other times (say, when you're jogging), try to think up interesting topics and titles for your next paper. And follow the advice of B. F.

Skinner, the renowned psychologist: "Use short sentences when you are talking to yourself."

Take study breaks. Which is better: sticking with a two-hour assignment until it's finished, or breaking it into half-hour periods with five-minute breaks in between? Breaking up a long assignment is better. Here's why: First, breaks keep you from getting tired and bored; second, just as in a sprint, you work harder and concentrate better in shorter spurts; third, five-minute breaks are great motivators; and fourth and best of all, the material you studied has a chance to *sink in* during the rest periods.

However, just as some baseball pitchers need a long time to warm up, some students take a long time to get into a long assignment. If such students broke long assignments into half-hour periods, they would need warming up at the end of every half-hour. Such students should study for a full fifty minutes or longer before taking a ten-minute break. It is better for them to be like marathon runners, to finish the long assignment all in one continuous stretch.

Before you take a break, review your underlinings and jottings. This will help the facts sink into your *long-term* memory. Or, just before a break, reread a particularly difficult problem or passage. This gets your mind working on the problem while you rest.

Use a month-at-a-glance calendar. Buy or make—but use—a calendar that shows the entire month on one page. For precise control, you need to see what's due and when at a glance. A page per week won't do. Above all, don't use a page for each day, because assignments hidden from view in next week's pages are out of sight and out of mind.

Obey the alarm clock. Don't play games with yourself. That's for kids. Once you have calmly reasoned and decided on a time to get up, don't argue the decision when the alarm rings the next morning. A sleepy mind will always make the wrong decision. Without further thinking, without stretching, yawning, or faking, make those feet hit the floor immediately. Five minutes later you'll be glad you did.

Write notes to yourself. Before you stop studying for the night, write a note to yourself indicating what to begin with at your next study period. You'll be surprised at how much time you'll save when you sit down to study and find a note from yourself, telling you exactly what to do. And you'll enjoy the boost that such a note provides.

Get a head start. Here are four more ways to save time:

1. Get your class schedule definitely set before classes start, so that you can plan your days and weeks.
2. Buy your textbooks immediately, before the campus store runs out of them; being without a textbook for a little while can be devastating.
3. Visit the building and room where each of your classes is to be held, so there'll be no mixup on the first day.

4. Make sure you never miss a class, for each class is a chapter in the "continued story."

GETTING THINGS DONE

A schedule, like an alarm clock, represents a plan. Just as the buzz of an alarm clock is the signal to get up, so sitting down at your desk should be a signal to begin to study. It all depends on your attitude. If you make a habit of getting started immediately and then studying vigorously, you will accomplish a great deal. Your achievement will make it much easier to get started next time.

This vigorous, aggressive approach must become a way of life in the classroom, the laboratory, the library, and elsewhere. Get what you came for! During a lecture, for example, you must be alert and work hard to capture the lecturer's ideas and get them down on paper.

In the library, some students wander about aimlessly or spend most of their time looking around and watching other students coming and going. If your purpose is to gather data for your research paper, then move on to the card catalogue, gather your references, secure the books, begin reading and taking notes. Get something done according to plan!

The intelligent use of time is a large part of academic success. Plan your time wisely, and then be sure to follow the plans that you make.

SUMMARY

Briefly, give us your opinion on using time.

I truly believe that success or failure depends on how you use your time. The key to success lies in your getting out of bed one hour before most people do. To do this, you have to begin your "day" on the night before: You must be in bed by 10 P.M. if you are to get up by 6 o'clock the following morning. This means absolutely no television, which is by far the greatest modern time waster.

A leisurely breakfast will set a calm and efficient tone for the rest of the day. Having gotten a head start on the day, you'll be able to keep actively and contentedly busy throughout the day, making use of every hour in some gainful way. And by 10 o'clock in the evening, you will have accomplished all you planned, and you'll be ready for a good night's sleep. And a good night's sleep is guaranteed because your mind will be free of worry and your body will be free of the chemicals (adrenaline and so forth) which fill the bloodstreams of students who get up late, rush or miss breakfast, and keep dashing frantically all day.

Must we have all three: goal, plan, and action?

Yes! They make up the three-legged stool: Knock out any one of the legs, and the whole structure topples. The action, which is the hardest part to bring about, must be directed toward a clear-cut goal, in accordance with a step-by-step plan.

Isn't it possible to get along without a schedule?

Yes it is. You can play it by ear, but at the price of inefficiency and anxiety. A schedule is the road map that takes you from morning to night in the most direct way so that you accomplish the most with your time and energy.

How many of the scheduling principles do we really have to use?

All of them. But remember that they are general principles. The specifics are up to you, and they depend on your individual circumstances.

Why bother with a master schedule when you have a daily one?

A master schedule is a must, because it is your reference sheet for the entire semester. Your daily schedule is based on it. The master schedule essentially shows your class and lab days and hours, and, as well, shows all your free hours; that is, hours that are free to use for studying and optional activities.

Does the daily 3 × 5 card system really work?

Yes, it does. Only a short time ago I ran into Steve, with whom I had had a couple of counseling sessions. I asked whether he was using the 3 × 5 card system.

"Yes, I'd be lost without my daily plan," he said as he showed me his card. He continued, "Filling in this card just before going to bed gives me a chance to review what I've done during the day and what I plan to do the next day. Best of all,

I always feel that I have firm control over my assignments, my baseball practice sessions, myself, and my day. It's a great feeling."

Looking at his watch and dashing off, he hardly left me the time to say "So long."

Is it true that the way we use our time is due to habit?

Yes, it is very true. The ways in which we talk, eat, behave, study, dress, walk, and so forth, are due to habits built up by the repetition of action after action. Old habits can only be broken when you have a strong desire to change, and the utmost of self-discipline is required.

Why can't we use our subconscious mind all the time?

The subconscious mind cannot communicate directly with the conscious mind; likewise, the conscious mind cannot directly communicate with the subconscious mind. They are not on the same wavelength, it seems. Some students think that when a thought originates in their subconscious mind during sleep, the thought remains there. They think that all they need to do is dredge it up. This cannot be done. In other words, it seems that the conscious mind can *suggest* things to the subconscious mind just before you go to sleep, but it cannot *command* and get action or information directly.

Do you use the spare-time thinking method?

Yes, I do. When I jog and during the mile-long walk from my home to my office, I concentrate on one or two preselected topics. And I used the method as a student. Honestly, the method works!

HAVE YOU MISSED SOMETHING?

1. **SENTENCE-COMPLETION.** Complete the following sentence with one of the three words listed below the sentence.

A study by A. A. Dole showed that the average student had about ten hours per day of unaccounted _____.

time   work   leisure

2. **MATCHING.** In each blank space in the left column, write the number preceding the phrase in the right column that matches the left item best.

_____ a. After class

_____ b. Consolidation

_____ c. Parkinson's law

_____ d. Intelligence

_____ e. Before class

_____ f. Procrastination

1. Pulling things together
2. Pitfall of excess time
3. Taking a clear direction
4. Prime study time for lectures
5. Putting things off
6. Best time to study for recitation

3. **TRUE-FALSE.** Write *T* beside the *true* statements and *F* beside the *false* statements that follow.

_____ a. It is possible to get along without a schedule.

_____ b. The master schedule should be updated daily.

_____ c. You should plan to do your assignments in about half the time.

_____ d. A leisurely breakfast can start a productive day.

_____ e. A good schedule is a plan for living, not just for studying.

4. **TIME ROBBERS.** Write "Yes" beside the time robbers only.

_____ a. Illness

_____ b. Laziness

_____ c. Hunger

_____ d. Procrastination

_____ e. Sidetracks

_____ f. Schedule planning

_____ g. Daydreaming

_____ h. Daylight Saving Time

5. **MULTIPLE-CHOICE.** Choose the phrase that completes the following sentence most accurately, and circle the letter that precedes it.

When you are trying to make a new habit, you need not

a. be determined.
b. carry pocket work.
c. use the habit as often as possible.
d. keep from making any exceptions.

PART II

YOUR MEMORY

Consider the postage stamp. It secures success through its ability to stick to one thing until it gets there.

—JOSH BILLINGS

4
Concentrating to Learn

Are you concentrating? If your answer is yes—if you answered at all—you're not concentrating. You may have been concentrating, but you aren't anymore. Concentration is that elusive. And yet no skill is more important. This chapter explains . . .

- The meaning of concentration
- What breaks concentration
- External distractions and
- Internal distractions, and
- What to do about them
- Techniques that help you concentrate
- Physical fatigue and its remedies
- Mental fatigue and how to prevent it

as well as
- The famous pencil technique

S TATED IN SIMPLE TERMS, concentration is thinking. And during our waking hours we are, with varying degrees of intensity, thinking all the time. Actually, we never run out of things to think and worry about. William James, the philosopher and psychologist, said that some thought or idea tries to gain the focus of our attention every two or three seconds. These thoughts and ideas bang, rattle, and knock on the door of our consciousness, trying to gain entry. No wonder it is so difficult to keep our minds on the job in hand!

Concentration is a slippery quality, because it is not a product or a process; rather it is a by-product. Concentration happens only when we don't think about concentration. For example, if you were thinking deeply about the principle of magnetism and suddenly realized that you were concentrating, then, at that moment of realization, you would have broken your concentration on the subject of magnetism.

What do you see in Figure 4.1? You will probably find your visual focus shifting every few seconds, so that you first see a goblet and then two profiles, and then the goblet again. It is difficult to focus visually on just one of the images and ignore the other. Similarly, it is hard for the mind to focus on just one idea at a time. Yet concentration is one of the keys to success. People who can focus their total thinking on the task before them have an infinitely better chance of completing the task more quickly and accurately than those who divide their attention, even when they don't mean to do so.

Concentration is the key in physical tasks as well as mental tasks. Watch a good bowler, for instance, as she takes her position and then gathers and concentrates all her thinking on the pins at the end of the alley. Or a professional quarterback concentrating only on getting a pass to an open receiver, in spite of the opposing linemen rushing at him from several directions. That's concentration!

Imagine reading your text so intensely that you speak out to the author: "That's not proof enough," or "Other writers explain it differently," or "I never thought about the problem that way before." That's concentration!

Trouble in concentrating may come from external or internal distractions, physical or mental fatigue, or lack of interest in the work to be done. Once recognized, each of these causes of poor concentration can be overcome.

EXTERNAL DISTRACTIONS

College study halls and libraries are full of external distractions, ranging from blue eyes to banging doors, so you must select your place of study carefully. Distraction can be minimized by following these suggestions.

Figure 4.1 A Goblet or Two Profiles?

A Place to Study

Itinerant preachers read their Bibles on horseback as they traveled from village to village. Abe Lincoln read by firelight. Most of us, however, need something more stable. We need a workbench or desk—a place of our own where pens, pencils, paper, and dictionary are at our fingertips, a place where we can leave books open and papers ready for the next study session. As a student, I used a flush door supported by two saw-horses—a wonderful space on which to work.

Psychologists emphasize that a conditioning effect is created between the desk and you: If you nap or daydream a lot while sitting at the desk, then the desk can act as a cue for napping or daydreaming. To avoid this type of negative conditioning, use your desk only for studying. When you want to nap or daydream, leave the desk and nap or daydream elsewhere.

Your place of study should be your workshop, a place where you feel secure and comfortable. Such a place will not distract you.

Equipment for Studying

More ink and more words have been wasted extolling the virtues of a straight-backed, hard-seated hickory chair than on any other single piece of study equipment. Forget it: Use a comfortable, well-cushioned chair. Keeping awake or falling asleep does not depend on your chair; rather, it depends primarily on the method of study, on your attitude and self-discipline, the light, and the room temperature. A hard, straight-backed chair can't take the place of these basic requirements.

An extremely practical piece of equipment is a book stand. I don't mean a book shelf or bookends; I mean a stand that is placed on your desk to hold the book in a tilted position with the pages held down so that they do not flip over. It can work for you in many ways: First, and very important, it can give you a feeling of readiness to study—a feeling of being a scholar in the traditional sense. This alone is worth many times the price of a stand. Second, the stand provides physical freedom. It eliminates the strain of continually holding the book open, pressing down on two sides to keep the pages from flipping over, tilting the book to avoid the glare, and trying to find something heavy enough to hold the book open so you can free your hands to make notes. It permits you to sit back with arms folded, to contemplate and reflect on the meaning of what you are reading.

Other basic equipment should include an up-to-date dictionary and such tools as books, a calculator, clock, and calendar. Some students struggle along without small but necessary items like paper clips, tape, rubber bands, erasers, an ample supply of note cards, and so on. Keep your desk well stocked so that you don't have to make unplanned emergency trips to obtain small items.

Lighting

The quality of the light by which you study is of crucial importance. Researchers report that poor lighting can cause eye strain, general tension, headaches, and sleepiness. Worst of all, these irritations interfere with concentration.

Lighting engineers find that there are three steps in creating a good quality of light.

1. *Eliminate glare.* Glare may come from the bulbs themselves or from shiny surfaces that reflect the light. So cover the bulb with a good shade, and put a light-colored blotter on your desk. An important way to reduce glare is to use indirect light. Indirect lighting is almost as good as daylight, which is, of course, best. Indirect lighting is light that is bounced down onto a lower reflector which, in turn, directs the light to an upper reflector or ceiling which, in turn, bounces the light down onto your desk. Two researchers found that studying by the light of an unshaded lightbulb for three hours can cause an 81 percent loss in clear vision. Glare must be eliminated!

2. *Eliminate contrasts between light and dark areas.* Contrasts and shadows on your book or paper also tire your eyes. Indirect light on your work area helps, but the best way to eliminate shadows is to have two light sources in the room. This can be done quite easily by having a floor lamp or a ceiling fixture to supply general light, and a desk lamp to light your study area.

3. *Eliminate flicker.* An incandescent light (standard tube) is a steady and constant light source, but it may flicker because of a loose connec-

tion. A fluorescent tube has a constant flicker (strobism), but in a double-tube fixture the synchronization of the two tubes eliminates visual flicker. With a single tube, fluorescent flicker cannot be eliminated. There is now a three-tube drafter's desk lamp, which provides superior light.

I use a double-tube fluorescent desk lamp of the drafter's type, with extension arms that permit me to position the light exactly where I want it. In this way, I eliminate just about all flicker and glare, and at the same time can regulate the intensity of the light by bringing it closer or farther away. A good investment! I bought it as a freshman almost forty years ago.

Some people prefer incandescent light. If you are one of them, make sure that the bulbs are shaded from your direct view. You can diffuse the light somewhat by using "soft-white" bulbs, but even these should be shaded. Drafter's lamps are available that take incandescent bulbs instead of fluorescent. And some companies manufacture study lamps with an intricate arrangement of reflectors and filters, so that even with an incandescent bulb you get a high quality of indirect light.

If you study under good light but your eyes still bother you, it would pay to have them examined by an ophthalmologist. Clear and comfortable vision is essential to good studying.

Noise

If you are a person who needs a quiet spot for efficient study, do your utmost to find one. If the library is the right place for you, then always go there. Nothing is more wasteful than going over the same paragraph again and again because there is too much noise for you to absorb what you are reading. Noise in your living quarters is one of the most serious obstacles to effective study.

Some students rationalize that it takes too much time to walk to the library. But two or three hours of efficient study in quiet surroundings does more good than ten hours in near bedlam. Many students find the walk to the library refreshing, and report that they can even concentrate on their studies and get something done as they walk.

One sure way to avoid being trapped in a noisy dormitory is to study in the library beginning with the *first* day of classes. And in the library, find a quiet spot that is free from other distractions.

Let's look at noise from the standpoint of health. You probably know that loud noise can seriously and permanently damage both your hearing and nervous system. But what is not so well known is that constant not-so-loud noise can do the same thing. And consider this: Constant noise can cause serious stress; it can disturb the body's chemical balance, causing physical damage.

Background Music

Many students use music from a radio or stereo as background for studying. Does background music help the learning process or interfere with it?

BACKGROUND MUSIC IN INDUSTRY.   Soft, wordless, nonstrident background music in industry provides a pleasant atmosphere that is often effective in maintaining productivity. The music helps overcome the drabness, boredom, and monotony of some jobs in assembly lines, supermarkets, and similar places. We must bear in mind that these tasks are routine and manipulative; they do not involve *conceptualizing* and *learning* tasks.

BACKGROUND MUSIC IN EDUCATION.   In a review of thirteen experiments on the effect of music on learning ability, the following results were gleaned.

1. In seven experiments, groups *without* music in the background achieved higher scores on a quiz than groups *with* music.
2. In five experiments involving some groups *with* and some groups *without* music in the background, tests showed that there were no significant differences in achievement.
3. In one experiment in which a bell was struck intermittently, a group of college students taking a thirty-minute intelligence test gained *slightly. The more intelligent students in the group, however, made more mistakes with the bell striking.*

The box score for background music is: one win (not really by music, but by the bell), five ties, and seven losses. A very poor record!

MY OPINION.   Click off the radio or stereo. In this business of studying, music is *noise*. Some students report that, all through high school, they studied successfully with music in the background. But success in passing high school courses is no proof that background music doesn't interfere. These students should be asked how much better they could have done without music. How much more could they have learned during the same period?

By exerting extra energy when the music is playing, you may be able to keep your mind on your studies 75 percent of the time. Then the music will capture only 25 percent of your attention. But your mind and body will be bombarded by the sound waves 100 percent of the time. Such bombardment is physically tiring. Why ask for problems when you are studying? It is hard enough to concentrate as it is.

INTERNAL DISTRACTIONS

Here are some suggestions for minimizing internal distractions. They have worked for many, many students.

1. *Plan ahead.* Indecision about when to study and which subject to study is a great time waster. It is also a sure way to create a negative attitude toward studying. You can hurdle this psychological barrier by planning ahead.

2. *Don't daydream.* One of the worst time wasters is daydreaming. Daydreaming is a way of escaping from hard work. Pleasant as it is, it can use up precious time in which you could be working toward your goals. It is far better to establish the positive habit of plunging directly and efficiently into your work. *This* is a habit which will stand you in good stead all your life.

3. *Deal with personal problems.* Each person must develop ways of dealing with personal problems that distract him or her from work. The suggestions in Chapter 2 are designed to help you cope with various emotional problems. If you cannot study because your mind is clogged with personal worries, positive action must be taken.

For example, if a problem intrudes on your thoughts while you are studying, write it out on a sheet of paper to deal with when you have finished your work. Then, after you have completed your work, attack the problem directly. If you cannot solve it yourself, get the help of friends or counselors. Decide on a plan of action, and follow it.

4. *Deal with anxiety caused by a course.* It is not unusual to have one course almost every semester that bothers you for one reason or another. It is surprising how quickly an initial feeling of discontent becomes a general anxiety that interferes with all your studies. One way to dispel anxiety in this situation is to talk the matter over with the instructor. There is a good chance that he or she will be able to help you.

For example, one student who came to me first reported that she liked the instructor and the course. About four weeks later, she said, "The instructor is too brusque; and, in his lectures, he doesn't stick to the topic." About five minutes later, almost as an afterthought, the real reason for her discontent surfaced. "And he wants everyone to lead a class discussion." Then she added, "I'll be home for the holidays, but I won't enjoy a minute of it thinking about having to get up in front of the class as soon as I get back." Almost to herself, she ended by saying, "Maybe I'll drop the course."

Realizing that for some students who haven't had some formal training in speaking such a venture could be traumatic, I suggested, "Go to the instructor, and sincerely put the cards on the table." At the time the student left my office, she had made no decision or promise of action; but, at least, she had an alternative to think about.

About two weeks later, the student re-entered my office, smiling and self-assured. "Well? What happened?" I asked.

"The prof said that he understood, and I could write a paper on my topic instead."

"I can see that you accepted the alternative assignment," I said.

"You bet I did. The prof even suggested a few up-to-date references. One of the references was an article written by him. Actually, we were kidding each other before I left."

5. *Set realistic goals.* Set up realistic goals for study. If a student has hardly been studying at all, it is not realistic for him to announce suddenly: "Tonight I plan to study for six hours." The chances are that the required effort will be too much for him, and he will only experience another discouraging failure. To succeed, the change in habits must be gradual. If that same student were to study for only two hours on that first evening, he would have a far better chance of achieving his goal.

6. *Use a reminder list.* To avoid worrying about the possibility of missing personal appointments, write them down on your daily 3×5 reminder card (this technique is discussed in Chapter 3). If an appointment is several days away, write it on a desk calendar. Having made a written reminder, you will no longer clutter your mind with these details.

CONCENTRATION TECHNIQUES

The following list summarizes other techniques that have helped students concentrate. Try one or two at a time to see whether they are for you.

1. *Have a positive attitude.* Try to look upon studying as an opportunity to learn, rather than as an unpleasant task to complete. Also, since you may be spending a great deal of time in your room, do not make it a prison; rather look to your room as a sanctuary. Remember, you are always free to take a well-earned break.

2. *Confine your shifts in attention.* It is quite natural for your attention to shift frequently. Probably this is an inheritance from our cave-dwelling ancestors, who had to be constantly aware of what was going on around them. There will be shifts in attention, but try to confine these shifts to the subject matter at hand.

3. *Use the spider technique.* A vibrating tuning fork held close to a spider's web will set up vibrations in the web itself. After the spider makes a few hurried investigations and finds no fly in the web, it learns to ignore the vibrations.

The next time that you are studying in the library and the door opens, don't look up. Controlling your impulse to look up will disturb your concentration the first few times. But very soon, like the spider, you'll learn to ignore these external disturbances.

4. *Ignore noise around you.* There will always be some noise around us. Avoid disturbances if you can, but do your best to ignore the noise you cannot avoid. By all means do not let yourself become annoyed. The internal irritation that you create has a more devastating effect on concentration than the external noises themselves.

5. *Make sure you have everything.* Before sitting down to study, make sure you have everything: sharp pencils, fresh paper and cards, necessary books. Then stay in your chair until you have studied an hour or so. In that way, you'll remain in the driver's seat—that is, in control.

6. *Use the no-room principle.* Imagine that the pathways of your mind are completely filled with thoughts about the subject in front of you. Then there will be no room for extraneous thoughts, and they will be turned away.

7. *Use the checkmark technique.* Have a sheet of paper handy by your book; then, when you catch yourself not concentrating, put a checkmark on the sheet. The mere act of doing this will remind you to get back to work. Students report that when they first tried this system, they accumulated as many as twenty checkmarks per textbook page; after one or two weeks, they were down to one or two checkmarks per page.

8. *Don't rely on will power!* Will power alone can't make you concentrate. You will be breaking concentration whenever you remind yourself, "I must use will power to concentrate!"

9. *Don't fight hunger.* Hunger is such a basic and persistent state that there is no sense trying to overcome it. Give in! Feed yourself; then go back to work.

PHYSICAL FATIGUE

There is little doubt that our general health affects our brain and, consequently, our ability to concentrate and learn. And general health depends mainly on diet, sleep, and exercise.

How's Your Diet?

Nutritionists remind us that *we are what we eat.* We often interpret this principle in physical terms, but the experts go beyond this. They say that nutrition determines whether we are grumpy or cheerful, radiant or dull, even young or old. And on the mental side, they say that nutrition determines the quality of thinking: whether it will be clear or confused. Nutrition, then, affects our whole being.

When you feel too tired to think, your blood-sugar is probably too low. Why blood-sugar? Well, that's what your body's cells use to produce energy. When you are tired, your immediate reaction may be to stoke the inner furnace with sugar or candy. Almost immediately your blood-sugar level will skyrocket. This high level will trigger your pancreas to cut down the excess sugar by pouring insulin into the bloodstream. Usually the insulin does such an efficient job that your blood-sugar level will be lower than before, leaving you feeling even more fatigued.

The only way to get out of this vicious circle is to add protein to your diet. Protein slows digestion and absorption, thus providing a steady supply of sugar (glucose) in the blood.

When should you add protein? At breakfast, say the nutritional chemists. Why breakfast? Because if you start the day feeling tired due to low blood sugar, you'll feel fatigued all day even though you may try to make up the deficiency by eating protein at lunch.

To find the just-right breakfast, two nutritional chemists[1] set up a two-year experiment using eight different breakfasts. After the first breakfast of unsweetened black coffee only, the blood sugar fell below the pre-breakfast level and the subjects reported hunger, weakness, headache, and lassitude. How about coffee and doughnuts? After two doughnuts and black coffee, there was a rapid rise in blood sugar followed by a plunge to below the pre-breakfast levels, resulting in weakness and lassitude.

The other six breakfasts were variations of the following *basic breakfast*. It looks good, but it's not good enough:

Food Items	Quantity
Citrus juice, unsweetened	1/2 cup
Bacon, broiled	2 strips
Bread, white, toasted	1 slice
Butter	1/2 square
Preserves	1 tablespoon
Coffee	1 to 2 cups
Cream, light	2 tablespoons
Sugar	2 tablespoons

Most people would consider this basic breakfast good, and obviously far better than coffee and doughnuts. But, surprisingly, this basic breakfast *did not* maintain the proper blood-sugar level. Even when oatmeal was added to the basic breakfast, the level of blood-sugar rose at first, but then plunged below the baseline and remained low all morning.

Finally, the researchers hit on an effective combination: eight ounces of whole milk, fortified with two and one-half tablespoons of nonfat pow-

[1]Elsa Orent-Keiles and Lois F. Hallman, "The Breakfast Meal in Relation to Blood Sugar Values," *U.S. Department of Agriculture Circular*, No. 827 (1949), 1–24.

dered milk, were added to the basic breakfast. Then the blood-sugar rose and stayed above the baseline throughout the entire morning. The experiment's volunteers reported a prolonged sense of well-being and satisfaction. In another combination, two eggs replaced the fortified milk and were added to the basic breakfast. Again, the blood-sugar rose and remained above the baseline throughout the morning.

The lesson to draw from these experiments is that we must include some protein in our breakfasts, such as milk and eggs (meat is okay, too, but bacon is very low in protein). Without protein, we short-change our entire system and drastically diminish the thinking power of the brain— not only in the morning but through the day.

How about lunch? All volunteers were given a sandwich of tomato, lettuce, and mayonnaise, with black coffee. Those who had the basic breakfast, reinforced by eight ounces of fortified milk or two eggs, showed not only an immediate increase in the blood-sugar level, but also maintained a high blood-sugar level all afternoon. On the other hand, those volunteers who did not have milk or eggs for breakfast, and whose blood-sugar levels became low during the morning, showed the following effects: the blood-sugar level increased for only a few minutes, then fell to a low level and remained there all afternoon. Moreover, hunger, weakness, headache, and lassitude were reported.

There's no getting around it. You must be nutritionally fit to gain learning that will stick in your mind permanently. And passing examinations doesn't necessarily mean you are learning. In the University of Minnesota Starvation Experiment, although the nutritional status of the subjects was low, they were still able to do the studying necessary to pass examinations.[2] But there was a total absence of any scholarly effort in what is called *advantageous learning*. Advantageous learning is learning done voluntarily and with enthusiasm for the purpose of just wanting to know. This type of learning is due to mental curiosity, a burning desire to learn something about a particular thing or topic.

Essential learning, on the other hand, is the learning of materials from textbooks and lectures, mainly by memorization in preparing for an exam. Such materials, though memorized, rapidly drop out of mind once the examination is over. The materials learned have served their purpose and are forgotten.

What distinguishes advantageous learning is the motivation behind it. The learner is not driven by fear of an examination; rather, he or she is driven by an inner urge to learn, to know and find out more about a thing or topic. This mental attitude makes all the difference in the world in helping one to learn material easily and to remember it almost permanently.

[2]Ancel Keys, Josef Brozek, Austin Henschel, et al., *The Biology of Human Starvation* (Minneapolis: The University of Minnesota Press, 1950), 2: 859–863.

Advantageous learning need not be used immediately. It can be stored for possible use later in life. It would seem that this type of learning is the only worthwhile learning—and it takes place only when one is well nourished.

How About Sleep?

Reports have it that Thomas Edison, Winston Churchill, and Napoleon got along with a minimum of sleep, yet put out a prodigious amount of work. It is true that they seldom slept for eight consecutive hours, but what is not reported is that they were free to nap at various times. An examination of the records shows that their catnaps often added up to about eight hours for every sixteen that they worked.

Everyone needs to sleep, no matter how important the task he or she is working on. Even astronauts sleep. The physiological reasons for sleep are not fully known, but it is obvious that sleep relaxes and refreshes both mind and body.

How LONG DO YOU NEED TO SLEEP EACH NIGHT? That is a matter for each individual to determine, but most people need to sleep seven to nine hours out of every twenty-four. You probably know how much you need, to feel at your peak.

Insufficient sleep can produce unpleasant effects, from loss of memory to muscular weakness. Experiments on sleep deprivation conducted at the Walter Reed Army Medical Center have shown the following:

1. After prolonged visual activity, the eyes tend to wander; we call this effect *visual attention fatigue.*
2. Brief periods of extreme drowsiness occur between midnight and dawn, and these interrupt any chain of mental operations.
3. Acquisition of new information is impaired.
4. A person "listening to a conversation may progressively lose his grasp of the situation, being dimly aware that people are talking but not of what they are saying. During this time, he is unable to comprehend the real situation, and he confuses external and internal events."[3]

Obviously, you can't stay up all night and expect to function well the next day.

A regular day-night rhythm is essential to health. If you normally are awake during the daytime and early evening, it would be difficult for you to go to bed at either 3 P.M. or 3 A.M. The mind and body come to de-

[3]G. O. Morris, H. L. Williams, and A. Lubin, "Misperception and Disorientation During Sleep Deprivation," *A.M.A. Archives of General Psychiatry* 2 (1960), 247–254.

pend on a stable rhythm of waking and sleeping. Changing your schedule disrupts you both physically and mentally. So if you normally go to bed at 10 or 11 o'clock, do so regularly. Otherwise you will have to pay the price.

Some students get so tense during the day that they are still tense when they go to bed. Then they have trouble going to sleep. This is especially true of very sensitive people who carry their arguments, their defeats, and their disappointments in their minds, playing and replaying the episodes over and over again. These replays simply heighten your feelings and emotions, causing you to get keyed up even more, and this stress-reaction may carry over into the night. Here is the way Dr. Hans Selye explains it:

> *Keep in mind that the hormones produced during acute stress are meant to alarm you and key you up for peak-accomplishments. They tend to combat sleep and to promote alertness during short periods of exertion; they are not meant to be used all day long. If too much of these hormones is circulating in your blood, they will keep you awake, just as a tablet of ephedrine would. (Incidentally, ephedrine is chemically related to adrenaline.) Your insomnia has a chemical basis, which cannot easily be talked away after it has developed; and at night in bed it is too late to prevent it from developing.*[4]

Is there anything you can do about insomnia? The ideal, of course, is to avoid those super-stress situations in the first place. But if you are already in bed and you just can't sleep, try this advice from Prof. Walter Rudolf Hess, Swiss mental specialist and Nobel Prize winner:

> *If you cannot sleep, resign yourself to it, arrange your limbs comfortably and enjoy the feeling of their relaxed heaviness. Occupy your mind with pleasant thoughts and memories, without worrying about the passage of time. Then sleep, too, will come.*[5]

This recipe is short, but it is distilled from years and years of experience with insomniacs. Notice that he does not say, "Go to bed determined to fall asleep." Rather he says, "Accept the fact that you . . . possibly won't fall asleep, but be comfortable in the meantime. Enjoy the physical feeling of rest." This is the simplest, most direct prescription that I have encountered. Try it, but gently.

Here are a few important results of studies regarding sleep:

Sleep and memory. A good night's sleep significantly helped subjects recall previously memorized material. Subjects who did not sleep did

[4]Hans Selye, *The Stress of Life* (New York: McGraw-Hill, 1956), p. 271.

[5]Thomas Kirk Cureton, *The Physiological Effect of Exercise Programs on Adults* (Springfield, Ill.: Charles C Thomas, 1969), p. 19.

poorly. However, good recall was accomplished only through nighttime sleep. Daytime sleep did *not* produce the same results.

Dreaming and sleeping. Some people believe that because they dream, they are not getting proper sleep and rest. Just the opposite is true. In one experiment, researchers awoke sleeping subjects as soon as they began to dream. Subjects were permitted to sleep when they were not dreaming, so the subjects were getting sleep, but no dreams. The result was that these subjects, deprived of dream sleep yet with plenty of non-dream sleep, felt tired and irritable. On the fourth day, the researchers just couldn't wake up the dream-starved subjects. The body and mind seemed intent on getting their share of dream sleep.

Caffeine and sleep. Many people are very sensitive to caffeine. If such people take in too much caffeine during the day, and especially in the evening, they have a hard time falling asleep. In addition, laboratory studies show that 200 to 500 milligrams of caffeine per day may produce headaches, nervousness, and gastrointestinal disturbances in some people.

You probably know that coffee is not the only substance that contains caffeine. Some carriers of caffeine are shown in Table 4.1.

RESIST THE TEMPTATION.   We have just finished exploring all the reasons why you should not use your sleep time for studying. Now I will emphasize

Table 4.1 Caffeine in Foods and Drugs

Source	Caffeine (milligrams)	Source	Caffeine (milligrams)
Beverages		Milk chocolate,	6
Coffee (5 ounces)		1 ounce	
Drip method	146	Baking chocolate,	35
Percolated	110	1 ounce	
Instant regular	53	*Soda (12-ounce cans)	
Decaffeinated	2	Diet Mr. Pibb	52
Tea (5 ounces)		Mountain Dew	52
(Loose or in tea bags)		Mellow Yello	51
One-minute brew	9 to 33	Tab	44
Three-minute brew	20 to 46	Shasta Cola	42
Five-minute brew	20 to 50	Dr Pepper	38
Ice tea, cans,	22 to 36	Diet Dr Pepper	37
(12 ounces)		Pepsi Cola	37
Cocoa and chocolate		Royal Crown Cola	36
Cocoa (made from	10	Diet Rite Cola	34
mix), 6 ounces		Diet Pepsi	34

Source: Copyright 1981 by Consumers Union of United States, Inc., Mount Vernon, NY 10550. Reprinted by permission from *Consumer Reports*, October 1981.

*Tests for caffeine content were done for the October 1981 issue of *Consumer Reports*. Since formulations of drinks can change, the figures given may not apply to current formulations.

that you not sleep when you are supposed to be studying. During study time, you're supposed to fight sleep to get the job done.

Most students find sleepiness one of their greatest problems. Sleepiness can result from real fatigue or from a subconscious desire to avoid a dull task. One way to fight sleepiness is to take frequent five-minute breaks. Another is to pace the floor slowly while reading a book or reciting a lesson aloud. Still another is to schedule recreation or academic assignments involving physical activity (such as rearranging your lecture and reading notes, writing in key words, or doing errands that you have been putting off) at hours when you ordinarily find it hard to study.

One word of warning: Many students rationalize that it is better to give in to the urge to sleep and that when they wake up they will be refreshed. Few students report this happy result. Rather, they awake to a formidable pile of undone work. It is far better to combat the desire to sleep, get the work done, and then go to bed at the usual time with a clear conscience. Then, after a productive evening of study, you have earned the right to a good night's sleep.

And Then There Is Exercise

A good workout promotes a keen appetite, keeps the brain and body in tone for alert studying and thinking, and triggers the organic clock when

Table 4.1 Caffeine in Foods and Drugs *Continued*

Source	Caffeine (milligrams)	Source	Caffeine (milligrams)
Coca-Cola	34	Pain relievers	
Mr. Pibb	33	Anacin	64
Cragmont Cola	Trace	Excedrin	130
7-Up	0	Midol	65
Sprite	0	Plain aspirin	0
Diet 7-Up	0	Tylenol	0
RC-100	0	Diuretics	
Diet Sunkist Orange	0	Aqua-Ban	200
Sunkist Orange	0	Permathene H_2Off	200
Patio Orange	0	Pre-Mens Forte	100
Fanta Orange	0	Cold remedies	
Fresca	0	Coryban-D	30
Hires Root Beer	0	Dristan	32
Nonprescription drugs		Triaminicin	30
(Standard dose)		Weight-control aids	
Stimulants		Dexatrim	200
Caffedrine Capsules	200	Dietac	200
NoDoz Tablets	200	Prolamine	280
Vivarin Tablets	200		

our regular bedtime rolls around. Then, after our night's sleep, we wake up alert for the day's academic work.

Exercise has these beneficial effects because it improves the circulation of the blood. Some people become mentally stale and physiologically old at a relatively young age. Why? Research unmistakably indicates that health, endurance, nutrition, and general well-being all depend on one thing—circulatory fitness. And the only way to achieve this is through *regular exercise.* Researchers report that physical exercise not only makes us feel better, but it is also *the only way* to keep our body chemistry in good condition.

The kind of exercise you get in college depends partly on the available facilities. Your school may not let you use the gym unless you are in an organized class or on a school team. Tennis courts may be available for casual play only during specified hours.

You may have to be a detective to find out what kinds of exercise are open to you. Perhaps you can schedule a course in basketball or swimming. Find a partner or two who can meet you for squash. Find out what the local "Y" and other community agencies have to offer. Even vigorous walking and bicycling can fill your need for exercise.

Don't settle for the required physical education courses. You will meet the requirement long before you are out of college, but you will still need regular exercise through your college years and beyond.

MENTAL FATIGUE

It is almost impossible to develop mental fatigue by studying, even by studying hard. We get "tired" readily enough, but this happens because we are bored with the subject, not because bodily wastes accumulate in the brain or the muscles. You may push away a textbook with the comment, "I'm exhausted! I can't read another word," then casually pick up a magazine or newspaper and read avidly, without any signs of fatigue, for an hour or so. Obviously, we tend to confuse *fatigue* with *boredom.*

Erle Stanley Gardner, the mystery writer and creator of Perry Mason, finds that he can best use his time and energies by working on three stories at once. He finds that he is more refreshed by switching from one story to another than by simply taking a rest break.

There are three lessons to keep in mind here: First, stay in good physical condition with the right kind of food, sleep, and exercise. Second, schedule your different subjects so that you don't study any one subject so long that you get bored with it. Third, be interested, or create interest in the subject in hand, so that you can keep working beyond the first symptoms of tiredness.

The American philosopher and psychologist William James developed this insight years ago. Basing his ideas partly on his background in medicine, he noted that most people do not use their mental energies in sufficient depth. He said that our reserves of energy are stored layer upon separate layer. In the physical (muscular) sense, after we use up most of the energy in the top layer by working or running, signs of fatigue relay the message for us to stop; but in cases of necessity when we do not stop to rest, a surprising thing happens: "The fatigue gets worse up to a certain critical point, when gradually or suddenly it passes away, and we are fresher than before. We have evidently tapped a level of new energy."[6] We have, in other words, gotten our *second wind*, and we continue to work or run almost effortlessly until we approach a third layer. We become tired again, but if we continue we can pierce through the resistance to gain a third and a fourth "wind." William James said that, in this process, there is an exact parallel between physical energy and mental energy.

The feeling of "tiredness" *occurring well before quitting time* may very well be a sign that you are *approaching* the second layer of mental energy. It is, however, *not* a sign that you are actually fatigued. At this point, William James might say, "Don't stop! Keep going! You are on the verge of tapping a new layer of reserve mental power that heretofore you never realized you had. Keep going, and you will attain your mental 'second wind,' enabling you to continue studying at a higher mental level and with relative effortlessness."

Most of us find it particularly hard to concentrate on a "boring" or "difficult" subject. The difficult subject is often the one that we are not interested in; consequently, we do not care to read and think about it. Frequently, the subject remains "boring" and "difficult" simply because our knowledge remains meager. Worse still, it pulls down our grades and upsets our composure and self-confidence. When we make the effort to break through this barrier, however, we are almost always pleasantly surprised. We soon find in it something of interest and value.

Here are some suggestions that will help you take a more kindly attitude toward a difficult subject. They may even help you gain a true education.

Try small group sessions. Find two or three other students who will meet with you to discuss briefly each assignment in the particular subject that is "boring" to you. During the give-and-take of the discussion you are bound to learn a great deal, and the subject may become "alive" to you. Also, the enthusiasm of some of the members might rub off on you. Once you begin to know something about the subject, your interest level will rise, and the vicious circle will have been broken. The only prerequisite for a group meeting is that every member do his or her homework. Only then can each person become an active contributor as well as a receiver.

[6]William James, *On Vital Reserves* (New York: Holt, Rinehart and Winston, 1911), p. 4.

Get some individual tutoring. Don't just "hang in" there knowing less and less, while almost everyone else is learning more and more. When you see that you are having trouble, find a classmate who is mastering the subject and arrange, for a modest fee, to be tutored. The tutor will probably be able to get you on your own in a short time.

Read alternative textbooks. The writing in some textbooks is more difficult to grasp than in others. Often it is the style of the author that causes the difficulty, not the abstruseness of the topic itself. In the library you will find many other books in which other authors discuss the very same topics. From personal experience, I know how helpful an alternative textbook can be. After reading the alternative textbook, however, it is important to go back to your regular textbook to read the assigned chapters. You will understand them then.

Use workbooks and programmed instructional materials. There are many supplementary materials on which to practice and to learn. These materials force you to take action. In programmed materials, especially, each step is a small problem that has to be solved on the basis of information presented in the previous steps. The ongoing sequence of problem solving forces you to concentrate and remember previous steps. And your solutions are immediately compared with the correct answers. In this way, wrong solutions are straightened out in your mind before they become embedded, and correct solutions are reinforced.

THE SECRET TECHNIQUE: THE PENCIL

I have saved the best for last.

A technique that has never failed any student over the past many years is the simple, humble *pencil technique.* The technique is this: *Whenever you are working to learn, study with a pencil in hand. And use it!* For example, if you are reading a textbook chapter, stop after several paragraphs and very briefly, in your own words, write down the key points made by the author. If, after reading several paragraphs, no words come to you, then you have no other recourse than to go back and read the passage again. This time, read with determination and concentration, to make sure that you learn the key points. The secret: Activity promotes and almost ensures concentration. The pencil provides the activity!

SUMMARY

What is concentration?   Concentration is losing yourself in the thought you're thinking, the activity you're doing, or the subject you're studying. In other words, when you give 100 percent attention to some one thing, you're concentrating.

What are external distractions?

External distractions are physical things (like people and pets) or actions (like people talking), outside your own body, that break in on your attention.

What articles do you find useful for studying?

First of all, I like to have a ream of clean paper at my fingertips; second, I need and constantly use a typewriter; and third, I like soft-lead pencils (hard lead takes too much pressing and still shows up lightly). But nothing is so important to me as a good light—and the "good light" to which I refer is my two-bulb flourescent lamp. With it, I can work without eye fatigue for hours and hours. Without good light, eye strain and headaches finish me off before an hour is up.

How does noise affect concentration?

Noise forces its way into one's system. The sound waves pound the eardrums, rattle the fragile bones of the inner ear, load the nerves with messages, and bombard the brain cells with codes. As long as the noise continues, a person continues to exert energy trying to ignore the disturbance. This makes it almost impossible for the conscious mind to give 100 percent attention to the job at hand.

Is music a noise?

As far as studying is concerned, yes! The human mind cannot concentrate on two different things at the same time. So if you are trying to concentrate on studying, the music will interfere. The solution, of course, is to do one thing at a time. Study in quiet surroundings. Later, listen to music; then you can do two things at once. You may look through a magazine, for example, and your concentration will dart back and forth from music to pictures. But don't try this bouncing back and forth with a textbook. You won't learn.

What are the biggest internal distractions?

Internal distractions are nonacademic thoughts and emotions that come from within. The most common internal distraction (usually mixed with emotion) is the personal problem. As humans, we all have personal problems, or we think we have. When thoughts about these problems keep bobbing to the surface, they break our concentration on academic work. Not only do they interfere with concentration, but they also drain us emotionally, so that we often have little enthusiasm for school work. The other great breaker of concentration and robber of time is the daydream. The more often we let daydreams enter our academic lives, the more frequently they will do so. In other words, daydreaming will become habitual.

We are what we eat: What does it mean?

It means that the kinds of food we eat have a direct effect not only on the muscles of our bodies, but also on our personalities and, more important, on our *brains*.

What is the importance of the level of sugar in the blood?

Digested sugars are picked up and carried by the blood to all the cells in the body, including the brain cells. The cells then convert the blood sugars into energy. If the blood-sugar level is low, then the body's cells work more slowly. That's when we feel "tired."

Does that mean we should eat sugar?

No! Eating plain sugar is not the answer. Raw sugar gets into the bloodstream fast and gives you a temporary lift, but only for minutes. Then the blood-sugar level falls below what it originally was, so you are worse off than when you started. What counts is the *slow* and *steady* feeding of the cells. This can be accomplished only by eating proteins, such as milk, eggs, and meat, that release their sugars slowly and steadily as they are digested.

Briefly, what's the difference between essential learning and advantageous learning?

Essential learning is the learning that we do to pass exams and get jobs. It is not voluntary learning based on "wanting to know," and it does not have much sticking power. Advantageous learning stems from an intense intellectual curiosity—a burning desire to learn something, to know. Such learning has great sticking power, but takes place only when a nutritionally balanced diet has led to a contented and glowing feeling of well-being.

Does lack of sleep affect academic performance?

Yes! It's a losing game in two ways: First, when you push yourself to study far into the night, learning becomes inefficient as you try to cram too much into a tired mind. Second, the next day, especially in the lecture hall, your sleepy mind will be unable to keep up with the lecturer. In addition, there is a health loss—you're giving a raw deal to your mind, nerves, emotions, and body.

How about taking short naps during the day?

Avoid doing so. Make full use of your daytime hours for studying. Remember, too, that daytime sleep is not equivalent to nighttime sleep. Furthermore, a daytime nap not only disturbs your nighttime sleep but also confuses the natural sleep rhythm that your body is used to.

Does coffee interfere with sleep?

The answer is yes! The caffeine in the coffee is a stimulant. Caffeine is also present in tea, cocoa, and cola drinks.

How does exercise help academically?

Physical exercise, such as playing squash or jogging, helps to ensure *circulatory fitness*. In other words, exercise improves your blood circulation and, thus, the delivery of oxygen and sugars to your brain cells. In addition, exercise keeps the body's muscles in tone, thus making for better studying, eating, and sleeping.

What is boredom?

Boredom is a psychological "tiredness" that we feel when we have, for example, studied a subject in which we are not too interested. We seldom feel bored when we do something we like. You can minimize boredom by following these techniques: First, don't study any one subject for too long at one time. Second, vary the types of studying you do; that is, do reading-type studying for half an hour, take a short break, and then switch to an active type of studying such as working math problems or even writing a paper. Third, try to dig down to rock bottom in each of your subjects, to get at the basic principles, and learn those principles cold. It seems that once you have learned something solid about a subject, you tend to like it rather than simply put up with it.

What is the secret of the pencil technique?

The secret of the pencil technique is *activity* and *expectancy*. Let me explain. With a pencil in hand while you're reading a textbook chapter, you are no longer a passive learner; you are an active learner. With a pencil in hand, you constantly have in mind the expectancy of underlining main ideas, writing in the margins, and so forth. With activity and expectancy to energize you and keep you alert, your concentration should be at its peak.

HAVE YOU MISSED SOMETHING?

1. **SENTENCE-COMPLETION.** Complete the following sentences with one of the three words listed below each sentence.

   a. Concentration is best described as a _____.

   product   by-product   process

   b. Physical fatigue comes from deficiencies in diet, sleep, and _____.

   caffeine   concentration   exercise

2. **MATCHING.** In each blank space in the left column, write the number preceding the phrase in the right column that matches the left item best.

   _____ a. "Spider technique"

   _____ b. Music

   _____ c. "Problems list"

   _____ d. Book stand

   _____ e. Caffeine

   _____ f. Workbook

   1. May divide or weaken concentration
   2. Makes monotonous subjects less troublesome
   3. Counteracts external distractions
   4. Counteracts internal distractions
   5. Creates a feeling of readiness
   6. Provides an artificial sense of alertness

3. **TRUE-FALSE.** Write *T* beside the *true* statements and *F* beside the *false* statements that follow.

_____ a. Sugar provides long-lasting energy when taken by itself.

_____ b. Dreams disturb the restfulness of sleep.

_____ c. Exercise is the only way to keep the body in good condition.

_____ d. "Boring" subjects can be made more interesting with small group sessions.

4. **MULTIPLE-CHOICE.** Choose the phrase that completes this sentence most accurately, and circle the letter that precedes it.

Internal distractions are such things as indecision, personal problems, and

a. bad lighting.
b. an uncomfortable chair.
c. a "problem" course or instructor.
d. your roommate's radio.

*The secret of a good memory is attention, and
attention to a subject depends upon our interest
in it. We rarely forget that which has made a
deep impression on our minds.*

—TRYON EDWARDS

5

Forgetting and Remembering

Would you like to transform your mind from a sieve to a snare? This
chapter shows you how much and how quickly we forget. Then it provides ten methods for clamping onto the information that you need to
know, by building a better memory . . .

- Motivated interest
- Selectivity
- Intention to remember
- Basic background
- Meaningful organization
- Recitation

- Consolidation
- Distributed practice
- Imagery: mental visualization
- Association

plus
- Mnemonics

S CIENTISTS DON'T KNOW how the brain stores, or memorizes, facts and ideas. But since we do have memories of previous experiences, the nervous system must somehow be able to make a record of these experiences. This record, in the brain, is called a *neural trace*. It cannot be seen, so we don't know much about it. For example, we don't know whether or not the neural trace disappears when we forget a fact, or whether we simply lose the ability to get to that particular neural trace.

However, it *is* known that everyone forgets most of what he or she learns. A psychologist, Robert S. Woodworth, found that, after only four weeks' time, people forget 98 percent of the totality of facts and ideas that they have experienced. This includes what they have read in newspapers, magazines, and books; what they have heard in conversations and lectures; what they have witnessed; what they have heard on radio and seen on television.

There are ways to overcome forgetting—to strengthen your memory. But before we begin to fight back, let's see what it is that we are fighting.

FORGETTING: THE RELENTLESS FOE

The Rate of Forgetting

Forgetting occurs very fast. Hermann Ebbinghaus, a German psychologist, investigated memory and forgetting over a period of many years. He used meaningless syllables (like GEP, JUK, KEV) in his research, to eliminate any effects of subjects' previous memorization. Ebbinghaus compiled the data in Table 5.1 (page 84), which indicate just how fast we do forget. For example, the first item shows that 47 percent of a memorized list of words was forgotten in just twenty minutes!

From his experiments, Ebbinghaus concluded that:

1. The greatest amount of forgetting occurs directly after finishing the learning task.
2. After the initial loss, forgetting slows down, but then, there's not so much left to forget.

But nonsense syllables are not the subject matter of college courses. How about textbook learning? H. F. Spitzer did a study in which 3,605 students learned—and then forgot—textbook material. Table 5.2 (page 84) tells the story. Notice how similar this table is to Table 5.1.

From Spitzer's experiment, we see that:

1. The greatest amount of forgetting occurs rapidly, during the first day.
2. Forgetting is still sizable during the first fourteen days.
3. Forgetting slows down after two weeks, but again there is not much left to forget.

Table 5.1 The Rate of Forgetting Meaningless Syllables

Time from First Learning	Percentage of Material Remembered	Percentage of Material Forgotten
After 20 minutes	53%	47%
After 1 day	38	62
After 2 days	31	69
After 15 days	25	75
After 31 days	22	78

Source: Hermann Ebbinghaus, *Memory* (New York: Columbia University Press, 1913). First published in German in 1885.

The results in Tables 5.1 and 5.2 might give you the impression that forgetting is caused by time. This just isn't true. To demonstrate that it isn't, the British psychologist Ian Hunter pointed out that "iron rusts in time" but rust is not caused by time.[1] Rust is caused by oxidation. Similarly, forgetting is not caused by time, but it happens as time passes.

You can, however, use time to your advantage when you study. For example, it is better to read two chapters in two succeeding nights than to read them both the same night. In the long run, you will retain more of what you study by *spacing* your work.

Listening and Forgetting

Remembering what you have *heard* is usually more difficult than remembering what you have *read*. In reading, you can slow down, pause,

Table 5.2 The Rate of Forgetting Textbook Material

Time from First Learning	Percentage of Material Remembered	Percentage of Material Forgotten
After 1 day	54%	46%
After 7 days	35	65
After 14 days	21	79
After 21 days	18	82
After 28 days	19	81
After 63 days	17	83

Source: Adapted from H. F. Spitzer, "Studies in Retention," *Journal of Educational Psychology* 30 (1939), 641–656. Copyright 1939 by the American Psychological Association. Reprinted by permission.

[1]Ian M. L. Hunter, *Memory: Facts and Fallacies* (Baltimore: Penguin, 1957), p. 61.

reflect, and even re-read. But in listening, you usually hear material only once, and you have to take notes, mental or written, to retain it. The following episode illustrates this point.

THE LEON-CLYDE EPISODE
(100 Percent True Story)

Characters: Leon, a psychologist; Clyde, a philosopher; Walter, the author of this book
Setting: Faculty lounge, after lunch

CLYDE: *Did you hear last night's lecture?*
WALTER: *No, I was busy.*
CLYDE: *Well, you missed one of the best lectures in recent years.*
LEON: *I agree. The four points that he developed were gems.*
CLYDE: *I never heard anyone make his points so clear.*
WALTER: *I don't want you to repeat the lecture, but what were those four points?*
LEON: *(Long silence) Clyde? (Passage of 2 or 3 minutes. Seemed like an hour.)*
LEON: *Well, I better get back to the office.*
CLYDE: *Me too!*
WALTER: *Me too!*

Both Clyde and Leon were brilliant men. Neither, however, was able to recall even a fragment of any point made in the lecture they had heard. The four points were forgotten because Clyde and Leon did not transfer them from short-term memory to long-term memory by *rehearsing* them. They did remember that the speaker was clear, forceful, and wise, and that he made four points; after the speech, they had rehearsed these generalities. However, they did not rehearse the four points by specifically thinking through them. As a result, they lost these points.

Pseudo-Forgetting

Whenever we cannot remember a name, telephone number, fact, idea, or even a joke, we automatically say, "I forgot." Yet, forgetting may not have anything to do with the problem. "I forgot" just seems to be a convenient, socially accepted explanation for these lapses. Let's look at two kinds of "forgetting" that are not real forgetting.

"YOU NEVER HAD IT" FORGETTING. Of course, it would be wrong to say "I forgot" about something when you never did have it in your memory in the first place. For example, you wouldn't expect to pull a $100 bill out of your wallet if you didn't put one there in the first place.

Similarly, you shouldn't expect to remember a name that was so mumbled during an introduction that you never did hear it clearly. Yet, you might later say, "I was introduced to him ten minutes ago, but I forgot his name already." Well, the truth is, you never had the name in your memory in the first place, so it's not forgetting. And this is also true of things you've briefly read in your textbook and briefly heard in a classroom lecture, without really grasping them, understanding them, and then making an effort to commit them to memory. That's not forgetting—it's never really knowing.

"MENTAL BLUR" FORGETTING.   This type of "forgetting" stems from grossly incomplete learning. You read a chapter straight through, but don't have time to go back to take notes. Next morning, when a question is asked in class, the best you can say to the instructor is, "I read it only last night, but I forgot most of it. I guess I have a poor memory."

You are wrong about forgetting and about having a poor memory. You see, you did read the words in the chapter, and you did understand the words, but you didn't stop to put these words together into ideas. So, instead of isolating the eight or ten important ideas in the chapter, you just saw a continuous string of words. It's like pointing a camera at the distant hills and rapidly swinging the camera to get in all the hills while you click the shutter. All you'll get is a blur. And your quick reading of the chapter, without stopping to get a separate mental picture of each idea, will result only in a mental blur of the entire chapter. If an idea or fact is to be retained in the memory, it must be impressed on the mind clearly and crisply at least once. A neural trace must be laid down in the brain. You cannot retain something that is not there in the first place.

What Causes Forgetting?

Most psychologists believe that forgetting is caused by interference—that is, old knowledge in the memory mingling with new knowledge. This means that new neural traces, formed when we learn new facts, dates, names, ideas, and so forth, mingle with and scramble older traces, causing forgetting.

Scientists have also shown that there are several varieties of interference. You should be aware of them so you'll have a fuller understanding of why forgetting is such a powerful foe:

1. *Retroactive interference.* In this process, new learning interferes with the recall of old learning. For example, I learned that the Pikes Peak gold rush took place in 1851. This is old learning, and there is a record,

a neural trace, of this fact in my brain. But today I read that gold was discovered at Sutter's Mill, California, on January 24, 1848, and started a big gold rush in 1849. If this new knowledge caused me to forget the date of the Pikes Peak gold rush, that would be retroactive interference.

2. *Proactive interference.* This kind of interference occurs when old knowledge interferes with the recall of new knowledge. It is just the opposite of retroactive interference. It would, for example, cause my memory of the Pikes Peak date to interfere with my remembering the California gold discovery date.

3. *Interactive interference.* Suppose I now learn that the Klondike gold rush took place in 1897. In interactive interference, my oldest knowledge (Pikes Peak) and my newest knowledge (Klondike) would tend to make me lose the intermediate knowledge (Sutter's Mill). In other words, interactive interference describes the bombardment of learning by both earlier and later learning. I can combat this interference by reviewing the three dates from time to time, to keep their mental traces clear, crisp, and sharp.

4. *Reactive interference.* This kind of interference arises from negative feelings or attitudes that we may have toward a disliked subject. Such feeling will not only make understanding more difficult, but also make the material difficult to remember.

The disliked subject is usually a required subject, so it must be learned. The way to cope with reactive interference is to study the subject in sprints. That is, work actively with paper and pencil for a disciplined effort of fifty minutes; then take a well-deserved ten-minute break. The rest period will allow the annoyance generated by the task to subside and disappear.

FIGHTING BACK USING TEN PRINCIPLES OF LEARNING AND REMEMBERING

Almost all the scientific studies and experiments on memory and forgetting indicate that you can combat forgetting only if you *learn the material thoroughly* in the first place. You must lay down a strong neural trace at the time the material is first learned. Without a neural trace, there is nothing to remember. And you must reinforce, or rehearse, what you wish to remember.

On the next several pages we discuss ten principles of learning and remembering. By applying these principles, you can learn to remember.

1. The Principle of Motivated Interest

Psychologists agree that to learn something thoroughly, you must have an *interest* in the material being studied. It is almost impossible to remember anything that does not interest you in the first place. In Chapter 1 you saw how interest in learning could be stimulated by a little academic success. In Chapter 4, I listed a few specific techniques for building interest in a distasteful subject. Here I simply want to emphasize the power of motivated interest.

I once interviewed a feeble-minded man who had been committed to an institution because he could not earn a living or function satisfactorily in the community. This man had a remarkable memory in one small area of knowledge. He could tell the day of the week for any date within a period of about twenty-five years. We could trace this ability back to an occasion when, as a boy, he had surprised his teacher by telling her that Lincoln's birthday would come on a Thursday. She praised him, and it was a rare thing for him to be praised for any mental accomplishment. He began to study the calendar, and soon he was able to amaze his classmates with day-and-date stunts. He continued to develop this ability, devoting all his spare time to it. In the institution he was regarded as a mental magician and was given the less unpleasant jobs for that reason. There was nothing miraculous about his ability; it was based on memory developed by intensive and prolonged effort—because he had a highly motivated interest in the feelings of success that his efforts brought him.

From James D. Weinland, How to Improve Your Memory *(New York: Barnes and Noble Division, Harper and Row, 1957), p. 6.*

The wizard of batting averages. In my home town, a young man achieved a townwide reputation for remembering every baseball player's batting average on a day-by-day basis in both the American and National leagues. Motivated interest: He was continually the center of enjoyable light-hearted attention.

Eight thousand names. When Charles Schwab was general manager of the Homestead Mill of the Bethlehem Steel Corporation, he knew by name all his 8,000 employees. Motivated interest: He believed in the dignity of the common working man; consequently he showed his respect by learning and using each man's name.

A college president. Charles W. Eliot, who was president of Harvard for forty years, year by year knew the names of all the students and faculty. Motivated interest: At one time he was so embarrassed by his inability to remember the name of one of his colleagues that he determined never to suffer the embarrassment again.

If you could study every one of your subjects with motivated interest, you would not have to worry about your final grades. If you are naturally interested in a subject, then you have no problem. If, however, you are not naturally interested, then create an artificial interest and enthusiasm.

(Read again the techniques described in Chapter 4.) Once you begin to learn something about a new subject, the chances are great that you will find it genuinely interesting.

The key point is to use the power of interest to work *for* you, not against you.

2. The Principle of Selectivity

According to this principle, you have to pare the job of learning down to manageable size. To do that, you must decide which facts to master and which ones you can safely ignore. This is a very difficult principle to follow, because of the tiring effect of constant decision making. But the deciding and selecting must be done if real learning and remembering are to be achieved.

It is impossible to learn and remember any subject with all its details. Any person who tries to do so will become bewildered and will end up remembering less than if he or she had tried to master less material in the first place. Over-conscientious students who set out to "learn everything in the book" actually sabotage their own efforts, because they run directly into some unyielding laws: In addition to the general laws of forgetting discussed in the previous chapter, there is the law of memory capacity for discrete items.

Hermann Ebbinghaus demonstrated this law when he recorded the *time* it took to learn different amounts of information.[2] He found that a list of seven syllables could be learned in three minutes. But when the list was lengthened to sixteen (slightly more than double), it took three hours and sixteen minutes—or *65 times as long!*—to memorize. And with a list of thirty-six syllables, the time consumed in learning them was thirteen hours and twelve minutes—or *264 times* the three minutes for seven syllables. Clearly, when you add just a few seemingly light bits of information to your learning load, you can make the job of memorization become a heavy burden—and it need not be.

What does this tell you? It should tell you to digest your textbook chapters and copious lecture notes exceedingly well, to come up with the essential details and ideas, and to commit them to memory—to practice the great law of parsimony (use the fewest to do the mostest).

Perhaps once again William James has said it best: "The essence of genius is to know what to overlook."

When urged to be selective, students often say, "What if I select the

---

[2]R. D. Williams and G. W. Knox, "A Survey of Dynamic Principles Governing Memory," *Journal of General Psychology*, 30 (1944), 167–179.

wrong ideas, facts, and details to memorize?" The answer to this question has six parts:

1. Have the courage to select and reject. You know that to try to memorize everything in a chapter will surely lead to failure.
2. As you evaluate the relative importance of each item, you will be thinking actively and consciously, and thus learning. That is the great bonus of this system.
3. With only a little practice you will become quite proficient in selecting the important ideas, facts, and details. If you don't begin using selectivity, you will be at the mercy of undifferentiated masses of material.
4. It is a lot easier to select the important points with the book open before you, than to do so during an examination, *without* the book in front of you. So, while you still have a chance, read thoroughly and make the best decisions that you can.
5. You have context on your side. Even in a new course, you have already listened to a lecture or two, heard general discussions, and perhaps skimmed the first and second chapters. So the subject matter and the course are not totally new. Now, in studying the next chapter, you have a general background that will help you make choices among ideas, facts, and details.
6. Some students use this variation: They go through a chapter the first time to select only the main ideas, thus establishing a strong framework. They then go through the chapter a second time to work into the framework the necessary details, and thus end up with the information in organized form.

The strength of this system is that general principles and main ideas are easier to remember because they involve understanding; your mind can associate them with all kinds of information already stored in your brain. The supporting details are more difficult to remember because that requires memorization through repetition. You can, therefore, establish a general principle as the magnetic center around which to cluster the supporting details. A unit is easier to remember than many separate details.

3. The Principle of Intention to Remember

Without an intention to remember, little worthwhile learning can take place. Many people have personally experienced the truth of this principle without realizing it. For example, many of us have helped a child memorize a poem or a speech by correcting his errors and prompting him when he forgot his lines. After spending as much time on the poem or speech as the child, we knew hardly any of it, but he had mastered it. The explanation: He *intended* to remember; we didn't.

One's mental attitude has a truly surprising effect on memory. In a carefully designed study, H. H. Remmers and M. N. Thisted worked with students who learned material with the intention of retaining it for only one day, as for an exam.[3] The retention of these students at the end of two weeks was lower than that of students who determined to remember the material for a two-week period.

The intention to remember is well illustrated by waiters in restaurants. They exhibit a remarkably good memory for what customers order, up to the moment they have paid their bills. Then the waiters jettison the entire transaction from their mind so that they can give full attention to the next customer. In this case, just as they intend to remember, they can intend to forget.

This concept of the intention to forget, so that one has room for new material, was succinctly put forth by Dr. Hans Selye:

> *It seems that to some extent* newly learned facts occupy the place of previously learned or subsequently learnable ones. *Consequently there is a limit to how much you can burden your memory; and trying to remember too many things is certainly one of the major sources of psychologic stress. I make a conscious effort to forget immediately all that is unimportant and to jot down data of possible value (even at the price of having to prepare complex files). Thus I manage to keep my memory free for facts which are truly essential to me. I think this technique can help anyone to accomplish the greatest simplicity compatible with the degree of complexity of his intellectual life.*[4]

The *intent to learn* is an overall positive attitude that automatically triggers several subsidiary attitudes, such as paying attention, getting a fact right the first time, and striving to understand.

ATTENTION. Attention is the mental set of giving yourself fully to the task at hand. Unfortunately, inattention is common in reading textbooks, especially when an idea in the book starts your mind dreaming down another road. Then your eyes move along the printed lines without comprehending them at all. Chapter 4 tackles this problem directly.

GETTING IT RIGHT THE FIRST TIME. All remembering depends on forming a clear neural trace in the brain in the first place. These initial impressions are vitally important because the mind clings just as tenaciously to in-

---

[3]H. H. Remmers and M. N. Thisted, "The Effect of Temporal Set on Learning," *Journal of Applied Psychology* 16 (1932), 257–268.

[4]Hans Selye, *The Stress of Life* (New York: McGraw-Hill, 1956), p. 269.

correct impressions as it does to correct impressions. Then we have to unlearn and relearn.

One helpful aid in getting it right the first time is to be attentive and cautious when it comes to learning new knowledge. Go very slowly at first. Place your emphasis on accuracy, not speed.

STRIVING TO UNDERSTAND.   You must make sure that you understand new material before trying to remember it. A good technique to ensure understanding is to recite or write the author's ideas in *your own words*. If you cannot, then you do not understand them. And you cannot remember what you do not understand. In other words, you cannot form a clear and correct memory trace from a fuzzy, poorly understood concept.

In the classroom, do not hesitate to ask the instructor to explain a point that is not clear to you. If the point is unclear to you, there is a good chance that it is unclear to others; so you will not be wasting anyone's time. Furthermore, most instructors appreciate the opportunity to slow down a lecture to answer questions.

4. The Principle of the Basic Background

Our understanding of what we *hear*, what we *read*, what we *see*, what we *feel*, and what we *taste* depends entirely upon what we already know—upon the knowledge and experience we have in our background. When listening to a speaker, we understand the successive points that he or she is making as long as we can interpret those points in terms of what we are already familiar with. But the moment the speaker refers to a concept like the *Zeigarnik effect*, or to a word like *serendipity*—a concept or a word that we do not have in our background—then we are lost. This concept or word stands alone as an isolated sound; we cannot attach an accurate meaning to it. At this point, we may need to stop the speaker and ask him or her to explain. Experienced speakers, however, usually know when they are putting forth concepts and words that are not popularly known, and they provide the audience with an example or analogy.

(To satisfy your curiosity, the *Zeigarnik effect* is the tendency to remember uncompleted tasks better than completed tasks. *Serendipity* is the faculty of making fortunate discoveries by accident.)

Many students make the mistake of thinking that the basic courses taken in their freshman year are a waste of time. These courses create the background essential for all their later courses. Budding technicians or engineers should realize that when they start studying these basic courses, they have already begun their careers. Your professional life begins with your freshman courses.

5. The Principle of Meaningful Organization

There is no better method for remembering large masses of material than the *personal organization* that you impose on the material. In other words, you should cluster facts and ideas into categories that are meaningful to you. The importance of organization is illustrated in Figure 5.1.

You were quickly able to see, no doubt, that list 1 would be most difficult to memorize because it contains groups of letters that simply don't make sense. List 2 would not be so difficult to memorize, since each word is meaningful, even though the words are unrelated. List 3, however, could be memorized most easily because all the words fit into a sentence, and the sentence makes sense.

So you need some sort of organizational system. But whatever system you use, make sure it's simple. A complicated system only adds to the burden of remembering; you have to remember the structure as well as the content. Here are some systems that have been found useful by students.

THE CATEGORY SYSTEM.   When reading or taking notes, first gather the facts and ideas. Then look them over with an eye toward clustering them under categories. For example, if you were asked to buy the following items at the market, you would have a difficult time remembering them:

Hamburg	Celery	Butter
Lettuce	Eggs	Pork chops
Milk	Steak	Carrots

Figure 5.1. Lists of Words and Nonwords. Which list would be most difficult for you to learn? Which would be easiest?

List 1	List 2	List 3
GIH	WHY	THE
WUK	ONE	BOY
NAF	THE	RAN
SIJ	TOO	TO
HUQ	CAN	THE
MAV	TEN	STORE
TIZ	HOW	TO
YEM	LET	BUY
NOL	NOW	A
LIW	ASK	CAN
DOF	OUR	OF
KAG	AND	MILK

But if you rearranged the items under natural categories, you would have very little difficulty in remembering.

Meats	Vegetables	Dairy
Hamburg	Lettuce	Milk
Steak	Celery	Eggs
Pork chops	Carrots	Butter

This category system of organization is very simple, but it has been of practical use to humankind for a long, long time.

THE MAGICAL NUMBER SEVEN THEORY.   Recent experiments have revealed the exciting possibility of remembering vast quantities of materials that are organized into categories or blocks. One researcher, G. A. Miller of Harvard, found that the immediate memory span of an adult appears fixed at approximately seven separate "bits" of information. It doesn't matter whether the seven bits are big or small; only the number matters. So the trick is this: Make each of your seven things into a big general category; then add bits of information within these categories. Later, by remembering the names of the categories, you'll also remember, by association, the *bits* of information that you previously attached to them.

These larger chunks must always be put in your own words and then rephrased in your own words, so that the seven chunks together form a continuous story in your mind. You are sure to find words that will bring together the seven chunks. As Miller says, "Our language is tremendously useful for repackaging material into a few chunks rich in information."[5]

FIRST AND LAST ON A LIST.   Here is something to remember about organizing information: The items that you place at the head of a list and those you place at the end of a list are recalled with greater accuracy than those in the middle of the list.[6] So when you recite a list of items to memorize it, give items in the middle of the list some extra attention and practice.

6. The Principle of Recitation

No principle is more important than *recitation* for transferring material from the short-term memory to the long-term memory.

Recitation is saying aloud the ideas that you want to remember. For

[5]G. A. Miller, "The Magical Number Seven, Plus or Minus Two: Some Limits on Our Capacity for Processing Information," *Psychological Review* 63 (1956), 81–97.

[6]B. B. Murdock, Jr., "The Retention of Individual Items," *Journal of Experimental Psychology* 62 (1961), 618–625.

example, after you have gathered your information in note form and have categorized and clustered your items, you recite them. Here's how: You cover your notes with a blank sheet of paper, expose only the title or name of one category, and then recite aloud the material in that category. After reciting, expose your notes and check for accuracy. You should not attempt to recite the material word for word. Instead, you should use the words and manner that you would use if you were explaining the material to your roommate. When you can *say it,* then you *know it.*

Recitation may also be used with a textbook. After you read through a headed or subheaded section consisting of a page or two, stop reading and test yourself on what you have just read by reciting aloud the key ideas. Once you have recited and seen that you understand the ideas thus far in the chapter, you will read and recite later portions with greater understanding and efficiency.

HOW RECITATION WORKS.   While you are reading the words in a sentence or paragraph, your *primary memory* (short-term memory) holds them in mind long enough for you to gain the sense of the sentence or paragraph. However, the primary memory has a very limited capacity; as you continue to read, you displace the words and ideas of the initial paragraphs with the words of subsequent paragraphs. This is one reason why we don't remember everything in the first part of a chapter by the time we reach the end of the chapter, when we read continually without pausing to recite.

However, when you *recite* or *contemplate* the idea conveyed by a sentence or paragraph, the idea has a chance (not guaranteed) of moving on into your *secondary memory* (a long-term storage facility). Actually, only part of the rehearsed (recited) material goes into your secondary (long-term) memory. The rest of it, usually the part you are least interested in, remains in limbo and then returns to the primary memory where it is forgotten.

Thus, whether new information is "stored" or "dumped" depends on (1) reciting it out loud and (2) your interest in the information.

WHY RECITATION WORKS.   Recitation is far more effective than merely reading and re-reading for the following reasons.

1. Since you know that you will stop to recite after reading each headed section within a chapter, you will be more motivated to understand.
2. Recitation lets you know how you are doing. A correct recitation is an immediate reward that helps keep motivation high. An incorrect recitation is punishment that motivates a student to avoid future punishment by studying harder.
3. Recitation strengthens the original memory trace, because your mind must actively think about the new material.

4. The physical activity of thinking, pronouncing, and even hearing your own words involves not only your mind but also your body in the process of learning. The more physical senses you use in learning, the stronger the neural trace in your brain.

IMPORTANCE OF PHYSICAL ACTIVITY.   To promote recall, it is important to make outward, physical motion a part of the learning process. Students who silently read their assignments, no matter how diligently, often wonder why they remember so little after several days have passed. They do not realize that it is inefficient and ineffective to use the eyes alone as a means of absorbing information. Reciting aloud or writing the information, even sketchily, is better by far.

HOW MUCH RECITATION?   How much time should you spend reading, and how much time reciting? The experiments of Prof. Arthur I. Gates, a famous educator, show that regardless of the kind of material studied, more material is retained when a greater proportion of the study time is spent in reciting.[7] Reciting ensures both immediate recall and long-term recall.

More specifically, Prof. Gates says that when you read a textbook chapter containing many facts, names, and principles, then 80 percent of the time should be spent in reciting and only 20 percent in reading. This proportion pertains to such subjects as economics, psychology, sociology, and history. When you are memorizing such reading material as biographies, then 60 percent of the time should be spent in reading and 40 percent in reciting.

Professor Gates also concluded that recitation should begin early in the learning process. In other words, you should not wait until all the material has been read before beginning to recite.

7. *The Principle of Consolidation*

Psychologists believe that neural traces need some time—from four or five seconds to about fifteen minutes—to jell or *consolidate.* Experiments with rats and hamsters offer concrete evidence of this phenomenon. In rats, the neural trace must persist in the brain for at least ninety seconds before a temporary memory can be converted or consolidated into a permanent one. In human beings the neural trace must persist for only a few seconds, perhaps four or five.

This principle of consolidation may well be at work when you *recite* or *write* the ideas and facts that you read. As you recite or write, you hold

[7]Arthur I. Gates, "Recitation as a Factor in Memorizing," *Archives of Psychology*, 7, No. 40 (1917).

each idea in mind for just the four or five seconds that are needed for the temporary memory to be converted into a permanent one.

Another practical application of the principle of consolidation is in reviewing your notes immediately after class. If the reviewing is done by recitation, you are not only consolidating the new information but also strengthening its neural trace in your brain.

A. M. Sones's experiment on the value of review is illuminating.[8] One group of students had no review immediately after a class meeting; a second group had only a five-minute review test. With only this five-minute advantage, the second group recalled one and a half times as much material as the group that had no immediate review, when both groups were tested six weeks later.

8. The Principle of Distributed Practice

In *distributed practice* the student uses relatively short study periods broken up by rest intervals. In *massed practice* the student studies continually until the task is completed. Many experiments show that, in general, there is an advantage to distributed practice. The optimal length of the study period, of course, varies with different individuals, as well as with the nature of the material being studied.

There are four apparent reasons why distributed practice is more efficient than massed practice:

1. Both physical and emotional fatigue are prevented.
2. Motivation is higher when we work within short blocks of time.
3. On subjects that are not very interesting, boredom is forestalled.
4. Once energized, the neural learning processes seem to continue working during the rest period.

A PRACTICAL APPLICATION. A practical application of the principle of distributed practice would be to make use of the small blocks of time (often only ten minutes) that occur between classes. When a lecture ends, while walking to your next class, try to recall the entire lecture—or as many of its ideas as possible.

IMMEDIATE AND LONG-TERM GAINS. In an extensive experiment, Irving Lorge found that, with the introduction of distributed practice, students im-

[8]A. M. Sones, "A Study in Memory, with Special Reference to Temporal Distribution of Reviews," University of Iowa, *Studies, Aims and Progress in Research*, No. 72 (1943) 65–72.

mediately improved their performance.[9] However, if distributed practice was stopped while the students were still working on the experiment, their performance decreased. There was an immediate reaction to both injection and withdrawal of distributed practice.

Bertram Epstein experimented to find out whether or not distributed practice had an effect on retention.[10] He tested his groups immediately after learning and then two weeks and ten weeks after the original practice. He found distributed practice to be superior to massed practice for both immediate and long-term retention.

USE OF MASSED PPACTICE.   In some cases, massed practice is superior to distributed practice. In work such as the writing of a paper, massed practice is often essential. For example, the exact locations of the little stacks of notes spread over the desk are held in mind with precision; the discrete bits of information are precariously suspended in mind to be fitted in like jigsaw-puzzle pieces at the appropriate time; and, the organizational pattern, though dimly perceived, is beginning to take shape. To stop at this point would be disastrous. The entire effort would collapse. So, in creative work, or work which needs to be overviewed at one sitting, it is far more efficient to overextend yourself—to complete that stage of the process—than to take a break or otherwise apply the principle of distributed practice.

9. The Principle of Imagery: Mental Visualization

"The human memory would be worthless without the capacity to make mental pictures," says Dr. Joseph E. Shorr.

We all know that the brain is divided into the left and right hemispheres. The left stores verbal information; the right stores visual information. Dr. Allan Paivio of the University of Western Ontario has done a great deal of research on memory and has come up with a "dual code theory."[11] He says that if you commit facts and ideas to memory through words only, then you are using only half your brainpower. But when the same fact or idea that you memorized through words (stored in the left

[9]Irving Lorge, *Influence of Regularly Interpolated Time Intervals upon Subsequent Learning*, Contributions to Education, No. 438 (New York: Bureau of Publications, Teachers College, Columbia University, 1930).

[10]Bertram Epstein, *Immediate and Retention Effects of Interpolated Rest Periods on Learning Performance*, Contributions to Education, No. 949 (New York: Bureau of Publications, Teachers College, Columbia University, 1949).

[11]Allan Paivio, *Imagery and Verbal Processes* (New York: Holt, Rinehart and Winston, 1971), pp. 522–523.

hemisphere) is also memorized through a picture or sketch (stored in the right hemisphere), you have set up a powerful combination in your memory. You can draw upon this combination later when you need to recall the fact or idea.

To use this principle, simply *make your own diagrams* as you read. For example, the following paragraph describing one of Faraday's experiments was not accompanied by a diagram:

> *In 1831, Michael Faraday, one of Britain's greatest scientists, did the experiments which completely demonstrated the close relationship between electricity and magnetism. One of his famous experiments was to take a coil of wire and connect the ends across an instrument capable of measuring tiny currents. By quickly pushing a bar magnet through the coil he was able to produce a small current in the coil and to measure that current. What he was really doing was to change the strength of the magnetic field in the coil by inserting and removing the magnet. The more rapidly he changed the field the more current he could generate.*[12]

Figure 5.2 shows how this description can easily be converted into a diagram for retention in the right hemisphere. In the process of drawing such a diagram, you will actually be breaking the description into its components. Thus you'll understand it far more thoroughly than you would through only reading and studying it.

Even when the material doesn't lend itself to diagraming, you can still devise a mental image. For example, if you need to remember that Abraham Lincoln was born in 1809, picture (or draw) a log cabin with the

Figure 5.2 A Descriptive Paragraph Diagramed.

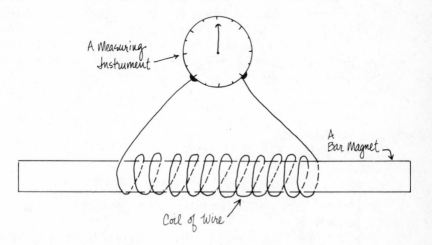

[12]J. D. Jukes, *Man-Made Sun* (New York: Abelard-Schuman, 1959), p. 33.

date 1809 over the doorway. The picture doesn't have to be a good one, it only has to be visualized.

10. The Principle of Association

Suppose you have just been introduced to a heavyset man named Mr. Perkins. To remember his name, you immediately associate it with a heavy coffeepot *perking*. You even visualize the perking pot and smell the aroma of freshly brewed coffee.

What you have done is tie the *new* information (Mr. Perkins) to *old* information (perking coffeepot) that is already well established in your memory. When you meet him at some future time, you will recall the perking coffee pot, which will prepare you to say, "Hello, Mr. Perkins, it is so nice to see you again."

Association is a strong principle. It was used by the Greeks and Romans and is the basis of many memorization techniques. As William James said, "The more other facts a fact is associated with in the mind, the better possession of it our memory retains." He also said, "Of two men of equal intelligence, the one who *thinks* over his experiences most, and weaves them into systematic relations with each other, will be the one with the best memory."

But how do you use this principle when you study? Simply by making a reasonable association when you come to a fact that you want to retain. Here's an example: "The boiling point of water varies with the air pressure and therefore with elevation. It is 212°F at sea level, and it decreases about 1°F for every 550 feet above sea level."

If I ran across this information while studying a textbook, I would make a strong association by saying *aloud*, "This is what I'd reply if I were asked a question about air pressure or elevation and boiling points." Then I would repeat the information, again aloud, in my own words. If I later read such a question on an exam, chances are that I'd recall the association and the information. There would be a linkage.

MEMORY NEEDS TIME TO CONSOLIDATE LEARNING

Here are the ten principles or methods for learning in summary form:

1. *Motivated interest.* You need a realistic goal and a strong thirst for knowledge.
2. *Selectivity.* Select principles and laws which, like powerful magnets, draw the details around them.

3. *Intent to remember.* Learn for permanency, not only for exams.
4. *Basic background.* The more you learn, the easier it is to learn more.
5. *Organization.* Learn and memorize ideas and facts in clusters and groups.
6. *Recitation.* Saying the facts and ideas aloud makes you *think* and makes you remember.
7. *Consolidation.* Like a warm rain, facts and ideas need time to sink in.
8. *Distributed practice.* Several short sessions of intense concentration are more productive than one long grinding-it-out session.
9. *Imagery.* Mental pictures and actual diagrams enable you to use 100 percent of your brainpower and memory power.
10. *Association.* Make a link between a new fact and some well-established old fact. Then, you will recall the old fact, which will pull the new fact up from the depths of your memory.

If you practice these ten methods but still find that at certain times the learning goes slowly, don't despair. This is not always the result of a poor memory.

No two people learn at exactly the same rate, yet the learning patterns for most people are quite similar. We all experience lulls in our learning. Progress is usually slow and steady at first, but then, for a period of time, there might be no perceptible progress even though genuine effort is being put forth. This so-called "no progress" period is called a *plateau.* After days, weeks, or even a month of effort, suddenly a surprising spurt in learning occurs and continues until another plateau is reached.

A generally accepted explanation for the plateau is that the individual skills, the bits and pieces, must undergo consolidation. During the plateau period they are gradually combined into a more or less unified whole, and then the stage is set for another spurt in learning. Plateaus can occur at any time in the learning cycle, and they can have short or long durations.

The reason for this discussion is to let you know that plateaus will occur and that you shouldn't lose heart. You may not see any progress, but learning is going on nevertheless. Once everything is in place, you'll be rewarded for your effort.

REMEMBERING THROUGH MNEMONICS

To combat forgetting, some students take memory courses given by commercial enterprises. Many others invent (or inherit) *mnemonic devices*—easily remembered words, phrases, sentences, or rhymes that are associated with difficult-to-remember principles or facts. Both memory courses and mnemonic devices have some good points and some that are not so good.

Mnemonic Devices

Almost all people use a mnemonic or two without realizing it. Probably the most widely used mnemonic device is the old jingle by which most of us learned the irregularities of our calendar:

> Thirty days has September,
> April, June, and November.
> All the rest have thirty-one,
> Except February alone.

Rivaling this days-in-the-month mnemonic is the one for spelling:

> *i* before *e* except after *c*
> or when sounding like *a*
> as in neighbor and weigh.

And many of us have private mnemonics, such as "surround the *r* with *a* for the word sep*a*r*a*te."

Though they are widely used for practical purposes, mnemonic devices have traditionally been contested with regard to scholarly learning. "Learn it directly," says one group, which feels that these extra associations only add to the amount to be learned. Other critics approach the controversy from an ethical point of view, noting that the use of mnemonics in place of good old-fashioned studying and memorizing is almost like cheating. Perhaps the strongest argument is that the mnemonic system ignores the meaning of the material being learned. That is, ideas, facts, and general information are simply compartmentalized, packaged, and mechanically brought forth when needed. Critics maintain that students learn little about information that they memorize in this way. If the same information were learned directly and meaningfully, students could integrate it into their general knowledge for use in relation to other facts and ideas.

Such unyielding critics overlook the fact that students are often exposed to material that is seemingly meaningless. How can they relate such material to something else? Should they just skip it? And suppose the information is too complex, or the data are too numerous, to hold in the memory; how are they to be remembered?

The cardinal rule for dealing with masses of information is to *organize* the data in some way that makes sense. If this cannot be done, then the use of a mnemonic would seem to be the next best choice. After all, a mnemonic device is an organizational system, pure and simple. It is an ordinary means to an important end. Moreover, since mnemonics are *organizational* systems, students who use them will discover the value of organization and be encouraged to use non-mnemonic organizational systems as well.

The Effectiveness of Mnemonics

Gerald R. Miller conducted a study to evaluate the effectiveness of mnemonic devices as aids to study.[13] His results were as follows:

1. Students who used mnemonic devices raised their test scores (by 77 percent in one case).
2. Students who made up their own mnemonics attained higher test scores than when they used no mnemonics.
3. Students who used mnemonics constructed by the instructor scored higher than when using mnemonics made up by themselves.

Miller recognizes that the use of too many mnemonics can overload the memory, thus reducing their effectiveness. Nevertheless, he argues that learning a large number of mnemonics well creates no greater hazard for the student than learning a large amount of material in the traditional way.

Devising Mnemonics

It is best to acquire knowledge through understanding, rather than by parroting. But occasionally you will be required to know facts that defy organization or that cannot be connected in a meaningful way. Then you will have to invent or adopt some mnemonic device to help you remember. When you do so, keep in mind that a mnemonic is an organizational device, and use your mnemonics only until you know the material so well that you no longer need them.

ASSOCIATIVE MNEMONIC. Sometimes you can associate a fact with something you know but which has no real connection with the fact. For example, to remember that the Tropic of Capri*corn* is in the Southern Hemisphere, you can associate it with the *corns* on your feet; that is, with *your* south. As another example, use the *n*'s to remember that lines of longitude run

---

[13]Gerald R. Miller, *An Evaluation of the Effectiveness of Mnemonic Devices as Aids to Study*, Cooperative Research Project No. 5-8438, University of Texas at El Paso, 1967. Supported by Office of Education, U.S. Department of Health, Education, and Welfare.

north and south; since the word latitude does not have an *n*, lines of latitude run west and east. (Here, this *is* a connection between longitude and north-south—all the better.)

MAKE-A-WORD MNEMONIC. In this type of mnemonic device, the letters of a "made" word help you remember key words. Here's an example:

The task is to make a mnemonic for these five ways to help prevent heart attack and stroke:

1. After <u>age 40</u>, get a medical checkup every year.
2. Do not <u>smoke</u>.
3. Keep your <u>weight</u> down.
4. <u>Exercise</u> moderately and wisely.
5. Get sufficient <u>rest</u>.

To devise a make-a-word mnemonic, we proceed as follows:

Step 1: Underline the key word in each item, as is done in the list above.

Step 2: Write down the first letter of each key word. Here, we have A, S, W, E, and R.

Step 3: Make a word or several words from the first letters of the key words. Change the order of the letters as necessary to do so. Here, we can make the word SWEAR, which will help us recall the five key words:

S moke
W eight
E xercise
A ge 40
R est

Your mnemonic may be a real word or a word that you just made up. When you use a made-up word, be sure you will be able to remember it.

MAKE-A-SENTENCE MNEMONIC. This is a variation on the make-a-word mnemonic. It is devised as follows:

Step 1: Underline the key word in each main point in your notes.

Step 2: Write down the first letter of each key word.

Step 3: Construct an easy-to-remember sentence using words whose first letters are the same as the first letters of the key words.

As an example, here are eight main points taken from a long article about what to do when you are in a building that is on fire. The key words are underlined.

1. In a burning building, feel the <u>door</u> with your hand. If it is hot, the room or hall on the other side is on fire.
2. If the door is cool, check the <u>air</u> coming under the door. If it is cool, there's probably no fire on the other side.
3. Still don't take chances. Open the door just a <u>crack</u> while kneeling, with your face turned away. Listen and smell for fire and smoke.
4. When you leave, <u>shut</u> all doors and windows.
5. If your room is smoke-filled, <u>crawl</u> with your nose about one foot above the floor.
6. Never use an elevator; use a <u>stairway</u>.
7. If you are trapped, use <u>wet</u> cloths to protect your face, hands, and breathing passages.
8. <u>Hang</u> something out of a window to attract attention.

The first letters of the key words are D, A, C, S, C, S, W, and H. An easy-to-remember sentence using words beginning with the first letters of the key words is

<u>D</u>anger <u>A</u>lways <u>C</u>auses <u>S</u>ome <u>C</u>ats <u>S</u>ome <u>W</u>here (to) <u>H</u>owl.

The letters need not appear in the same order as the key words. However, here the sequence of steps was considered to be important, so the order was preserved.

In general, it is easier to make a sentence using the initial letters of the key words than to mold the initial letters into a word or two, especially if the order of the points is to be maintained. Of course, if the initial letters are mainly consonants, both can be difficult. To get around the problem of too many consonants, try to choose some key words that begin with a vowel.

Classic Mnemonic Devices

Here are some mnemonic devices that have been handed down and used by generations of students:

Astronomy. In astronomy, the favorite of students is the sentence that reminds them of the order of the planets (Mercury, Venus, Earth, Mars, Jupiter, Saturn, Uranus, Neptune, Pluto):

<u>M</u>en <u>V</u>ery <u>E</u>asily <u>M</u>ake <u>J</u>ugs <u>S</u>erve <u>U</u>seful and <u>N</u>umerous <u>P</u>urposes.

Biology. The first letters of the words in the following sentence stand for *kingdom, phylum, class, order, family, genus, species, variety:*

<u>K</u>ings <u>P</u>lay <u>C</u>ards <u>O</u>n <u>F</u>airly <u>G</u>ood <u>S</u>oft <u>V</u>elvet.

Geography. Remembering the names of the Great Lakes is not too difficult, but remembering them in order is not so easy. Here's a mnemonic device that organizes them from West to East (Superior, Michigan, Huron, Erie, Ontario):

<u>S</u>uper <u>M</u>achine <u>H</u>eaved <u>E</u>arth <u>O</u>ut.

History. The royal houses of England (Norman, Plantaganet, Lancaster, York, Tudor, Steward, Hanover, Windsor) are most difficult to remember without this mnemonic device:

<u>N</u>o <u>P</u>lan <u>L</u>ike <u>Y</u>ours <u>T</u>o <u>S</u>tudy <u>H</u>istory <u>W</u>isely.

Mathematics. Students of mathematics use this rhyme to remember the value of pi, the ratio of the circumference of a circle to its diameter (3.1415926535895 +). The key is the number of letters in each word:

  3   1   4   1   5   9   2   6   5
How I wish I could determine of circle round

  3   5   8   9   5
The exact relation Arkimedes found.

Medicine. Even doctors and pharmacists have jingles to keep certain chemicals straight. To distinguish between cyan*ates*, which are harmless, and cyan*ides*, which are extremely poisonous, they use this device:

—ate, I ate;—ide, I died.

Spelling. The greatest number of mnemonic devices center around spelling. Here's how to remember the correct way to spell two words that confuse many students:

A princi<u>pal</u> is a <u>pal</u>.
A princip<u>le</u> is a ru<u>le</u>.

In using mnemonic devices, you must make certain to memorize the sentence, word, or jingle thoroughly, for the slightest error can throw you off completely.

How Commercial Memory Courses Work

Many students prefer to combat forgetting by taking memory courses given by commercial enterprises. The techniques used in such memory courses vary, but the majority require the memorization of a master list of words called *pegs*. Each of these words is numbered, and a strong association is made between the number and the word. For example, *one* is *bun*, *two* is a *shoe*, *three* is a *tree*, *four* is a *door*, *five* is a *hive*, and so forth. To remember a shopping list consisting of butter, sugar, sausage, bacon, and bread, you would form a bizarre image associating the first peg word with the first item on the list, the second peg word with the second item, and so on. For example, for butter you might visualize a pound of butter atop a *bun* left out in the sun with the butter melting all over it. For sugar, you could visualize a *shoe* filled with loose sugar.

In the supermarket, to recall the grocery items you would simply recall the well-memorized peg words in numerical sequence. Almost automatically, with each peg word would come to mind the item associated with it. However, if you went to the store the next day for milk and eggs, you would have to associate the milk with the bun, and yesterday's butter might interfere with today's milk.

In other words, because the same symbols are used for many different lists, the peg system is useful only for things that you want to remember for a short time. Obviously, this system is all right for grocery lists. However, it has two important limitations with regard to school work: First, it can be used with only one list of items for only one exam at any time. Second, no permanent knowledge is gained, for items so memorized are quickly forgotten. I believe that peg words should be used only when you have to survive a battle (quiz or exam), so that you can stay on to win the war (pass the course).

SUMMARY

What's a neural trace?

A neural trace is the record, in the brain, of an experience. No one has ever seen a neural trace. However, we do remember our experiences, so some record of them must be made. That record is what we call the neural trace.

What's the great value of Ebbinghaus's experiment?

Ebbinghaus showed that, of all forgetting that occurs during the entire one-month period after learning, 60 percent occurs in the first twenty minutes. This evidence indicates loudly and clearly that the prime time to review, recite, and reflect is immediately after you learn something, before forgetting sets in. Notice that only 3 percent of the forgetting occurs in the last fifteen days of that first month.

What's the value of the Spitzer study?	It shows that textbook material is forgotten just as rapidly as the artificial words in Ebbinghaus's experiment. In Spitzer's experiment, 46 percent of the material read was forgotten after one day, and 81 percent after one month! Such massive forgetting shows why you have to study long and hard to recapture so much, especially before final exams.
Why did you include the Leon-Clyde episode?	Its purpose is to emphasize that forgetting, even 100 percent forgetting, can occur after you have just listened to a lecture. The simple lesson: Take notes while you listen to lectures.
What is pseudo-forgetting?	*Pseudo* means fake or nonreal. Pseudo-forgetting is so-called forgetting that is not really forgetting. It is an inability to recall information that you never really had in the first place.
What causes forgetting?	All your thoughts, ideas, dreams, and emotions have a way of interfering with your ability to recall any particular fact. It is this interference that causes forgetting. So, the more you know, the more potential interference you have. (The more stuff you have jammed into a crowded closet, the harder it is to find a particular item.) *Retroactive* interference takes place when later learning interferes with the recall of previously learned material. *Proactive* interference takes place when previous learning interferes with the recall of later learning. *Interactive* interference occurs when older and newer learning interfere with the recall of intermediate learning. Finally, *reactive* interference occurs when a negative attitude interferes with the recall of learning.
How important is motivated interest to learning?	Of utmost importance! Without genuine interest in a subject or in improvement in your performance, there will be almost no retention and thus almost no learning. You'll only go through the academic motions of learning, and even these will be a

waste of energy and time. In other words, you must *want to learn!* You must *want to improve!*

Isn't selecting the right ideas to remember difficult?

Yes, it's difficult, but if you have the *courage* to start doing so, you'll be surprised how expert you can become in a short time. If you want to become an independent self-learner, you must stand or fall by your personal judgments. In your selecting, be stingy. Use the fewest to do the mostest.

Doesn't everyone intend to remember?

Wishing to remember and *intending* to remember are two different things. Intending takes determined effort. And intending means having a game plan: First, pay 100 percent attention to the task of learning. Second, strive hard to understand each fact or idea, in your own words. Third, make sure you end up with a correct, clear, crisp concept to store in your memory. In other words, don't just sit there—*take action!*

A basic background: Why is it important?

Everything you hear, read, see, feel, and taste is interpreted in light of what you already know. For example, if you were asked about the taste of a new ice cream, you might say, "It's a cross between raspberry and banana." But, to say that, you must have had basic background knowledge of the tastes of banana and raspberry. In sum, the old is the key to the meaning of the new.

Why is organization important?

Organization is important because it helps you remember more information longer and better, for three reasons: First, mentally handling each piece of information to see where it best fits and then placing it into a category, you become very familiar with the information. Second, as you think through and design your organizational plan, you get familiar with the information and with how it fits in the overall picture. Third, organizing ties all the ideas, sub-ideas, and details in a neat package, which is many times easier to remember than scattered bits of information.

What is recitation and how does it help us remember?

Recitation is simply saying aloud, in your own words, the principal points that you read in a book or hear in a lecture, without looking at the book or your lecture notes. Recitation helps retention by making you think, by creating strong memory traces, and by providing time for the ideas to move from your short-term memory to your long-term memory.

What does consolidation imply about learning?

Before an idea, detail, or activity can become a permanent part of your memory, it has to pass from the short-term memory into the long-term memory. For this to happen, the idea must be held in the mind for a period of time, maybe four or five seconds. And this process can occur only when you *think over* the idea, detail, or activity, as you recite or write it, or as you review lecture notes.

What's the story on massed versus distributed practice?

Generally speaking, breaking a study session of, say, three hours, into six half-hour sessions with five-minute breaks between sessions, is better than trying to do the job all in one sitting. Taking breaks is good because it relieves boredom and fatigue and gives you time to "recharge your batteries" for another strong effort. However, if you can stick with study sessions for longer periods of time, that's okay. And some assignments should be done all in one sitting, because to stop would mean losing the facts and thoughts already held at the tip of your memory. In other words, you must use your judgment about breaks.

Can drawing a picture help you to remember?

Yes! Dr. Allan Paivio calls it the "dual code" theory. If you remember with words alone you're using only half your brain. Add a diagram, and you're suddenly making use of the whole brain. When it comes to memory, the combination of words and pictures is hard to forget.

How does association work?

Association is the mind's glue. To remember a new fact, you glue it to a fact you already have in your memory, through association.

What makes mnemonic devices work?

Mnemonic devices work on the principle of *association*. Each part of a mnemonic device is a direct cue to the facts or ideas that you want to remember.

Can almost all things be learned without mnemonics?

The answer has to be yes. Sometimes, however, the result may not be worth the memorization effort. Most things should be learned through understanding and organization, but items that defy organization or are too complex can be remembered through mnemonics.

What are the main criticisms of mnemonics?

The criticisms are three: that material memorized by rote lacks understanding; that mnemonic devices just add to the memory's overall load; and that material learned through mnemonics is soon forgotten.

What's good about mnemonics?

At least two things: First, mnemonic devices are sound and effective ways to organize your material and keep it straight. Second, when information that was learned through mnemonics is used frequently, it becomes a permanent part of your knowledge.

Do mnemonics help in exams?

Yes! In one study, all students using mnemonics raised their test scores over scores they attained without using mnemonics.

HAVE YOU MISSED SOMETHING?

1. **SENTENCE-COMPLETION.** Complete the following sentences with one of the three words listed below each sentence.

   a. The most important feature of a rest period is its _____.

      length   regularity   location

   b. In textbook study, recitation is best when it is done after every

      _____.

      chapter   sentence   sub-topic

c. The main strength of mnemonics lies in _____.

organization   rhymes   literature

2. **MATCHING.** In each blank space in the left column, write the number preceding the phrase in the right column that matches the left item best.

_____ a. Mnemonic

_____ b. Organize

_____ c. SWEAR

_____ d. Imagery: mental

visualization

_____ e. Distributed practice

_____ f. Association

_____ g. Selectivity

_____ h. Pseudo-forgetting

_____ i. Leon-Clyde episode

_____ j. Neural trace

_____ k. Interference theory

_____ l. Reactive interference

1. Cardinal rule for memory
2. Peg is one type
3. Mnemonic for health
4. Using old facts as hooks for new information
5. Reading a textbook chapter over several evenings
6. Making use of the old law of parsimony (fewest to do the mostest)
7. A diagram that accompanies a difficult explanation in a text
8. A battle of old and new ideas
9. An illustration of forgetting
10. "You never had it"
11. A memory record
12. Fueled by negative feelings

3. **TRUE-FALSE.** Write *T* beside the *true* statements and *F* beside the *false* statements that follow.

_____ a. Forgetting is caused by time.

_____ b. Spaced reading is best with long-term assignments.

_____ c. Distributed practice is recommended for every assignment.

_____ d. Recitation transfers information from short-term to long-term memory.

_____ e. Personal organization will help you to remember.

_____ f. Without mnemonics, the memory runs the risk of overloading.

4. **INTERFERENCE.** The following statements are examples of the four types of interference. Two are "imposters"; write "No" beside these two.

_____ a. Forgetting Communist arguments because you don't agree with them

_____ b. Allowing a distinct memory to be stored in the brain

_____ c. Letting last term's trigonometry confuse your understanding of this term's calculus

_____ d. Confusing memories of yesterday with those of this morning and last week

_____ e. Learning French II while forgetting French I

_____ f. Forgetting a textbook chapter that you skimmed over quickly

5. **MULTIPLE-CHOICE.** Choose the phrase that completes this sentence most accurately, and circle the letter that precedes it.

One advantage of recitation is that it

a. serves as a substitute for motivation.
b. retains information in the primary memory.
c. builds the body as well as the mind.
d. lets you know how you're doing.

PART III

YOUR NOTES

He listens well, who takes notes.

—DANTE

6

Listening and Notetaking

Listening and notetaking are inseparable partners. Any experienced reporter will confirm this. The only way to take notes is to listen; listen without taking notes and you'll quickly forget. This chapter shows you how to listen, how to take notes, and how to combine the two into a powerful pair. It contains . . .

- The case for taking notes
- Listening and concentrating
- How to go about notetaking
- Twenty notetaking guidelines

and

- The Cornell System for notetaking

plus

- Speaking up in class

W HAT GOES ON IN THE CLASSROOM is just as important as what goes on in a textbook—and sometimes even more so. Yet many students don't see it that way. Students who would never skip an assigned textbook chapter may routinely stay out of class. It appears to be standard practice to skip classes to study for examinations, to get another hour's sleep, or to take the full number of allowable "cuts."

Even more serious is the skipping that goes on inside the classroom: skipping the opportunity to take good notes, or skipping most of the discussions by letting the mind wander where it will. The problem may be the informality of the classroom, which creates a take-it-or-leave-it climate. Although most students "take it," far too many "leave it."

WHY TAKE NOTES?

Your objective in taking notes in class is to capture the instructor's ideas in the order in which they are given, so you can take them back to your room to study and master. You have to take notes or else you'll forget what you've heard. Incidentally, you should ignore the complainers who argue that notetaking prevents you from listening. These are the very same students who consistently find themselves at the bottom of the class. Instead, look back at the beginning of Chapter 5, and note again how rapidly and how massively forgetting takes place.

As for the complainers, you might ask them what grades they earn in the courses in which they don't take notes.

In any event, rely on your own judgment. Do your own thinking. And consider the following episode, which shows all too clearly the amount of forgetting that takes place in a general discussion.

A secret recording was made of a discussion. Two weeks later, those who took part in the discussion were asked to write down all they could recall about it. The recollections were checked against the recording, and it was found that the average number of specific points recalled by an individual was only 8.4 percent of the total. Moreover, 42 percent of the recalled points were incorrect to some degree: Happenings were reported that never took place; casual remarks were greatly expanded; points were reported that had only been hinted at; and so forth.

In sum, only fragments were recalled, and even these fragments were distorted. And the people who forgot 91.6 percent of the specific points raised in the discussion? They were highly educated members of the Cambridge Psychological Society.[1]

---

[1] Ian M. L. Hunter, *Memory: Facts and Fallacies* (Baltimore: Penguin, 1957), p. 83.

LISTENING IS THE FIRST STEP

To take good notes, you have to be a good listener, and good listeners are not so common as you might think. It is not enough simply to hear all the words. You have to transfer the *ideas* from the short-term memory to the long-term memory. And you have to be able to see and interpret all ideas—main ideas *and* sub-ideas—in the context of the whole lecture.

Research shows that an average student remembers about 50 percent of a ten-minute lecture when tested immediately, and only 25 percent when tested forty-eight hours later. These poor results are due to students not knowing how to "package" the lecturer's ideas into more easily remembered units. However, listening is a skill, and it can be improved. One way to do so is to eliminate ten well-researched bad listening habits and to adopt in their place the habits of good listeners.

Ten Bad Listening Habits

Ralph G. Nichols, an internationally known expert on listening, identified the ten bad listening habits that are paraphrased below.[2] Eliminate them, and you'll be a better listener.

1. *Calling a subject dull.* A poor listener will "turn off" as soon as he or she decides a lecture is going to be dull. And such a decision is usually based on ignorance rather than knowledge.

A good listener will listen closely for information that can be important or useful, even in a seemingly dull presentation.

2. *Criticizing a speaker.* A poor listener will find fault with the speaker—perhaps a rumpled suit or a monotonous voice—and infer that such a speaker can't have anything important to say.

A good listener will realize that a lecture is not a fashion show. He or she will look for ideas, not for things to criticize.

3. *Overreacting.* A poor listener will become so involved in disagreeing with the speaker that he or she will miss most of the lecture.

A good listener will listen with the mind, not with the emotions. He or she will simply jot down a disagreement, to ask about later, and then go on listening.

4. *Listening for facts only.* A poor listener wants only facts and considers the "big picture" as nothing more than someone else's opinion.

A good listener wants to see how facts illustrate principles; how examples illustrate ideas; and how evidence supports arguments. He or she realizes that facts are important, but only in relation to principles, ideas, and arguments.

[2]From *The Supervisor's Notebook* by Ralph G. Nichols, Vol. 22. Copyright © 1960 by Scott, Foresman and Co. Reprinted by permission.

5. *Outlining everything.* A poor listener tries to force every lecture into a rigid mold through detailed outlining. He or she is so busy with form and style that the content is missed.

A good listener adjusts his or her notetaking to the speaker's topic and organizational pattern.

6. *Faking attention.* A poor listener will lock his or her eyes onto the speaker and then relax, expecting to get the information out of the textbook later, during study time.

A good listener realizes that each lecture is a chance to get, in fifty minutes, facts and ideas that the speaker took hours to assemble.

7. *Yielding to distractions.* A poor listener will use every little distraction—footsteps, a door opening or closing, a cough, a dropped pencil—as an excuse to stop listening to the instructor.

A good listener disciplines himself or herself to shut out distractions and to concentrate on the speaker's message.

8. *Choosing only easy stuff.* To a poor listener, it's too much trouble and hard work to follow the instructor's complex arguments and ideas. Such a student wants entertainment, not learning.

A good listener is intellectually curious, wants to see how the speaker proves his or her points, and is not afraid of tough, technical, or complex ideas.

9. *Overreacting to emotional words.* A poor listener overreacts, almost blows up, at personally emotional words, such as *communist, income tax, Nazi,* or *evolution.* His or her blood pressure rises, and listening comes to an end.

A good listener hears the same emotion-laden words but will listen even more intently, to follow the message or argument and see where the speaker's prejudices lie.

10. *Wasting thought speed.* Even a poor listener realizes that thinking proceeds at a much higher rate than speech (actually about four times as fast). The poor listener usually moves along lazily with the speaker or uses his or her thought speed to solve personal problems. Often, this results in the poor listener falling behind the speaker and giving up for the rest of the lecture.

A good listener uses his or her thought speed and any pauses in the lecture to distinguish supporting material from main ideas, make fast summaries of the lecture's highlights, and anticipate the lecturer's next point.

The Listening Attitude

Attitude is probably the most important requirement for effective listening. So assume a positive mental attitude. You must convince yourself that the lecturer has something useful to say. Begin by realizing how lucky you are to have such an easy way of obtaining so much information. The lecturer had to do the searching, reading, selecting, discarding, and organizing of information from dozens of books, spending perhaps hundreds of hours.

The most productive attitude is the sympathetic one. Show that you are *with* the speaker by having a pleasant expression on your face, keeping your eyes on the speaker when you're not writing notes, and nodding your head when you agree. Your reward? You'll be treating the speaker as you would want to be treated; you'll immediately notice a more enthusiastic flow of words and ideas from him or her; and—most important— you'll be concentrating like you've never concentrated before.

Hearing versus Listening

Hearing is strictly mechanical. We don't have to learn to hear, for physically we are equipped to do so right from birth. In fact, studies have shown that we hear even during sleep. However, unless they are unusually loud, most of us won't remember the sounds that we heard during the night.

Listening, on the other hand, is the absorption of the *meanings* of words and sentences by the brain. This, in turn, leads to the understanding of facts and ideas. But listening takes (1) attention, or sticking to the task at hand in spite of possible distractions, and (2) concentration, which is the focusing of your thoughts upon one problem. Concentration does not mean thinking only one thought. Various ideas will flash into your mind, and you can either discard or pursue them. Concentration means holding a central issue or problem in mind and having ideas that are related to that issue.

A good way to begin concentrating is to anticipate the lecture. Look over your notes from the last lecture, and then take two minutes to answer the question, "What is she going to talk about today?" Or, if the lectures follow your textbook, peek ahead to see what's coming next. Then, once the lecture starts, let your mind dart ahead (during pauses) to anticipate what's coming next. You'll be alert, engrossed in the material, and concentrating 100 percent. And remember this: You cannot attain concentration by concentrating on the act itself. Your attention must focus on the data and ideas.

With this head start on concentration, and with a desire to learn, you have already begun the process of serious listening. To keep it going, show up in the classroom with sharp pencils and a good-sized notebook. Then begin taking notes the moment the speaker begins. To take intelligent notes, you will have to listen attentively, with natural concentration. And you will be combatting the boredom that leads to sleepiness and daydreaming.

NOTETAKING

Here are three important findings from studies concerned with notetaking. First, notetaking does not interfere with listening and comprehension; in fact, it helps you listen. Second, students who study their lecture notes using the recitation method remember one and a half times more after six weeks than students who do not review. Third, students who take no notes, or do not study their notes, forget approximately 80 percent of the lecture by the end of two weeks. From these findings we can conclude that students who take copious notes and then study them, both directly after the lecture and several additional times before an examination, stand a good chance of remembering between 90 and 100 percent of the material! In other words, if you don't take notes, then you put yourself at a disadvantage.

How to Take Notes

Begin with anticipation: Preread the textbook chapter so you'll easily be able to follow the development of the material. In the classroom, take a seat near the lecturer, to hear better and see the board better. Then begin taking notes as soon as the lecture begins, and don't stop until you have notes on the entire lecture.

Do not try to take down the lecture word for word. Instead, write in telegraphic style, using both your own words and those of the lecturer. Make special note of all vivid or striking words that the lecturer uses; they will help you recall the lecturer's statements later. Remember that your purpose is to record the lecturer's ideas for later study. Don't waste valuable time trying to find synonyms for the lecturer's precise words, simply to have paraphrased them. You can use your own words later, when you have the time to think, write, and understand the ideas more fully.

Make notes on main ideas and on sub-ideas, examples, and details. You need to come away from the lecture with enough information to form each concept as fully as possible. If you can detect the lecturer's main headings and subheadings, write them down. They will help you organize your ideas and facts. But don't use an inability to detect these headings as an excuse for not taking notes.

Listen carefully as you make your notes, but don't stop to ponder the ideas presented. By the time you have finished reflecting on idea number one, the lecturer will probably be on idea number four or five. It is important that you do consider these ideas, but the time for reflection is *after* classes. Your job in the classroom is to capture the lecturer's ideas.

If a particular lecturer talks too fast for normal notetaking, try the two-page system. On the left-hand page record only the main ideas in a bold, nonformal way. Make sure that you grasp the key words. Immediately after the lecture, as well as during pauses in the lecture itself, record on the right-hand page as many details as you can recall. Place them opposite the main ideas that they support. You will end up with the important information from the lecture in brief form on the left, which will serve you when it's time for review. And you'll have the supporting details on the right.

Don't try to get around notetaking by using a tape or cassette recorder. You'll end up spending more time. When a lecture is recorded, you can't review it in five or ten minutes; you have to replay the entire lecture. Moreover, you will lose the benefits of notetaking—the attention, concentration, and organization this act provides—and you won't be able to see relationships among various ideas that become evident when they are set down on paper.

Again, to save time you should not take lecture notes in shorthand. Nor should you allow your notes to get sloppy in the expectation that you will retype them. Both transcribing shorthand and retyping notes take energy and time that you could use for studying or having fun; they also require you to do some chore before you can use your notes. In contrast, longhand notes can be used immediately.

Your notes should be legible and complete enough so that you can make sense of them several months later. They should be neat enough so that a classmate who missed the lecture can understand them. Then, when you are reviewing your notes and trying to concentrate on their meaning, your mind will not be bogged down in deciphering them. With messy notes, you'll have to review some and decipher some, then review some more and decipher some more. And so on. You'll not only waste time, but seriously drain your energy doing unnecessary work.

HOW TO MAKE NEAT NOTES

The breakthrough in my own notetaking came when I saw an instructor write on a blackboard using a modified printing style. Her writing was not only surprisingly rapid, but also amazingly clear. I immediately began to write in a similar style—without needing practice at all. I believe anyone can adopt this style, and use it to write neatly and clearly.

Here is how the individual letters are formed in this modified printing style:

a b c d e f g h i j k l m n o p q r s t u v w x y z

And here is the style as used in a paragraph:

There are four advantages to using this modified printing style. First, it is faster than cursive writing; second, it is far neater, permitting easy and direct comprehension; third, it saves time by precluding rewriting or typing; and fourth, it permits easy and clear reforming of letters that are ill-formed due to haste.

Even today, I almost always write this way because the style is the easiest, swiftest, and neatest of any I've tried.

Review Your Notes

Notetaking helps you concentrate on the lecture, but it also provides you with a valuable learning resource. To use this resource to full advantage, you must review your notes several times.

Begin as soon as you leave the lecture. While you are walking to another building for your next class, try to recall the points made by the lecturer. Visualize the classroom and the lecturer—even the lecturer's gestures, emphases, and blackboard notes. This will help you set the lecturer's points and ideas in your mind and clarify vague points. Ask yourself what the lecturer was getting at. What was his or her central point? Before your next class starts, jot down any questions you think you'd like to ask the lecturer, or any points about which you are not sure.

Then, as soon as you have a chance, review your notes carefully. With the lecture still fresh in your mind, you can fill in gaps in your notes, or answer some questions that arose during your mental review of the lecture. Write down other questions that come up during this review. Use the review to complete your overall picture of the lecture, to find its central point or idea. (You'll find that many points take on greater meaning when you review the lecture as a whole.) Add to your notes as necessary to make them complete. Also arrange to see the lecturer, either before class or in his or her office, to discuss your questions. Add these answers to your notes; otherwise they will continue to elude you.

This review may take ten or fifteen minutes of your time. It will perhaps save you hours of struggling to understand your notes later, when they are "ice cold." The review will also serve as preparation for the next lecture, which will probably continue where this one ended.

Also go back over your notes whenever you need a refresher, and *study* them in preparation for exams. That is, look upon your notes as a handwritten book, and use it in the same way you use your text. If you have taken good notes, they will serve you well. Remember that instructors examine you on the ideas in their course, regardless of whether these ideas come from the text or the lecture.

Make It a Habit

A pile of raw, scribbled, and unorganized notes is almost worthless. To be of use, your notes must be organized so that you can easily find what you need and understand it immediately. This requires disciplined orderliness. The twenty general notetaking suggestions that follow mean, in essence, be alert, be orderly, be systematic, and don't ever let things slide.

1. Attend lectures faithfully. The lecture system is the backbone of almost all courses, and a complete set of notes, in your handwriting, is crucial to success.
2. Consolidate your notes. Keep the notes for each course in one place, in a separate notebook.
3. Use large note paper to give yourself room to indent, and to see the pattern of your notes. The standard size for a large notebook is 8½ × 11 inches.
4. Record the name and number of the course, the date, and the lecturer's name on the first sheet for each lecture. This safeguards against loss or a mix-up of notes.
5. Do not doodle or knit in the classroom. Manual activity of this kind inhibits notetaking, interferes with concentration, and breaks eye contact with the lecturer.
6. Be academically aggressive. *Work hard* at concentrating and taking notes on the lecturer's development of each topic.
7. Discover the lecturer's pattern. The lecturer usually speaks from a set of notes, so he or she is following an organized pattern. Try to spot it.
8. Write legibly to save time later when you review.
9. Make your notes complete and clear enough so that they will have meaning for you weeks and months later. You need not write in full

sentences, however, since notetaking is a process of selection, condensation, and compression.

10. Leave blanks for words, phrases, or ideas you think you may have missed. Directly after the lecture, ask the instructor or a fellow student to help you fill the gaps.

11. Develop your own system of enumeration and indention. Don't indent so far that you are crowded into a small area at the right-hand side of the page.

12. Develop abbreviations of common words and recurring terms. This will give you more time both to listen and to write.

13. Use a symbol (such as an asterisk, arrow, or underline) to mark ideas the lecturer emphasizes.

14. Mark off assignments that are mixed in with the lecture. Similarly, note and mark off any books or other references the lecturer mentions; these will be valuable guides to further reading.

15. Separate your own thoughts from the lecturer's. It is an excellent practice to jot down questions and your own examples, ideas, and references; but make sure you bracket or otherwise label these as yours, not the lecturer's.

16. Be alert for clues. Often an instructor will say, "You'll see this later," or "This is important," or "This is a common pitfall." Use such clues to note important statements with an asterisk or other symbol in the margin. Listen for enumerations such as "The four steps in the process are as follows." Listen for words such as "finally," "therefore," and "furthermore," which may warn that an important point is about to be presented. Listen for other transitional words, phrases, or sentences that may signal the end of one main idea and the beginning of another.

17. Always record the lecturer's examples. They often clarify abstract ideas. Indicate the fact that they are examples with a special notation like *Ex.*

18. Pay as close attention to the end of a lecture as to the beginning. Lecturers do not always pace themselves accurately, and they may have to cram half the content into the last five or ten minutes. Record such packed finales as rapidly as you can. If necessary, stay in your seat for a few extra minutes to write down as much as you can remember.

19. Record additional ideas of your own immediately after the lecture.

20. Review your notes after the lecture, and improve the organization if necessary.

Like any technique, listening and notetaking improve with practice. If you really try, you will soon be able to keep up with the fastest lecturer.

THE CORNELL SYSTEM
FOR TAKING NOTES

The Cornell System puts into practice most of the concepts discussed in this chapter. It is a simple and efficient procedure for both taking and reviewing notes. It is not the only available notetaking system, but it is one that you should consider if you have not yet developed a personal system of your own.

The First Step: Preparing the System

Use a large loose-leaf notebook. The large size provides ample room for writing meaningful notes, recording examples, and drawing diagrams. The loose-leaf feature enables you to insert mimeographed "hand-outs" and assignment sheets in topical or chronological order.

If you don't want to lug around a large loose-leaf binder, just carry a good supply of sheets on which to take your notes. Then fit the note-filled sheets into the binder after classes. Make sure, however, that you label, number, and date *each sheet.*

Spiral-bound notebooks don't work as well in the Cornell System. But if you insist on using them, keep a separate notebook for each subject. Since these notebooks all look alike, have a large, easy-to-distinguish label on the face of each, so that you won't find yourself taking notes in the wrong book.

Use one side of each sheet only. This will allow you to spread out the pages, to see the pattern of the lecture, when you are reviewing. Draw a vertical line about 2½ inches from the left edge of each sheet. This sets off the *recall column.* Classroom notes will be recorded in the space to the right of the line. Later, key words and phrases will be written to the left of the line (see Figure 6.1 on page 128).

Before each lecture, take a few minutes to look over your notes on the previous lecture, to provide continuity with the lecture you are about to hear.

The Second Step: During the Lecture

During the lecture itself, follow these simple directions.

1. Record your notes in simple paragraph form or in one of the other forms discussed below. Your object should be to make your notes complete and clear enough so they will have meaning for you weeks and months later.

Figure 6.1 The Cornell System Format.

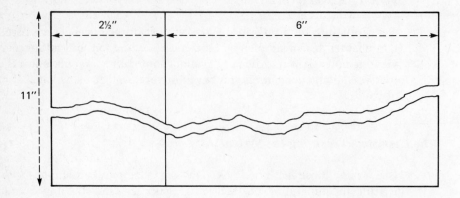

2. Do not bother to make elaborate outlines, using Roman numerals, capital letters, Arabic numerals, small letters, etc., with various indentations. If you have to worry about which number or letter comes next, you'll miss part of the lecture.

3. Strive to capture general ideas rather than illustrative details. In this way, you will be able to follow the train of the argument or development of an idea. You can get names and dates from the textbook.

4. Skip lines to show the end of one idea and the start of another. Indicate sub-ideas and supporting details with numbers or letters under the major idea.

5. Use abbreviations to give yourself extra time to listen and write. But avoid using too many abbreviations or ones you might have trouble deciphering weeks or months later. (See the list on pages 136 to 138 for ideas.)

6. Write legibly. Try using my modified printing style if your writing gets hard to read.

The Third Step: After the Lecture

Consolidate your notes during your first free time after class, or during the same evening at the latest. First read through your notes, make any scribbles more legible, and fill in spaces you purposely left blank. Then underline or box in the words containing the main ideas.

Now, you are ready to use the recall column on the left side of the page. In this column, jot down key words and key phrases that will serve as cues for the ideas and facts on the right. In making these jottings, reread all the lecturer's ideas, rethink them in your own words, and reflect on them so that you will come up with words or phrases that will work for you. In doing so you will have organized and structured the lecture, both in your notebook and, more important, in your mind.

Now (not later) cover up the right side of each sheet, exposing only the jottings in the recall column. Use the jottings as cues or "flags" to help you recall and *recite aloud* the facts and ideas of the lecture as fully as you can, in your own words, and with as much appreciation of the meaning as you can. Then uncover the notes and verify what you have said.

Finally, take the sheets for the day's lecture out of the binder, and overlap them so that only the recall columns are exposed. The key words and phrases in the recall columns are your organizational framework. Glance up and down these columns; notice the sequence of categories; see how they hang together to make an integrated whole. By acquiring this mental picture of the whole, you will be far more likely to remember the material.

Review these splendidly organized notes from time to time, to keep your retention at a high level. And make full use of them in reviewing for the final exam.

Types of Notes

The type of notes you take depends on the nature of the material presented in the lecture.

DEFINITION-TYPE NOTES.   In Figure 6.2 (page 130), the material consists of definitions and explanations of words; consequently, most of the notes are short. Long explanations were not needed.

At first glance, it may appear that the notes follow a formal outline, but this is not really so. The lecturer announced a main topic, *animism*, then went on to explain its unique features. The numbering and the lettering were used to keep items separate, not to indicate any relationship among them. If these items had been recorded in sentences and paragraphs, they would have been too tightly packed.

SENTENCE-TYPE NOTES.   Figure 6.3 (page 131) shows the use of sentences for notes on ideas and concepts. It also shows how assignments, diagrams, and bibliographic items can be worked into a page of notes.

TOPIC-AND-IDEA-TYPE NOTES.   The material in Figure 6.4 (page 132) fell naturally into a topic-and-idea format. The lecturer mentioned a topic and then expanded on it. Again the student made no attempt to follow a formal outline. The numbering and the lettering are there just to show separations of topics, not to show relationships among them.

Figure 6.2 Lecture Notes in the Cornell System: Short phrases for definitions and terms.

	October 10, (Mon.) – Soc. 102 – Prof. Oxford
	A. Animism
Stick has mind-power.	1. Object has supernatural power.
	2. Belief object has mind – a power.
Power – mana	3. Animism associated with Polynesia.
	4. Power called mana. (not limited to objects)
	a. Objects accumulate mana.
	Ex. Good canoe has more mana than poor one.
Can gain or lose mana	b. Objects can lose mana.
	c. People collect objects with lots of mana.
	d. Good person's objects collect mana.
	e. People, animals, plants have mana, too.
	Ex. Expert canoe builder has mana –
	imparts mana to canoe.
Good people have lots of mana	f. Chief has lots of mana – too dangerous to
	get too close to chief – mana around head.
Too much mana = Tabu.	5. Tabu
	a. Objects with powerful mana are tabu.
	b. Chief can manipulate mana – If certain
Use Tabu to regulate economy	animal becoming scarce, can place tabu
	on animal for a while.
	B. Magic
Cause & Effect (mixture) (rain)	1. Science of primitive man – cause & effect.
	2. Make mixture (cause); Then it rains (effect).
	a. Don't know why it works, but when mixture
	made, rain comes.
Sympathetic = clay model	3. Two kinds magic.
	a. Sympathetic – make model or form of
	person from clay, etc., then stick pins
	into object to hurt symbolized person.
Contagious = fingernail clippings	b. Contagious magic
	(1) Need to possess an article belonging
	to another person.
	(2) Ex. Fingernail clippings. By
	doing harm to these objects, feel
	that harm can be thus transmitted.
Good or evil uses.	c. All magic not necessarily evil – can
	be used for both good and evil.

Figure 6.3 Lecture Notes in the Cornell System: Sentences for ideas and concepts.

Key Terms:	Romantic Masterworks – Abrams 9/30 (Thurs.)
apocalypse	Topic: Background for Reading Apocalyptic Literature

Key Terms:
apocalypse
millennium
regenerate
cataclysmic

Def. of
Apocalypse

Origin of idea
of apocalypse

Idea of
apocalypse in
theories of
history:

2 greek ideas:
1. ——
2. ——

Hebrew view —

2 peculiarities
of Hebrew view:

(Biblio.)

Modern idea —
man taking
over.

Romantic Masterworks – Abrams 9/30 (Thurs.)
Topic: Background for Reading Apocalyptic Literature

Assignment:

Read Genesis and Revelations before next class meeting.

I. Def. of apocalypse: a vision of a new world — the last days in which world is regenerate and (in New Testament) all time stops and we're back in infinity.

II. Idea of apocalypse a Hebrew invention. Greeks had nothing like it.

III. Various views of hist. & how apocalyptic idea figures in them.

  A. First greek view: the "cycle pattern" — "everything repeats itself;" "there's nothing new under the sun." Goes on w/o end:

  B. 2nd greek view: the "primitivists" – the best days were in the beginning & things going from bad to worse ever since.

  C. Hebrew view:
    1. History has beginning & an end – this peculiar to them: In the beginning, a heaven & earth – in the end, a new heaven & earth:
    2. Diagram of Hebrew view:

    but restoration delayed until "second coming." After the end, time stops and those deserving return to eternity — either to heaven or hell.
    3. Two peculiarities
      a. beginning and end – finite.
      b. right angle – fall and restoration sudden, not gradual. History changes at once.
    4. Like second greek view in that best was in beginning — but Hebrew fall is sudden rather than gradual.

In Pursuit of the Millenium (Sp?)

  D. 17th Century idea (up to modern times)
    1. Gradual progress can be brought about by man's own efforts. Man can achieve return to felicity by getting rid of evil — man, by taking things in his own hands, can change environment and change it from bad to perfect. [Note: God left out of this scheme. Man, not god, effects change.]

Figure 6.4 Lecture Notes in the Cornell System: Topics and supporting ideas.

Economics 105 - Professor Terry - Oct. 27 (Wed.)   ①

<u>Some Basic Laws & Principles</u>

1. Composition
indiv. → groups
generalization

1. Fallacy of Composition
   a. What seems to be true or good for individuals is not always good for society.
   b. Dangerous to generalize from indiv. cases.

2. Diminishing Returns -
   ‑point where extra inputs...
   ‑Malthus pop‑land‑food
   ‑Improved
   ‑methods
   ‑Technology

2. Law of Diminishing Returns
   a. Refers to amount of extra output we get when we add additional inputs; but, <u>after a point</u>, the extra inputs yield decreasing amounts of extra output.
   b. Malthus's views depended on this law. Just so much land, but population could increase more rapidly than food supplies.
   c. Improved methods of production have offset the law of dim. ret. in many instances, eg. Malthus.
   d. Industry - improved technology overcomes dim. ret.

3. Money
   a. Medium of exchange; measuring rod of values
   b. Barter = no guarantee that desires of two parties will coincide.
   c. Commodities - hard to det. equivalent values.
   d. Paper money = convenient; social invention, value easily recognized.

PARAGRAPH-TYPE NOTES.   The notes in Figure 6.5 are written in paragraph form. But notice that the paragraphs are not standard literary paragraphs with grammatically complete sentences. The purpose here is to get away from the outline form, which can slow down your notetaking if you try to impose a logical outline on information that is not structured in outline form in the first place. Remember, your purpose is to capture the lecturer's ideas on paper in the way that's most efficient for you. Write short telegraphic sentences and phrases, but be sure they will make sense to you the next day or the next month, when you're reviewing them for an exam. In Figure 6.5 the sentences are telegraphic, but they are in sufficient detail to permit instant and easy rereading and reviewing.

Summaries in the Cornell System

As you probably know, writing summaries is a sure-fire way to force yourself to think about and come to grips with the ideas in your notes.

Figure 6.5 Lecture Notes in the Cornell System: Topics and paragraphs.

When you write summaries, you can't end up with fuzzy, half-understood ideas. Best of all, however, is that written summaries make studying for exams a breeze. The work of studying for exams is already 80 percent done!

Figure 6.6 (page 134) shows how to rule and set up your Cornell System sheets with space for a summary at the bottom. You may, of course, leave more or less room depending on your personal needs. You'll be able to determine those after a few lectures.

Actually, you have three options with regard to summaries: First, you can summarize at the bottom of each sheet; second, you can summarize the whole lecture at the bottom of the last sheet; and third, you can summarize at the bottom of each sheet and then summarize the whole lecture at the bottom of the last sheet.

I believe that the third option will yield the greatest reward. When you review your notes for exams or otherwise, you'll be able to see the steps you've taken to arrive at your final, last-page summary.

Figure 6.7 (page 135) is an example sheet of paragraph-type notes with a one-sheet summary. Notice how valuable the summary will be when the sheet is used to study for an exam. Notice also that, by leaving

Figure 6.6 Summaries in the Cornell System.

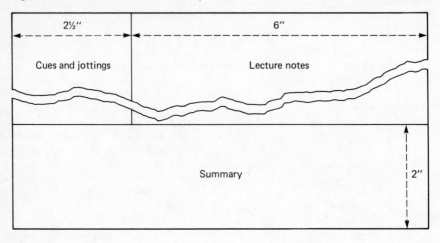

space for a summary, you make it an easy and natural step in your note-taking and review.

Incidentally, the lecturer must have announced the assignment in the middle of the lecture. So, rather than scrambling for an assignment book, the student embedded the assignment directly into the notes, making sure to box the word *assignment*, so it would not be overlooked. After the lecture, or that evening, the student should have transferred the assignment to his or her assignment book, or to the front of the notebook where assignments are kept in running order.

Combining Textbook and Lecture Notes

The format shown in Figure 6.8 (page 136) is ideal for lectures that mainly explain and amplify the textbook.

Notes on a previously assigned textbook chapter are recorded first, in the middle column. Then, when you take lecture notes in the right-hand column, you can avoid repeating material you already have, while you add the lecturer's explanations, examples, and supplementary comments. When you become accustomed to the lecturer's ways, you will be able to judge how much space to leave between items in the middle column, to keep lecture notes and textbook notes directly opposite each other.

When you write your cue words or flags in the left column, you should combine the two sets of notes to weave and blend them into a whole.

Figure 6.7 Lecture Notes in the Cornell System: Topics, paragraphs, and summary.

American Philosophy 333 — Sept. 23, 1983 - Prof. Murphy

What Am. Phil. is + what part it plays in Am. culture

Man's phil.- way he looks at life - based on daily experience	**1. Some terms + concepts :**
Phil. —Truth-based on principles	Man's phil.— way he looks at and evaluates the world.
Definite relationship betw. culture + phil.	Philosophy — pursuit of truth—attempt to investigate reason or justification for our ultimate beliefs—push reason back as far as possible until we get at self-evident proofs. [See Collinwood on presuppositions]
1. culture insecure	Ultimate beliefs - are usually the influence of our times.
2. tensions arise	As ideas chg., the traditional ideas are challenged.
3. questions asked	When challenges arise, then philosophies appear to find some fundamental truth — to bring truth
4. phil. answers	into focus. Examine, adjust, throw out, chg. current thinking + beliefs.
Opinions of market- place influence people	Climate of beliefs —these are beliefs people hold without inquiry or investigation.
	Assignment: Jonathan Edwards for Fri. 1st five selections— last 4 important. Suppl: H. Schneider, Hist. Am. Phil.
Edwards-Calvinist predeterminism	**2. Jonathan Edwards** — Calvinist theologian
	Doctrine: Absolute sovereignty of God —will + motion are predetermined by God. [Look up predestination]
Is there Free Will?	People started to think about free will. If God does everything, what can the human Will do? Nothing? Conflict!
To conserve estab. faith, Edwards gave basic reasons for faith	Edwards a conservative. Wanted to justify the established faith + bring into relation with current thought. Felt need of giving reasons for beliefs; didn't simply say "This is revealed."
	Example: When Jefferson severed connections with Britain, he gave reasons based on "self-evident" truths. (more)→

A country does not necessarily develop its culture according to an a priori set of philosophical principles. More likely the culture develops first, then philosophical principles are brought forth to support the culture. Furthermore, as the culture grows and changes, so do the philosophical principles which support it. ————————————→

Figure 6.8 Lecture Notes in the Cornell System: Combining textbook and lecture notes.

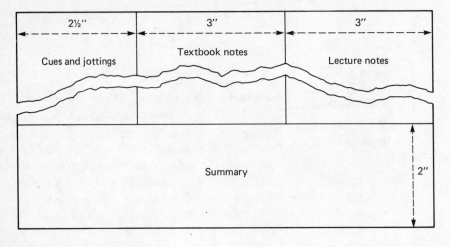

Abbreviations and Symbols

Here are some abbreviations and some rules about abbreviations. You should use only those that fit your needs and that you will remember easily. A good idea is to introduce only a few abbreviations into your notetaking at a time. Overuse may leave you with a set of notes that is difficult to read.

1. Symbols are especially helpful to students in engineering and mathematics. Lists are given in most texts and reference books.
   $\neq$ does not equal
   f   frequency
2. Create a family of symbols.
   $\bigcirc$ organism
   $\odot$ individual
   $\circledS$ individuals
3. Leave out the periods in standard abbreviations.
   cf   compare
   eg   for example
   dept   department
   NYC   New York City
4. Use only the first syllable of a word.
   pol   politics
   dem   democracy
   lib   liberal
   cap   capitalism

5. Use the entire first syllable and only the first letter of a second syllable.

subj	subject
cons	conservative
tot	totalitarianism
ind	individual

6. Eliminate final letters. Use just enough of the beginning of a word to form an easily recognizable abbreviation.

assoc	associate, associated
ach	achievement
biol	biological
info	information
intro	introduction
chem	chemistry
conc	concentration
max	maximum
rep	repetition

7. Omit vowels from the middle of words, and retain only enough consonants to provide a recognizable skeleton of the word.

bkgd	background
ppd	prepared
prblm	problem
estmt	estimate
gvt	government

8. Use an apostrophe.

gov't	government
am't	amount
cont'd	continued
educat'l	educational

9. Form the plural of a symbol or abbreviated word by adding "s."

□s	areas
chaps	chapters
co-ops	cooperatives
$\underline{f}$s	frequencies
/s	ratios

10. Use "g" to represent *ing* endings.

decrg	decreasing
ckg	checking
estg	establishing
exptg	experimenting

11. Use a dot placed over a symbol or word to indicate the word *rate*.

$\dot{\updownarrow}$	vibration rate
$\dot{f}$	frequency rate

12. Short words should generally be spelled out. Symbols, signs, or abbreviations for short words will make the notes too dense with "shorthand."
    in, at, to, but, for, key
13. Leave out unimportant verbs.
14. Leave out the words *a* and *the.*
15. If a term, phrase, or name is initially written out in full during the lecture, initials can be substituted whenever the term, phrase, or name is used again.
    Initial writing: Modern Massachusetts Party
    Subsequently: *MMP*
16. Use symbols for commonly recurring connective or transitional words.

&	and
w/	with
w/o	without
vs	against
∴	therefore

SPEAKING UP IN CLASS

All this careful notetaking will do more for you than increase your interest and your grades. Notetaking will provide you with the kind of background that should make you a full participant in class discussions. And that will help to increase your interest and grades even more!

Don't let stage fright keep you from learning and growing. Asking and answering questions in class and participating in discussions are powerful ways to learn and remember. Don't sabotage yourself by keeping silent.

Do You Want to Overcome Stage Fright?

If you do, here's how: *Give your total attention to what's going on in class.* In a lecture, for example, you are listening, thinking, and anticipating—concentrating and taking notes on what's taking place. Whenever you don't understand a point in the lecture, or differ with one, place a question mark at that point in your notes. Then, at the first opportunity, raise your hand *without hesitation* and ask for clarification or modestly state your view on points with which you differ.

During an ongoing class discussion, it is even easier to say a few words. Again, *give your total attention to what's being said* (above all, don't silently rehearse or practice what you're going to say). At the moment the speaker stops, raise your hand to add your "two bits."

The best time to start is immediately, so speak up on the first day of class. The longer you wait, the harder it becomes to break the ice.

How to Handle Questions

When an instructor asks you a question in class, a good and fair technique is to begin by paraphrasing the question, that is, restating the question in your own words. This helps you in three ways: First, you will make sure you are on the right track; if you're not, the instructor will have a chance to set you right. Second, by rephrasing the question, you will warm up your thinking on the subject. Third, you will gain some time to compose a reasonable opening statement and gather your thoughts, instead of blurting out an unreasoned comment.

SUMMARY

Why take notes in class?	Because humans forget what they hear. We forget rapidly (in a matter of minutes) and massively (in some studies, 47 percent in twenty minutes). Obviously, without written notes, you cannot recapture, study, and learn what was presented in the lecture. Without notes, you're stuck.
Isn't listening something we do automatically?	No! You might be confusing *listening* with *hearing*. Hearing is automatic, but listening is a learned skill. For example, you may be hearing the sound of the lecturer's voice, but if your mind is on tomorrow's exam or tonight's date, you are not listening.
How do you acquire the skill of listening to a classroom lecture?	It is relatively easy, if you do these two things: First, be fully *aware* of the ten "bad listening habits." Second, and most important, *concentrate, like a reporter,* on the lecturer's facts and ideas in the sequence in which you hear them. Your goal is to be able to repeat the lecture later, in your own words, to yourself or to others. Remember, "like a reporter": Don't interject your own

thoughts and opinions. You can do that later after reviewing the facts and ideas *as presented.*

In what ways do I benefit by becoming a better listener?

You benefit in at least six ways: You will (1) learn faster and remember more; (2) improve your ability to reason; (3) experience less disappointment and frustration; (4) save study time by having gained knowledge in the classroom; (5) build a larger background of knowledge and build it faster; and (6) create healthy attitudes toward instructors and your courses.

Is there ever a good reason for not taking notes?

No! There is no reason, no excuse, no argument strong enough to keep students from taking notes of classroom lectures.

How many notes to take?

Take enough notes to enable you to repeat the lecture in your own words, main idea by main idea. It is much, much better to take too many notes than to take too few. Too many notes will provide excellent context, and in relearning the lecture, you can overlook what you don't need.

What's the objective in taking notes?

Your objective is to capture the instructor's ideas and facts in the order in which they are presented, so you can take them back to your study area to learn them.

How about using shorthand or cassettes?

A big *no* to both. They both waste time. To get one little fact from a cassette recorder, you may have to play the whole thing. And shorthand characters are no earthly good until they are transcribed into English, which is what your notes should be written in from the start.

How does one get the most out of every lecture?

Take notes continually, yet concentrate hard on the lecturer's words, following the step-by-step development of the topic. Never mind the lecturer's mannerisms or appearance; just extract the knowledge and wisdom embedded in his or her ideas. Don't prejudge; just listen, concentrate, and write.

How can we make the most of our notes?	By organizing them so that they make both visual and logical sense—that is, so they are immediately understandable. The moment you look at them, your eyes should be able to draw up meaning, the way cool milk is drawn up through a straw.
What's the big advantage of the Cornell System?	Its clear, clean structure guides you through an organized, step-by-step learning and remembering process, thus saving time and effort both when you make and review your notes and when you use them to study for exams.
Which Cornell System format is best?	They are all good. Actually, you might want to use several of them, depending on the courses you take and how the lecturers present their material. If you're choosing only one, choose the one that best fits the way you work. Of course, I recommend using the summary section with all of them.
What about speaking up in class?	The concentration you develop for notetaking will keep you aware of—and help you give total attention to—what is going on in the classroom. Participation in discussions will soon become natural. Stage fright, which is usually due to lack of preparation (real or supposed) will be a thing of the past.

HAVE YOU MISSED SOMETHING?

1. **SENTENCE-COMPLETION.** Complete the following sentences with one of the three words listed below each sentence.

   a. In two weeks, a student who listens to a lecture without taking

   notes will lose _____.

   80 percent   20 percent   interest

   b. Only after reading, thinking, reflecting, reciting, and jotting down

   key words are you ready to _____.

   memorize   continue   rehearse

2. **MATCHING.** In each blank space in the left column, write the number preceding the phrase that matches the left item best.

_____ a. Consolidation	1. Recommended for the Cornell System
_____ b. Recall column	2. Creates a point of departure for questions
_____ c. Summary space	3. Integrates lecture and textbook notes
_____ d. Loose-leaf notebook	4. Should be done as soon as possible
_____ e. Three-column format	5. Answers "What did I learn in this lecture?"

3. **TRUE-FALSE.** Write *T* beside the *true* statements and *F* beside the *false* statements that follow.

_____ a. Classroom lectures are as important as textbook readings.

_____ b. During a lecture, notes should be taken constantly.

_____ c. While you are listening to a lecture, it's best to take only brief notes.

_____ d. Notes should always be taken in your own words.

_____ e. It is a mistake to let one or two words stand for an idea.

_____ f. The outline form speeds up the notetaking process considerably.

4. **MULTIPLE-CHOICE.** Choose the phrase that completes the following sentence most accurately, and circle the letter that precedes it.

Research on notetaking indicates that

a. notetaking does not interfere with the ability to listen.
b. students who take notes but don't recite them do very well.
c. boring lectures are remembered better than interesting lectures.
d. students who make neat notes often miss points or facts.

In all matters, before beginning, a diligent preparation should be made.

—CICERO

7

Surveying Your Textbook

If a baseball pitcher didn't warm up before the game, his priceless arm would quickly turn to gelatin. Few activities should begin without a warm-up. But how do you warm up for a new textbook? This chapter tells you . . .

- How to get a head start with your text
- How to get the most out of the preface
- How to read and reread a book's introduction
- How to warm up before reading a chapter
- How to survey your textbook

as well as

- The magic of asking questions

A RE YOU ABLE TO COPE with your textbook assignments, or are they harder to face every day? Is each day's assigned chapter more difficult to study than the previous one? With all the practice you have, you should get better and better at studying your textbook. If this is not the case, you probably need a system that you can use over and over again, to study chapter after chapter, in book after book. Or, if you have a system but you are still having trouble, maybe it needs to be corrected or modified.

In this chapter and the next several chapters, you'll read about various study systems. Compare these systems with what you are now using. You may want to trade your system in for a ready-made system; or, you might want to construct a new system of your own from parts of several systems. In any event, find or concoct a system that fits your way of studying. Then try it out. You'll be able to tell when a system is right for you, because then your work will go along surely and smoothly, and you'll get better at it day by day.

WARMING UP BEFORE THE SEMESTER STARTS

In an earlier chapter, I suggested that you buy all your textbooks immediately after you register for your courses. One important reason for doing so is to get a head start—by reading the prefaces and introductions to all your books. Read carefully and thoughtfully; underline important words and sentences, and make notes in the margins.

Then, while you still have the time, leaf through each of your books. Look at the pictures, tables, and diagrams, and read their captions. Read the chapter titles and the headings and subheadings that interest you. This will give you a good idea of what the book is like and where you will be going during the semester. Later, you'll be glad you took the time to do so—for you'll be able to see how the various parts of the course fit together.

Reading the Preface

In most textbooks, the authors are dealing with serious subjects. Consequently, they write in a somber, serious, scholarly vein. They may be warm and congenial people, but they can appear, in their writing, to be cold and faceless. The only place where most authors can drop their scholarly style and let their hair down is in the preface. There you have a chance to meet and get to know the authors as people. Once you do, you'll find you can converse and even argue with them as you read the text. You'll find yourself blurting out, now and then, "No, I don't agree with that statement" or "What do you mean by that?" But, you wouldn't make such a statement to a cold unanswering textbook if you couldn't visualize a live hand behind the writing.

I've often thought how much more meaningful every textbook would be if the authors could visit your classroom and give a short informal talk. Thereafter, your textbooks would have far greater meaning. Since personal appearances are out of the question, the next best thing is to let the authors talk with you in the preface. So don't miss the chance.

Here are some other things you can find in the preface. They are illustrated, by number, in Figure 7.1 on page 146.

1. *What the author's objective is.* It is a tremendous advantage to know the author's objective, for then you'll read and interpret the text from the correct point of view. Otherwise, reading could be quite a struggle, and the facts could seem to be completely unconnected. In Figure 7.1 the author is saying, "Keep your eye on the *perspective*, not on the facts."

2. *What the author's objective is not.* Being told what the author is *not* trying to do helps make the objective even clearer. In Figure 7.1 the author says, in effect, "No, this is not a list of facts, as many other books are." Being so warned, you'll refrain from drifting into the wrong pathways of thinking while reading.

3. *The organizational pattern of the book.* Having the organizational pattern is like having a road map. You'll know not only what the authors are doing but also where they are going. In Figure 7.1 you're also told what patterns the author is not following, which makes the plan of the book even clearer.

4. *How and why the book is different.* This, too, is valuable information. It is easy to think that a new book on a subject is just "some more of the same stuff." So, when the authors point out why their book is different and why their version or approach is necessary, you will read with greater awareness and, thus, with greater comprehension.

5. *The author's qualifications.* Writers usually try, in some subtle way, to let the reader know that their book is written by a scholar, an expert on the subject. In Figure 7.1, the writer develops a very fine logical point in an interesting manner, saying that though a writer knows the broad field, he is still an expert only on one phase of it. And if he wrote on only that one phase, we'd have each expert presenting only a narrow slice of the field. A book written in that way would be "choppy" and difficult to read.

As a practical exercise, you might find it interesting to go back and read the preface of this book, if you haven't done so already. See how

Figure 7.1 The Function of a Preface

① Objective = to present a perspective ⟶

This little book aims to give a certain perspective on the subject of language rather than to assemble facts about it. It has little to say of the ultimate psychological basis of speech and gives only enough of the actual descriptive or historical facts of particular languages to illustrate principles.[1]

② Not the objective = not mainly descriptive or historical facts. ⟶

③ Organization = along psychological lines ⟶

This book is organized, therefore, neither along chronological lines nor the less obvious logical line of proceeding from simple narration to varying emphases. The arrangement is, if anything, psychological.[2]

④ How book is different and why it is necessary ⟶

Many histories of philosophy exist, and it has not been my purpose merely to add one to their number. My purpose is to exhibit philosophy as an integral part of social and political life; not as the isolated speculations of remarkable individuals.

⑤ Competence = "I know the field as well as anyone." ⟶

It is obviously impossible to know as much about every philosopher as can be known about him by a man whose field is less wide; I have no doubt that every single philosopher whom I have mentioned, with the exception of Leibniz, is better known to many men than to me. If, however, this were considered a sufficient reason for respectful silence, it would follow that no man should undertake to treat of more than some narrow strip of history.[3]

[1]*Source:* Edward Sapir, *Language* (New York: Harcourt, Brace, Jovanovich, 1921), p. v.

[2]*Source:* William M. Sale, Jr., James Hall, and Martin Steinmann, Jr., eds., *Short Stories: Tradition and Direction* (Norfolk, Conn.: New Directions, 1949), p. xii.

[3]*Source:* Bertrand Russell, *A History of Western Philosophy*, p. x. Reprinted by permission of Simon and Schuster, Inc., New York, and George Allen Unwin, Ltd., London.

much you can gain toward understanding not only the book, but also the author.

Reading the Introduction

Prefaces deal with matters broad and general, but introductions deal with matters narrow and specific.

The introduction in Figure 7.2 (page 148) bristles with specifics and with solid instruction of great and immediate value for the sharper reading of textbooks. It is from a book titled *Six-Way Paragraphs*.[1] The book's sole purpose is to teach students how to ascertain main ideas. One hundred paragraphs are provided for practice. To prepare students for such practice, the introduction strives to explain the ins and outs of the paragraphs found in textbooks. As you read it, be aware not only of *what* the writer says, but also *how* he says it and his *purpose* for saying it.

Here are four good reasons for reading introductions:

1. They are usually well written, because the writer knows that the introduction is the book's show window—especially for prospective customers looking the book over to decide whether to buy it.
2. Having only limited space, the writer packs it with facts and ideas. As a reader, you will get a lot out of reading a relatively few pages.
3. You gain a firm footing for the rest of the book, making future assignments easier, spending less time, and achieving a higher level of mastery than could otherwise be achieved.
4. With your underlinings and notes in the margin, you can quickly review the introduction time after time, to give yourself a warm-up as well as a door into each assigned chapter.

WARMING UP ONCE CLASSES START

For an athlete, warming up is more than just limbering up the muscles and achieving coordination. There are psychological and intellectual aspects as well. Psychologically, when the warm-up period goes well, the athlete performs with a *positive attitude*. Intellectually, a *mental set* is achieved which ensures that the mind works smoothly with the muscles.

All these advantages can be yours, too, if you engage in a bit of pre-study warm-up. I say *a bit* purposely, because that's all it takes. Research

[1]Walter Pauk, *Six-Way Paragraphs* (Providence, R.I.: Jamestown, 1974), pp. 7–8. Material reprinted by permission of Jamestown Publishers.

Figure 7.2 The Specifics of an Introduction

what: wants you to focus on the paragraph – unit

how: brings you and the writer together

purpose: wants you to look at the paragraph through the eyes of the writer

The paragraph! That's the working-unit of both writer and reader. The writer works hard to put meaning into the paragraph; the reader works hard to take meaning out of it. Though they work at opposite tasks, the work of each is closely related. Actually, to understand better the job of the reader, one must first understand better the job of the writer. So, let us look briefly at the writer's job.

what: each paragraph has but one main idea

how: shows you how a writer thinks

purpose: to convince you to look for only one idea per paragraph because writers follow this rule

To make his meaning clear, a writer knows that he must follow certain basic principles. First, he knows that he must develop only one main idea per paragraph. This principle is so important that he knows it backwards, too. He knows that he must not try to develop two main ideas in the same, single paragraph.

what: the topic of the main idea is in the topic sentence, which is usually the first one

how: the writer needs to state a topic sentence to keep his own writing clear and under control

purpose: to instill confidence in you that the topic sentence is an important tool in a writer's kit and convince you it is there, so, look for it!

The next important principle he knows is that the topic of each main idea must be stated in a topic sentence and that such a sentence best serves its function by coming at or near the beginning of its paragraph. He knows, too, that the more clearly he can state the topic of his paragraph in an opening sentence, the more effective he will be in developing a meaningful, well-organized paragraph.

what: developing main ideas through supporting material

how: "more to a writer's job", still keeps you in the writer's shoes

purpose: to announce and advance the new step of supporting materials

Now, there is more to a writer's job than just writing paragraphs consisting of only bare topic sentences and main ideas. The balance of his job deals with *developing* each main idea through the use of supporting material which amplifies and clarifies the main idea and many times makes it more vivid and memorable.

what: (a) main ideas are often supported by examples, (b) other supporting devices listed.

how: still through the writer's eyes

To support his main ideas, a writer may use a variety of forms. One of the most common forms to support a main idea is the *example*. Examples help to illustrate the main idea more vividly. Other

Figure 7.2 Continued

purpose: to develop the new idea of supporting materials

supporting materials are anecdotes, incidents, jokes, allusions, comparisons, contrasts, analogies, definitions, exceptions, logic, and so forth.

what: paragraph contains (a) topic sentence, (b) main idea, and (c) supporting material

how: transfer the knowledge from the writer to you, the reader

purpose: to summarize all the three steps

To summarize, the reader should have learned from the writer that a textbook-type paragraph usually contains these three elements: a topic sentence, a main idea, and supporting material. Knowing this, the reader should use the topic sentence to lead him to the main idea. Once he grasps the main idea, then everything else is supporting material used to illustrate, amplify, and qualify the main idea. So, in the final analysis, the reader must be able to separate the main idea from the supporting material, yet see the relationship between them.

has shown that far greater learning takes place following a *small* (rather than large) amount of warming-up activity.

How can you limber up your brain and its neural pathways? Follow the practice of Edward Gibbon, who wrote the *History of the Decline and Fall of the Roman Empire*, published in six large volumes and translated into many languages. Before beginning to write, Gibbon would take a long walk or sequester himself in his study, to bring to mind everything he knew on the subject he was getting ready to write about.

Here are the more essential and more traditional warm-up steps. Generations of students have found them effective. And business executives report that surveying or skimming, for example, is the most valuable reading tool they have.

Surveying the Chapter

This step goes under various names. Some writers use the word *overview*, others use *preview*, while still others use *skim*. They all mean to *survey* the chapter.

Although this step is almost always advocated, most students strongly resist it. They feel that surveying a chapter is a waste of time. Instead, they want to dig directly into the first paragraph of the assigned chapter to get on with the job. In view of this strong resistance, let us begin this discussion with the advantages of surveying.

WHY SURVEY, OVERVIEW, PREVIEW, OR SKIM?   Here are two practical reasons why skimming can make a real and immediate difference in your reading.

1. *Surveying creates a background.* When you don't have some prior knowledge about the subject matter in an assigned chapter, reading and understanding the chapter are slow and difficult. But when you come to a familiar point in such a chapter—something that you recognize from prior learning—you read faster and with more comprehension. The difference is the prior background, and surveying can give you an instant background.

When you survey a chapter, you spot and pick up topics by reading the headings and subheadings of sections and paragraphs; you pick up the ideas by reading the first and last sentences of paragraphs; you become familiar with the names of people and places by skimming the words; you obtain the general objective by reading the introductory paragraph; and you get an overview by reading the summarizing paragraph at the end of the chapter. You won't know any of these facts and ideas cold, of course. But when you meet them again on your next careful reading, you will recognize them almost like old friends, and this familiarity will give you confidence and understanding.

In addition to familiarity, surveying provides *vision*. Once you have viewed the broad canvas, you will see more clearly how the individual ideas fit into the complete picture.

2. *Surveying provides advance organizers.* Familiarity with the general contents of a chapter creates what Ausubel, a learning-theory psychologist, calls *advance organizers.* This means that the familiar landmarks act as topics or categories within which you can cluster ideas, facts, and details. They provide what John Livingston Lowes calls "magnetic centers" around which the ideas, facts, and details cluster like iron filings around a magnet.

HOW TO SURVEY A TEXTBOOK CHAPTER.   Surveying has various uses, but its greatest use is in mastering textbook assignments. It is the "grease" that makes subsequent reading and studying more efficient. A good scholar would no more begin reading a chapter without first skimming it than an automotive engineer would run a car without first greasing it. The grease does not supply the power, but without it the gasoline would not be of much use.

In the first chapter of this book we introduced Linda, a sophomore who wanted to become an elementary school teacher. Although she had trouble with her studies in some ways, she developed the technique of surveying almost to a fine art. Here is her account.

I first spend two or three minutes trying to get the full meaning out of the title of the chapter. I even wonder briefly why the author picked such a ti- tle. Then I shove off by saying to myself, "Let's see what he has to say about this subject."

Next, I read the first couple of paragraphs in the regular way. If I don't do this, it's like coming into the middle of a conversation: I can't make head or tail of it.

Then I let the printer guide me. My eyes dart to the big-type headings and subheadings. I read them because I know that they are like the small headlines for newspaper items. They are little summaries. I then read a sentence or two underneath these headings. My eyes float over the rest of the material looking for other islands of information. They might be marked by clues such as italicized words, underlined words, and changes in the type.

When I first started to skim, I used to skip all the illustrations, charts, and diagrams. But after getting burned on exams, I found I could learn a lot very easily just by reading the captions and noticing what the lines on the diagrams and graphs meant. At least for me, illustrations stick in my mind better than words do; so during an exam, I take advantage of this. I close my eyes and see the illustration on the blackboard of my mind.

I'm always careful to read the last paragraph or last section marked "summary." That's where the author gathers together all the main ideas of the chapter.

Finally, I pause for a few minutes to bring all these pieces and frag- ments together before I begin reading and taking notes on the chapter. Sometimes to bring things together, I go back to the beginning of the chapter and leaf through the pages without reading, just looking at what I have already looked at.

There are a few other things that skimming does for me. First, I no longer put off studying. Skimming is easy, so I don't mind getting started. Second, once I get into the chapter, I find that most of the chapters con- tain some interesting information, so I become interested. Third, because I am interested in the material, I concentrate better. And fourth, the topics that I find by skimming somehow make good topic headings for my notes.

An important aspect of surveying is the way it overcomes inertia. Many students find it difficult to open a textbook and begin studying. If you are one of them, start with the easy step of surveying, which is less demanding than getting-down-to-brass-tacks reading. Use surveying to ease yourself into studying.

You need not always survey an entire chapter as the first step. But you should begin by surveying at least the first part, before you read it. Later, as you work your way through the chapter, you may want to skim further ahead, page by page, as you read and study to understand and to take notes.

When you skim, don't dawdle. Move along with good concentration, but do go slowly enough to get the facts, ideas, and principles accurately. Once you assimilate a mistake, it is hard to eradicate.

Asking Questions Before and During Reading

The people who have *answers to give* when they have finished are usually those who had *questions to ask* before and during their reading! This is an amazing and valuable technique for attaining high comprehension.

Asking questions works for one main reason: The questions force you to concentrate and to keenly, directly, and selectively observe the words you read. When you don't have a question in mind, your eyes just glide over the words of a paragraph, and you never realize that those self-same words contain all manner of answers. If the question isn't asked, there can be no answer.

You should interrogate the writer, not simply stare at the words. You must go into each paragraph like an inquiring reporter, with definite and searching questions; the better your questions, the better your comprehension. And here's an added bonus: Coming up with answers to your own questions is the most basic, the most essential step in the whole process of *remembering.*

How do you formulate warm-up questions as you read and study a textbook? One well-known technique is to turn each heading into a question. For example, the main heading "Basic Aspects of Memory" could instantly be turned into the question, "What are the basic aspects of memory?" It sounds simple, and it is—but it works.

Here are some additional examples:

Subtopic heading	*Question formulated*
The Memory Trace	What is a memory trace?
Rate of Forgetting	How fast do we forget?
Organization of Recall	How is recall organized?
Decay Theory	What is the decay theory?

Once you have turned a heading into a question, you read the material under that heading to answer your question. If the question is answered early in the discussion, ask another, based on what you have read. And turn each heading into a question as you come to it. You will never reach the bottom of a page without some new facts or ideas.

There are also general questions that you can use in reading almost any topic. Some readers prefer to ask these general questions to elicit specific facts and ideas. Other readers just enjoy conversing with the writer through the use of a general question-and-answer technique. In either case, an active searching attitude is created. Here are some of the general questions:

> What does this paragraph tell me?
> How does this paragraph fit in with this chapter?
> What questions might I be asked about this paragraph?
> What are the important supporting details?
> Does this example make the main point clear?
> If this fact or idea is true, then what logically follows?
> If it is true, how does it affect my existing knowledge?
> What evidence does the writer give?
> What is the underlying principle?

Some practical readers ask not only "What is the author saying?" but also "How can I use this information?" When you ask such questions, however, make it a rule to try to answer them. Say something. Say anything that seems to make sense to you. Without effort, there's no gain.

A great deal is said these days about learning how to think. Books are written about thinking, lectures are given, and teachers remind us to think. I believe, however, that the entire subject of thinking can be summed up in one sentence: *Thinking at its highest level is asking the the right, relevant question.*

SUMMARY

If what I'm doing seems to work, should I change my way of studying?

Conventional wisdom says "If it works, leave it alone." But, that's the "head in the sand" approach, because there's always room for improvement. If you don't try to improve, you'll stay where you are. Furthermore, what worked in high school, won't necessarily work in college; and what worked in undergraduate studies won't necessarily work in graduate studies.

Why read the preface and introduction? They'll be forgotten by the time I get into the chapters.

That's true! They'll be forgotten, but it will take only minutes to recapture the important points if you have underlined selectively and made thoughtful marginal notes. That's the reward for doing it right in the first place. Going back to the preface and introduction before beginning each new chapter can do wonders by keeping your mind on the target—the main point of the text. And, best of all, your prior reading of the preface and introduction pays dividends in insight over and over again with every reading of every chapter. What an investment!

What should I look for in a preface?

At least five things: (1) a glimpse of the writer's personality; (2) the main objective of the book; (3) the organization of the book; (4) how the book is different; and (5) why it is different.

Why bother with introductions?

The introduction often contains information which pertains to *every chapter* of the book. It would be too repetitive for the writer to remind you of the same thing at the beginning of every chapter. So, the best place to present this important information is at the very beginning of the book—in the introduction. Having said it carefully and with emphasis once, the writer expects the reader to carry this important message through chapter after chapter.

Is skimming really like an athlete's warming up?

Yes, there's great similarity. For athletes, warming up means stretching the *muscles*, buoying up their psychological *attitude*, and achieving *mental* concentration. In the same way, skimming a chapter helps your muscles, attitude, and mind. Skimming gets you going physically, warms up your attitude toward the assignment, and oils and revs up your mind's wheels.

Besides warming us up, what else can skimming do for us?

Skimming a chapter creates an instant background; that is, you become familiar with some of the ideas and facts. Then, when you begin to read the chapter systematically, you will meet familiar "faces" and thus read with greater interest and comprehension. In addition, familiar words, facts, and ideas make rallying points (advance organizers and magnetic centers) around which to cluster details as well as facts and ideas.

Why will asking questions help us understand more and remember better?

In one word, asking a question makes you *concentrate*! The bonus effect is that answers gained through reading or hearing while concentrating are long remembered.

Actually, concentration is the basic requirement for all learning. Without concentration there is no learning in the first place, so memory never even comes into the picture.

HAVE YOU MISSED SOMETHING?

1. **SENTENCE-COMPLETION.** Complete the following sentence with one of the three words listed below the sentence.

   Studying a textbook efficiently requires a _____.
   teacher   system   preface

2. **MATCHING.** In each blank space in the left column, write the number preceding the phrase that matches the left item best.

   _____ a. Preface
   _____ b. Introduction
   _____ c. "Good Reader"
   _____ d. Positive attitude
   _____ e. Advance organizer

   1. Interrogates the writer
   2. Serves as an anchor for new facts
   3. Deals with matters broad and general
   4. Helps the warming-up process
   5. Deals with matters narrow and specific

3. **TRUE-FALSE.** Write *T* beside the *true* statements and *F* beside the *false* statements that follow.

   _____ a. There is a strong student resistance to skimming.
   _____ b. The longer you warm up, the better.
   _____ c. Asking questions helps to focus your concentration.
   _____ d. Successful students ask questions before and as they read.
   _____ e. Surveying should always be the beginning step.

4. **MULTIPLE-CHOICE.** Choose the phrase that completes the following sentence most accurately, and circle the letter that precedes it.

   The following description is *not* a characteristic of a preface:
   a. is well written and packed with facts.
   b. often reveals the author's personality.
   c. explains how and why the book is different.
   d. outlines some of the author's objectives.

8

Learning from Your Textbook

Almost anything is easier to digest when you divide it into bite-sized pieces. Textbooks should often be read a chapter at a time and considered paragraph by paragraph. This chapter deals with . . .

- Learning paragraph by paragraph
- Textbook troubleshooting
- The Corson Plan
- Using an alternative text

as well as

- Reciting,
- Reviewing, and
- Reflecting on textbook material

plus

- Five textbook study systems

156

*T*HE OBJECTIVE OF THE WARM-UP STEPS in the previous chapter is to prepare you to sit down at your study table, draw your textbook toward you, and lose yourself in a serious study session. Now you must converse with the writer to try to comprehend his or her facts and ideas. You must try to draw yourself into the words of the writer until, as Professor James A. Winans says, "The words may come to mean as much to you as to the writer." Then, to combat forgetting, you must recite, review, and reflect.

THE PARAGRAPH-BY-PARAGRAPH READING METHOD

Since most writers present their ideas paragraph by paragraph (usually one main idea to a paragraph), you are most certain to achieve success when you read paragraph by paragraph. After overviewing the chapter, return to the first paragraph and read it thoroughly enough to answer only one question: "What did the author say in this paragraph?" If you are unable to answer this question at first, you must re-read the paragraph until you can; otherwise you will not gain a functional understanding of the paragraph.

This is the most crucial step in the entire process of studying a textbook. You must not move ahead to succeeding paragraphs if that means leaving the present paragraph unsettled. You may push on beyond a problem paragraph for the purpose of understanding its context, but always with the intention of coming back to the problem paragraph. Remember that a succession of comprehended paragraphs leads to comprehension of the chapter.

Guard against the practice of moving your eyes over the lines of print without truly understanding the writer's ideas. This common practice is a carryover from the reading of novels, in which the action is vividly portrayed so that the reader doesn't have to exert much effort to understand the book. In a textbook, you have to read for the ideas and concepts behind the words, not merely for a good story. One way to do so is to ask questions (see Chapter 7). Another is to view each paragraph as though you were going to teach the material to someone else. Pause at the end of each paragraph, or at the end of a series of paragraphs that go together, and in your own words describe the writer's main idea together with the supporting details. Answer the question, "What did I learn in this paragraph?" When you have described, you have understood.

Don't forget to use the topic sentence to help you break into the meaning of each paragraph. After all, the topic sentence is there for you to use. It often contains the main idea or points to the main idea.

The paragraph in Figure 8.1 (page 158) could have been taken from a

Figure 8.1 An Example Paragraph

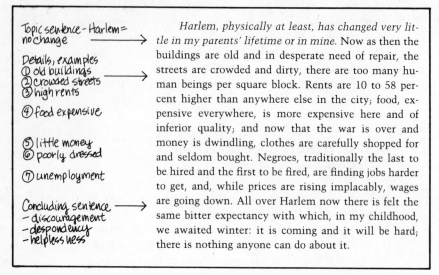

Topic sentence - Harlem = no change ⟶

Details, examples
① old buildings ⟶
② crowded streets
③ high rents

④ food expensive

⑤ little money
⑥ poorly dressed

⑦ unemployment

Concluding sentence ⟶
- discouragement
- despondency
- helplessness

Harlem, physically at least, has changed very little in my parents' lifetime or in mine. Now as then the buildings are old and in desperate need of repair, the streets are crowded and dirty, there are too many human beings per square block. Rents are 10 to 58 percent higher than anywhere else in the city; food, expensive everywhere, is more expensive here and of inferior quality; and now that the war is over and money is dwindling, clothes are carefully shopped for and seldom bought. Negroes, traditionally the last to be hired and the first to be fired, are finding jobs harder to get, and, while prices are rising implacably, wages are going down. All over Harlem now there is felt the same bitter expectancy with which, in my childhood, we awaited winter: it is coming and it will be hard; there is nothing anyone can do about it.

Source: James Baldwin, *Notes of a Native Son* (Boston: Beacon Press, 1955), p. 57.

sociology textbook. Note how the topic sentence, which is the first sentence, gives the main idea of the paragraph. Then comes the body of the paragraph, which is a long list of concrete examples. Each example supports the main idea that Harlem hasn't changed much. Notice, too, that the last sentence is not a continuation of the list; rather, it rounds out or completes the paragraph. Incidentally (but importantly), notice how the writer has maintained the *mood* of despondency right from the opening sentence, through the examples, and even more poignantly into the last clause of the last sentence.

Textbook Troubleshooting

As you read and study your textbook, your businesslike side should keep checking, by asking "Am I getting it?" If the answer is something like "It's getting pretty vague," you should take immediate action: First, go back a couple of paragraphs to pick up the thread of the writer's ideas again. Second, read ahead a couple of paragraphs to see where you're going. Third, open the dictionary and look up any words that you are not sure of, and that might be holding you back. Fourth, re-read the troublesome paragraph aloud, using exaggerated expression and emphasis to get at the meaning of what's being said. Such reading aloud, especially with expression, brings concentration back to a 100 percent level. And fifth, if you're still not getting it, use the Corson technique: Determine specifically what it is that you do not understand. (This technique is explained a little later in this chapter.) It is a good idea to write out what's bothering you, so you can ask a classmate or your instructor about it the next day.

While You Are Reading

Here are some additional points that can be of help to you in your reading:

In reading sentences, make full use of organizational clues. If a sentence or paragraph begins "On the one hand," watch for the inevitable "On the other hand," which introduces the other side of the argument. Innocent little everyday words such as "since," "because," and "although" are as important in relating parts of a sentence as a plus, minus, or square-root sign is in a math equation. Ignoring or misreading them can get you into serious trouble.

If you get bogged down in a really difficult sentence or paragraph, try reading the material without any modifying phrases. Find the simple subject of the sentence, the verb, and the simple object, to avoid getting lost in a maze of language. When the framework shows through clearly, so that you can grasp the main idea, then go back and read the material with all its "trimmings," to get its full sense.

After you finish a paragraph and summarize it, don't plunge immediately into the next paragraph. Pause for a minute or two, to think about the meaning of the paragraph you just read. Such a thinking pause provides time for the main idea to consolidate, to sink into your memory.

Whenever you encounter a difficult, unusual, or new word or term in your textbook, look it up in a glossary or dictionary. Put these words and terms, with their definitions, on 3×5 cards. You will learn them cold by carrying them around in your pocket and looking over the cards whenever you have a chance. Each word is a concept, and you must know it precisely, not fuzzily. Otherwise, the subject will become harder and harder and you'll never know why.

When you feel bored, do not "reward" your boredom by slamming your book shut and leaving empty-minded. Above all, don't reward yourself by going to a movie. If you get bored, give yourself the limited objective of extracting one nugget of knowledge, be it ever so small. Then, with that *accomplished*, you have *earned* the right to a break or a movie.

Making Notes

Paragraph-by-paragraph reading is the first step in taking good notes on your reading. As you read and ask questions, write down your answers immediately. Otherwise they will soon be forgotten, and you'll have to do the same work over again when you study for the next exam. Note-taking is so important that I have devoted a full chapter to this technique.

An Alternative Text

If you should happen to have an unusually difficult textbook, go to the library and look through books that cover essentially the same topics. If you find several, the chances are good that one of them will be written in language that is much easier to read and understand.

Now, don't simply substitute the easier-to-read book for the assigned one. Instead, do this: First read the assigned topic in the easier book, to grasp it fully. Then turn to the assigned text, and there underline the key points and make marginal summaries or take separate notes. The obvious point is that once you understand the topic, you can turn to the difficult text with so much confidence that you'll say, "Oh, yes! I see what the author's *trying* to say." You will reap an additional bonus, too: This double exposure to the same topic will make your understanding deeper and your remembering stronger.

WHEN YOU DON'T UNDERSTAND

Dale Corson, former president of Cornell University and dean of the College of Engineering, said that engineers and other students in science and mathematics must often "crack" the meaning of an idea or concept one sentence at a time. If comprehension does not occur even at this snail's pace, then you must ask your instructor for help. "But, before you do," says Dr. Corson, "ask yourself this question: What is it that I don't understand?"

Under no circumstance should you go to the instructor, open the book in front of him or her, even politely, and with a general sweep of the hand say, "I don't understand this portion." When you go for help, you should be able to say, "I understand and follow the writer's idea up to this point and even beyond this point, but I don't make heads or tails out of this particular portion."

Then you have told the instructor a lot. You have said that you've wrestled realistically with the problem and have done as much as you could, but that there's an insurmountable obstacle. And you have pointed out the problem, so the instructor can deal with it. Effective help will be forthcoming.

This Corson Plan has a wonderful by-product. After analyzing and verbalizing your problem, after you have viewed it from several angles, you will most likely have solved it yourself. You may not have to discuss it with anyone but yourself!

RECITATION

You must believe, without an iota of doubt and without a moment of hesitation, that *forgetting* is and will continue to be your major academic concern. Forgetting erodes, corrodes, and thwarts learning. But we have a powerful weapon that can stop it almost dead in its tracks. That weapon is recitation.

Recitation is reciting aloud, *in your own words*, the main points and details of a paragraph you have just read, without looking at the printed page for help. Numerous studies show that alternately reading a paragraph and then reciting, then reading the next paragraph and reciting, and so on, leads to quicker learning and better remembering.

Reciting after each paragraph triggers mental and physical action that (1) promotes *concentration*, (2) forms a sound basis for understanding the next paragraph, (3) provides time for the memory trace to consolidate, (4) ensures that facts and ideas are remembered accurately, and (5) provides immediate feedback on how you're doing. And when you know that you're doing well, you will make progress. Moreover, experiments have shown that the greater the proportion of reciting time, the greater the learning. For example, groups of subjects who spent 20 percent of the time reading and 80 percent reciting did much better than groups that spent less time reciting.

When you recite, simply cover up the printed paragraph in your textbook. If you have written cue words in the margin (see Figure 8.1), leave them exposed. Then repeat the ideas of the paragraph—*aloud*—in your own words. *Avoid mental mumbling;* express the ideas in complete sentences and paragraphs, inserting the proper transition words. When you recite a list of ideas and facts, enumerate them by saying "first," "second," and so on.

If you are a truly conscientious student, you may want to write the ideas and facts, as if you were writing answers in an examination, as you recite them. This would cement the ideas even more strongly in your long-term memory. If you recite while you write, you will be learning through three channels: ears, eyes, and muscles.

Do not ever fall into the trap of believing that re-reading can take the place of reciting. Re-reading is simply doing the same thing over again. You set a mental pattern, with regard to what is in the chapter or paragraph, during the first reading; after that, the eyes and mind see only the same things over and over again. A different approach to the same material is necessary if efficient learning is to take place, and that different approach is recitation.

REVIEW

Alternating reading and recitation is a first step in the war against forgetting, which begins the moment after you learn something. But just as forgetting is a continuous process, your fight against it must be continuous. Reviewing is a weapon that you can use immediately after you have read and recited a chapter, as well as at later times.

The Immediate Review

After you have worked two or three hours to master a chapter, it doesn't make sense to allow yourself to lose a good percentage of it almost immediately. You must protect your investment of time and effort by reviewing immediately. And, if necessary, you must overcome any psychological resistance to a review by launching automatically into one, whether you feel like it or not. The time you spend on reviewing (and it should not be much time) will save a lot of relearning time that might be needed later if you skip a chapter review.

Why does an immediate review cut down on forgetting? Simply because it gives you a chance to put together all the separate parts of the chapter—to snap them together like the parts of a jigsaw puzzle and see the chapter as a whole. Then, instead of having umpteen separate things to remember, you have one unified "picture" of the chapter.

The immediate review is simple to conduct. Begin as soon as you have finished reading the chapter paragraph by paragraph. Cover the first page of the chapter with a sheet of paper, but leave marginal notes exposed. Use your marginal or separate notes as cues to recite aloud, in your own words, the ideas, facts, and details contained on that text page. Then uncover the page to pick up and correct any errors or omissions. Go through each page of the chapter in this way, and you will end up feeling that you know the sequence and flow of the chapter's ideas. And you will remember them!

The Later Reviews

The immediate review is important—very important—but it is not enough. You should review thoroughly and often. Later reviews should be conducted in the same way as the immediate review: using cues, one page at a time, aloud, and in your own words.

These later reviews will keep you in a state of preparedness for quizzes (especially unannounced quizzes) and exams. There will be no need to cram your head full of ideas and facts on the night before an exam; they will have been there all the time. All you'll need is a refresher, in the same form—one more review.

As you review, look for ways to connect or categorize, to put like things together and to place opposite things opposite each other. Look for common characteristics, differences, or functions by which to categorize facts and ideas. This puts you in control and gives you the chance to use your creativity—to bring the textbook to life and bring order to the mass of information you are required to learn in college. Categorizing also puts to practical use the finding that the immediate memory seems to be limited to seven categories, but these categories can be *as big as we care to make them.* (We discussed this in Chapter 5.)

The best time for a fast review of your textbook is the half hour before going to bed. Things learned then have a way of lingering in the conscious mind during the time before sleep comes, and in the subconscious mind after sleep comes.

REFLECTION

After you learn facts and ideas through recitation and immediate review, let your mind reflect on them; let it speculate or play with the things you have learned. To engage in reflection is to bring creativity to your learning. Ask yourself such questions as these:

> What is the significance of these facts and ideas?
> What principle are they based on?
> What else could they be applied to?
> How do they fit in with what I already know?
> What can I see beyond these facts and ideas, but based on them?

When you reflect in this way, you weave new facts and ideas into your existing knowledge. They then become part of your regular stock of "thinking tools."

Prof. Hans Bethe, nuclear physicist and Nobel Prize winner, said, "There's a world of difference between proficiency and creativity. A student can become proficient by studying his textbooks and lecture notes, but he will never be creative until he attempts to see beyond the facts, tries to leap mentally beyond the given. He must reflect on the facts and ideas, for creativity comes only through reflection."

So, seeing new material in the light of what you already know is the only road to creative ideas, for having an idea is nothing more than discovering a relationship not seen before. And it is impossible to have an original idea without reflecting—without thinking reflectively. Best of all, *reflection* not only glues facts and ideas into your permanent memory, but also converts them into true wisdom.

You can and should use reflection often. Reflection is a skill that you can take with you wherever you go, and make use of in spare moments. You can reflect while walking from one building to another, standing in line, waiting for a friend, or riding a bus. People who have made great discoveries have reported that some of their best insights came in unlikely places and at odd times.

Begin with the facts and ideas you have learned, and become curious about them. Look at them in different ways, combine them, separate them into the basics, try to find out what would happen if the opposite were true, and so on. This may be difficult at first, but it will become easier as your creativity grows. Continue your reflection, each time, until your ideas take definite shape. Don't leave them vague. If you need more information, an encyclopedia or a standard source book on the subject will often give you what you need to bring fuzzy ideas into focus.

Scientists have recently uncovered a crucial fact about learning: The only type of learning that not only becomes a permanent part of you but also increases your innate wisdom is *advantageous learning*. And that means learning which occurs when you take a voluntary, extra step beyond the mere memorization of facts—the extra step that is *reflection*.

This great and essential concept of reflection is exactly what the famous philosopher Schopenhauer was referring to when he wrote in one of his *Essays*, "A man may have a great mass of knowledge, but if he has not worked it up by thinking it over for himself, it has much less value than a far smaller amount which he has thoroughly pondered."

FIVE STUDY SYSTEMS
FOR TEXTBOOKS

Chapter 7 and the first part of this chapter contain a number of study techniques and principles. I recommend each and every one of them, but I do not recommend that any one person try to use them all. In fact, you should not use any of them mechanically, without considering how they fit your needs. Nor should you try each of them, one after the other, simply to sample them all. My purpose is to introduce you to the available techniques and the reasons they work. Your job is to select only the techniques you need and can benefit from.

Beware of an overload! Don't be like the knights of old, overburdened by armor. A fully armored knight was as well protected as an armadillo, but as heavy as a hippopotamus and as slow as a snail. Worse yet, the heavy armor often kept him from doing the job he was supposed to do. Don't let this happen to you; don't let the weight of techniques and systems keep you from doing your main job—studying to learn and remember. Pick and choose among the five textbook study systems that follow. If you find one that exactly fits your personality, style, and academic needs, then use it. If you can't find a perfect fit, then select, modify, and adjust parts of these systems to tailor one that is just right for your needs.

Remember, you have only one goal in studying any textbook chapter. When you have finished it, you must be able to explain—orally or on paper—the ideas and supporting details of that chapter. And, of course, you must do so without looking at your text. But explaining the substance of a chapter requires a lot of preliminary work. The explanation is like the visible one-eighth of an iceberg; the invisible seven-eighths is the hours of study that make the explanation possible.

The 3Rs for Academic Survival

Sometimes a direct approach to textbook study is best. Not all material needs or deserves to be transferred to your long-term memory. When this is the case, you can use the 3Rs system to obtain a general understanding of the material. And, if you like its simplicity, you can also use the 3Rs system to implant facts and ideas in your long-term memory. Just emphasize the third step: Keep reciting the facts and ideas until overlearning occurs.

THE 3Rs SYSTEM

Here is a lean and wiry system containing all the essential techniques for mastering textbook assignments. This is an "exam passer."

R_1	READ	*Read the chapter paragraph by paragraph. Read and re-read until you can answer the question, "What did the author say in this paragraph?"*
R_2	RECORD	*Once you are able to describe what is in the paragraph, you will want to retain that learning by* under- lining, making notes in the margin, or making notes in your notebook. *Be courageously selective in your note- making.*
R_3	RECITE	*Cover up your notes or printed page and recite aloud. Remember: If you can't say it now, you won't be able to say it tomorrow in class or write it on an exam. So, while you still have the chance, keep trying until you can say it right.*

The SQ3R System

The SQ3R system is probably the first truly systematic method for studying a textbook (it was devised in 1941). It became popular not only because of its sound academic principles, but also because its name made the steps easy to remember. SQ3R was developed by an Ohio State University psychologist, Francis P. Robinson. Almost all textbook study systems are either partially based on or inspired by this work.

You will see that this system lacks the *reflection* step, which recent studies have found indispensable for true growth in intellect and wisdom. It is, however, a very fine and sound method, as far as it goes. If it appeals to you, simply add to it the reflection step from either the SUPER SIX Rs system or the OK5R system.

Robinson had this to say about the benefits of the SQ3R system:

> These five steps of the SQ3R system—survey, question, read, recite, and review—should result in faster reading, and fixing of the important points in the memory. You will find one other worthwhile outcome: Quiz questions will seem familiar because the headings turned into questions are usually the points emphasized in quizzes. By predicting actual quiz questions and looking up the answers beforehand, you know that you are effectively studying what is considered important in the course.[1]

THE SQ3R SYSTEM

S   SURVEY   Glance through all the headings in the chapter, and read the final summary paragraph (if the chapter has one). This survey should not take more than a minute, and it will show you the three to six core ideas on which the discussion will be based. This orientation will help you organize the ideas as you read them later.

Q   QUESTION   Now begin to work. Turn the first heading into a question. This will arouse your curiosity and thereby increase comprehension. It will bring to mind information you already know, thus helping you understand that section more quickly. The question also will make important points stand out from explanatory details. You can turn a heading into a question as you read the heading, but it demands conscious effort on your part.

[1]Francis P. Robinson, *Effective Study*, 4th ed. (New York: Harper and Row, 1970), p. 32.

R_1	READ	*Read so as to answer that question, but read only to the end of the first section. This should not be a passive plodding along each line, but an active search for the answer.*
R_2	RECITE	*Having read the first section, look away from the book and try briefly to recite the answer to your question. Use your own words, and cite an example. If you can do this you know what is in the book; if you cannot, glance over the section again. An excellent way to do this reciting from memory is to jot down brief cue phrases in outline form on a sheet of paper.*
		Now repeat the second to fourth steps for each successive section: That is, turn the next heading into a question, read to answer that question, and recite the answer by jotting down cue phrases in your outline. Read in this way until the entire lesson is completed.
R_3	REVIEW	*When you have read through in this way, look over your notes to get a bird's-eye view of the points and their relationships to each other. Check your memory by reciting the major subpoints under each heading. This can be done by covering up your notes and trying to recall the main points. Then expose each major point and try to recall the subpoints listed under it.*

Source: *Adaptation of "Steps in the SQ3R Method" (pp. 32–33) from* Effective Study, 4th Edition, *by Francis P. Robinson. Copyright 1941, 1946 by Harper & Row, Publishers, Inc. Copyright © 1961, 1970 by Francis P. Robinson. Reprinted by permission of the publisher.*

The PQRST Study Plan

Here is a system that you can adopt as is, or from which you can choose a step or two for your own system.

The first step, *preview,* is what we called "surveying the chapter" in Chapter 7. In the second step, *question,* you write out questions that come to mind during the preview; some may only require turning a heading into a question. During the third step, *read,* you pick out the answers to your questions, and in the fourth step, *summarize,* you make brief notes to help you answer your questions. You then use these notes to summarize each paragraph and the selection or section as a whole.

The fifth and last step, *test,* is a review. As usual, you do the review without looking at your detailed notes. And the test that you make up will further prepare you for a real test.

THE PQRST STUDY PLAN

P   PREVIEW   *Read the title, headings, and first and last sen-*
                     tences of each paragraph. Read the introductory
                     and summary paragraphs completely.

Q   QUESTION   *During the preview, write out questions that you*
                     will answer in the next two steps. One way to
                     form questions is to turn headings into questions.

R   READ   *Read to answer the questions you have written.*

S   SUMMARIZE   *During your reading, make brief notes that will*
                     help you answer your questions. State, in your own
                     words and in one brief sentence, the central idea of
                     each paragraph. Then combine your paragraph-by-
                     paragraph summaries into one general summary
                     for the selection.

T   TEST   *Try to answer each of your original questions*
                     without looking at your notes. Then make up a
                     true-false quiz on the selection.

Source: *Paraphrased and condensed from George D. Spache and Paul C. Berg,* The Art of Efficient Reading *(New York: Macmillan, 1966), p. 93.*

The OK5R System

The OK5R system is the result of my first attempt to include reflection in a study system. I was eager to bring in this valuable step, because it seemed to be so important to the people who had accomplished the most, throughout human history. The idea for the system was derived from Prof. Robinson's SQ3R.

The first step, *overview*, is again a chapter survey. The second step, *key ideas*, was designed for those who prefer the direct approach of reading a paragraph and then extracting the writer's main thought. The third step, *read*, is designed to help you with chapters that don't have headings, or that have very few. Of course, if a chapter does have plenty of headings, and you feel comfortable making questions out of them, by all means do so.

The fourth step, *record*, is important. Your immediate and later reviews will be based on the notes you make at this point.

The fifth step, *recite*, is now included in almost every study system. I hope we have discussed recitation sufficiently to convince you not to skip it. And the sixth step, *review*, is exactly what we discussed earlier in this chapter. Here, I will only caution you not to put off your immediate review, owing to tiredness or any other reason. If you do, you will be throwing away more than half the work you have put into the chapter.

The seventh step, *reflect*, has a dual purpose: to help you remember by weaving new ideas into your old, existing memory, and to foster creativity through the use of what you have learned.

THE OK5R SYSTEM

O   OVERVIEW   *Sample the chapter to find out what it is all about. Glance at the headings and subheadings to determine what ideas are being explained, what problems raised, and what questions posed. Get the big picture. Don't burrow into paragraphs. Headings and subheadings will be future categories (advance organizers). Overview to overcome inertia and gain momentum for studying.*

K   KEY IDEAS   *All textbook writing is made up of just three literary elements:* main ideas, supporting material, *and* transitions. *Your main job is to separate the main idea from the mass of supporting material.*

R_1 READ   *Read only a paragraph or short section. Then stop to ask: What is the main idea? How do the supporting materials support it? Which transitional words point to the main idea and organize the supporting material? Finally, what is it in this paragraph that I need to know, to describe what I have read?*

R_2 RECORD   *Make marginal notes, and underline only key words and phrases. Better still, summarize main ideas and supporting materials in your notebook. Don't summarize each sentence. Summarize ideas, not words.*

R_3 RECITE   *To counteract forgetting, recite! Cover your textbook or notebook page, exposing only your notes in the margin. Then, using your own words, recite the ideas and supporting material aloud. After reciting, check on how accurate you were. Read, record, and recite paragraph by paragraph, until you complete the chapter.*

R_4 REVIEW   *Immediately after reciting, take a fresh look at your notes to fit them into the overall picture. It is easier to remember one complete jigsaw picture than a multitude of separate, seemingly unrelated puzzle pieces. A review now will give you the total picture. And review occasionally to keep your retention at a high level.*

R_5 REFLECT   *Now, mentally manipulate these ideas, turn them over, speculate on them, compare one with the other, notice where they agree and differ. Organize and reorganize them into larger categories, or compress them into smaller units. Finally, free these ideas from the chapter and the book by weaving them into your existing knowledge.*

The SUPER SIX Rs System

Here's another way of naming and combining the textbook study steps—
easy to remember (six Rs in a row) and easy to use. Once you know the
steps, you'll move automatically from one to the next. Think of the first
step, *reconnoiter*, in the military sense, that is, scout around the territory
in advance. Follow it with *read, recite, record, review,* and *reflect,* and
you are sure to win the battle against forgetting.

SUPER SIX Rs

R_1	RECONNOITER	*This means "to examine with the eye; to make a preliminary examination or survey." So survey, overview, or skim to warm up.*
R_2	READ	*Read paragraph by paragraph. If you read a chapter straight through you will remember only 50 percent of what you read. Convert headings and subheadings into questions, and then read the paragraph to answer the questions.*
R_3	RECITE	*Recite the main ideas and facts in each paragraph. And recite immediately after reading each paragraph.*
R_4	RECORD	*Make notes on your recitation. Capture your words while they're still fresh, and use them over and over for reviewing.*
R_5	REVIEW	*Now that you have read, recited, and recorded, go over all your notes to gain a picture of the whole chapter. Don't close your book until you do so.*
R_6	REFLECT	*Consider the facts and ideas from every angle, separately and in groups or categories. Make them a part of you and they will be yours to command.*

SUMMARY

*Why not read each
chapter straight
through?*

There are several reasons: First, the writer
used a paragraph structure to put one idea
in each paragraph. So it is natural to reverse the process and make sure you have
extracted the idea from each paragraph be-

fore reading on. Second, if you don't stop to test yourself after each paragraph, you may believe you've grasped the main idea just because you understood every word in the paragraph. Third, forgetting takes place rapidly, even as you read, and present information blocks out the memory of previous information. To grasp the idea in the paragraph you've just read, you have to stop and begin to set it in your memory.

Do topic sentences really help us get the meaning?

Yes. Topic sentences are put there by writers to help them stay on target, so they point out the main idea. And, by concentrating on finding the topic sentence, you are automatically concentrating on the entire paragraph.

What makes the Corson Plan work?

The secret element is making you think, making you solve a problem. As you analyze what you don't understand, the chances are great that you will get the answer by yourself. The plan knocks out fuzzy thinking and won't let you get away with vagueness due to laziness or tiredness.

Should we make notes in the margin or in a notebook?

Notebook notes are better. Taking notes is a must, but taking too many can break the camel's back. Then nothing is gained, and hard work is lost. Always make your notes brief and to the point, and be highly selective—be *courageously* selective. In addition, you should jot cue words in the margins of your text.

Is reciting as important as you say?

Yes, and even more so. In a word, reciting is effective because it makes you *think*, for without thinking there's no learning, which is the reason for reading in the first place.

Why the big rush for an immediate review?

To fight *forgetting*. The bulk of forgetting takes place in the few minutes after you learn—after you finish a chapter, for example. So, before forgetting robs you of the result of your effort, you must protect it with an immediate review.

Why all the emphasis on categorizing?

Without putting facts, ideas, and details into categories, you're relying on brute memory to remember. But by thinking through and analyzing each item, seeing similarities and differences and classes, and then categorizing them all, you are using intelligence. Almost by the time you've classified your facts, you've committed them to memory.

In brief, what does reflection do?

Three great things! It's the way to (1) wisdom, (2) creativity, and (3) a bear-trap memory.

What's the main strength of the 3Rs system?

It's a straightforward system designed for the student who wants a clean, hard-hitting, step-by-step guide for textbook mastery. It includes all the ingredients of other systems, except reflection, which can be added to it.

What's the main strength of the SQ3R system?

Without a doubt, this system is known for its *question-asking* step—that is, turning each heading and subheading into a question, and then reading to answer the question. Its only weakness is its lack of a reflection step.

What's the main strength of the PQRST system?

The fourth step, *summarize,* is the special strength of PQRST. But you should be aware that it is not easy to pull together an entire selection or section of a chapter. Nor can it be done in texts that are packed with many separate ideas, facts, experiments, names, outcomes, and so forth. Nevertheless, even the attempt to make a summary can help you see the big picture, and help you remember the specific facts and details.

What are the strengths of the OK5R system?

This system emphasizes the importance of writing cue words in the margins of textbooks. It also uses reflection as an integral part of a textbook study system.

What's the main strength of the SUPER SIX Rs method?

I believe that this system is *complete,* in the sense that it includes the very best of what is known about effective reading and studying.

HAVE YOU MISSED SOMETHING?

1. **SENTENCE-COMPLETION.** Complete the following sentences with one of the three words listed below each sentence.

   a. By reading paragraph by paragraph, you parallel the way the book was first _____.

   published   written   read

   b. In the SQ3R system, you turn headings into _____.

   questions   textbooks   reflections

2. **MATCHING.** In each blank space in the left column, write the number preceding the phrase that matches the left item best.

   _____ a. Read

   _____ b. SQ3R

   _____ c. 3Rs

   _____ d. Reflect

   _____ e. Recite

   _____ f. Reconnoiter

   1. To examine with the eye
   2. Best for quick study before an exam
   3. Simple way to counteract forgetting
   4. Present in every system
   5. Forerunner of recent reading systems
   6. Distinctive feature of OK5R and SUPER SIX Rs

3. **TRUE-FALSE.** Write *T* beside the *true* statements and *F* beside the *false* statements that follow.

   _____ a. You should recite after every paragraph.

   _____ b. The best time to review is one-half hour before going to bed.

   _____ c. Reflection is an involuntary response.

   _____ d. Re-reading can be used effectively in place of reciting.

   _____ e. Boredom should seldom be rewarded with a rest.

   _____ f. The 3Rs system takes an indirect approach.

   _____ g. The *record* step works best with a cassette player.

   _____ h. The *summarize* step in PQRST calls for a single main idea.

4. **MULTIPLE-CHOICE.** Choose the phrase that completes the following sentence most accurately, and circle the letter that precedes it.

When you alternate your reading and reciting, paragraph by paragraph, you test yourself and

a. reflect at the same time.
b. check that your notes are accurate.
c. allow your brain some consolidation time.
d. practice advantageous learning.

5. **REFLECTION.** Pick out the advantages of reflection by writing "yes" next to each of them.

_____ a. Weaves new material with old

_____ b. Fosters creativity

_____ c. Turns headings into questions

_____ d. Increases intelligence

_____ e. Keeps ideas in short-term memory

A picture shows me at a glance what it takes dozens of pages of a book to expound.
—IVAN TURGENEV

9

Understanding Visual Materials

Many students skim over graphs and diagrams as though they were empty pages. The graphic depiction of a principle, object, or idea can be a crucial part of the text. What's more, it can often simplify otherwise complicated ideas. This chapter explains . . .

- How graphic materials are designed
- How to read graphic materials
- Some things to watch out for
- The four basic types of graphs

plus
- Tables and diagrams

S IZABLE PORTIONS OF BOOKS in the sciences, in sociology and psychology, and in business and economics are devoted to tables, graphs, diagrams, and pictures. Such visual materials can convey a great amount of information in a relatively small space. This information is as important as verbal information, and maybe more so; yet many students who feel pressed for time will simply flip past a table or graph, thinking "Ah! Here's a page that I don't have to read," and speed their way toward the end of the chapter.

When you flip past a page of visual material with no more than a passing glance, you are shortchanging yourself in two ways: First, you are missing important information, and second, you are skipping a first-rate opportunity to do some pure thinking. Here's why: Since the page contains *visual* information, you must transform it into *verbal* information. You have to stop and do all the thinking, but once it is done you will have thought through the information and stored it as both verbal and visual data. You will understand it and remember it with great clarity for a long time.

The very best way to learn to master nonverbal material is through intensive study of every table, graph, diagram, and picture that you encounter in your assigned reading. This may sound like the hardest way to learn, but actually you will be accomplishing several things. You'll be learning a skill which will be useful to you today, tomorrow, and in many future assignments. And, as you use this skill, you'll become more and more proficient. Furthermore, you'll be learning important material directly and efficiently—material that you need to learn anyway. Finally, there will be the motivating reward of a job well done, and done well in advance of exam time.

GRAPHIC MATERIALS
ARE EASY TO READ

It is not at all difficult to read graphic materials. These materials are devised by specialists who build four important qualities into each graphic item:

1. *Directness.* Visual materials are designed to draw the attention of readers immediately to the information that is to be seen.
2. *Simplicity.* The information is organized tightly, and needless details are avoided.
3. *Clarity.* Both visual format and meaning are set forth clearly.
4. *Accuracy.* Data are carefully checked, and only graphic forms which do not distort the data are used.

With these built-in qualities, visual materials should be neither complex nor confusing to you. But you still have to know how to read them.

Once you do, you'll find that reading graphics is both a pleasure and a welcome break from the constant bombardment of printed words.

How to Read Graphic Materials

Here are some suggestions for reading graphics, especially tables:

1. *Survey the graphic.* Look it over to get a general impression.
2. *Read the title.* Read carefully, for the title often tells you *what* the data represent, *where* they were collected, and *when*. Of course, the title gives you the subject matter.
3. *Determine the units of measurement.* There is a big difference, for example, between percentages of the whole and actual measurements. Also note whether graphs begin at zero or at some other measurement.
4. *Check headings or captions.* Read the headings over columns (vertical) and alongside rows (horizontal) in tables, to be sure you know what they represent. Read the captions alongside the axes in graphs.
5. *Read the footnotes and headnotes.* If present, footnotes or headnotes provide further information, and often a key to symbols.

How to Read Pictures

Most readers give pictures no more than a passing glance. But pictures should be analyzed systematically. Here's how:

1. Read the title of the picture and the place it depicts. Also read all notations and explanations.
2. Make a general survey, looking for the "message."
3. Now look closely at the different parts of the picture. Like Sherlock Holmes, take in detail after detail. You'll be surprised at what you'll discover.
4. Try to find the connection between the picture and the text. Ask yourself, "Why did they include it?"
5. Strive to make generalizations and draw inferences from the information you have gleaned.

Some Things to Watch Out For

Factual data—especially statistics—can be placed in graphic formats that distort the data. Unscrupulous people may use this device to strengthen arguments or make data appear favorable to their cause. The book *How* to *Lie with Statistics*[1] exposes some of the devious tricks that are used and is also fun to read.

For example, you should be wary of the word *average,* and you should try to find the highest and lowest figures that went into each average. Two companies may have an average salary of $29,000. But if the range of salaries in one company is $6,000 to $90,000, whereas in the other company it is $20,000 to $35,000, then the salary policies of the two companies are quite different.

Don't be overly impressed by the steepness of the lines in graphs. Look at the side of every graph, to find the scale—the value of each increment. Units of $100 will make a line much steeper than units of $1,000. And always convert what you see into words; otherwise you'll remember the steepness or flatness, but not the real information that is being presented.

Remember that visual relationships can be tricky. The frame around a diagram can actually change the way you see the diagram. For example, this is a diamond-shaped figure:

But notice that when the same figure is placed in a frame,

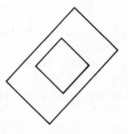

it becomes a square. The size and shape of a chart or graph can also affect what you see. Data that may, in fact, be quite neutral or ordinary can be made to look startling by the form and scale of the graphic. But if you read graphics carefully, you'll see them the proper way, rather than as someone else may expect you to see them.

[1]Darrell Huff, *How to Lie with Statistics.* Pictures by Irving Geis, 1st ed. (New York: Norton, 1954).

TYPES OF GRAPHS

In your reading, you'll come across dozens of graphs which seem to differ in a variety of ways. On closer inspection, however, you'll find that they are all modifications of four basic types. In this section we'll look at these basic types.

Bar or Column Graphs

These graphs have two scales. The horizontal scale usually measures time, while the vertical scale measures some quantity or amount.

Figure 9.1 is a graph that you can read easily and directly. Instead of using a vertical scale, the artist placed the amounts at the tops of the columns. What aspect of this graph is most forceful and prominent? Isn't it the unbroken upward steps showing increases in unemployment, month by month? Furthermore, the column graph shows such trends better than the line graph and much better than words in a paragraph.

Figure 9.2 (page 180) is a fine example of a bar graph, with the horizontal scale measuring time and the vertical scale measuring quantity. Using a ruler, you can readily see that imports for 1975 were 12 million short tons. Notice, too, that the source of the statistics is always given.

Figure 9.1 Unemployment in Pittsburgh

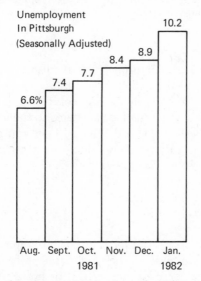

Source: Pittsburgh Office of Employment Security. From *The Wall Street Journal,* Eastern Edition CXCIX, No. 51, March 16, 1982, p. 31. Reprinted by permission of *The Wall Street Journal,* © Dow Jones & Company, Inc. 1982. All Rights Reserved.

Figure 9.2 U.S. Imports of Iron and Steel Mill Products

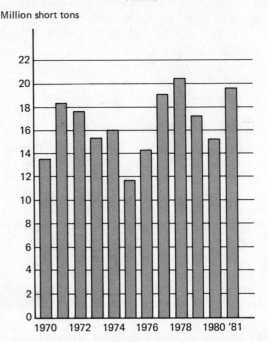

Volume

Million short tons

Source: American Iron and Steel Institute and U.S. Department of Commerce. From Federal Reserve Bank of Chicago *International Letter*, No. 468, February 26, 1982. Reprinted by permission.

Figure 9.3 is a column graph that shows the relation between two quantities as well as their magnitudes. The relation is shown directly, clearly, and forcefully by placing columns side by side. Since the values are in millions, you must add six zeros to the numbers shown on the vertical scale. Notice the grid lines to help you assess values quickly and easily. Notice, too, the key, which distinguishes the columns for "Net Earnings" and for "Cash Dividends Paid."

Circle or Pie Graphs

No graph can do a better job than the pie graph when it comes to showing the *proportional parts* of the whole. It is probably the easiest of all graphs to read, since there are no vertical or horizontal lines to follow or any amounts to interpolate. The chart clearly shows the proportions, and the amounts are given directly.

Figure 9.3 Net Earnings and Cash Dividends Paid

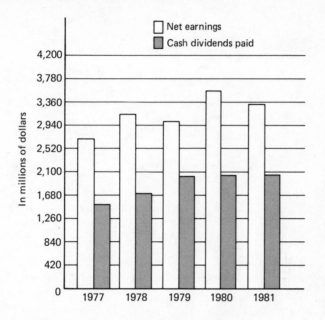

Source: International Business Machines Corp. *Annual Report 1981*, p. 25.

Figure 9.4 (page 182) accompanied an article which pointed out that there are 350,000 acres of green lawn area in New York State. To maintain these lawns on an annual basis means millions of dollars of income to manufacturers of such products as weed controls, fertilizer, machines for cutting grass, tools for maintenance, and work clothes.

Incidentally, the amounts in Figure 9.4 do not add up to a neat 350,000. Thus you can assume that there were many more acres scattered among many other categories. They were omitted so as not to obscure the main point with too many details.

Line Graphs

These graphs are widely used because they can be adapted to all kinds of quantitative data. The line graph has two scales at right angles, one vertical and the other horizontal. If time is one of the variables, it is usually shown on the horizontal scale.

In Figure 9.5 (page 182), the sentence below the line graph immediately orients you to the graph's full meaning. Notice, on the horizontal scale, that each year is divided into months. By placing a ruler on the

Figure 9.4 Lawn Care Is Big Business in New York State (Figures in acres).

Parks
48,000

Home lawns
128,000

Highways
13,000

School
grounds   16,000

Commercial sod
production
5,000

Cemeteries
40,000

Golf
courses
40,630

Industrial,
public, private,
gov't grounds
57,000

Source: Research and Education, New York State College of Agriculture, Cornell University.

Figure 9.5 Hourly Earnings

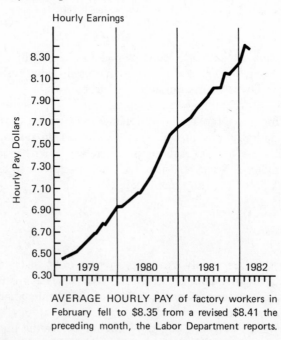

Hourly Earnings

Hourly Pay Dollars

8.30
8.10
7.90
7.70
7.50
7.30
7.10
6.90
6.70
6.50
6.30

1979   1980   1981   1982

AVERAGE HOURLY PAY of factory workers in
February fell to $8.35 from a revised $8.41 the
preceding month, the Labor Department reports.

Source: The Wall Street Journal, Eastern Edition CXCIX, No. 51, March 16, 1982, p. 1. Reprinted by permission of *The Wall Street Journal,* © Dow Jones & Company, Inc. 1982. All Rights Reserved.

graph, you can get a fairly good idea of the hourly wage for any of the months shown. Why didn't the artist use a column graph to show the wages month by month? Simply because such a graph would have been too crowded if thirty-eight columns, one for each month, had been jammed into the space allotted to the figure. Here, a single line makes a clean, inviting graph.

The two graphs in Figure 9.6 were used to show the stockholders of IBM that profits shrank when the money earned in two countries was converted into U.S. dollars. Notice that no effort was made to show months on the horizontal scale. The purpose of the graphs was not to show precise conversions in any month, but only to show the overall *plunging* movement of the foreign currencies. IBM felt that a picture was worth a thousand words.

Combination Graphs

Some graphs are neither bar graphs nor line graphs, but may have characteristics of both. The makers of graphs often use great imagination and creativity to put forth complex information in an easy-to-understand form. The graph used to show the daily Dow Jones Average (of the prices

Figure 9.6 Foreign Currency Valued in U.S. Dollars

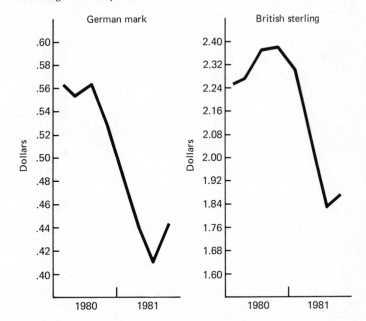

Source: International Business Machines Corp. *Annual Report 1981*, p. 31.

of thirty industrial stocks on the New York Stock Exchange) is a fine example of this type of ingenuity.

The symbol used to show the daily averages is a short line, which is explained at the top right-hand corner of Figure 9.7. The top of the daily line indicates the highest stock average reached during the day. The bottom of the line indicates the lowest average for the day. And the little horizontal projection indicates the average at the close of the day. Notice that on January 8 the closing average was very near the low average for the day. The horizontal scale is marked in weeks. There are usually five lines in each week, since the stock market is closed on Saturdays, Sundays, and legal holidays.

TABLES

Tables are used to present a large amount of factual information (usually statistics), in a compact, orderly arrangement that makes complex relationships immediately clear. For example, Table 9.1 shows how life ex-

Figure 9.7 The Dow Jones Averages

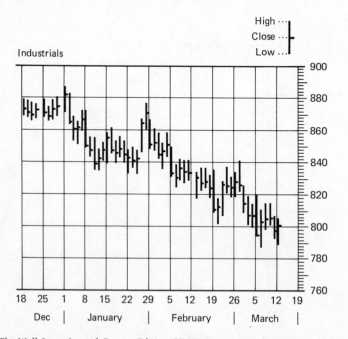

Source: The Wall Street Journal, Eastern Edition CXCIX, No. 51, March 16, 1982, p. 47. Reprinted by permission of *The Wall Street Journal,* © Dow Jones & Company, Inc. 1982. All Rights Reserved.

Table 9.1 Expectation of Life at Birth: 1920 to 1978

Year	Total			White			Black and Other		
	Total	Male	Female	Total	Male	Female	Total	Male	Female
1920	54.1	53.6	54.6	54.9	54.4	55.6	45.3	45.5	45.2
1930	59.7	58.1	61.6	61.4	59.7	63.5	48.1	47.3	49.2
1940	62.9	60.8	65.2	64.2	62.1	66.6	53.1	51.5	54.9
1950	68.2	65.6	71.1	69.1	66.5	72.2	60.8	59.1	62.9
1955	69.6	66.7	72.8	70.5	67.4	73.7	63.7	61.4	66.1
1960	69.7	66.6	73.1	70.6	67.4	74.1	63.6	61.1	66.3
1965	70.2	66.8	73.7	71.0	67.6	74.7	64.1	61.1	67.4
1970	70.9	67.1	74.8	71.7	68.0	75.6	65.3	61.3	69.4
1971	71.1	67.4	75.0	72.0	68.3	75.8	65.6	61.6	69.7
1972	71.1	67.4	75.1	72.0	68.3	75.9	65.6	61.5	69.9
1973	71.3	67.6	75.3	72.2	68.4	76.1	65.9	61.9	70.1
1974	71.9	68.1	75.8	72.7	68.9	76.6	67.0	62.9	71.3
1975	72.5	68.7	76.5	73.2	69.4	77.2	67.9	63.6	72.3
1976	72.8	69.0	76.7	73.5	69.7	77.3	68.3	64.1	72.6
1977	73.2	69.3	77.1	73.8	70.0	77.7	68.8	64.6	73.1
1978	73.3	69.5	77.2	74.0	70.2	77.8	69.2	65.0	73.6

Source: Statistical Abstract of the United States 1980, U.S. Department of Commerce, Bureau of the Census, Washington, D.C., p. 72.

pectancy varies with age, race, and sex. As you can see, this table is easy to read, and it contains a tremendous amount of information within a relatively small space.

DIAGRAMS

Some textbooks—science and engineering texts, for example—contain diagrams on almost every other page. A labeled diagram of an insect or a carburetor is of great help in visualizing and understanding the complex relationships of the parts. The student who studies such diagrams so thoroughly that he or she can reproduce them from memory is the student who will know the subject cold, not only for the next exam but also for the long pull.

Figure 9.8 (page 186) is a diagram of a "cold storage" room designed for the preservation of vegetables and canned foods. It illustrates the tremendous power of a diagram to help you visualize quite easily things that would require much effort to convert from word descriptions to mental images.

Figure 9.8 Storage Room

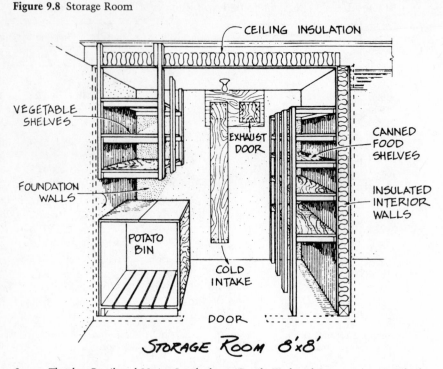

CEILING INSULATION

VEGETABLE SHELVES

EXHAUST DOOR

CANNED FOOD SHELVES

FOUNDATION WALLS

INSULATED INTERIOR WALLS

POTATO BIN

COLD INTAKE

DOOR

STORAGE ROOM 8'x8'

Source: Theodore Brevik and Marion Longbotham, "Family Work and Storage Areas Outside the House," *The Yearbook of Agriculture 1978.* U.S. Department of Agriculture, Washington, D.C.

SUMMARY

Why are graphic materials used?

Graphic materials provide you with instant visualizations, which lead to better understanding and longer remembering. In addition, they pack a great deal of information into a relatively small space.

What makes graphics such good learning devices?

Since graphics are not presented in words, you have to supply the words. And to do that you *must* think. So you end up not only understanding the fact or idea more deeply, but also remembering it longer because you have entered it into your long-term memory right at the start.

What makes graphics easy to read?

You don't have paragraphs of words to interpret or misinterpret. In graphics, you have plain lines and plain figures, so the chance of a mistake is reduced to the minimum. Furthermore, the makers of graphics strive mightily to be direct, simple, clear, and accurate.

What's the best way to read a graphic?

Look over the graphic generally, and then read and understand the title, the footnotes, and any descriptions. Next, read all headings or captions, and determine the units of measurement. Finally, enter into the graphic itself and sample it. Determine how its various parts (rows and columns, lines and axes, or photo subjects) are related.

HAVE YOU MISSED SOMETHING?

1. **SENTENCE-COMPLETION.** Complete the following sentences with one of the three words listed below each sentence.

   a. Pictures should be studied _____.
      briefly   systematically   infrequently

   b. Before studying a graph carefully, you should give it a general ____.
      survey   inference   title

2. **MATCHING.** In each blank space in the left column, write the number preceding the phrase that matches the left item best.

   ____ a. Line graph

   ____ b. Combination graph

   ____ c. Table

   ____ d. Diagram

   ____ e. Circle graph

   ____ f. Bar graph

   1. Best at showing proportions
   2. Quite common in science texts
   3. Mixture of bar and line graphs
   4. Most used graphic
   5. Holds a great deal of information
   6. Related to the column graph

3. **TRUE-FALSE.** Write *T* beside the *true* statements and *F* beside the *false* statements that follow.

   ____ a. The horizontal axis is traditionally reserved for time.

   ____ b. Graphic material is always more understandable in paragraph form.

_____ c. Graphs, tables, and diagrams provide instant visualization.

_____ d. Nonverbal materials should be mastered with intensive study.

_____ e. Unlike paragraphs, graphs provide only objective information.

4. **MULTIPLE-CHOICE.** Choose the word that completes the following sentence most accurately, and circle the letter that precedes it.

Understanding a graphic involves transforming the visual into the

a. mental.
b. vocal.
c. verbal.
d. rational.

5. **GRAPHICS.** Pick out the four characteristics of good graphics and write "yes" beside them.

_____ a. colorful

_____ b. direct

_____ c. simple

_____ d. small

_____ e. clear

_____ f. accurate

Read, mark, learn, and inwardly digest.
—THE BOOK OF COMMON PRAYER

10
Making Notes On (and From) Your Textbook

Marking textbooks isn't simply a matter of scribbling in the margins or turning certain sentences yellow with a marker. Poor textbook marking can create confusion instead of eliminating it. And sometimes it's better to take separate notes. Read this chapter to find . . .

- When to mark or take notes
- Guidelines for marking and notetaking
- How to use symbols
- Sample markings and textbook notes
- How to study collateral materials

and

- How to use notes once you have them

WHEN YOU READ FOR PLEASURE, you can sink back into a soft, luxurious easy chair, put your feet up, and let the book or magazine do the work. But when you read to learn, you must put as much into the process as you expect to get out of it. Reading to learn is an active process; mental and physical activity are what make it work. Keeping a pencil in your hand as you read will provoke both kinds of activity. It will serve as a constant reminder that you must do something with it— underline and make marginal notes in your text, or take separate notes on the important ideas, facts, and principles. Why do you need such notes? Because without them you can't use any of the study systems of Chapter 8. Without notes you can't review, and studying for each quiz or exam then requires reading the chapter all over again—starting again from square one.

Mental activity enters the picture because you have to concentrate to take notes. You have to find the important ideas, facts, and principles, and you have to separate them out and make them yours. So the concentration leads to thinking, which leads to reasoning, which leads finally to comprehension.

MARK THE TEXT OR
TAKE SEPARATE NOTES?

Most students prefer to mark their textbooks, underlining important words, phrases, and sentences and making brief notations in the margins. However, many students prefer to leave their books unmarked; instead, they make sentence-type notes in a separate notebook. Some of those who prefer notetaking claim that it helps them to be more active, systematic, and thorough readers. For others, the writing of a one-sentence summary for each paragraph breaks up the task of reading a whole chapter. They also like the idea of having all their notes on a few sheets of paper, rather than scattered throughout the twenty or so pages of each textbook chapter.

A few students both mark the textbook and take separate notes. These students claim that underlining and making marginal notes gives them a thorough understanding of the chapter as a *whole*. Then, based on their markings and this understanding, they are able to make concise and unified notes in a separate notebook. These students depend almost entirely on their notebook notes for periodic reviews and to prepare for exams. They also refer back to their well-marked textbooks whenever necessary to amplify a fact or idea.

I also know of a few students who have used all three systems (textbook marking, separate notes, and a combination of the two), depending on the nature of the course, the textbook, and the emphasis of the instructor. You should be aware of all three, but use the one or ones that work best for you.

GUIDELINES FOR
TEXTBOOK MARKING

1. *Finish reading before marking.* Never mark until you have finished reading a full paragraph or headed section and have paused to think about what you just read. This procedure will keep you from grabbing at everything that looks important at first glance. While you are reading, it is difficult to determine whether the author is stating a new idea or merely stating the same idea in different words. You will be able to spot these duplications by looking back *after* you have finished the paragraph or section.

2. *Be extremely selective.* Don't underline or jot so many items that they overload your memory or cause you to try to think in several directions at once. Be stingy with your markings, but don't be so brief that you'll have to read through the page again when you review.

3. *Use your own words.* The jottings in the margins should be in your own words. Since your own words represent your own thinking, they will later be powerful cues to the ideas on the page.

4. *Be brief.* Underline brief but meaningful phrases, rather than complete sentences. Make your marginal jottings short and to the point. They will make a sharper impression on your memory, and they will be easier to use when you recite and review.

5. *Be swift.* You don't have all day for marking. Read, go back for a mini-overview, and make your markings. Then attack the next portion of the chapter.

6. *Be neat.* Neatness takes conscious effort, not time. Later when you review, the neat marks will encourage you and save time, since the ideas will be easily and clearly perceived.

7. *Organize facts and ideas under categories.* Items within categories are far more easily memorized than random facts and ideas.

8. *Try cross-referencing.* For example, if you find an idea on page 64 that has a direct bearing on an idea back on page 28, draw a little arrow pointing upward and write "28" by it. Then, turn back to page 28 and, alongside the idea there, draw an arrow pointing downward and write "64" by it. In this way you'll tie the two ideas together, in your mind and in your reviewing.

9. *Be systematic.* Figure 10.1 (page 192) contains twelve suggestions for marking textbooks. Note especially the single and double underlines; the use of asterisks, circling, and boxing for important items; and the uses of the top and bottom margins for longer notations. If some of these

Figure 10.1 Suggestions for Marking Textbooks

EXPLANATION AND DESCRIPTION	SYMBOLS, MARKINGS, AND NOTATIONS
1. Use double lines under words or phrases to signify main ideas.	<u>Radiation can produce mutations</u> . . .
2. Use single lines under words or phrases to signify supporting material.	<u>comes from cosmic rays</u> . . .
3. Mark small circled numbers near the initial word of an underlined group of words to indicate a series of arguments, facts, ideas—either main or supporting.	Conditions change . . . ① <u>rocks rise</u> . . . ② <u>some sink</u> . . . ③ <u>the sea dashes</u> . . . ④ <u>strong winds</u> . . .
4. Rather than underlining a group of three or more important lines, use a vertical bracket in the margin.	had known . . . who gave . . . the time . . . of time . . .
5. Use one asterisk in the margin to indicate ideas of special importance, and two for ideas of unusual importance. Reserve three asterisks for principles and high-level generalizations.	* When a <u>nuclear blast</u> is . . . ** People <u>quite close</u> to the . . . *** The main <u>cause of mutations</u> . . .
6. Circle key words and terms.	The (genes) are the . . .
7. Box words of enumeration and transition.	[fourth,] the lack of supplies . . . [furthermore,] the shortage . . .
8. Place a question mark in the margin, opposite lines you do not understand, as a reminder to ask the instructor for clarification.	? | The latest . . . | cold period . . . | about 1,000,000 . . . | Even today . . .
9. If you disagree with a statement, indicate that in the margin.	Disagree | Life became . . . | on land only . . . | 340 million years . . .
10. Use the top and bottom margins of a page to record ideas of your own that are prompted by what you read.	Why not use carbon dating? . . . . Check on reference of fossils found in Tennessee stone quarry.
11. On sheets of paper that are smaller than the pages of the book, write longer thoughts or summaries; then insert them between the pages.	Fossils Plants = 500,000,000 years old Insects = 260,000,000 " " Bees = 100,000,000 " " True fish = 330,000,000 " " Amphibians = 300,000,000 " " Reptiles = 300,000,000 " " Birds = 150,000,000 " "
12. Even though you have underlined the important ideas and supporting materials, still jot brief cues in the side margins.	Adapt — . . . . fossil — . . . . layer — . . . .

ideas appeal to you, work them into your marking system, one or two at a time. But use them consistently so you will remember what they mean at review time.

CAUTION!

A word of warning is in order. Textbook marking can be a useful aid to study and review, but it must be done with thought and care. Otherwise it becomes mere busywork—just another dodge to avoid genuine recall, reflection, and review. Drawing underlines and boxes, or inserting symbols and question marks, can give you a false sense of accomplishment if you are not thinking deeply about what you read. Besides, if you over-mark your book, you will defeat the purpose: quick identification of important points. When you come to re-read, you will find yourself deciphering a code instead of reviewing ideas. Figure 10.2 (page 194) shows a page that has been sadly overmarked.

A final point is that the "you" that marks the book will not be quite the same "you" that reviews it. You will grow in knowledge; many things that seemed so important to underscore, box, circle, star, question, comment on, or disagree with in October or November will be accepted as commonplace by January or June. Then your earlier marks may only hamper your review. So use the help that marking can give you, but don't go overboard.

SAMPLE MARKED PAGES

On the following pages are samples of appropriately marked textbook pages. You can learn something about good marking by reading my comments on the samples, but you will learn even more by studying the samples themselves.

Figure 10.3 (page 195) shows how a brief marginal note can expand a title into a summary that will be invaluable for review. It gives the dates of the Crusades, since dates are important, and ties them to a date that is instantly meaningful—1492. The cryptic "13C" is an abbreviation for "thirteenth century." Notice also the summary notes in the margin and the circles representing concepts and geographical locations to be looked up. Underlining is used sparingly and effectively, so that review will be easy.

Figure 10.4 (page 196) shows how material can be organized by numbering key concepts. If they are already numbered for you in the text, that's great. If they are not, then impose your own organization. Add your own numbers—and letters, too, if they are needed for subtopics. In any case, carry the numbers and letters over to your marginal notes, so that

Figure 10.2 Too Much Marking. A well-meaning but overconscientious student can defeat the purpose of marking. When you try to emphasize too much, you emphasize nothing.

I. Color vision in people.
A. Can't explain how we see color
B. All shades matched through mixing primary colors
C. No proof all people see color in same way — assume they do — can't assume with animals

Disagree? what kind of proof is needed that all people experience color in same way? If all people call something red, isn't that proof?

II. Color vision in animals.
A. Can animals see light of a given color?
1. Chickens
2. honeybees

B. Can animals distinguish color?
1. bees can distinguish colors

2. other animals which can

Color Vision in Animals

Color vision is extremely puzzling to the physiologist; we have no satisfactory theory of color vision, nor can we explain how we see color. For example, we cannot explain why we see white light if we mix spectrally pure red (656 mμ) and blue-green (492 mμ), or why the sensation of spectral green can be perfectly matched by a mixture of yellow and blue. We do know, however, that all shades of color can be matched by appropriate mixtures of three so-called primary colors: red, yellow, and blue. A deviating color vision, known as color blindness, is associated with reduced acuity for shades of green or red (or both). It is quite common in man, occurring in about 8 per cent of all males and 0.6 per cent of females.

From our own experience, each of us knows that he sees colors and that these colors have names, and by inference we assume (although we have no proof) that when somebody says "red" he has the same experience we have. Such inference, however, is completely unjustified when it comes to animals of a different species, with whom we cannot talk; but even so, we can discover some facts about color vision in animals. We really want the answers to two questions: first, whether an animal can see light of a given color at all and, secondly, whether different colors are perceived differently so that they can be distinguished.

Some simple tests can often answer our first question. If a chicken is fed in a darkroom that has rice grains scattered on the floor and the grains are illuminated with spectral colors, the animals will pick up all the grains in red, yellow, and green light, but not the ones in blue light, although these are clearly visible to us. Evidently the chicken eye is not able to perceive blue as light. In a similar fashion we can show that honeybees are insensitive to red, and, by using red light, we can observe their life in the "darkness" inside the hive without disturbing them. On the other hand, bees are sensitive to ultraviolet, which we do not see.

Our second question—can animals distinguish colors? —has been answered by training experiments. If, for example, bees are trained to feed from a dish of sugar solution placed on a yellow disk, they will rapidly learn to seek food on a yellow background. If the full dish is now placed on a blue background and an empty dish on the yellow, the bees will continue seeking food on the yellow background. With a careful application of this and other training experiments, we are able to show that bees can distinguish colors (although we do not know what they see). In similar ways, it has been shown that at least some teleost fishes can discriminate colors, but elasmobranchs cannot. Turtles, lizards, and birds have color vision, but most mammals, except man and monkeys, are unable to discriminate color.

Source: Text from *Animal Physiology* by Knut Schmidt-Nielsen, pp. 89–90. Copyright © 1960 by Prentice-Hall, Inc., Englewood Cliffs, N.J. Reprinted by permission of the publisher.

Figure 10.3 Simple Marking of a Textbook Page

The Crusades

1096 -
to late 13C.
-and 200
years before
Columbus

From the time when they occurred to the present, the crusades have commanded public attention and called forth innumerable chronicles, histories long and short, and even poems. Their place in the historiographical tradition of Europe is thus assured, and the very word crusade has become familiar in our vocabulary. But if <u>historians,</u> mediaeval and modern, have <u>agreed</u> that the crusades were <u>interesting</u> <u>and important,</u> they have <u>differed</u> widely in explaining their <u>origins</u> and interpreting their <u>significance.</u> Indeed, it might be questioned whether they belong in a discussion of the mediaeval church. They were, however, <u>launched originally</u> <u>by the papacy;</u> and the <u>church's role,</u> though it diminished, was <u>never negligible.</u> In this brief account it will be possible only to summarize the more generally accepted conclusions.

Causes
1. Seljuks

|First,| it is clear that the <u>eight large expeditions</u> from <u>1096</u> to the <u>later</u> years of the <u>thirteenth</u> century, as well as the many less important ventures, were <u>occasioned by</u> the political and military <u>successes of Islam.</u> In particular, they were a response to a comparatively new menace presented in the <u>second half of the eleventh century by the Seljuk Turks.</u> The (Seljuks) had overrun the Bagdad (caliphate) and as a consequence of a resounding victory over a Byzantine army

Manzikert

at <u>Manzikert in 1071</u> opened the way to the conquest of Asia Minor. <u>Byzantium</u> had faced Islam across the straits before, but never had it <u>lost the entire hinterland of</u>(Asia Minor.)

2. 11 C
energy;
Cluny;
Expansion

|Second,|the crusades were <u>made possible</u> by the religious, political, and economic <u>energy</u> so characteristic <u>of the</u> <u>eleventh century.</u> The(Cluny)reform reached a climax in the second half of the century, and it was not difficult for an ecclesiastically militant church to direct its forces to the military defense of Christendom and the recovery of the Holy City, Jerusalem. <u>Politically and economically,</u> eleventh-century Europe was entering one of those <u>periods of expansion</u> which have characterized its civilization down to modern times.

Source: Reprinted from Marshall W. Baldwin, *The Mediaeval Church.* Copyright 1953 by Cornell University. Used by permission of Cornell University Press.

Figure 10.4 Marking a Textbook: Numbers and Letters

Memory

1. Three stages of
memory
a) acquisition
b) retention
c) retrieval

To begin with, we must distinguish among ^{1.}three stages which are implied by any act of remembering. Consider a person working on a crossword puzzle who is trying to recall an eight-letter word meaning "African anteater." If she does, we can be sure that she succeeded in all three stages of the memorial process. The first is acquisition. To remember, one must first have learned; the subject must somewhere have encountered this particular item of biological exotica. During this acquisition stage, the relevant experiences presumably left some enduring record in the nervous system, the **memory trace.** Next comes retention, during which the information is filed away for later use (until the next crossword puzzle). The final stage is retrieval, the point at which one tries to remember, to dredge up this particular memory trace from among all others. Many failures to remember are failures of retrieval and not of storage. Our subject may be unable to come up with the correct answer at the time, but when she later sees the solution she realizes that she knew it all along. "Of course, Aardvark!"

2. Methods of
retrieval
a) recall
b) recognition

A previously acquired item of information can be ^{2.}retrieved in two ways: recall and recognition. An individual who is asked to recall must produce an item or a set of items. "Where did you park your car?" or "What is the name of the boy who sat next to you in third grade?" are examples of recall questions. The experimental psychologist typically tests for the recall of materials that were learned in the laboratory; this assures that any failures in recall are not simply failures of original acquisition. Thus a subject might have to learn a dozen unrelated adjectives which he will later be asked to recite. Recall need not be verbal. An example is the retention of a motor skill such as playing golf; here memory is best assessed by observing how the subject hits a golf ball and not by how he talks about his swing. Another example is the memory of visual patterns. This is sometimes tested by the method of reproduction in which the subject tries to draw what he has seen. (Unfortunately, such reproduction failures may only prove that he cannot draw and not that he cannot remember.)

A memory trace can also be tapped with a recognition test. A person who is shown an item must indicate whether he has encountered it before, either in general ("Did you ever see this face before?") or in a particular context ("Is this one of the girls who played on your high school field hockey team?"). In the laboratory the subject is usually asked to pick out the previously learned item from among several false alternatives. Examples are multiple-choice or true-false tests which clearly put a greater premium on recognition than do essay or short-answer fill-in examinations, which emphasize recall.

Source: Reprinted from PSYCHOLOGY by Henry Gleitman, by permission of W. W. Norton & Company, Inc. Copyright © 1981 by W. W. Norton & Company, Inc..

later you can recall the entire "package." In this instance, only the bare key words were placed in the margin, primarily for use as cues in reciting. Too much information in the margin will make reciting too easy.

GUIDELINES FOR MAKING NOTES ON TEXTBOOKS

1. *Use the Cornell format.* Mark a 2½-inch margin on the left of your paper, leaving a six-inch-wide area on the right in which to make notes. Use the margin for key words (see Chapter 6). This is the ideal format for recording, reciting, and reviewing. Figures 10.5 and 10.6 (pages 198 and 199) illustrate this format.
2. *Finish reading before you take notes.* Never write a note until you have finished reading a full paragraph or a headed section. This will keep you from summarizing everything that looks important at first glance.
3. *Be extremely selective.* Pick out the essentials and write them concisely. This rule is probably the most difficult of all, because to be selective you must read critically and think about what you have read. Then you'll be able to summarize each paragraph in *one sentence.* Don't try to master every idea, fact, and detail in the book; get the important ideas and the basic principles. And don't try to rewrite the textbook in longhand, for you won't be accomplishing a thing. Simply read the paragraph and re-read it if necessary, decide *at that time* what is important, and write your one-sentence summary.
4. *Use your own words.* After finishing the paragraph or section, ask "What is the author's main point?" Recite it, and then quickly write it in the words you just spoke. Do not mechanically transfer words from the textbook to your notebook. You will be bypassing your mind and wasting time and energy.
5. *Write full sentences.* Don't make notes in outline form. Rather, write full sentences expressing full thoughts: This is what you will have to do during an exam. Also, when you review and restudy, you will be able to perceive each idea instantly. Neat writing will also be of help when you review.
6. *Be swift.* You don't have all day and night for notetaking. So keep alert and press for efficiency: read, go back for a mini-overview, recite the author's idea, and write it. Then attack the next portion of the chapter.
7. *Don't forget visual materials.* Important diagrams, like important facts and ideas, should be transferred to your notebook, recited, and reviewed. In biology, for example, a sure way of memorizing the structure of the amoeba is to sketch it, with all parts labeled. Take

notes regarding the important aspects of maps, charts, and tables as well; they are vital parts of your text.

SAMPLE NOTES

Figure 10.5 shows the kind of notes you might use for material that requires an orderly listing of facts, principles, or rules. Though at first glance the notes in this sample may appear to be a formal outline, this is not the case at all. The facts under "general rules for contour lines" form a simple list, and the sentences are almost complete.

Figure 10.6 shows notes on material that deals more with ideas and their relationships than with facts. Here you would be reading for concepts and theories that are likely to span many paragraphs. You would skim in your overview, to get an idea of what the main concepts are and how extensively they are treated. Your task then would be to summarize and condense many paragraphs into one or two, as shown in the sample.

Slow readers often find that notetaking forces them to concentrate better, and they go through each chapter faster than before. Rapid readers slow down a bit, but they learn to read with a new thoroughness.

Edward W. Fox, Cornell University's great teacher, lecturer, and historian, had this to say about notetaking:

> . . . Notes are a means to an end and not the end in themselves. Some system is desirable, but a very common failing among beginning students is to develop a method so complicated and formal that it wholly defeats its purpose.
>
> Notes taken in paragraph form on a page with a wide left-hand margin are the most generally useful. Elaborate arrangements tend to confuse, and the traditional topical form, the use of Roman numerals, capital letters, Arabic numerals, and small letters, etc., with much indentation, has a fatal tendency to imply a logical analysis rather than elicit one.

Figure 10.5 The Cornell Format Used for Material Emphasizing Facts

Key Words	Notes on the Chapter
Contour Lines	General Rules for contour lines
1. steep slope	1. Steep slope — lines close together.
2. gentle slope	2. Gentle slope — lines are spread.
3. cross	3. Lines never cross
4. streams	4. Lines crossing streams — bend upstream.

Figure 10.6 Notes on Material Emphasizing Ideas and Relationships

Key Words	Notes on the Chapter
Song of Roland defeat french valor magic horn no love story knighthood	Song of Roland (medieval epic) One of the noblest poems in Europe. Celebrating a *defeat*, the french fought with such supreme valor that the defeat was vindicated. Roland had a magic horn which Charlemagne could hear. Poem is wonderfully concentrated on a single incident. Virtually no love story. A rugged, primitive poem. The finest ideals of knighthood have been crystalized in it.

The most useful aspect of the topical outline [is] annotation in the process of review. Topical headings, brief lists of points, and critical comments may be penciled in the margin of the notes during review in preparation for an examination. Most students find this an effective device. It forces them to select and extract the most important points, to keep their attention closely focused on the material, and to fix material in their minds through the mechanical process of writing it in summary form.[1]

So you see, it is not only the study-skills experts who advocate notetaking. Figure 10.7 (page 200) is an example taken from Prof. Fox's book *Syllabus for History*. In this example, the telegraphic style is combined with categorization, for more powerful notes. Notice, however, that the notes preserve the basic elements of regular sentence structure, even though they are telegraphic. The abbreviations "imp." and "impt." both mean "important."

COLLATERAL MATERIAL: READING AND NOTETAKING

In many undergraduate courses, assignments and lectures revolve around a single textbook. But instructors will often give outside reading assignments, in other publications. They do not expect you to master such col-

[1]Edward W. Fox, *Syllabus for History* (Ithaca, N.Y.: Cornell University Press, 1959). Reprinted by permission of the author.

Figure 10.7 Telegraphic, Categorized Notes. The student will jot key words in the left margin during review.

Chester G. Starr, Jr., <u>The Emergence of Rome</u>, Ch. I:
  "Geography and People of Ancient Italy"
Geography is very influential factor. Italy, long-narrow peninsula in center of Med. Sea.

<u>Physical Aspect</u>:
Italy divided into 2 sections — peninsula — Med. land imp. in ancient times, other — north of Po R. impt. medieval and modern times. Plains in Italy very hilly — stone villages on hillsides so more room for farming.
<u>Climate</u>: Winter — westerly winds with rainstorms. Spring — Sahara blast — drought in summer. Rome: two months without rain. Po Valley — water from Alps.

Source: Adapted from Edward W. Fox, *Syllabus for History* (Ithaca, N.Y.: Cornell University Press, 1959). Reprinted by permission of the author.

lateral material in the same way that you master your one and only textbook. However, there are reasons for assigning the extra work. Here are some of them:

1. To *amplify* topics treated in your textbook or taken up in classroom lectures.
2. To go into greater *detail,* for example, by assigning original documents or sources as readings.
3. To expose students to another *point of view* or a different *philosophy.*
4. To bring background material into discussions.

How to Cope with the Assignment

The assignment has been made, and you must cope with it. But how? In addition to the collateral reading, you have all your regular assignments to do; consequently, you cannot spend an inordinate amount of time. But still, you must extract something definite from your reading. Here are some suggestions for doing so.

First, try to figure out why the book was assigned. You might ask the instructor. If you find out, then you can skim the book looking for pertinent material, disregarding all the rest.

Second, read the preface. As you already know, the preface provides a great deal of "inside" information. It may tell you how this book is different from your text.

Third, study the table of contents. Notice especially the titles of chapters, to see whether they are like the ones in your textbook or whether some are different. If the chapters with similar titles contain the same information as the chapters in your textbook, then read the chapters not included in your textbook. Do this with topics covered in your classroom lectures, too.

Fourth, if you have not found an "angle" so far, then read the summarizing paragraph at the end of each chapter. Make brief notes on each chapter from the information thus gained. With these notes spread out before you, try hard to see the overall pattern. And from the overall pattern, come up with the author's central thesis, principle, problem, solution, or whatever.

Fifth, don't leave the book with only a vague notion of what it is all about. You must come up with something so definite that you can talk about it the next day, or write about it two weeks hence. Do not waste time on details, but be ready to answer general questions: What was the author's central approach? How was it different from that of your textbook? How was it the same? Look for the central issues around which everything else is organized.

Sixth, have the courage to think big. If you lack courage, you'll waste time on minor details that you won't remember anyway. Select the big issues and concentrate on them.

Taking Notes on Collateral Material

When a highly condensed summary of a book or long selection is required, you need a special approach. The introduction–thesis–body–conclusion sequence is useful in forcing you to clearly understand the material and the way the author develops and supports it. Furthermore, a summary that follows this sequence can be highly condensed; you may be able to capture the main ideas of a collateral book in only a page or two of notes. Figure 10.8 (page 202) is an example.

NOW THAT YOU HAVE NOTES, USE THEM

When you have read and comprehended the assignment and summarized the central points, you are ready to practice the active recall that will convert facts and concepts into knowledge you can retain and use. Read over your notes to be sure (1) they say what you mean and (2) they are

Figure 10.8 Notes in the Form of a Highly Condensed Summary

I. Introduction

Experiment in living close to nature.

Thoreau voluntarily withdrew from a civilization which he felt was getting too complicated. He spent 2 yrs., 2 mos., and 2 days living at Walden Pond to regain the simplicity of life which comes when one lives close to the soil.

II. Thesis

Each man should pause to decide just how he should spend his life. Is he paying too dearly for unessentials?

In a complex civilization, the fast flowing current of unessentials stemming from custom, tradition, advertising, etc., somehow sweeps a man away from the genuine goals in life.

Only by temporarily cutting oneself off from civilization, could man realize that his life need not be so complex. By getting back to nature to rethink the basic issues of life, man could chart his course, and attempt to steer his life in accordance with these standards (not the expediencies set up by the pressures of complex civilization).

III. Body

Thoreau did not wish to hold up progress or civilization; rather, he wished that man would be more contemplative and selective in his actions.

Man should awaken and become aware of real life.

Live simply & you will live more fully.

Thoreau chronicled his experiences at Walden Pond. He wanted to become familiar with nature.
  a. He built his own hut.
  b. Average cost of living a week was 27 cents.
  c. He observed nature: trees, birds, animals, etc.

He believed that every man ought to measure up to the best he could do. What the best is, depends upon the individual. To have a standard to measure up does not mean that all must have the same, but every man should measure up to a standard in the best way he is able to.

IV. Summary

Urged people to reject unessentials, and get back to fundamentals.

Thoreau wanted to demonstrate that many so-called necessities were not necessary at all. He wanted man to observe, appreciate, and evaluate what was important in life. Once man had set his sights upon the good life, he should follow it without compromising.

clear enough to mean the same thing weeks and even months later. Write summarizing notes and recall cues in the left-hand column. Now study one section of your notes at a time: Cover the section with a piece of paper and, from the cues, try to recall the section, reciting aloud or even writing it out. Look again at your notes to see what errors you made or what you forgot. Repeat the process until you can accurately repeat the material in your own words. (This is the same process that I recommended for effective study of lecture notes.)

There is no better way to prepare for an examination than by training yourself to reproduce your notes without looking at them.

SUMMARY

What makes textbook marking work?

Activity. Since marking is both a physical and mental activity, you are consequently awake, alert, thinking, and deciding. If you marked your textbook well, you will have underlined the bare outline that the author used in writing the book.

Why is marking the textbook so important?

Forgetting is bound to take place. Careful marking of a textbook chapter will enable you to review the chapter and regain the information with the minimum expenditure of time and effort.

What principle should guide us in marking a textbook?

Selectivity! You must have real courage to resist underlining what "looks" important, and mark only what *is* important.

How about using symbols and abbreviations?

In marking a book, do make use of a good, familiar set of symbols and abbreviations— those which deliver their meaning *to you* immediately and accurately. Use them with consistency so that they will mean the same thing to you time after time.

What are the advantages of writing separate notes over marking a textbook?

Greater involvement and more activity. You not only select the main points, but also convert them into your own words. And you'll be writing your notes just as you'll be writing answers for an exam.

Why draw diagrams in textbook notes?

To learn. A diagram in a book looks obvious. But when you try to reconstruct it without looking, you will find you've missed a lot of the information that was packed

Why should collateral readings be treated differently?

into it. The only way to remember a diagram is to reproduce it from memory.

Collateral readings are meant to supplement your textbook, so you need to find only those points that are different from what's in your textbook.

To remember my textbook notes, do I have to recite them?

Yes! Cover up the body of your notes, leaving exposed only the jottings or cues in the left-hand margin. Glimpse a cue, then recite the body of information that the cue stands for.

HAVE YOU MISSED SOMETHING?

1. **SENTENCE-COMPLETION.** Complete the following sentences with one of the three words listed below each sentence.

   a. Marking should be done after you read each _____.

      sentence   paragraph   chapter

   b. In notetaking, it's best to underline phrases that are _____.

      long   colorful   meaningful

   c. One sure way to remember a picture is with a _____.

      sketch   paragraph   bookmark

2. **MATCHING.** In each blank space in the left column, write the number preceding the phrase that matches the left item best.

   _____ a. Underlining   1. Can be written during review
   _____ b. Collaterals   2. Prime organizational device for ensuring memorization
   _____ c. Categories   3. Should be done very selectively
   _____ d. Cues   4. Help make textbook marking systematic
   _____ e. Symbols   5. Supplement standard textbook

3. **TRUE-FALSE.** Write *T* beside the *true* statements and *F* beside the *false* statements that follow.

   _____ a. The power of marking comes from physical and mental action.

   _____ b. There is really no such thing as "too much marking."

_____ c. Too much information in the margin makes recitation too easy.

_____ d. Slow readers find that notetaking helps them to speed up.

_____ e. Collateral material should be mastered in the same fashion as your text.

_____ f. Notes should be written in short phrases.

4. **MULTIPLE-CHOICE.** Choose the phrase that completes the following sentence most accurately, and circle the letter that precedes it.

In both marking a textbook and taking textbook notes, you should

a. be accurate, rather than neat.
b. write or mark quickly to save time.
c. use the author's words whenever possible.
d. mark or note everything that looks important.

PART IV

TESTS AND EXAMINATIONS

Dig a well before you are thirsty.
—Chinese Proverb

11
Preparing for Tests

Exams. You may be one of those people whose palms begin to sweat just at the sound of that word. Or perhaps you've got a system for coping with exams, but you'd like to improve it. In either case, you've come to the right place. This chapter helps you with everything but answering the questions. It provides tips on . . .

- Being prepared
- Making summary sheets
- Organizing your time
- Predicting exam questions

and even
- Cramming

along with
- What to do during and after the exam

*H*OW DO YOU TAKE EXAMS? Calmly, knowing that you are well prepared for them. And seriously, making use of the experience and
ideas of experts who have provided research results, hints, and tips on
taking tests and examinations. In this chapter we shall look at what to
do before an exam, during the exam, and even after the exam. We'll concentrate mainly on final exams, but the ideas given also apply to tests
and quizzes. The only difference is the amount of information on which
you will be tested.

The day or two before the final exam have far more value than any
other day or two during the semester. To do well, you must use this time
to organize and consolidate facts and ideas you have gained throughout
the course. If you use up this time on tasks that should have been done
earlier, *you* subtract from the grade that you could have attained. So your
preparation for the exam should actually begin on the first day of classes
and continue through the semester, as you keep the decks cleared for
your pre-exam activities.

BE PREPARED

From the beginning of the course, you should take classroom notes on
every lecture (Chapter 6). From time to time throughout the semester,
spend five or ten minutes reviewing these notes, using the key notes and
phrases that you have written.

You should take notes on each textbook chapter, or mark your text
as your read (Chapter 8). Again, these notes or markings should be reviewed occasionally—at least several times during the semester.

As a result of your notetaking and marking, you will have a set of
well organized notes ready for immediate study. In addition, the periodic
reviews should keep your remembering at, or near, the 80 percent level.
That is, you will retain about 80 percent of what you have read and
learned—instead of the 20 percent that you might remember without
notetaking, recitation, and review. Now your notes and the information
you have retained will form a solid base for your study in the week or so
before the exam.

BEFORE THE EXAM

How should you study for your final exams? Where should you start?
Suppose you are taking five courses, each consisting of about forty classroom lectures and twenty textbook chapters. That's two hundred lectures
and one hundred textbook chapters for which you are responsible. How
do you organize your notes and your time to study all this information?

Organizing Your Notes

The best way I know of to study for an exam is to consolidate your lecture and textbook notes into sets of summary sheets, and then recite them. As you make up the summary sheets, you are accomplishing three things. First, you are reviewing the notes you took throughout the semester, adding to the information you have retained. Second, you are categorizing information under specific headings, which will help you retrieve it from your memory during the exam. Third, you are preparing a condensed set of notes that you can use as a refresher immediately before the exam.

One set of summary sheets should be prepared for your lecture notes and one for your textbook notes, for each course. By categorizing notes into blocks of information, you should be able to reduce each of these sets of notes to about ten pages. The details and background information will be in your mind, rather than on the summary sheets. But the summary sheets will contain all the cues; therefore, they are ready for use with the recitation study technique.

CORNELL SYSTEM SUMMARY SHEETS.   Figure 11.1 is a Cornell System summary sheet that represents more than ten pages of notes taken during two lectures. Notice how the various points are categorized by century on the sheet, and placed side by side for ease of comparison. The key words are brief, as they should be; they hint at, but do not supply, each comparison.

Figure 11.1 Summary Sheet for Classroom Lecture Notes: Cornell System

	Sociology 103 – Dr. Lind	
	19th CENTURY	20th CENTURY
Head of family	1. Patriarchal. Father head of family.	1. Now, individualistic & democratic
Stable - non extended fam. -	2. Family stable.	2. Family less stable.
	3. Many children and relatives under one roof = extended family	3. Smaller in size. Only two generations (parents & children)
non-mobile -	4. Non-mobile. Rarely moved "Old family homestead"	4. Mobility increased & residence changes often
women & work	5. Women: housework and children	5. Women: work outside & care for children after hours
sex -	6. Puritanical on sex matters.	6. Increasingly liberal
family types -	7. Family types in community alike	7. Greater variability in family type
family functions	8. Family had many functions: political, religious, economic	8. Now: function- procreation and socialization

Figure 11.2 shows a Cornell System summary sheet derived from textbook markings. The subcategories, "Advantages" and "Disadvantages," were supplied by the student who took the notes. The material in each of these subcategories was originally scattered throughout the chapter.

To use one of these summary sheets for recitation, place a blank

Figure 11.2 Summary Sheet for Textbook Chapter: Cornell System

Economics 102 – Professor Maxwell

I. Single
   Adv:
   1. freehand
   2. profits-his
   Disadv:
   1. liable
   2. "venture capital"

I. Single proprietorship
   ADVANTAGES
   1. Can do what desires
   2. All profit goes to owner
   DISADVANTAGES
   1. All losses hurt owner (unlimited liability)
   2. Commercial banks ordinarily will not provide "venture capital"

II. Partner –
   Adv:
   1. Common pool
   2. "vertical integration"
   3. "horizontal   "   "
   Disadv:
   1. death & change
   2. liable

II. Partnership
   ADVANTAGES
   1. Pool wealth, profits, losses
   2. "Vertical integration" = gain control of resources, become own wholesaler
   3. "Horizontal integration" = buy out competitors; add products; improve products
   DISADVANTAGES
   1. Each time a member dies or leaves, a new partnership needs to be formed
   2. Unlimited liability, even if own a small share

III. Corporation
   Adv:
   1. legally formed
   2. stock-capital
   3. limited liability
   4. perpetual – board
   Adv. to society:
   1. production-eff.
   2. continuation
   3. creates capital
   4. pays taxes

III. Corporation
   ADVANTAGES
   1. Easy to form (legal permission needed)
   2. Issue stock to raise capital; banker underwrites stock issue and sells to public.
   3. Limited liability – Corp., distinct from its owners, can sue and be sued.
   4. "Perpetual succession," or existence. Board of directors.
   ADVANTAGES TO SOCIETY
   1. Technical efficiency – production of goods & services
   2. Pool business risks – Continuation of production
   3. Creates further capital for expansion or finance new
   4. It is taxed

piece of paper over the right-hand column, look at the key words on the left, and recite. When you have recited the entire sheet, remove the blank paper to check if you covered all the points.

MODIFIED-OUTLINE AND PARAGRAPH FORMS.   Figure 11.3 (page 214) is an example of a summary sheet in which the cue-word column is omitted. The key words themselves *are not omitted,* however. They are used as the headings and subheadings in this modified-outline format.

To use this kind of summary sheet for recitation, place a blank sheet of paper over it. Then draw the blank sheet down to expose the first heading (*A. Speech*), and recite. After reciting, expose the notes under the heading to check your accuracy. Then draw the blank sheet down to expose the next heading, recite, and so on to the bottom of the sheet.

Once you have reached the bottom of the page, take a few minutes to cast your eyes over the page, to see the relationships and continuity among the various categories. This will give you a mental view of the whole.

The type of summary sheet in Figure 11.4 (page 215) can be reviewed in the same way. The only difference between this sheet and that in Figure 11.3 is that this sheet is in paragraph form. The main topics are still easy to identify and use as key words. The format you use should depend on the material and on your personal preference.

Organizing Your Time

Begin by scheduling the time available to you in the week before finals. Make up a form like that in Figure 11.5 (page 216). Then fill in the time blocks that will be taken up by meals, meetings, job (if you have one), and recreation. Next fill in the classes that you must attend. Under no circumstances should you miss any of these. You'll be responsible for the lectures themselves, and you will want to hear the instructor's answers to students' questions about the exam.

Fill in the time you will need to complete term papers and other assignments. Make sure you get them done *before* exam week. You don't want unfinished business to interfere with your study or to distract your thinking during exams.

You should find that some extra time is available toward the end of this week. Use it to study for your exams. Fill in the exact study times and subjects. Instead of simply writing "Study" in the time blocks, write exactly what you will study: "Study economics, chaps 1 to 10" or "Summarize sociology notes." Make a schedule that you'll be able to follow, and then follow it.

Toward the end of the week before finals, make up another schedule—this one for exam week. Fill in the times for your exams, and for

Figure 11.3 Summary Sheet in Modified-Outline Form. The separate column of key words has been omitted because the key words are in the outline.

The Hopi

A. <u>Speech</u>
1. Uto-Aztecan family (Ute, Paiute, Shoshone)

B. <u>Subsistence – Economic Life</u>
1. Skillful farmers — growing maize (mainstay), beans, squash,
2. Main fields not irrigated — small gardens irrigated. Cotton.
3. Domestic animals not important.
  a. turkeys — for feathers.
  b. sheep — for wool.
4. Wild flora — onions, potatoes, tobacco — yucca for soap.
5. Hunting
  a. rabbit

C. <u>Settlement & Houses</u>
1. Proximity of water
2. Desire for security — mesa residence.
3. Clay, sandstone, mud — terraced effect — hole in top
       reached by ladder.
4. Only women own houses.
  a. matrilocal residence — brings together matrilineal kin.
  b. kinship groups are strong.

D. <u>Crafts</u>
1. Basketry (not too good).
2. Loom work — wool has become the principal textile material.
3. Pottery (coiled) painted.

E. <u>Division of Labor</u>
1. Men
  a. most of farming.
  b. spin, weave, tan skins, make clothing for selves & wives.
  c. housebuilding: both sexes work.
2. Women
  a. make pottery.
  b. tend gardens.

F. <u>Trade</u>
1. Other Pueblo
2. Paiute, Apache, Navaho.

G. <u>Society — Lineage & Clan</u>
1. Typical matrilocal residence. — Underlie the clan system.
2. Houses owned by women.   —   "   "   "   "
3. All-important ceremonials associated with maternal lineage.
4. Clans are exogamous.
5. Clans have totemic names, but do not believe descended from
       totem.

H. <u>Family & Clan</u>
1. Boy accompanies father to cornfields; learns from him.

I. <u>Government</u>
1. Chief — head of Flute ceremony.
2. Power vested in hierarchical council of headmen.
3. Town chief must learn long ceremonial chants.

Figure 11.4 Summary Sheet in Paragraph Form

> *Greek Race*
>
> <u>Unity, well-rounded</u>
> The early Greeks were a vigorous people who constantly strove to achieve a well-rounded life — a unity of human knowledge. The Greeks did not have a departmental view. They believed that one man should know all things in one lifetime. The well-rounded Greek, in addition to being well versed in the arts, had to be an athlete, soldier, and statesman.
>
> <u>Competition</u>
> The Greeks loved competition. For example, they got together for athletic games each year. The athletic competitions best known to us were the games held at Mount Olympus and at Delphi.
>
> <u>Human-Image</u>
> A strong religious force permeated their lives. The early Greek religion was an interpretation of nature — polytheism. The Greeks invested the gods with a human image in order to define these forces as tangible beings. These gods had greater power than humans, but they possessed human frailties. There was a close connection between government and religion. Every city was supposed to have been established by some god. For example, Athena was supposed to have founded Athens and the people were descended from her.

your meals and recreation. Remember that you must be in tip-top shape mentally, emotionally, and physically if you are to do your best on the exams. Don't skip meals, recreation, or sleep to get in more study.

By finals week, the bulk of your preparations should be completed, and most of your summaries should be in order. Leave a block of time immediately before each exam to review the summary sheets for that exam. The less time you allow between this last review and the exam, the less forgetting will take place. Review calmly and thoughtfully, and carry this calm, thoughtful behavior pattern right into the exam room.

Helping Yourself

Here are some more things you can do before your final exams, to ensure that you do your best on the exams:

1. Find out as much as you can about each exam. Ask your instructor about the types of questions (objective, essay, or both) that will be on the exam. Find out whether your instructor will allow partial credit, how long the exam will take, and whether textbooks, notes, calculators, or other equipment will be allowed in the exam room. See if you can get copies of last semester's exam, to see what kinds of questions were asked

Figure 11.5 Sample Weekly Schedule Form

	M	Tu	W	Th	F	S	S
7:00							
8:00							
9:00							
10:00							
11:00							
12:00							
1:00							
2:00							
3:00							
4:00							
5:00							
6:00							
7:00							
8:00							
9:00							
10:00							

and the proportions of each, and to make sure you know the meanings of the words that are used in the directions. (For example, *interpret* doesn't mean the same thing as *evaluate* in an essay question.) Use all this information to direct your study effort and to make sure you have the equipment you need to take the exam.

2. As you recite from your summary sheets, pause between key words and ask yourself, "What kind of question would I ask on this material if I were the instructor?" Then write out your questions on a separate sheet of paper. You may end up with twenty or even thirty questions for each course. Use part of your study time for each course to sit down and answer these questions, as if they were the exam. Write out your answers just as you would for the exam itself. Then check your answers to see that they are complete and accurate.

Don't worry about how close your questions might be to the actual questions. They will be close enough. And the more questions you make up and answer, the greater the chance that you'll encounter similar questions on the exam. Since those exam questions will already be familiar to you, you'll answer them surely and swiftly, without any "exam anxiety."

3. Study in the same way for both objective- and essay-type exams. Some students believe objective-type exams are easier, and they tend to study less for them. Others believe they should study details for objective exams, and relationships for essay exams. I have found that you need to master the material just as thoroughly for one type as for the other.

4. Don't study by re-reading the textbook. Re-reading is not efficient or effective as a study method. Use your notes, underlinings, and marginal key words to study through summarization and recitation—they are hard to beat because they get you actively involved in your studying.

5. Think positively. Your attitude will influence how you do on an exam. And a positive attitude begins with your feeling of preparedness. But even if you feel you haven't studied as successfully as you should have, don't think negatively. Remind yourself that you do know a good portion of the material, and that your healthy physical, mental, and emotional state will help you think through the rest.

6. Don't expect to be helped in any way by going to a so-called relaxing movie on the night before an exam. Any such activity can only interfere with remembering. Instead, take a "grand tour" of the summary sheets for tomorrow's exam. That is, spread out the summary sheets and try to see the overall picture; try to get a panoramic view of the course. Then go to bed and get a good night's sleep. Next morning, have a leisurely and nourishing breakfast, take a last tour through your notes, and do well on the exam.

CRAMMING

Should students cram? Yes, if they don't know their material. But cramming, sometimes an unfortunate necessity, must be done according to a system if it is to be of any use.

An Extreme Case of Nonpreparation

Suppose that a student has taken notes on almost every lecture, but has not recited or reviewed her notes since they were taken. Also, she has skimmed through each assigned textbook chapter, has underlined the chapters indiscriminately, but has not taken any separate notes.

With the passage of time and with no reviews of the material, her retention is probably at the 10 percent level. Two days before the examination, she will be starting almost from scratch.

With all five of her courses in this state of nonpreparation, she has an almost impossible task before her. If she foolishly tries to study day and night to learn every idea, fact, and detail for each course, she will learn almost nothing. The mind simply is not built to take in such chunks of undigested material in such a short time.

The Selectivity System

If your only chance to pass a course is to cram, then the one word to remember is *selectivity*. You must avoid falling into the trap of trying to learn too much. It will be extremely difficult to resist picking up important-looking bits of information along the way, but that is what you must do. Concentrate on essential facts, and use as much of your time as possible for *remembering* them.

Each textbook chapter has to be skimmed and searched, and the main ideas and pertinent supporting materials must be ferreted out and written, in your own words, on a separate summary sheet ruled in the Cornell format. The same must be done with your lecture notes.

When all the highlights have thus been noted, push aside the books and notebooks. Leave in front of you only the ten or so sheets of notes you took on the textbook, and the ten sheets of notes taken from your classroom notes.

Now recite, recite, and recite. The notes you have selected will do you no good unless you embed them in your mind so that you can mentally carry them into the examination room. To make these notes your own, glance at the key words in the left margin, and recite the ideas, principles, and supporting details over and over again until you know them cold.

It is true that you have taken a chance by selecting only certain ideas, principles, facts, and supporting materials. My point, however, is that if you try to remember too much, you will end up with almost nothing; you cannot possibly memorize so much in such a short time. By judiciously selecting the very top ideas and memorizing them, you give yourself a good chance of passing the examination. You may not remember much after the exam, but the objective is to survive the battle so that you can come back next semester to continue the war.

Cramming Doesn't Replace Regular Study

Experiments have shown that people do not learn well or react logically in a crisis. These results apply directly to the student who tries to learn under the pressure of cramming. During the crisis of the examination, on questions that require thinking beyond the facts or with different facts, the student will be panic-prone and will answer a question with wrong material, or make false, frantic starts, or just "freeze." It seems that studying under intense pressure stifles flexibility in thinking and acting.

Through organized notetaking, regular recitation, and systematic review, you can be ready to study for your final examinations. Then a few days spent with your summary sheets will organize vast amounts of material in your mind—far more than you could ever learn by cramming. Moreover, you will be rested, confident, and ready for the exams.

DURING THE EXAM

Getting Ready

Arrive at the examination room early, to get a good seat. Sit where the light is good for you; where the proctor will not disturb you as he or she paces up and down; where you can see the blackboard; and where there will be a minimum of distractions.

Do not sit near a friend. Friends are distractions. Any conversation before the exam is likely to interfere with the mental set you have developed for the exam. And, during the exam, you are likely to break concentration if your eyes meet those of your friend. Then, if your friend leaves the room early, you may be tempted to leave early too, so you can discuss the exam. Finally, there is the danger of being accused of cheating because of a friendly but harmless word or smile.

Until the exam itself is passed out, silently rehearse some of the facts, formulas, and ideas that you've studied. This kind of thinking keeps distracting thoughts out. It also warms up your thinking apparatus, so that you will be able to give your full attention to the exam.

If you feel tense before or during the exam, use the doctor's method to get rid of your anxiety. This method, which is discussed in Chapter 2, consists of three steps: (1) breathe in until your lungs feel completely full; (2) take a sudden, quick, extra breath through your open mouth; (3) let your breath out slowly. Repeat the three steps five, six, or seven times, depending on what feels right for you. They are hardly noticeable to others.

Listen carefully for additional instructions, before—and even after—you receive your copy of the exam. The instructions that are written on the examination itself are not always complete, or they may require clarification. If you have already received your copy, you may be tempted to read the exam, giving only half an ear to the spoken instructions. It pays to stop reading and listen, because the proctor's oral instructions may change or even negate some written instructions. You would, for example, be in hot water if you missed the proctor's instruction to "Do only three out of the five essay questions."

If the directions are not clear, and the exam hasn't started yet, immediately ask about them. Don't start any test with such a doubt in your mind. If the exam has already started, and you have a question—especially about procedure—raise your hand high. When the proctor comes to you, whisper your question.

Answering the Questions

Before you answer any questions, *read the directions carefully*. Then skim the entire exam, just enough to become slightly familiar with the types of questions asked and to see how much weight is assigned to each question. Next, quickly decide how much time you should spend on each question. Finally, begin answering the questions, but *do the easy questions first*. You will save time because you'll be able to get to work immediately; you'll feel better about the exam once you put a question or two behind you; and, with your thinking processes limbered and oiled, you'll be in a better position to attack the harder questions.

Check the time occasionally to see that you are keeping up with your question-answering schedule, but don't get worried if you're a bit behind. Use any time you gain to go back and check your answers, and to make sure that your answers are numbered to correspond with the question numbers.

Don't get upset when you run into a question that you can't answer, and don't sit and ponder the question forever. Both these responses are time wasters, and your time should be used for earning exam points. When you come to a tough question, read it again carefully. Then, if you can, quickly outline some kind of logical or reasonable response and carry the response as far as possible, hoping to get some credit for the effort. Then put the question and answer out of your mind, and go on to the next question. If you can't write anything at all, either because your memory is "blocked" or because you just don't know, then go on to the next question immediately. Return to the skipped question later.

Always take the full time allowed for the exam. If you finish early, go back to the questions you've skipped, and try to answer them. When there is no penalty for guessing wrong in a multiple-choice exam, leave no question unanswered. When there is a penalty, use this system. If five possible choices are given and you can eliminate two as being incorrect, then guess. If four choices are given and you can eliminate one, then guess. But if you cannot eliminate any choices, skip the question.

You can also use any extra time to re-read the questions, to make sure you understood the real intent of each one. And you may want to change some of your answers. Research shows that students improved their scores by changing answers on objective tests *after giving the questions more thought*. (In one study, using a true-false test, the changing of *true* to *false* was more often correct than changing *false* to *true*.) So, after calm thought, if you think you should change an answer, do so. But don't change an answer simply because you are nervous about your original response.

Standardized Tests

Standardized tests are preprinted tests, usually prepared by firms that specialize in testing. They are generally answered on machine-readable answer sheets. For example, the SAT or PSAT tests are standardized tests. Definite standard procedures are used to administer, score, and evaluate them, so that the test scores of all students all across the country can be compared without bias.

Here are five tips for taking these tests:

1. To record your answer, make a dark mark in the space provided, with *one firm stroke* of the pencil from top to bottom.
2. Since stray marks on the answer sheet may be picked up by the machine as incorrect answers, erase such marks cleanly.
3. If you change an answer, erase your previous mark thoroughly.
4. Occasionally check to see that you are recording your answers in the spaces that correspond to the proper questions in the test booklet.
5. Keep your test booklet very near the answer sheet to make the marking faster and more accurate.

AFTER THE EXAM

Directly after the exam, while your memories are still fresh, it is a good idea to talk over the exam with several of your friends. The bigger the group the better, for then you'll be getting more information about how the others interpreted the questions and how they answered them. You'll benefit from knowing the techniques and thinking and reasoning processes they used. You'll see where and why you made mistakes, and where you succeeded. In addition, you'll be reviewing the subject matter of each question. Like other, more formal, reviews, this one too will help you remember the important facts and ideas.

Most final-exam papers are not returned to students, but tests and quizzes usually are returned. When you get back a test or exam paper, don't simply note the grade and file it "for future reference." It's yours and you "paid" for it, so use it to learn even more:

1. Go first to the questions you missed. Read and analyze them carefully to find out specifically what was wrong with your answers. Were they incomplete? Did you make careless mistakes? Did you really know the material?

2. Learn from your mistakes by taking the time to outline (or even write) better answers. You might reap an unexpected bonus by doing this, because instructors often repeat, on the next test, a question that many students missed.
3. Learn from your correct answers by analyzing why they were correct. You'll be pleasantly surprised at how much you can learn with this seldom-used technique.
4. Check to see which types of questions you did or did not do well with: definitions, interpretations, discussions, mostly facts, mostly ideas, and so forth. Check also to see where the questions came from: lectures, textbooks, outside readings, or discussions. Use this information to study more effectively for the next test.
5. Determine which of your study and testtaking techniques worked, and which did not work. Modify your study and testtaking strategies accordingly, beginning right now.

If you feel the need to discuss your exam with the instructor, by all means do so. Before your meeting, write out the questions you want to ask; then ask them in a constructive manner. Find out what the instructor was trying to test with the questions, what ideas or facts he or she thought were important. This will help you to "read" future exam questions with greater accuracy. Above all, don't be negative. Don't argue with the instructor, or complain about the wording of the questions. Don't explain that you knew the answer, but the time ran out. Such negative arguments cannot possibly help you.

Finally, the most impressive thing you can do in any course is show steady progress. Few instructors give a term grade based only on cumulative average; the last examination in a course is usually far more important than the first. Suppose student A starts with an 85, dips to 75, rises slightly to 80, and on the final exam staggers through with a 72. Student B fails the first test with a 60, pulls up to 75, then to 80, and is a class leader with a 90 on the final. Student A actually has the higher average. But wouldn't you give the higher semester grade to student B if you were the instructor?

SUMMARY

How can we overcome exam jitters?

Don't treat each exam as a separate crisis. Have a game plan (a study plan) which you can use to prepare for any exam. Then, when an exam is announced, you will immediately be able to direct your time, thoughts, and energy toward following your plan. Because each step is familiar to you, you will face the exam with calmness and readiness.

What's a good game plan?

First, make up a reasonable study schedule for the exam. Make sure it includes everything you need to do, and follow it. Then organize your notes on summary sheets, and use them for recitation. Finally, make use of the other tips included in this chapter.

Why make a schedule for the week before final exams?

Because deliberate, planned study is far more effective than hectic, panic-ridden study. Time is precious, and you must be in control of both your time and yourself. Studying for an exam is too important to leave to chance.

Why is time more valuable close to exams?

Because that's when you stop working with details and concentrate on basic ideas and facts. Unless you use this time wisely, the weeks and months of lectures and textbook study will be mostly wasted.

What's the best way to make the "final countdown" go smoothly?

There are only two cardinal rules. The first is to be consciously aware that from the very first note in your notebook and the very first underlining in your textbook, you are deliberately getting ready for an exam. The second cardinal rule is to finish each day's work on that day, *without exception*. Together they add up to being prepared for your pre-exam study.

What are summary sheets?

Summary sheets are sheets of notes that have been carefully selected and condensed from your lecture notes and textbook notes or markings. Writing out the summary sheets makes you re-read all your notes, which is an excellent review. Then you must decide what to leave out and what to summarize, and that means you have to think about the material. And the result, about ten pages of solid information, is something you can handle in your study for the exam.

What is the biggest argument against cramming?

With too much to learn and with too little time to learn well, you overload your memory with half-memorized material. You can easily forget such material when you are faced with a difficult examination question. Furthermore, partially remembered information can only be repeated; it can't be *used* to answer exam questions.

Should we ever cram?

Of course, if you're unprepared, your only chance of survival is to cram. But if you cram, do it with courage. Use the courage to select only the main ideas or concepts; then recite this handful of main ideas till you master them, for then you'll know at least that much *well* and confidently. If you lose courage and try to take in too many ideas and details, you'll only sabotage your efforts.

How do we avoid anxiety just before and during an exam?

You don't avoid it, you control it. Before the exam you work gainfully according to your schedule, eat reasonable meals, and get your regular eight hours of sleep each night. And remind yourself occasionally that you're getting things done. On exam day, get to the exam room early, and choose a seat that you will be comfortable in—without distractions. Review, in your mind, some of the easiest of your "things to remember," to occupy your mind with work. Then, if you feel you need it, use the doctor's method to get rid of any lingering tension.

In taking an exam, what's the one most important rule to follow?

Don't get stuck! Give each question good, serious thought and analysis. Then, if it doesn't yield to your attack, move on to the next question. Put the tough question out of your mind, knowing you'll get back to it later if there is time.

Why do the easiest question first?

Three reasons: First, because you'll make better use of your time by getting something done immediately. Second, an immediate success will dispel anxiety and promote confidence. Third, it will clear the decks so you can tackle the harder questions.

How about changing answers?

Change an answer only after giving the question some additional thought. Don't change answers impulsively.

Is it okay to guess?

If there is no penalty for guessing, leave no question unanswered. If there's a penalty, guess if you can eliminate two out of five options or if you can eliminate one out of four options.

What's the most important thing to do when exams are returned?

Read, think about, and analyze each question and answer, to see what worked and why, and to see what did not work and why. Then, use your results to plan how you'll *study* for and take the next exam.

HAVE YOU MISSED SOMETHING?

1. **SENTENCE-COMPLETION.** Complete the following sentences with one of the three words listed below each sentence.

   a. Summary sheets should be made up from your _____.

   textbook   notes   exams

   b. Knowing that you've mastered your facts will help you avoid ____.

   questions   studying   panic

2. **MATCHING.** In each blank space in the left column, write the number preceding the phrase in the right column that matches the left item best.

   _____ a. Rationalizing

   _____ b. "Grand tour"

   _____ c. Objective

   _____ d. Cramming

   _____ e. Difficult

   _____ f. Movie

   1. Questions that should be done later
   2. Should only be done systematically (and as a last resort)
   3. Waste of time that gets you nowhere
   4. Questions that require 100 percent precision
   5. Not recommended for the night before the exam
   6. Recommended for the night before the exam

3. **True-False.** Write *T* beside the *true* statements and *F* beside the *false* statements that follow.

_____ a. During exam week, you need not allow time for recreation.

_____ b. Certain summary sheets work better without the cue column.

_____ c. You should master your notes only to prepare for objective exams.

_____ d. On an exam the biggest time waster is getting and staying stuck on a question.

_____ e. It's helpful to choose an exam seat by a friend.

_____ f. Easy exam questions can serve as warm-ups for harder ones.

4. **Multiple-Choice.** Choose the phrase that completes the following sentence most accurately, and circle the letter that precedes it.

In preparing for an exam, it is *not* important to

a. read and summarize your notes carefully.
b. ask your instructor whether the exam will be fair.
c. know the types of questions that will be asked.
d. make up and answer your own exam questions as you study.

To be able to discern what is true is true and what is false is false; this is the mark and character of intelligence.

—EMANUEL SWEDENBORG

12

Answering True-False, Multiple-Choice, and Matching Questions

---

Do you know right from wrong? Can you recognize a correct answer when you see one? This chapter will help you do both—on tests and exams. It tells you . . .

- What to look for in true-false questions
- How to analyze multiple-choice questions
- How to study for and take a matching-question test

and

- When and how to guess

*T*RUE-FALSE QUESTIONS, multiple-choice questions, and matching questions provide a very efficient way to test a student's knowledge of facts. With these types of questions, a fifty-minute test can cover a great deal of ground. Such questions are easy to grade, and the results depend only on knowledge. That is, the student's writing ability doesn't get in the way of his or her answers.

The three types of questions are similar in one respect. That is, all the answers are given; you have to either choose the correct answers or sort the answers out:

True-false: You are presented with a statement, and must choose from the two possible answers *true* (meaning "the statement is true") and *false* (meaning "the statement is false").

Multiple-choice: You are usually given a partial statement along with four or five possible endings. You must choose the correct (or most correct) ending.

Matching: You are given two columns of words or phrases. You must match the items in one column with those in the other column, according to some stated relationship.

In spite of this similarity, different techniques are used to analyze and answer these three different types of questions.

TRUE-FALSE QUESTIONS

In its simplest form, a true-false question is a statement that attributes a property or quality to one or more persons or things. Here are three true-false questions that are presented in this most basic form:

T   F   Birds can fly.
T   F   Students are creative.
T   F   Snakes are poisonous.

In the first statement, the ability to fly is attributed to (or connected with) birds. In the second, the quality of creativeness is connected with students. And, in the third, the property of being poisonous is attributed to snakes. On an exam you would circle *T* in all three cases, because all three statements are true. That is, there are birds that can fly; there are students who are creative; and there are snakes that are poisonous. You should have no trouble with such simple, straightforward statements.

The problem is that very few (if any) true-false statements are written so simply. Most contain qualifiers, negatives, or strings of qualities that make them more difficult to handle.

Watch Out for Qualifiers

Here's what happens when we add *qualifiers* to our basic true-false questions:

T   F   *All* birds can fly.
T   F   *Some* students are creative.
T   F   *Most* snakes are poisonous.

In each case, one small word—the qualifier—makes a big difference in the basic statement.

The first statement, "All birds can fly," is false, because such birds as the ostrich and the penguin cannot fly. The qualifier *all* overstates the connection between birds and flying. The second statement is true because *some* students are indeed creative. The qualifier *some* does not overstate or understate the situation. The third statement, "Most snakes are poisonous," is false; of the 3,000 different kinds of land snakes, only about 250 are poisonous. Here again the qualifier leads to overstatement.

Qualifiers may be grouped into sets, and the six most-used sets are:

All—most—some—none (no)
Always—usually—sometimes—never
Great—much—little—no
More—equal—less
Good—bad
Is—is not

Within each set, the qualifiers may overstate a true-false statement, understate it, or make it just right. Memorize the six sets, and they will help you answer many true-false questions.

Whenever one qualifier from a set is used in a true-false statement, substitute each of the others for it, in turn. In this way, determine which of the qualifiers in the set fits best (makes the statement just right). If that is the given qualifier, the answer is *true*; otherwise, the answer is *false*.

For example, suppose you are given the question

T   F   All birds can fly.

Substituting the other qualifiers in the "all" set gives you the four statements

All birds can fly.
Most birds can fly.
Some birds can fly.
No birds can fly.

The statement beginning with the word *most* is just right, but that is not the statement you were given. Therefore, the answer is *false.*

There are some qualifiers that I call "100 percent words." They imply that the statements they appear in are true 100 percent of the time. These words are:

No	Every	Only
Never	Always	Entirely
None	All	Invariably
		Best

Such qualifiers are almost always connected with a false statement, because there are very few things in this world that are 100 percent one way or the other. Here are two examples:

All chickens make clucking sounds.
No true chicken can swim.

Always watch out for these qualifying words, but don't automatically consider a statement wrong simply because it contains one of them. To keep you honest and alert, some instructors will occasionally use them in true statements:

All stars are surrounded by space.
All human beings need food to survive.
No human being can live without air.

So, while you watch out for these 100 percent qualifiers, remember that instructors know you are wise to them. Most instructors will try to keep them out of exams.

Qualifying words that fall between the extremes are generally used in true statements. Here are some in-between qualifiers:

Seldom	Most	Usually
Sometimes	Many	Generally
Often	Few	Ordinarily
Frequently	Some	

Here are two items in which these words are used:

T   F   *Many* birds fly south for the winter.
T   F   A balanced diet *usually* leads to better health.

To test your ability to recognize and work with qualifiers, do the exercise in Figure 12.1.

Check Each Part of the Statement

If any part of a true-false statement is false, then the whole statement is false. Be suspicious of a statement that contains a string of items, but

Figure 12.1 An Exercise in Key Words (Qualifiers)

The following quiz (from Clifford T. Morgan, *Introduction to Psychology*, McGraw-Hill, New York, 1961, p. 2), specifically designed both for students who have had a course in psychology and for those who have not, illustrates the importance of key words in objective questions. Take the quiz, picking out the key words and writing them in the space provided. In most cases, there is only one key word, but in a few instances, there are two or three. Also indicate in the right-hand column whether you think the statement is true or false. When you are finished, look below for the correct answers.

1. Geniuses are usually queerer than people of average intelligence. _____ ___

2. Only human beings, not animals, have the capacity to think. _____ ___

3. Much of human behavior is instinctive. _____ ___

4. Slow learners remember what they learn better than fast learners. _____ ___

5. Intelligent people form most of their opinions by logical reasoning. _____ ___

6. A psychologist is a person who is trained to psycho-analyze people. _____ ___

7. You can size up a person very well in an interview. _____ ___

8. When one is working for several hours, it is better to take a few long rests than several short ones. _____ ___

9. The study of mathematics exercises the mind so that a person can think more logically in other subjects. _____ ___

10. Grades in college have little to do with success in business careers. _____ ___

11. Alcohol, taken in small amounts, is a stimulant. _____ ___

12. There is a clear distinction between the normal person and one who is mentally ill. _____ ___

13. Prejudices are mainly due to lack of information. _____ ___

14. Competition among people is characteristic of most human societies. _____ ___

15. The feature of a job that is most important to employees is the pay they get for their work. _____ ___

16. It is possible to classify people very well into introverts and extroverts. _____ ___

17. Punishment is usually the best way of eliminating undesirable behavior in children. _____ ___

18. By watching closely a person's expression, you can tell quite well the emotion he is experiencing. _____ ___

19. The higher one sets his goals in life, the more he is sure to accomplish and the happier he will be. _____ ___

20. If a person is honest with you, he usually can tell you what his motives are. _____ ___

ANSWERS FOR EXERCISE IN KEY WORDS

The key words for each question were as follows: (1) usually, (2) only, not, (3) much, (4) better, (5) most, (6) psychoanalyze, (7) very well, (8) better, (9) in other subjects, (10) little, (11) stimulant, (12) clear, (13) mainly, (14) most, (15) most important, (16) very well, (17) usually, best, (18) quite well, (19) sure, happier, (20) usually. All the statements are false. The reasons for their being false can be found in the book from which they were taken or, very likely, in any general course in psychology.

Source: Quiz reproduced by permission of McGraw-Hill Co., New York.

don't conclude that it is false only because it contains the string. Here are two examples of statements with strings:

> A long-term sales chart shows the dollar sales and sales trend by weeks, months, and years.

> A warm-climate product, cocoa is grown in the Gold Coast of Africa, Nigeria, Brazil, Colombia, Venezuela, and in southern Norway.

The first statement is true because a long-term sales chart does show both dollar sales and the sales trend, which is indicated by the up-and-down movement of the graph. In addition, the time scale on the chart is marked in weeks and months as well as years.

The first nineteen words of the second statement are true. The last two words, "southern Norway," are false because cocoa grows only in warm climates—and all of Norway, both northern and southern, is freezing cold in winter. This one false item makes the entire statement false.

Some tricky (and usually false) statements are made up of two "substatements," both of which may be true; the two substatements are connected by a conjunction such as *therefore, thus, because, consequently,* or *so,* or a phrase such as *as a result.*

What generally makes the statement false is that the second substatement doesn't logically follow from the first. In other words, the two parts are not directly related, although the statement is presented as if they are. For example, consider the statement:

> Thomas Edison invented the ticker-tape machine for recording stock prices and, *as a result*, he became famous.

It is true that Edison invented the ticker-tape machine and that he became famous in his lifetime. However, his fame was not due directly to his ticker-tape machine, but to other inventions, including the electric light bulb, the phonograph, and the storage battery. For this reason, the statement is false.

Beware of the Negative

True-false statements that contain negative words and prefixes are difficult to sort out and answer: The negatives can upset or complicate your thinking. Negative words include *not* and *cannot,* and the negative prefixes are *dis-, un-, in-, im-, il-, ir-, non-,* and *dis-,* as in *inconsequential* or *illogical.*

Notice, in the following three statements, how the addition of negatives increases the difficulty of understanding what the statements mean—let alone deciding whether they are true or false.

Thomas Edison's fame was due to his many practical inventions.
It is illogical to assume that Thomas Edison's fame was due to his many practical inventions.
It is illogical to assume that Thomas Edison's fame was not due to his many practical inventions.

When you are confronted with such a statement, begin by circling the negative words and negative prefixes. Then try to get the meaning of the statement without the negatives. Finally, re-read the sentence to find out if it is true or false in its entirety. Here, the first statement is true, the second is false, and the third is true.

Think True—and Guess When You Must

Most true-false tests contain more true statements than false statements, simply because they are made up by teachers. Since teachers would rather leave true information in your mind, they tend to stack the test with true statements. Of course, some teachers will fool you, but after the first test you'll know for sure.

On a true-false test, it is a good idea to guess at answers that you don't know, even if credit is subtracted for wrong answers. According to the laws of probability, you should get 50 percent right when you guess, even if you know nothing about the subject matter. If you can make intelligent guesses—knowing that there are more true than false statements—you should be able to do much better than that.

MULTIPLE-CHOICE QUESTIONS

Most multiple-choice questions[1] are of the incomplete-statement type: A partial statement (called the *stem*) leads grammatically into four or five sentence endings, or options, listed directly under it. One of the options is the correct answer. The other (incorrect) options are called *distractors* or *decoys*.

Here is an example of a well-constructed multiple-choice question:

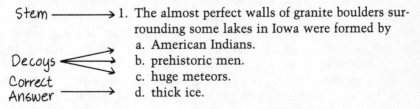

Stem ————→ 1. The almost perfect walls of granite boulders surrounding some lakes in Iowa were formed by
    a. American Indians.
Decoys ⇔   b. prehistoric men.
Correct   c. huge meteors.
Answer ————→   d. thick ice.

[1]Some of the ideas in this section were inspired by James F. Shepherd, *The Houghton Mifflin Study Skills Handbook* (Boston: Houghton Mifflin, 1982), pp. 230–270.

This incomplete-statement-type question exhibits good construction in the following ways:

1. All options are grammatically consistent.
2. The stem is long, and the options are short.
3. Extraneous material is excluded from the stem.
4. The stem contains one central problem.
5. Double negatives are not used.
6. All options are plausible.
7. The correct option is no longer or shorter than the others.
8. Only one option is the correct or best answer.[2]

When the use of the incomplete-statement form would lead to an awkward stem or options, the more usual question form is used. The options are again listed below the question.

Answering Multiple-Choice Questions

Before you even look at a question on a multiple-choice test, you must *read the directions carefully*. Some say, "Mark the one best answer," whereas others may require that you "Mark all correct answers." You will lose credit if you mark more than one answer in the first case, or if you miss a correct option in the second case. If the directions are not clear, then *ask*.

Begin each question by reading the stem all the way through. Then read the options all the way through. Don't be in a rush to mark the first option that sounds good. In some questions, *all* the options may be correct, and you have to choose the best one; you won't find it unless you read them all.

You should read all the options even when the question seems unfamiliar. One of them might provide you with a hint as to what the question is about. Furthermore, there's information in the options themselves—information that might help you remember what you need to know.

After you read the stem and the options, spend no more than a brief few seconds puzzling over the question. If it resists answering, cross out any options you have eliminated, mark the question so you will be able to find it easily later, and move on to the next question. But don't leave any question so fast that you do not give it the calm consideration it deserves. If you merely go through the *motions*, you're wasting time. The idea is to convert the easier questions into quick point-getters and leave enough time to go back to the questions you skipped.

[2]William D. Hedges, "How to Construct a Good Multiple-Choice Test," *The Clearing House*, September 1964, pp. 9–11.

When you have worked your way through the test, go back to the questions that you marked for reconsideration. This time, however, concentrate on eliminating options. The more distractors you can eliminate, the better your chance of finding the correct answer.

If you can somehow eliminate all the distractors, then you will, of course, have isolated the correct answer. If you can eliminate only one or two of the options, then you should guess at the correct answer. In the long run you will come out ahead by doing so, even if, say, 25 percent credit is subtracted for each incorrect answer.

Here are some additional hints that may be of help to you in eliminating distractors and choosing the correct answer.

Try to Apply the True-False Technique

To use the true-false technique, you make a complete statement from the stem plus each option, in turn. An option that results in a false statement is eliminated as a distractor. One that results in a true statement is probably the correct answer.

As an example, consider this multiple-choice question:

> 2. Because of its lack of lumber, Syria has many "beehive" homes built of
>   a. metal.
>   b. concrete.
>   c. marble.
>   d. mud brick.

To judge the correctness of the first option, you would complete the stem as follows: Because of its lack of lumber, Syria has many "beehive" homes built of metal. Since Syria is a hot, dry, and rather poor country, you would probably decide that this statement is false. Metal (and concrete and marble as well) are too expensive, and not readily available to the vast majority of people. The last option, *mud brick,* undoubtedly produced locally, would be inexpensive and available and would hold up in a country where the rainfall is so meager. (The correct answer is *d.*)

When you use this technique, don't be too quick to eliminate options; do so only after sufficient consideration. And, if you have eliminated three options but don't like the remaining option, you must go back and reconsider them all.

Stick to the Subject Matter of the Course

When a multiple-choice question includes options that you don't recognize or that seem out of place, don't get panicked into choosing one of them. The chances are great that these misplaced options are distractors. Here's an example:

3. Which of the following does not have satellites (moons)?
   a. Venus
   b. Cassiopeia
   c. Mars
   d. Perseus

You might reason as follows: "We've been studying planets and their rotation around the sun. I've heard of Cassiopeia, but we haven't studied it. I never even heard of Perseus. I bet both are decoys—I'll cross them off. We did study Venus and Mars. They are planets, but I don't remember which one has satellites and which one doesn't. Well, at least I've boiled things down to a fifty-fifty chance. I'll mark this question and come back to it later."

Later, when you have returned to the question, you might remember that Mars has a ring of satellites or moons around it. That would eliminate Mars, leaving Venus. You still might not remember whether or not Venus has satellites, but since that's the only option left, you would choose it. (*Venus* is the correct answer.)

Watch out for Negatives and Extreme Words

We discussed these words in relation to true-false questions, and our discussion applies here as well. Whenever you find negative words such as *not* or *except* in the stem or the options, circle them so they'll stand out. Then make sure you take them into consideration when you choose your answer. Here's an example:

4. Which materials are (not) used in making saddles?
   a. Linen, canvas, serge
   b. Wood and leather
   c. Rubber and cork
   d. Iron and steel

(The correct answer is *d*. The materials in *a*, *b*, and *c* are all used in saddles.)

Always circle such 100 percent words as *never, no, none, best, worst, always, all,* and *every*. And be very suspicious of the options in which you find them. In fact, if you have to guess, first eliminate all the options that contain absolute words. Then choose your answer from the remaining options.

As an example, see if you can answer this question:

5. The author suggests that the desert
   a. climate is unpredictable.
   b. heat is always unbearable.
   c. is totally devoid of rain.
   d. earthquakes pose a constant danger.

You should have circled the *always* in *b*, *totally* in *c*, and *constant* in *d*, to obtain *a* as the correct answer. You didn't even have to know what the question is about.

Foolish Options Are Usually Incorrect

I've never been able to understand why test writers occasionally include a silly—and sometimes insulting—statement as an option. Most likely, they become tired and simply dash off foolish statements to fill space. You should almost always view such statements as distractors worthy of being immediately crossed out. Here's an example:

6. The most important reason why the travel agents tested the Camel Caravan was to
   a. judge the safety aspects of the trip.
   b. better foreign relations with the Arabs.
   c. get a free vacation.
   d. test the appeal of the Caravan for tourists.

The foolish option, of course, is *c*. The correct option is *d*. Notice that options *a* and *b* make true statements, but the word *most* in the stem calls for option *d*.

The Option "All of the Above"
Is Usually Correct

This option is frequently used by test writers when all the reasonable candidates for options will make the statement true. From personal experience, I can tell you that it greatly simplifies the writing of such a question. Here's an example:

7. Until the first half of the second millennium B.C., an army laying siege to a city made use of
   a. scaling ladders.
   b. seige towers.
   c. archery fire.
   d. all of the above

(The correct option is *d*).

One way to confirm the choice of "all of the above" is to find two correct answers in the options. For example, suppose you were sure that ladders and towers were used, but you weren't sure about archery fire. Then, if only one answer were permitted, that answer would have to be *d*, because *d* is the only option that includes *a* and *b*.

Numbers in the Middle Range
Are Usually Correct

When all the options in a multiple-choice question are numbers, the answer is easy if you have memorized the correct number. Otherwise, you'll probably have to do some guessing. If you have no other information to go on, your chances of guessing correctly are increased if you eliminate the highest and lowest numbers. For some reason, test writers usually include at least one number lower than the correct answer and at least one number higher than the correct answer.

This "rule" allows us to eliminate half the options in the following example:

8. The "Great Pyramid" originally stood how many feet high?
   a. 281
   b. 381
   c. 481
   d. 981

We would eliminate 281 as the lowest number and 981 as the highest, leaving two middle-range numbers 381 and 481. At this point we have a fifty-fifty chance of choosing correctly. Can we do better?

We could compare the two remaining options to something we know—say, a football field. Then, 381 feet is slightly greater than a football field, perhaps not so high for a pyramid. But 481 feet is over 1½ times as high as a football field is long. That would really make a "Great Pyramid." (If we stuck with 481 feet, we would be correct.)

Check for Look-Alike Options

Test makers occasionally include, in one question, two options that are alike except for one word. Such a pair seems to indicate where the test maker's interest was focused, so it is logical to assume that one of the pair is the correct answer. The other options should, of course, be read carefully; they should be eliminated in favor of the look-alikes only in a guessing situation. For example, consider this question:

9. The author considers himself an authority on
   a. touring the Middle East.
   b. Middle East rug dealers.
   c. Middle East rug bargains.
   d. behavior patterns of tourists.

If I had no inkling of the correct answer, I would eliminate *a* and *d* and choose from the similar pair *b* and *c*. (The correct option is *b*.)

The test writer can keep you from using this technique, simply by inserting *two* pairs of similar options. Then you would have to deal with four options as always:

10. The author considers himself an authority on
    a. behavior patterns of merchants.
    b. Middle East rug dealers.
    c. Middle East rug bargains.
    d. behavior patterns of tourists.

Check for Longer or More Inclusive Options

In multiple-choice questions, the correct option is often longer or more inclusive of qualities or ideas than the decoys. The length or inclusiveness results when the test writer must qualify or amplify a simple statement. So, be alert for a tightly packed or overly long option, as in this question:

11. The author says that rug buying in the Middle East is like courtship in that
    a. both parties fool each other.
    b. both parties must trust each other.
    c. both parties desire the same thing but begin with expressions of disinterest.
    d. in rug-buying, as in courtship, one dresses in one's best.

(Here, option *c* is correct.)

MATCHING QUESTIONS

Matching questions provide a most efficient way to test knowledge in courses such as history (in which events, dates, names, and places are important) and psychology (for which numerous experiments, experimenters, results, and special terms and definitions have to be remembered). In a matching question, two vertical lists of items are placed next to each other. Each list contains a half dozen or more words or phrases, in random order. The task is to match the items in one list with those in the other list, according to a relation that is given in the directions for answering the question.

Figure 12.2 contains a matching question that will test your knowledge of inventors and their inventions. You may want to try it now, before you read the next section.

How To Answer a Matching Question

The following sequence of steps will help you work through any matching questions systematically and efficiently.

1. Read the directions. Then run your eyes and mind down both columns, just to get a brief overview of the specific items you will be working with.
2. Read the top item in the left-hand column. Then look carefully and thoughtfully down the right-hand column until you find a match for it. Don't stop at the first likely match; instead, continue through to the end of the right-hand column, to make sure there is not a more

Figure 12.2 Matching: Inventors and Inventions

Match the inventions in the right-hand column with the inventors in the left-hand column by writing the proper letter in the space provided alongside each inventor's name. Use each item in the right-hand column only once.

Inventor	Invention
_____ 1. Eli Whitney	a. Automobile assembly line
_____ 2. James Watt	b. Telephone
_____ 3. Robert Fulton	c. Vulcanizing of rubber
_____ 4. Cyrus McCormick	d. Six-shooter revolver
_____ 5. Elias Howe	e. Steel plow
_____ 6. Henry Ford	f. Steamboat
_____ 7. James Hargreaves	g. Motion pictures
_____ 8. Richard Arkwright	h. Cotton gin
_____ 9. Samuel Colt	i. Dynamite
_____10. Charles Goodyear	j. Steam engine
_____11. Alfred Nobel	k. Telegraph
_____12. Thomas Edison	l. Sewing machine
_____13. Guglielmo Marconi	m. Spinning frame (textiles)
_____14. John Deere	n. Radio
_____15. Samuel Morse	o. Spinning jenny
_____16. Alexander Bell	p. Grain-reaping machine
	q. Locomotive (train)

Answers: (1) *h*, (2) *j*, (3) *f*, (4) *p*, (5) *l*, (6) *a*, (7) *o*, (8) *m*, (9) *d*, (10) *c*, (11) *i*, (12) *g*, (13) *n*, (14) *e*, (15) *k*, (16) *b*.

perfect match. (If the right-hand column has the longer entries, you can save reading time by looking for the matches in the left-hand column.)

3. When you are *certain* that you've found a match, fill in the proper letter or number. (If you match the wrong items you'll not only lose credit on that match, but you will run into more trouble later.) If you're not sure, skip the item and come back to it later.

4. This is the secret: Continue down the left column, filling in all the matches *that you're sure of.* This will drastically and immediately reduce the number of items that are left when you have to make the more difficult matches. And the fewer the items, the better your chances of being correct.

5. As you use each item in the right column, circle its letter or number to show that it has been used. (You may also want to add the number or letter of the item with which it has been matched. This "keying" of your matches will help you check your answers later.)

Don't do any guessing until you are almost absolutely sure you're completely stumped. Here's why: If you make an incorrect match too soon, you'll remove a "live" item from later consideration; then a second match, which would have made use of that item, will also be wrong. So first do your very best; then, using common sense and hunches, go ahead and guess at the remaining matches.

In case you're not an expert on inventions, Figure 12.3 contains a

Figure 12.3 Matching: Personalities

Match the activities in the right-hand column with the names in the left-hand column by writing the proper letter in the space provided alongside each name. Use each item in the right-hand column only once.

Names		*Activity*
_____ 1.	Jesse Owens	a. Tennis
_____ 2.	Brooks Robinson	b. Swimming
_____ 3.	Bronko Nagurski	c. Hockey
_____ 4.	Kareem Abdul-Jabbar	d. Aviation
_____ 5.	Bobby Hull	e. Basketball
_____ 6.	Althea Gibson	f. Movies
_____ 7.	Gertrude Ederle	g. Football
_____ 8.	Amelia Earhart	h. Opera
_____ 9.	Joan Crawford	i. Baseball
_____10.	Beverly Sills	j. Boxing
_____11.	Joe Louis	k. Track
		l. Soccer

Answers: (1) *k,* (2) *i,* (3) *g,* (4) *e,* (5) *c,* (6) *a,* (7) *b,* (8) *d,* (9) *f,* (10) *h,* (11) *j.*

matching question that features famous personalities of the past and present. If you didn't use the matching-question sequence for Figure 12.2, try it here.

How to Study for Matching Questions

If you know that your instructor includes a long matching question in almost every exam, here's the best way to prepare for it. As you read and mark your textbook, be alert for facts and ideas that are associated with people's names. On a separate sheet, list the names and facts opposite each other, so that you end up with two distinct vertical columns, as in the following example:

Names	Facts or ideas	(Subject)
Susan B. Anthony	Woman's movement	(Sociology)
Jack London	*Call of the Wild*	(Literature)
George W. Carver	Agricultural chemist	(Science)
Lewis & Clark	American explorers	(History)
George A. Miller	Magical number seven	(Psychology)
William James	Pragmatism	(Philosophy)
Mozart	*Marriage of Figaro*	(Music)

To master your list, cover the fact column with a sheet of paper. Look at each item in the name column, and recite and write the corresponding fact or idea. Then, to make sure that you learn the material both ways, block out the name column and use the facts as your cues. As you can see, my example includes items from various subject areas. The same steps can be taken in any single subject area.

SUMMARY

What makes some true-false questions so hard to answer?

The difficulty often occurs when the test maker uses such qualifying words as *all, most, some,* and *none.* You must not only know the main fact, but also whether the qualifying word overstates or understates the fact, making the statement false. Be especially watchful for words that allow no exceptions—that is, such words as *never, all, always, none,* and *every.* These words can change an otherwise true statement into a false one.

What if half the statement is true and half is false?

Then the statement is false. Always judge the entire statement. Be especially careful when a statement contains a long list of items.

What else should we watch out for?

Watch out for negative and extreme words within the statement. To make sure you take them into consideration, begin your analysis of the question by drawing a circle around every negative word and prefix.

Should we guess on true-false tests?

Yes. You have a fifty-fifty chance anyway, and knowing something about the subject matter should give you the winning edge.

How should we answer multiple-choice questions?

Begin by reading the directions carefully. Then read each question carefully—both stem and options. Eliminate options (distractors) where you can. Try to use the options as clues, and try the true-false technique—it works.

Should we answer each question before moving on?

No. Don't waste time on a question that you can't answer in a reasonable amount of time. Instead, cross out options you have eliminated, mark the question so you can come back to it later, and go on to the next question.

What should we do when we return to a multiple-choice question?

Concentrate more on eliminating distractors. Make full use of probability techniques by looking for foolish options, "all of the above," and look-alike and long options. Guess when you are able to eliminate at least one option in a four-option question, or two in a five-option question.

What's the best way to work a matching question?

Carefully! First read the instructions and all the listed items. Then mark only the matches you are sure of, one by one. Next, go back to those items that you have skipped, and try to match them. Guess only when you're completely stumped.

Why is it we can study for matching questions, but not for the others?

You can study for all types of questions; that's what this book is about. But you can do some special studying for matching questions by making a list of likely matches and then learning your list.

HAVE YOU MISSED SOMETHING?

1. **SENTENCE-COMPLETION.** Complete the following sentences with one of the three words listed below each sentence.

   a. Negative and absolute words should be _____.

   avoided   circled   defined

   b. In matching questions, the fewer the remaining choices, the better

   your chances of being _____.

   incorrect   correct   alert

2. **MATCHING.** In each blank space in the left column, write the number preceding the phrase in the right column that matches the left item best.

   _____ a. Stem

   _____ b. Qualifier

   _____ c. Guessing

   _____ d. Distractor

   _____ e. Overstatement

   _____ f. Understatement

   1. Incorrect multiple-choice option
   2. Risk of the word *none*
   3. Correct option makes it a true statement
   4. Risk of the word *all*
   5. A word like *usually* or *some*
   6. A "last resort" for matching questions

3. **TRUE-FALSE.** Write *T* beside the *true* statements and *F* beside the *false* statements that follow.

   _____ a. Qualifiers make true-false statements easy to answer.

   _____ b. More complicated true-false statements are usually false.

   _____ c. Guessing is advised when you don't know the answer to a multiple-choice question.

   _____ d. In a well-constructed multiple-choice question, the correct option is always the shortest.

   _____ e. In a matching question, answers you've used should be circled or marked in some fashion.

   _____ f. In a matching question, you should immediately guess at matches you are unsure about.

4. **MULTIPLE-CHOICE.** Choose the phrase that completes the following sentence most accurately, and circle the letter that precedes it.

In a multiple-choice question, an option is usually correct if it is

a. longer and more inclusive than the other options.
b. one of two look-alike options.
c. the only nonabsolute option.
d. all of the above.

Brevity is the soul of wit.
—SHAKESPEARE

13

Answering Sentence-Completion and Short-Answer Questions

Shakespeare knew what he was talking about: It takes a certain knack to answer questions briefly but accurately. In this chapter you'll find out . . .

- How to analyze and answer completion questions
- How to write short answers

and, again,

- How and when to guess on a test

*T*HE TYPES OF QUESTIONS discussed in Chapter 12 require only that you *recognize* the answer (or recognize that a statement is true or false). The answer is already on the test paper, waiting for you to pick it out. To answer the questions that are discussed in this chapter, you must first find the correct information in your memory, and then write it concisely:

> *Sentence completion:* You are given a statement containing one or more blanks. You must fill the blanks with words or phrases that make the statement correct.
>
> *Short answer:* You are given a key word or phrase and must define, describe, or explain it in a few sentences.

Some students worry that having to supply the answers makes these types of questions more difficult. But the truth is that only guessing is more difficult on completion and short-answer tests; you have to know the information to do well on *any kind of test.*

SENTENCE-COMPLETION QUESTIONS

You really have to supply very little information to answer a sentence-completion question—one or two words, or perhaps a phrase. On the other hand, the test writer has to pack enough information into the incomplete statement so that you will know exactly what is wanted. All this information should be full of clues that will draw the correct answer up out of your memory. And sometimes even the physical makeup of the question can help you find the correct answer.

Finding the Clues and Filling the Blanks

ONE-BLANK STATEMENTS.   Most sentence-completion statements contain only a single blank, so you need to supply only one word. The easiest to complete are those in which the missing word comes at the very end of a sentence; then you have the uninterrupted context of the sentence to help you find the answer.

Here's a long one-blank statement:

> In China there are about 80 million people named Chang; in France, the most common last name is Martin; in Germany, it's Schultz; in Spain it's Garcia; in Russia it's Ivanov; and in the United States
>
> there are 2,400,000 _____.

This statement provides a number of clues. There should be no doubt in your mind that what's wanted is the most common name in the United States, which is, of course, Smith. (Here, *Smiths* is the required answer.)

Two-blank statements.   Two blanks with only a space between them indicate that a two-word answer is required. Often the two words are the first and last names of a person, as in the following example.

The first person to suggest the use of daylight saving time was

_____   _____.

Notice that both lines denoting implied words are of the same length. A careful test writer will make sure that all missing-word lines are of the same length, regardless of the actual lengths of the missing words. This is done to ensure that the lines don't serve as clues to the answers. (Here, the answer is *Benjamin Franklin*.)

When two blanks in a sentence-completion question are widely separated, you must treat them as if they occurred in separate sentences. There may or may not be a direct relationship between the missing words, so make sure that each filled-in word makes sense in its own part of the statement. Here is an example:

Corn is the second most widely grown crop on earth today, after

_____, and in the United States corn is the largest crop;

however, no one in Europe knew about corn until _____ returned from the New World.

In the first portion of the sentence, the word *corn* tells you you're dealing with a grain. If you had read your textbook carefully (or if you hadn't, but used your common sense), you'd know the answer is *wheat*. The second blank demands a person's name; in this case, it is *Columbus*.

A long blank.   A long blank indicates that a long answer is desired—a phrase, a clause, or even the equivalent of a sentence. Here is an example:

Wedding rings have been worn on the third finger of the left hand since the days of ancient Greece, because the Greeks believed

_____.

To fill in this long blank, you would have had to read your assignments, because guessing wouldn't be practical or rewarding. However, you won't often find long blanks in completion questions, for two reasons: (1) they are difficult to grade because correct answers can vary so much; and (2) instructors don't want to get into arguments with students who claim that their answers are just as plausible as the so-called correct answer. (The answer is: *that a vein in this finger runs directly to the heart*.)

Grammatical clues.   Occasionally, a word in the incomplete statement will give you a clue to the missing word. For example, note the form of the verb that follows the blank in this question:

About 75 million meteors enter our atmosphere each day, but usually no more than _____ ever reaches the ground.

Because "reaches" is a singular form, the answer must be *one*.

Sometimes, though less and less frequently these days, a completion question will provide you with the *a*-or-*an* clue. This can help you reduce the number of possible answers. Here's an example:

In addition to being one of this country's greatest statesmen, Benjamin Franklin also made lasting contributions to modern life as an

_____.

After you finish reading this question, you should begin to run through Franklin's various interests. He was a diplomat, a philosopher, a printer, an author, an autobiographer, and an inventor. Right away you can see that the first three possibilities won't work. The word *an* in the question requires an answer that begins with a vowel. That leaves author, autobiographer, and inventor. Now you have to do a little thinking, based on the more important clue, "lasting contributions." As an author, Franklin wrote *Poor Richard's Almanack*, whose proverbs are still quoted occasionally. ("A penny saved is a penny earned" is probably the most famous of these.) His autobiography is no longer very popular. What about inventions? Among other things, Franklin discovered electricity, invented the lightning rod, and developed bifocals. Modern life would be quite different without these items, so *inventor* seems to be the best choice. (The correct answer is, indeed, *inventor*.)

The Question-Asking Strategy

Whenever you are genuinely unsure as to what specifically is wanted in a sentence-completion question, don't be afraid to ask. Before you raise your hand, however, have your question formulated in such a way that you can get the desired answer and, with it, the clue you need. As an example, here's a relatively simple completion question.

Today, most of the olives we eat come from _____

or _____.

Though the sentence is well constructed, it is nevertheless unclear. The problem is that you know that olives are grown in Spain, Italy, Portugal, Morocco, Libya, Algeria, and all along the northern African coast, but you wonder whether you should write in the two continents of Europe and Africa, or the names of the two major olive-producing countries.

At this crucial point you should *not* call the instructor over and say, "I don't understand what you want!" If you do, you won't get much help. The instructor will simply tell you to do the best you can. Instead you should say something like, "I have answers for this one, but I'm not sure whether you want me to list the continents or specific countries." In this case the instructor would tell you to list specific countries. Then you would fill in the blanks with the two largest exporters of olives. (The correct answers are *Spain* and *Italy*.)

When Should You Guess?

You should begin every test by moving quickly through it once, to answer the questions you are reasonably sure of. Take the time to read each question carefully, and mark those you skip so you will be able to find them later. Then go through the test a second time, give each unanswered question some thought, and write as reasonable an answer as you can. You have nothing to lose, because there is usually no penalty for guessing on a sentence-completion question. A blank space is worth zero; but a good guess, based on common sense, can earn you some points.

Here's an example:

By using a system of rivers, bays, and canals called the _____

_____, it is possible to travel by ship from New England to Florida, without once entering the usually rough open seas.

This sentence is long enough and descriptive enough to help you come up with a good guess, in the event you don't know the official name for the system. You might call it the "Inland Waterway." That's not the exact name, but it is very close; I'm sure you'd get almost full credit for it. (The answer is *Intracoastal Waterway*.)

SHORT-ANSWER QUESTIONS

Figure 13.1 shows part of a typical short-answer test. Note that, as is usual, only a limited space is provided for each answer. To save time and space, and to make sure you don't have to do any massive erasing, *think* before you write. Give direct answers, concentrate on presenting information, and write in telegraphic sentences (unless the instructor specifically asks for complete sentences). Even when you do write full sentences, make them simple; concentrate more on packing information into your answers than on graceful literary style.

As usual, you should work through a short-answer test twice—once to answer the questions you are sure of, and the second time to work on those you skipped. When you go back to a question, *think* about it, and then write down any fragments of information that you may recall. Try to put the fragments in some logical order, to show that you know what you are doing. Make a stab at questions you are not sure about, but do so

Figure 13.1 Short-Answer Questions with Answers

NAME, AND BRIEFLY DISCUSS OR DESCRIBE, THE FOLLOWING ANIMALS.	
Fastest animal:	The cheetah. For short distances, can top 70 miles per hour.
Fastest bird:	The swift, which can top 106 miles per hour; the fastest of all living creatures.
Non-flying birds:	The ostrich of Africa, the penguin of the Antarctic, the emu and the cassowary of Australia, the rhea of South America, and the kiwi of New Zealand.
Most poisonous snake:	The Australian tiger snake is the most poisonous snake in the world. There's enough venom in its glands to kill 300 sheep.
Most common domesticated animal:	The chicken, formerly a jungle fowl from Asia, domesticated about 1500 B.C. Now, about four billion chickens on earth. About 400 million in U.S. and about 560 million in Russia.

quickly; guesses usually don't earn many points on these almost-essay-type questions.

The best way to study for short-answer tests (and other types as well) is to make and recite summary sheets as we discussed in Chapter 11.

SUMMARY

What's the trick in answering sentence-completion questions?

There are very few tricks or gimmicks that will help you. Your best bet is to know your facts and ideas cold!

What's the best clue to use in answering these questions?

The best clue is *context*—the incomplete sentence itself. So read the sentence thoughtfully, trying to get as much meaning out of it as possible. Even individual words can spark the recall of the correct answer.

How about guessing on completion questions?

When you are sure there is no penalty for guessing, fill in reasonable and serious answers to questions that stump you. But never give a "cute" or "wise" answer. It will almost always affect the test marker negatively.

What's the prime advantage of short-answer questions?

They enable the instructor to cover more ground on an exam, in less time than it would take to answer one essay question. So a short-answer test more fairly represents the course material.

What's the secret to writing short answers?

Think before you write; then write telegraphic sentences, packed with as much information as possible. If you're going to guess, do so quickly and then move on to the next question.

HAVE YOU MISSED SOMETHING?

1. **SENTENCE-COMPLETION.** Complete the following sentences with one of the three words listed below each sentence.

   a. In a completion question, the most important clues come from the

   _____.

   context   lines   instructor

   b. Unless the instructor specifies otherwise, your short answers should be _____.

   literary   telegraphic   humorous

2. **MATCHING.** In each blank space in the left column, write the number preceding the phrase in the right column that matches the left item best.

   _____ a. Information

   _____ b. Space

   _____ c. Question

   _____ d. Zero

   _____ e. Guessing

   _____ f. Recitation

   1. Limited in a short-answer test
   2. Study method for all kinds of tests
   3. Normally awarded to a blank that is left blank
   4. More important than style in short answers
   5. Used intelligently, it can clarify a confusing answer
   6. Of limited value in a short-answer test

3. **TRUE-FALSE.** Write *T* beside the *true* statements and *F* beside the *false* statements that follow.

_____ a. Two-blank statements often require a person's first and last name.

_____ b. You can depend on line lengths for clues in completion questions.

_____ c. Blanks that are widely separated are best treated as if they appear in separate incomplete statements.

_____ d. There's an element of the essay question in a short-answer question.

_____ e. If you do guess on a short-answer question, you should spend plenty of time on it.

_____ f. In a short-answer test you should strive for direct answers.

4. **MULTIPLE-CHOICE.** Choose the word that completes the following sentence most accurately, and circle the letter that precedes it.

Unlike a multiple-choice question, a short-answer question involves

a. recognition.
b. recall.
c. revision.
d. reflection.

It is possible for a handful of questions to break the bank of our answers.

—Antonio Machado

14

Answering Essay Questions

"In your own words." That's perhaps the scariest aspect of the essay question. There are no blanks to fill in or answers to choose from. Everything must come from you and what you've learned. This chapter discusses . . .

- How essay exams are graded
- The mechanics of answering an essay question
- The content of an essay answer

and

- How to interpret key words in essay questions

*T*O ANSWER AN ESSAY QUESTION, you must write (from one or two paragraphs to several pages) about a given topic. You are required not only to *recall* ideas and facts, but also to *organize* them into thoughtful, forceful sentences and paragraphs.

HOW ESSAY EXAMS ARE GRADED

I was once invited by Prof. Fox to observe how his staff prepared to grade over two hundred examination papers in History 103–104, a popular introductory course. The exam had been given the day before. Each staff member had time to scan, but not to grade, the answer booklets. At their meeting, each grader read aloud what he thought was the one best answer for each question. A model answer for each question was then agreed upon by the staff. The essential points in the model answers were noted by all the graders, for use as common criteria in grading the responses.

During the reading of the answers, one grader remarked, "Yes, this student mentioned points five and six . . . but I think he didn't realize what he was doing. He just happened to use the right words as he was explaining point four."

I distinctly remember that I gasped and thought, "Brother, if I ever take another essay examination and if I have five points to make, I'll number them, bold and dark—1, 2, and so on. And I'll organize my points, and use transitional words to show how I got from one to the next. No one is going to think I just stumbled onto any of my points."

But graders don't simply count facts, ideas, and dates. Most essay questions require *reasoning*, and graders look for it in students' answers. In one survey, 114 college teachers were asked what they look for most when grading answers to essay questions. Here's how they responded:

Specific Quality	Number of Responses
Reasoning ability	103
Factual accuracy	84
Relevance to question	73
Good organization	71
Complete answers	71
Clarity	64

Note that four of these point-getters are related to *how* students answer, and only two are related to *what* they answer. Of course, you must know your facts cold, because you can't reason and organize well or be clear and relevant if you don't know what you're writing about. But you must also present your facts in such a way that your answer exhibits the other important qualities. The remainder of this chapter tells you how to do so.

PLAN BEFORE YOU ANSWER

There are a number of things that you can do to help yourself once the essay exam has begun, but before you have started to answer the questions. These actions will get you ready for the questions, get you into the first question, and even help you go through them efficiently.

1. *Make notes on the back of the exam sheet.* Even before you read the exam questions, unburden your mind by quickly jotting on the back of the exam sheet the ideas, facts, and details that you have memorized but think you might forget. This is almost like putting down a summary of your summary sheets. Furthermore, it is a positive action that will involve you in the exam immediately. Do not, however, spend more than a minute or so making these notations.

2. *Read the examination directions carefully.* Notice especially whether you must answer all the questions, and whether there are any time limits. Frequently, you may be given a choice of questions.

3. *Read all the questions.* Before you write anything, read all the questions. If you have a choice among questions, select those for which you are best prepared. As you read the instructions for each question, underline or circle the *key words*, which tell you the form in which the answer is wanted. Then check the key words before you begin to answer the question. (A list of key words and their meanings is given in Figure 14.1.)

4. *Jot cues alongside each question.* While reading each question, quickly note a few words or phrases that immediately come to your mind. Later, when you begin writing, use these jottings and those on the back of the exam sheet to organize your answer.

5. *Plan your time.* It takes less time to follow these suggestions than to read them—especially in relation to the time you will gain through efficient handling of answers. Find out how much time is left after following these steps; then decide how much time to give to each question, and *stick to your plan.*

6. *Start with the easiest question.* Nothing inspires confidence and clear thinking more than getting off to a flying start with one question well answered. Don't sit and stare at the first exam question! Seize on an easy one, number the answer correctly, and start writing.

Figure 14.1 Key Words in Essay Questions. This alphabetical list contains key words encountered in the directions for essay questions, along with brief explanations.

KEY WORD	EXPLANATION
Apply a principle	Show how a principle works, through an example.
Comment	Discuss briefly.
Compare	Emphasize similarities, but also present differences.
Contrast	Give differences only.
Criticize	Give your judgment of good points and limitations, with evidence.
Define	Give meanings, but no details.
Demonstrate	Show or prove an opinion, evaluation, or judgment.
Describe	State the particulars in detail.
Diagram	Show a drawing with labels.
Differentiate	Show how two things are different.
Discuss	Give reasons pro and con, with details.
Distinguish	Show main differences between two things.
Enumerate	List the points.
Evaluate	Discuss advantages and disadvantages, with your opinion.
Explain	Give reasons for happenings or situations.
Give cause and effect	Describe the steps that lead to an event or situation.
Give an example	Give a concrete example from your book or experience.
Identify	List and describe.
Illustrate	Give an example.
Interpret	State the meaning in simpler terms, using your judgment.
Justify	Prove or give reasons.
List	List without details.
Outline	Make a short summary with headings and subheadings.
Prove	Give evidence and reasons.
Purpose	How something fulfills an overall design.
Relate	Show how things interconnect.
Relationship	Connection between events, the linkage.
Review	Show main points or events in summary form.
Show	List your evidence in order of time, importance, logic.
Solve	Come up with a solution based on given facts or your knowledge.
State	List main points briefly without details.
Summarize	Organize and bring together the main points only.
Support	Back up a statement with facts and proof.
Trace	Give main points from beginning to end of an event.

HOW TO ANSWER
AN ESSAY QUESTION

Hugo Hartig suggests the following ten rules for answering essay questions.[1] The rules are not meant to tell you *what* to write, but rather *how* to compose and word your answers.

1. *Understand the question with precision.* It is important to read the question very carefully, so that you are clear about the *exact* idea that the professor is trying to get at. A good essay question is never vague or ambiguous, and if there is anything unclear about the question, do not hesitate to ask for a clarification from the instructor. You are going to be graded very largely on the *clearness* and *precision* of your answer, so obviously the question must also be clearly and precisely understood.

2. *Strive for a complete answer.* State your ideas explicitly. Do not leave anything to be inferred or concluded by the reader. Also define your terms as you go, to show that you know the full meaning of all the words that you are using. Explain all significant statements, to show that you know why they are significant. Show the complete process of your thinking. If your instructor has to "read between the lines" in order to get your point, he will mark you down. Make sure that every sentence actually has a definite point and definite purpose.

3. *Use facts and logic, not vague impressions or feelings.* Your personal likes or dislikes, emotions, attitudes or "feelings" are of no interest to anyone except yourself. Also, they are private: no instructor has the right to demand that you reveal your feelings in any way. Students sometimes believe that the purpose of a course is to teach them to "like" the subject, but this is absolutely not the case. Even in a course such as "Music Appreciation" the purpose is not to teach students to *like* music, but rather merely to *understand* it. In an essay exam, then, it is important to remember that liking or disliking is irrelevant; understanding is all important. The reason for this is the simple fact that teachers are not preachers, and, therefore, they are not in the business of persuading you to like anything or to believe in anything.

4. *Avoid unsupported opinions.* An opinion that is not supported by some kind of logical or factual evidence is not worth anything at all, even if it is absolutely correct. For example, if you make the statement: "*Huckleberry Finn* is a masterpiece of American literature," and do not give any good reason to show that the statement is true, you get a zero on the statement. It is important to make significant statements, but it is equally important to show that they are either true, or untrue, on the basis of some convincing evidence or argument.

5. *Be concise.* The most impressive answer is invariably the one

---

[1]This section is quoted, with permission, from Hugo Hartig, *The Idea of Composition* (Oshkosh, Wisc.: Academia, 1974), pp. 29–32.

that manages to get at the exact "heart of the matter" in the most direct and straightforward manner. It is important to make complete answers, and to explain and support everything you say; but it is even more important to say exactly the right thing, and not hide this gem of thought in a rambling discussion. If you must write out your ideas, to get them organized in your mind, do so on a sheet of scratch paper, and then write out your concise answer when you really have discovered the single most significant idea.

6. *Write carefully so as to avoid errors.* Teachers almost without exception are very prone to make snap judgments about your general intelligence on the basis of your writing style. If you misspell common words, and make clumsy errors in sentence structure, or even if you write paragraphs that lack unity and coherence, many of your instructors are going to take it as a sure sign that you are sadly lacking in basic academic ability. Once a teacher thinks this about you, you will not get much credit for your ideas, even if they are brilliant. English teachers tend to be especially prejudiced in this regard.

7. *Be natural and sincere.* Avoid the use of high-sounding jargon, super-elegant language, phony fancy style or so-called "fine writing." This does not impress anybody in regard to either your literary ability or your intelligence. On the contrary, many teachers will be insulted by it, because they will believe that you are trying to give them a "snow job." Any teacher who has read hundreds or thousands of papers becomes very sensitive to phoniness in student writing, because he sees so much of it.

8. *Organize your answer intelligently.* Focus on either one central idea, or on several main points. In either case, follow the principle of "one idea—one paragraph." Write *deductive* paragraphs, in which you first state your important idea clearly and precisely, with adequate explanation. Then follow this statement immediately with factual or logical evidence that will support it adequately and convincingly. Sometimes it is helpful to underline your key statements in order to show that you are thinking systematically; but do not overdo it, or it will be less effective. In some cases, it may be helpful to use a brief introductory paragraph that states clearly in your own words exactly what the problem is that you are going to try to solve. A concluding paragraph that answers the "So What" question, may also be effective.

9. *Keep it simple.* Do not get involved in deep philosophical profundities. Especially avoid vague and fuzzy speculations that cannot be squared with ordinary common sense. Quite difficult and subtle ideas can be expressed in straightforward and simple language. If you can do this, your writing will be most impressive.

10. *Understand the instructor's pet ideas.* In general, every instructor uses only a few basic approaches to his subject, and he probably keeps repeating these over and over again in his discussion of various aspects. An alert student can easily identify these "pet ideas" and work them out carefully in his own words. The student who does this is prepared not only to see through the instructor's questions quite readily, but

he also knows exactly how to answer them, using the teacher's own methods of problem solving! Perhaps this is the very essence of grade getting in any course that depends heavily on essay exams.

THE CONTENT OF AN ESSAY ANSWER

Your answer must demonstrate first, that you understand the question with precision; second, that you know the necessary facts and supporting materials; and third, that you can apply reasoning to these materials. Your only way to demonstrate that you "know your stuff" is through an organized answer. The following suggestions should help you "get organized."

1. *Do not write an introduction.* Don't start your essay with an introductory paragraph, nor even with a high-sounding sentence such as, "This is, indeed, a crucial question which demands a swift solution; therefore. . . ."

Such a general approach forces you to scatter your ideas, whereas the instructor is looking for a sharp focus. He or she wants to know *how you answer the question.* It follows, too, that without a sharp focus, you will do serious damage to the *unity* of your answer. The result could be an answer that contains all the necessary details, but so mixed up that they will not convince the instructor that you know what you are talking about.

2. *Answer the question directly and forcefully in the first sentence.* Then develop your essay from this single sentence. The key to the technique of a direct answer is in a partial repeat of the question itself; that is, by using the question as the stem of your answer, you cannot help but write a direct answer.

You can see how this principle works in the example in Figure 14.2. The question asks for the student's opinion; therefore, it is quite correct to start the sentence with "I believe." Notice that the first line in the answer includes some of the exact words that are used in the question. Such an approach keeps you honest; there can be no partial or off-focus answers. You have committed yourself to a direct answer.

Figure 14.2 A Direct Answer

Question: What do you think is the purpose of studying sociology?

Answer: I believe that the purpose of studying sociology is to make us aware and conscious that the people of the world are not one conglomerated mass; rather, that people fall into various groups, societies, and economic systems.

3. *Expand on the first sentence.* Now all you need to do is put down your ideas, facts, and details to support your first sentence. Notice how easy and natural this approach is. When everything you write pertains to the first sentence, you cannot help but achieve unity; that is, everything is not only pertinent, but it also hangs together.

In Figure 14.3, the question is directly answered in the first sentence. The answer revolves around the "characteristic shapes" of dunes. All the other sentences in this short essay are on the right track as they amplify the main point: the shape. Note too that this question has two parts; one part asks for a yes-no answer, and the other asks the student to "describe." Simple diagrams would have been appropriate to help describe the different shapes of the dunes.

The essay in Figure 14.3 is a one-paragraph essay. For an extended essay (fifteen to thirty minutes), it is even more important that your direct answer come first, but now in the form of a full paragraph rather than a sentence. Then each of your subsequent paragraphs should expand on one of the sentences in the first paragraph. Again, the organization of the essay will develop easily and naturally.

In the opening sentence of Figure 14.4 (page 262), the student places his answer in context. Then he immediately states his thesis sentence: "To help my students improve their reading skills. . . ." He next outlines the points he plans to cover and connects them with the rest of his answer by using the transitional sentence, "I shall discuss each of these methods briefly." Notice how the student makes his points stand out by lettering them, and note his use of examples. These examples are supporting material; they definitely convey to the instructor the student's full grasp of the area under discussion.

4. *Use transitions.* Transitions are often called "directional words"; they point to the turn in the road that the reader should take. When transitions lead the instructor from one idea to the next, he or she finds the

Figure 14.3 A Paragraph-Length Essay

Question: Are dunes recognizable after they have been covered with vegetation? Describe.

Answer: Yes, dunes can be recognized in the field after they have been covered by vegetation because dunes have characteristic shapes which cannot be entirely obscured or obliterated by vegetation. Dunes have a definite crest or summit, usually having a long windward slope and a much steeper leeward slope. They would be easier to recognize if they were barchans (crescent-shaped dunes). By studying the shape of the dunes it is often possible to determine the direction of the prevailing winds over a region; thus a person can ascertain the present direction of the prevailing winds to see whether the windward slope and the winds coincide. Shape therefore indicates much more than whether a desert feature is or is not a dune.

Figure 14.4 A Longer Essay Answer

Question: Name and briefly describe several specific methods that a classroom teacher may employ to aid students in improving their reading skills. Consider this question in the context of the subject area in which you plan to teach.

Answer: I plan to teach high school English. To help my students improve their reading skills, I would teach them word analysis, how to read between the lines and interpret what they are reading, how to read with a purpose—and for different purposes—and how to better understand the structure of what they are reading. I shall discuss each of these methods briefly:

(A) Reading ability is greatly improved when the student has a grasp of most of the words with which he is dealing. To increase my students' working vocabulary I would teach them how to analyze words in context. We would learn prefixes, suffixes, and roots and would learn how to analyze these and put them together. Word analysis would also involve figuring out words from their contexts. By practicing these skills, the students should be better able to handle new words in their future reading.

(B) Interpretative reading or reading between the lines is another means of improving reading. To help students interpret what they read, I would have them read practice passages—especially of poetry—and have them answer such questions as "What was the author's attitude toward Silas Marner, as reflected in her description of him?" or "What did the poet think of the girl about whom he wrote, 'Your face is like a rose.'?"

(C) Reading with a purpose is basic to comprehension in any field. To get students used to reading with a purpose I would ask specific questions about the material, specifically about setting, character, etc. To get them used to reading for various purposes, I'd introduce various material—magazines, novels, poems, etc.

(D) I would try to improve students' reading skills by teaching them the structure of writings—the kinds of paragraphs, location of topic sentences, etc. Practice in writing would be beneficial.

To sum up, I would help my students improve their reading skills through word analysis, interpretive reading, reading with purpose, and analysis of the structure of writing.

---

paper clear, logical, and refreshing. A number of transitional words are listed in Figure 14.5; try to use them when you have the chance.

5. *Don't save the best for last.* Avoid the mistake of saving your best idea for a big finish. If it is not included in your direct answer in the first few lines, your point may never become clear to the instructor. Also, your point may never be worked into the organizational pattern of your answer; then this precious concept you were saving for last might end up unused.

6. *End with a summarizing sentence or two.* The final sentence or two in your answer should summarize (as in Figure 14.3) or repeat (as in Figure 14.4) the points made in your opening sentence or paragraph. Notice the transitional phrase "to sum up" in the last sentence of Figure 14.4; it clearly labels that sentence as a concluding statement.

Figure 14.5 Transitional Words and Expressions

The experienced writer knows that transitional words provide directional clues for the reader, that they show the relationship between sentences in a paragraph. For example, the word *furthermore* says, "Wait! I have still more to say on the subject." So the reader holds the previously read sentences in mind while reading the next few sentences. The following list suggests other words and expressions that you might find valuable.

Intention or Relationship	Transitional Words and Expressions
Amplification	For example, in other words, that is
Cause and effect	Accordingly, because, consequently, for this reason, hence, since, thus, therefore, if . . . then
Concession	Accepting the data, granted that, of course
Contrast or change	In another sense, but, conversely, despite, however, nevertheless, on the contrary, on the other hand, still, though, yet
No change	Similarly, moreover, also, too, in addition, likewise, next in importance
Emphasis	Add to this, besides, in addition to this, even more, to repeat, above all, indeed, more important
Equal value	At the same time, likewise, similarly
Increasing quantity	Also, besides, furthermore, in addition, moreover, too
Order	First, finally, last, next, second, then
Summary	For these reasons, in brief, in conclusion, to sum up
Time	Then, since then, after this, thereafter, at last, at length, from now on, afterwards, before, formerly, later, meanwhile, now, presently, previously, subsequently, ultimately

SOME IMPORTANT ODDS AND ENDS

1. *Be neat.* A neat and legible paper or answer booklet does influence the grade. In a carefully controlled experiment, a group of teachers was instructed to grade a stack of examination papers on the basis of content and to disregard poor handwriting. Placed randomly within the stacks were word-for-word duplicate papers: one paper in good handwriting and the other in poor handwriting. In spite of their instructions, on the average the teachers gave the neater papers the higher grades—by a full letter grade.

2. *Use ink.* Pencil is not appropriate for a written exam.

3. *Write on only one side of each sheet.* When both sides are used, the writing usually shows through, giving the paper a messy look. In addition, in an exam booklet, if you need to change or add something, you

can write it on the blank page and draw a neat arrow to the spot where you want it inserted on the facing page.

4. *Leave a generous margin, especially on the left side.* You will have a neater paper and provide space for the instructor's comments.

5. *Leave space between answers.* This will allow you to add an idea or fact that may occur to you later. Such an idea may be blended into the answer by using an appropriate transitional phrase, such as, "An additional idea which pertains to this question is. . . ."

6. *Watch the time.* If you think you may run out of time, just outline your remaining points to show the instructor that you did, in fact, have the necessary material in mind. You will gain points. And, if you have time left over, use it to go back over your answers to correct points of grammar or to insert clarifying words or phrases.

SUMMARY

What's the most important step in writing an essay answer?

Without a doubt, starting your first sentence with a full or partial repeat of the question is the most important step you can take to keep your answer on target. Furthermore, it forces a natural organizational pattern upon your writing. In other words, your opening sentence is a topic sentence, and all you do after that is expand it by explaining it, giving examples, and supporting it in general. Then, don't forget that last strong concluding sentence which tells the grader that you're in control right to the finish line.

How can I show the grader I'm thinking?

First, of course, you must put down your facts accurately. In addition, you must show that you can reason on the basis of those facts by organizing your essay well, keeping your comments relevant to the question, and writing clearly and neatly (without an abundance of erasures and cross-outs). When you reason beyond the facts, make sure you identify the reasoning or opinions as your own.

How can we be sure we've read the essay question correctly?

There are two steps to take: First, make sure you underline key words such as *list*, *evaluate*, and *compare* in the instructions. Then fix in your mind exactly how you will comply with these specific directions. Second, quietly ask the instructor about anything you do not understand for certain, including whether you have interpreted the question correctly. If you are fuzzy about the question, your answer is almost guaranteed to be equally fuzzy.

HAVE YOU MISSED SOMETHING?

1. **SENTENCE-COMPLETION.** Complete the following sentences with one of the three words listed below each sentence.

   a. In essay questions you are graded on your _____.

   reasoning   handwriting   evaluation

   b. Your answer to an essay question must demonstrate that you understand the _____.

   facts   question   directions

2. **MATCHING.** In each blank space in the left column, write the number preceding the phrase in the right column that matches the left item best.

_____ a. Neatness	1. Explain in simpler terms
_____ b. Key words	2. Requires opinion plus evidence
	3. Has been known to affect essay grades
_____ c. Evaluate	4. Calls for arguments plus details
_____ d. Transition	5. Says "Come along to this next sentence"
	6. Should be underlined or circled in essay
_____ e. Interpret	instructions
_____ f. Discuss	

3. **TRUE-FALSE.** Write *T* beside the *true* statements and *F* beside the *false* statements that follow.

   _____ a. Vague impressions or feelings are helpful in an essay answer.

   _____ b. Comparisons can include differences as well as similarities.

   _____ c. It helps to be aware of the instructor's "pet" ideas.

   _____ d. Graders sometimes use "model" answers to essay questions.

   _____ e. It's best to tackle the toughest question first in an essay exam.

4. MULTIPLE-CHOICE. Choose the phrase that completes the following sentence most accurately, and circle the letter that precedes it.

In taking an essay exam, you should

   a. begin writing as soon as the exam begins.
   b. avoid unsupported opinions.
   c. write quickly and correct your errors later.
   d. add philosophical asides to spice up your answers.

How should you go about preparing for, taking and learning after the exam.

PART V
YOUR VOCABULARY

*The difference between the right word and the
almost right word is the difference between
lightning and the lightning bug.*

—MARK TWAIN

15

Assessing Your Vocabulary

Do you have a lightning vocabulary or a lightning-bug vocabulary? Do
you know the precise meaning of every word you use? This chapter tells
you why you need a precise vocabulary, both as a student and after you
graduate. It shows how your vocabulary affects . . .

- Your speaking, reading, and learning
- Your thinking

and includes

- Two tests to help you assess your vocabulary

N UMEROUS RESEARCH STUDIES, in both the academic and business worlds, show a close relationship between a good vocabulary and success. Here are two examples:

A survey in an eastern engineering college showed that the students who improved most in vocabulary during their freshman year averaged three or four places nearer the top of their class in academic standing during the sophomore year; those who did not improve at all in vocabulary averaged 7.5 places nearer the bottom.[1]

The Human Engineering Laboratory, a company that specializes in testing business executives, found a very significant correlation between high vocabulary scores and success at the top executive level.

These and similar findings demonstrate that a good vocabulary is a valuable asset both in college and after college. But what exactly is a good vocabulary? First and foremost, it is a precise vocabulary, in which the exact meaning of each word is known with certainty. The size of a person's vocabulary is also important—the larger it is, the better it can be. But precision comes first.

THE IMPORTANCE OF A GOOD VOCABULARY

Words are the tools with which we communicate. We speak, read, and hear words, so we learn through words. We even think with words. A poor vocabulary tends to place a limit on our ability to understand; with a good vocabulary, however, the sky's the limit.

In Speaking

It is easy enough to talk about the weather; but it is not so easy to talk about ideas and concepts. How many times have you heard someone say, "I know what I mean, but I just can't express it." This is an open confession of an inadequate vocabulary. Plato said that to transmit ideas, a speaker must paint pictures in the minds of listeners through the use of precise words.

A person who can explain a job process clearly to a machinist is more valuable to his or her company than someone who cannot. At higher levels in business, the person who can present ideas clearly at a staff conference will almost naturally emerge as a leader. In college, a good oral re-

[1]Cited in *Word Study*, Copyright © 1958 by G. & C. Merriam Co., publishers of the Merriam-Webster Dictionaries.

port or a clear, precise contribution to a class discussion has far more impact than vague generalities. And the knowledge that you have something to say and are saying it well can do wonders for your ego.

In Reading

Reading generally requires greater use of a person's vocabulary than any other act of communication. So in reading it is especially easy to misinterpret meanings because of an imprecise vocabulary. Take the word *fulsome*, for example. Do you know what it means? Would you stop reading to consult a dictionary if you came across this sentence: "The mayor spent considerable time giving *fulsome praise* to the chairman of the finance committee."?

Such words as *fulsome* are extremely deceptive, because the parts are familiar. Many people would leap to the conclusion that *fulsome* is only an elaborate way of saying *full*; consequently, *fulsome praise* would be misinterpreted as "full of praise." The dictionary meaning of *fulsome*, however, is this:

> **ful•some** (fŏŏl′ səm) *adj.* **1.** Offensively excessive or insincere. **2.** Offensive to the senses; loathsome; disgusting.[2]

Such errors can lead to the complete misinterpretation of an author's presentation. And that, in turn, can result in a memory full of fuzzy thoughts, instead of crystal clear concepts.

In Learning

Without an adequate vocabulary, no one can master important principles and ideas. The fundamental building blocks of learning and knowledge are words—words with precise meanings. Get the meanings wrong, and you have learned false information. If you have no idea of the meanings, then you will have to work harder to learn. Moreover, an inadequate vocabulary can limit your ability to conceptualize; that is, though you may hear and recognize individual words, you will have difficulty grasping the sequence of concepts being developed by a speaker or an author.

In Thinking

J. B. Watson, a noted psychologist, said that thinking is silent speech. This means that you think with actual words, and not with some mys-

[2]*The American Heritage Dictionary of the English Language,* (Boston: Houghton Mifflin Company, 1973), p. 532.

terious, fluffy "thinking stuff." Your thinking is usually accompanied by slight movements of the speech muscles and organs. The words may not be audible, and your lips may not move; nonetheless, this subvocal monologue sends words racing through your mind. Obviously, then, if your vocabulary is limited or imprecise, your thinking will be limited or imprecise as well.

The next section contains two vocabulary tests that I've included to allow you to assess your own vocabulary. You can also use them to demonstrate to yourself that thinking is done with words. Try to keep track of your thinking as you go about answering the first five or six questions in each test. You should notice that you are using a constant stream of speech—words rather than concepts or images. You may also find that audible speech is more effective than silent speech.

TWO VOCABULARY TESTS

The tests in this section will give you a chance to test your vocabulary in private. These tests are much more difficult than the traditional ones, in which you are given a test word and are required to choose a second that most nearly matches it in meaning. Here, you must choose the word or phrase that is most nearly *opposite* in meaning to the test word. Thus, you will be working with antonyms. And you'll have to hold the meaning of the test word in your mind while searching the options for its opposite.

In the quiet of your room, and without the pressure and exposure of a classroom, observe how you handle each test question. Notice whether the test word is familiar, vaguely familiar, or totally unfamiliar. If it is familiar, can you pick out its opposite with confidence? Do you know the meanings of some of the words in a vague, general sense, but not specifically? Are you able to pronounce each word accurately and with confidence?

Determine what your weaknesses are, and then do something about them by starting a systematic vocabulary-building program. Remember, vocabulary is not a fixed trait like the color of your eyes or hair. A vocabulary is something that you can design and build in accordance with your personal specifications. The first step is to get a dictionary, keep it at your elbow, and use it whenever you hear or read a word that you really aren't sure of.

We'll discuss vocabulary building in much more detail in the next two chapters. For now, take the tests in Figures 15.1 and 15.2. The correct answers are given in Tables 15.1 and 15.2 (see Appendix B in this text), along with the percentages of students who answered each question correctly. As you can see, most of us need to work on our vocabulary.

Figure 15.1 PSAT Vocabulary Test

For each question in this section, choose the best answer and blacken the corresponding oval on the answer sheet.

Each question below consists of a word in boldface, followed by five lettered words or phrases. Choose the word or phrase that is most nearly <u>opposite</u> in meaning to the word in boldface. Since some of the questions require you to distinguish fine shades of meaning, consider all the choices before deciding which is best.

Example:

good: (A) sour   (B) bad   (C) red
    (D) hot   (E) ugly

1. **promptness:** (A) excessive modesty
    (B) extreme rigidity
    (C) reluctance or apathy
    (D) hesitation or delay
    (E) embarrassment or shame

2. **indulge:** (A) adhere   (B) abstain
    (C) divulge   (D) exonerate   (E) expiate

3. **commonplace:** (A) genuine   (B) illogical
    (C) enormous   (D) intermediate
    (E) extraordinary

4. **deaden:** (A) join   (B) justify   (C) stimulate
    (D) guard carefully   (E) alter significantly

5. **rove:** (A) whisper   (B) nourish   (C) close up
    (D) squeeze dry   (E) settle down

6. **relinquish:** (A) retain   (B) conform
    (C) persuade   (D) send forward
    (E) move together

7. **shrewd:** (A) glum   (B) witless   (C) sinister
    (D) penniless   (E) mischievous

8. **outclass:** (A) initiate   (B) oppress
    (C) keep secret   (D) be inferior
    (E) arrange in order

9. **monochromatic:** (A) polygamous
    (B) multicolored   (C) multitudinous
    (D) syndicated   (E) bilateral

10. **foreshadowed:** (A) unwanted
    (B) unrecognizable   (C) unobserved
    (D) unintentional   (E) unanticipated

11. **dwindling:** (A) enterprising
    (B) advantageous   (C) instructive
    (D) impulsive   (E) growing

12. **desecration:** (A) isolation   (B) decision
    (C) consecration   (D) declaration
    (E) modification

13. **overt:** (A) hidden   (B) ordinary   (C) prone
    (D) barren   (E) accidental

14. **flaccid:** (A) mountainous   (B) fertile
    (C) thin   (D) firm   (E) young

15. **stoic:** (A) patriarch   (B) mediator
    (C) progenitor   (D) confederate
    (E) sensualist

16. **pique:** (A) prefer   (B) show   (C) carry
    (D) placate   (E) startle

17. **cogent:** (A) unconvincing   (B) uniform
    (C) argumentative   (D) unthinkable
    (E) meditative

18. **castigation:** (A) belief   (B) adroitness
    (C) propagation   (D) adulation
    (E) indoctrination

19. **dichotomy:** (A) monotony   (B) union
    (C) infinity   (D) termination
    (E) abnormality

20. **ancillary:** (A) principal   (B) irregular
    (C) subjective   (D) contemporary
    (E) consonant

Source: PSAT test questions are from the *PSAT/NMSQT Student Bulletin,* College Entrance Examination Board, 1981. Reprinted by permission of the Educational Testing Service, copyright owner of the sample questions. Permission to reprint the sample PSAT material does not constitute review or endorsement by Educational Testing Service or the College Board of this publication as a whole or of any other sample question or testing information it may contain.

Figure 15.2 SAT Vocabulary Test

For each question in this section, choose the best answer and blacken the corresponding oval on the answer sheet.

Each question below consists of a word in boldface, followed by five lettered words or phrases. Choose the word or phrase that is most nearly <u>opposite</u> in meaning to the word in boldface. Since some of the questions require you to distinguish fine shades of meaning, consider all the choices before deciding which is best.

Example:

good: (A) sour   (B) bad   (C) red
(D) hot   (E) ugly

(A) ● (C) (D) (E)

1. **ordinary:** (A) numerical   (B) rational
   (C) impolite   (D) staunch   (E) abnormal

2. **ban:** (A) borrow   (B) regret   (C) permit
   (D) conquer   (E) exaggerate

3. **compression:** (A) equality   (B) expansion
   (C) exposure   (D) endurance
   (E) excitement

4. **flicker:** (A) rise slowly   (B) burn steadily
   (C) warm completely   (D) fume
   (E) collide

5. **atheist:** (A) believer   (B) scholar
   (C) recluse   (D) expatriate   (E) pauper

6. **fraudulent:** (A) dynamic   (B) masterly
   (C) possible   (D) genuine   (E) abundant

7. **parasite:** (A) expert   (B) imposter
   (C) instigator   (D) self-assured snob
   (E) self-sufficient individual

8. **sparse:** (A) thick   (B) tidy   (C) wealthy
   (D) round   (E) sticky

9. **denounce:** (A) overstate   (B) acclaim
   (C) destroy   (D) refuse   (E) hasten

10. **serrated:** (A) undervalued   (B) aggressive
    (C) smooth and even
    (D) loose and flexible
    (E) supremely confident

11. **fly-by-night:** (A) unbalanced   (B) moderate
    (C) permanent   (D) incredible
    (E) modern

12. **sterile:** (A) venal   (B) productive
    (C) generous   (D) variegated
    (E) unalloyed

13. **rejoice:** (A) defend against   (B) shrug off
    (C) criticize   (D) bemoan
    (E) discriminate

14. **cosmopolitan:** (A) indecisive   (B) ineffectual
    (C) antagonistic   (D) parochial
    (E) deferential

15. **fanaticism:** (A) optimism   (B) hedonism
    (C) penitence   (D) didacticism
    (E) apathy

16. **vestigial:** (A) fully developed
    (B) publicly announced   (C) offensive
    (D) provincial   (E) miraculous

17. **hypocritical:** (A) guileless   (B) eccentric
    (C) perspicacious   (D) untrustworthy
    (E) sagacious

18. **ebullient:** (A) staid   (B) anxious
    (C) feminine   (D) unique   (E) respectful

19. **accolade:** (A) appetizer   (B) censure
    (C) recoil   (D) seizure   (E) referendum

20. **propound:** (A) remove from consideration
    (B) defend without evidence
    (C) avoid without reason
    (D) view with humility
    (E) rescue from imprisonment

21. **divert:** (A) bore   (B) rescue   (C) espouse
    (D) judge fairly   (E) question relentlessly

22. **exculpate:** (A) require   (B) yield
    (C) reinstate   (D) vivify   (E) convict

23. **hackneyed:** (A) integrated   (B) appealing
    (C) inventive   (D) acceptable
    (E) improper

24. **alacrity:** (A) indolence   (B) bravery
    (C) wisdom   (D) pungency   (E) retention

25. **burgeon:** (A) fail to prove
    (B) shrivel and die
    (C) pursue and capture
    (D) disobey regulations
    (E) speak incoherently

Source: SAT test questions are from *Taking the SAT*, College Entrance Examination Board, 1981. Reprinted by permission of Educational Testing Service, copyright owner of the sample questions. Permission to reprint the sample SAT material does not constitute review or endorsement by Educational Testing Service or the College Board of this publication as a whole or of any other sample question or testing information it may contain.

Note that students taking this kind of test are usually given separate answer sheets on which they indicate their answers by blackening an oval with a pencil. Readers of this book, lacking answer sheets, can simply circle the correct answers on the test.

SUMMARY

Why is there such a strong relationship between success and vocabulary?

Communicating, learning, and thinking all require words and are important elements of success. The person who has a good, precise vocabulary will do all these things well and will naturally be successful.

Are words really used to think with?

Yes! Strange as it may seem, thinking is done with actual words. The two vocabulary tests should have shown you that. And, since thinking is done with words, it stands to reason that if your vocabulary is limited, your ability to reason and to think on a higher level will also be limited.

Why use a dictionary?

To find the precise meanings of words. One solid way to create a strong dictionary habit is to have a dictionary within easy reach at your place of study. When you need it, you can quickly flip pages, get the word, pronounce it aloud, read the definition aloud, go back to the sentence, and read the sentence aloud using the dictionary meaning instead of the textbook word. Then you'll have it!

HAVE YOU MISSED SOMETHING?

1. **SENTENCE-COMPLETION.** Complete the following sentences with one of the three words listed below each sentence.

    a. The greatest test of a person's vocabulary is in _____ .

    reading   writing   speaking

    b. The purpose of having a dictionary is to use it to obtain _____.

    understanding   wisdom   definitions

2. **MATCHING.** In each blank space in the left column, write the number preceding the phrase in the right column that matches the left item best.

_____ a. Precision

_____ b. Misinterpretation

_____ c. Fulsome

_____ d. Success

_____ e. Dictionary

_____ f. Vocabulary

1. Offensively excessive or insincere
2. Related to good vocabulary
3. Can be built to personal specifications
4. Vocabulary-building tool
5. More important than size in vocabulary
6. Can lead to fuzzy thinking

3. **TRUE-FALSE.** Write *T* beside the *true* statements and *F* beside the *false* statements that follow.

_____ a. The person who can present ideas clearly often ends up as the leader.

_____ b. In a vocabulary, what you don't know *can* hurt you.

_____ c. Although we speak in words, we think entirely in concepts.

_____ d. A poor vocabulary cannot keep you from drawing correct conclusions.

_____ e. Without an adequate vocabulary, mastery of important ideas isn't possible.

4. **MULTIPLE-CHOICE.** Choose the phrase that completes the following sentence most accurately, and circle the letter that precedes it.

A precise vocabulary is important for

a. speaking and reading.
b. thinking and learning.
c. college and beyond.
d. all of the above.

We must think things not words, or at least we must constantly translate our words into the facts for which they stand, if we are to keep the real and the true.

—OLIVER WENDELL HOLMES, JR.

16
Exploring and Analyzing Words

Our language is the product of centuries of growth and change. Many of the words we use have acquired their present meanings only relatively recently. The story behind some of them can be as captivating as a historical novel. This chapter tells you about . . .

- Becoming interested in words
- Books on words
- The histories of words
- Dictionary-mindedness

and

- Word prefixes and roots

WORDS ARE THE TOOLS of communication, learning, and thinking. Like a mechanic with an inadequate tool kit, a student with an inadequate vocabulary just cannot get the job done effectively or efficiently. (Do you know the difference between *effectively* and *efficiently?*)

Fortunately, the similarity ends here. You don't have to go out and buy new words to complete your kit of communication tools. You simply need to be alert as you listen or read, and you'll find word after word that you will want to add to your vocabulary. When you do find such a word, gather it in immediately. Write it down—in the sentence in which you found it, so you'll have its context. Then, as soon as you can, look it up in an unabridged dictionary.

Don't be satisfied with the definition alone. The dictionary will probably tell you something about the history of your word—earlier meanings, perhaps, or the origins of its prefix and root. Learn all you can about the new word, from the dictionary and from other sources such as books about words. For example, see what one word book says about the word *bribe* (Figure 16.1). As you explore and analyze each new word, it will become a lifelong friend and a useful part of your growing vocabulary.

BECOME INTERESTED IN WORDS

You can begin to gather in words immediately by becoming attentive and *interested* in them. Prof. Lee Deighton, of Columbia University, says in effect that to learn a word genuinely, you need the following essential ingredients: a keen sense of *interest*, a sense of *excitement*, a sense of *wonder*, and a feeling of *pleasure* when you choose words and words choose you.[1]

Notice that Professor Deighton listed *interest* first. And for a very good reason. A genuine interest in words is the surest path to a close kinship between you and words. The spark that ignites your interest in words will occur in different ways at different times—often by chance and occasionally by luck. It can also come about because you want it to happen.

For me, the critical incident was a remark I heard when I was very young. While talking about the perennial topic of weather, a man said, "It will stop raining by this afternoon, and we'll have sunny skies. I'm an optimist." I suddenly became aware that one's thoughts and personality could be expressed in interesting, thoughtful, and precise terms. Although I didn't know the definition of *optimist* until later that day when

---

[1]Lee C. Deighton, *Vocabulary Development in the Classroom* (New York: Teacher's College Press, 1959), p. 59.

Figure 16.1 Bribe

Bribe

Bribe: once only a scrap of bread
   The word *bribe* has degenerated morally while acquiring greater importance financially. It was once an honest scrap of bread. That was in the Late Latin form *briba.* The French borrowed it (*bribe*) in the sense "a lump of bread," "leavings of meals," something that might be given to beggars. When *bribe* first came into English it meant "a gift begged," then "a present." In modern use the "present" is frequently a large amount of money, and its purpose is to corrupt a person in a position of trust.

Source: From *Picturesque Word Origins,* © 1933 by Merriam-Webster Inc., publishers of the Merriam-Webster® Dictionaries.

I looked it up, I knew immediately that this was a man who was not just uttering clichés. He was thinking as he was speaking. And to think well, I realized, a person had to have a good vocabulary.

   You can create your own interest in words by reading (or just looking through) books like *Picturesque Word Origins,* which I was fortunate enough to stumble upon. The book contains brief histories of words and, even better, excellent pictures that illustrate some of the words and help you remember their meanings.

   I was so impressed by *Picturesque Word Origins* that I decided to lend my copy overnight to each of the high-school juniors and seniors who were in my six-week summer course in study skills at Cornell University. At the beginning of the course and again at the end, all students took the Cooperative Reading Test, which includes a vocabulary subtest. Summer after summer, the improvement in vocabulary was both surprising and gratifying. Some classes averaged about 35 percent, and one class averaged a whopping 64.6 percent improvement.

Here is a list of books, including *Picturesque Word Origins,* that are almost guaranteed to arouse your interest in words while they enhance your vocabulary. They are separated according to whether they are in print or out of print at present. The out-of-print books are worth looking for in libraries; those still in print can be obtained from their publishers.

Books Still in Print

Ciardi, John, *A Browser's Dictionary and Native's Guide to the Unknown American Language.* Published in 1980. Hard cover. The author discusses about a thousand words, including *baker's dozen* and *swindle.* Information and copies: Harper & Row Publishers, Inc., Keystone Industrial Park, Scranton, PA 18512.

Funk, Charles E., *A Hog on Ice, and Other Curious Expressions.* Published in 1948. Hard cover. The author discusses about 750 phrases, such as *kick the bucket* and *kangaroo court.* Some illustrations or drawings. Information and copies: Harper & Row Publishers, Inc., Keystone Industrial Park, Scranton, PA 18512.

Funk, Charles E., *Thereby Hangs a Tale, Stories of Curious Word Origins.* Published in 1950. Hard cover. The author discusses about 650 words such as *alligator* and *Yankee.* Information and copies: Harper & Row Publishers, Inc., Keystone Industrial Park, Scranton, PA 18512.

Funk, Wilfred, *Word Origins and Their Romantic Stories.* Published in 1950 by Funk & Wagnalls Co. Hard cover and paperback. The author discusses about three thousand words such as *aardvark* and *zwieback.* Easy to read. Information and copies: Harper & Row Publishers, Inc., Keystone Industrial Park, Scranton, PA 18512.

Holt, Alfred H., *Phrase and Word Origins.* Published in 1961. Paperback. The author discusses over one thousand words and phrases from *armed to the teeth* to *wet your whistle.* Information and copies: Dover Publications, Inc., 180 Varick Street, New York, NY 10014.

Laird, Charlton, *The Word: A Look at the Vocabulary of English.* Published in 1981. A look at how words enter and leave our language. Information and copies: Simon & Schuster, Inc., 1230 Avenue of the Americas, New York, NY 10020.

Maleska, Eugene, *A Pleasure in Words.* Published in 1981. A look at the origins and meanings of thousands of words in our language by a distinguished educator, author, and current crossword puzzle editor of *The*

New York Times. Copies: Simon & Schuster, Inc., 1230 Avenue of the Americas, New York, NY 10020.

Mathews, Mitford M., *American Words.* Published in 1959 and again in 1976. Hard cover. The author discusses about two hundred words such as *podunk* and *hickory,* and many are illustrated by drawings. Information and copies: Philomel Books, 200 Madison Avenue, Suite 1405, New York, NY 10016.

Partridge, Eric, *A Dictionary of Catch Phrases.* Published in 1979. Chock full of common phrases, together with their origins and uses. Copies: Stein & Day, Scarborough House, Briarcliff Manor, NY 10510.

Shipley, Joseph T., *Dictionary of Word Origins.* Published in 1979. Paperback. The author discusses about two thousand words such as *arsenic, assassin,* and *whippersnapper.* Information and copies: Littlefield, Adams & Co., 81 Adams Drive, Box 327, Totowa, NJ 07511.

Train, John, *Remarkable Words with Astonishing Origins.* Published in 1980 by Clarkson N. Potter Books. Copies: Crown Publishers, Inc., 1 Park Avenue, New York, NY 10016.

Out-of-Print Books

Chapman, Bruce, *Why Do We Say Such Things?* Published in 1947 by Miles Emmett, New York. The author discusses about a thousand words such as *acrobat* and *stooge.*

Ernst, Margaret S., *In a Word.* Published in 1939 by Alfred A. Knopf, New York. The author discusses (and James Thurber illustrates) about 250 words, such as *abundance* and *whiskey.*

Ernst, Margaret S., *More About Words.* Published in 1951 by Alfred A. Knopf, New York. The author discusses (and W. A. Dwiggins illustrates) about 250 words, such as *abracadabra* and *jinx.*

Funk, Charles E., and Charles E. Funk, Jr., *Horsefeathers and Other Curious Words.* Published in 1958 by Harper & Brothers, New York. The authors discuss such words and phrases as *Annie Oakley* and *woodchuck,* with occasional illustrations. About 1,300 words are discussed.

Garrison, Webb, *What's in a Word?* Published in 1965 by Abingdon Press, Nashville. The author discusses about 500 words grouped in such categories as sports, adventure, farming, and frontier. Occasional illustrations.

Picturesque Word Origins. Published in 1933 by G. & C. Merriam Company, Springfield, Mass. One hundred fifty-eight words are fully discussed, and forty-eight more are interestingly but briefly discussed under the categories of flowers, birds, animals, cloth, and gems. Forty-five of the words are graphically and meaningfully illustrated. (See Figure 16.1 on page 279.)

LEARN THE HISTORIES OF WORDS

Words, like facts, are difficult to remember out of context. Remembering is greatly facilitated when you have a body of information with which to associate either a word or a fact. For words, interesting origins or histories will help provide a context. For example, a *hippopotamus* is a "river horse," from the Greek *hippos*, meaning "horse," and *potamos*, meaning "river."

Indiana is called the *Hoosier State*, and its people *Hoosiers*. Why? In the early days, the pioneers were gruff in manner; when someone knocked at the front door, a pioneer's voice would often boom, "Who's yere?"

You may have wondered why runners on a cross-country track team are called *harriers*, especially by sports writers. Actually, a harrier is a swift-running dog, useful in hunting rabbits.

If you were offered a *Hobson's choice*, would you know what was meant? Here's the story: Thomas Hobson owned a livery stable in seventeenth-century England. He loved his horses, and to prevent any one horse from being overworked, he hired them out in turn, beginning with stall number one. Customers had to take the horses they were given. So, you see, *Hobson's choice* means no choice at all.

The following excerpt indicates what is to be found in the history of words.

To the man who knows its origin, every word presents a picture. Not only do these stories make interesting reading, but to know them will give you an effectiveness in speaking and writing that can come in no other way. When you know the origins and the essential meanings of words, your own use of words will become more forceful, accurate, and colorful.

Back of almost every word in the English language there is a "life story" that will come to many as a fascinating revelation. Our words have come to us from a multitude of sources. Some of them have lived for thousands of years and have played their parts in many lands and many civilizations. They may record ancient superstitions. They may be monuments to customs dating back to classical antiquity. They may reveal our ancestors' manners and beliefs, shrouded in the mists of ancient history. Words that you use today may have been the slang of Roman soldiers twenty centuries ago or the lingo of savages. They may have been used by an Athenian poet or by an Anglo-Saxon farmer.

From Interesting Origins of English Words, Copyright © 1959 by G. & C. Merriam Co.

BE DICTIONARY-MINDED

Many scholars and business executives attribute their interest in words to the old-time "vest-pocket" dictionary.

Eddie Rickenbacker, who left school when he was only twelve, nevertheless made it a habit to carry a small dictionary in his pocket. Here is his own account:

> *Though much of my association was with mechanics and other drivers, I also had the opportunity to converse with men in higher positions, automotive engineers, and company officials. . . . I listened carefully and marked well the way such men constructed and phrased their thoughts. I carried a dictionary with me always and used it. I have never slackened in the pursuit of learning and self-improvement.*[2]

Get yourself one of these small pocket dictionaries (for example, the *New Webster's Vest Pocket Dictionary* or *Webster's New World Vest Pocket Dictionary*). Carry it with you always. Instead of reading the print on cereal boxes, or looking at advertising placards on buses and subways, or just staring into space, take out your dictionary and *read it*. Its definitions will be terse, consisting mainly of synonyms, but its value lies in fostering a lifelong interest in words, as well as increasing your vocabulary. Of course, a pocket dictionary is no substitute for a larger dictionary; but as a portable teaching tool, it is worth its weight in gold.

Every college student should also own a good desk dictionary for ready reference. I especially recommend the following:

> *The American Heritage Dictionary of the English Language* (Houghton Mifflin Company)
> *The American College Dictionary* (Random House)
> *Webster's New Collegiate Dictionary* (G. & C. Merriam Company)
> *Webster's New World Dictionary of the American Language* (World Publishing Company)

Keep your dictionary within easy reach as you study, and develop the habit of consulting it.

For intensive word study there is no substitute for an unabridged dictionary. Locate the unabridged dictionaries in your library—normally you will find them in the reference room—and use them to supplement your own abridged desk dictionary. An unabridged dictionary gives more definitions, more about the derivations of words, and more on usage. Good one-volume unabridged works include *Webster's New International Dictionary of the English Language* and the *New Standard Dictionary of the English Language*. *The Oxford English Dictionary*, in ten volumes plus

---

[2]From the book *Rickenbacker* by Edward V. Rickenbacker. Published by Prentice-Hall, Inc., Englewood Cliffs, N.J.

supplement, is indispensable for the historical study of words, but more detailed than you will need for most purposes.

The reference librarian can also help you find specialized dictionaries on various subjects. They list technical terms not always found even in unabridged dictionaries. However, your textbooks are the best sources of the definitions for such terms.

You can probably get some idea of the meaning of a new word from its context—how it is used in your reading material. Use context when you can, but be aware that it has its limitations. Lee Deighton points out three: First, context provides only the meaning that fits that particular situation; second, you often end up with a synonym, which is not quite the same as a definition; and third, when you have to infer the meaning of a word, you can be slightly (or greatly) in error.[3] The safest bet is to avoid all the guesswork and go straight to your dictionary.

Buy and use the best abridged dictionary you can afford. Whenever an unabridged dictionary is nearby, use it. But also remember that no word is ever fully defined. The dictionary meaning is good and necessary, but it is only an operational meaning that will solve your immediate problem. Words have shades of meaning that add richness but that we come to understand only by reading, hearing, and using words in a variety of contexts.

As you study, consult your dictionary whenever you come to a word that you don't know precisely. Find the exact meaning you need; then go back to your textbook and reread the paragraph, with the *meaning* substituted for the word. If you become interested in a particular word, write it on a 3×5 card. Later, go back to the dictionary and investigate it. Write its meanings on the card, and keep the card and other like cards to look through and study occasionally. But don't break into your studying for a long session with the dictionary; save that for later.

GET TO KNOW
WORD PREFIXES AND ROOTS

A word *root* is the core of a word, the part that holds the basic meaning. A *prefix* is a word beginning that modifies the root. As you work to make your vocabulary more precise, you will appreciate more and more the value of prefixes and roots. Soon, some of them will become old friends, and you will recognize them almost daily as you read and listen. And when you recognize one of them as part of a new word, you will be well on the way to grasping its meaning. One well-understood root word can help you learn an entire "constellation" of words. Figure 16.2 shows such

[3]Deighton, *Vocabulary Development in the Classroom*, pp. 2–3.

a constellation, based on the root *duct,* from the Latin *ducere* (to lead). Notice how the various prefixes, and suffixes, or word endings, modify the root to make the different words.

A number of commonly used prefixes and roots are listed in Tables 16.1 and 16.2. They can help you understand definitions more precisely. They will also be of use in unlocking the meanings of unknown words that you find in your reading. But you must look up such words in a dictionary anyway. Here's why.

Over the centuries, many prefixes have changed in both meaning and spelling. In other words, "of the 68 prominent and commonly used prefixes there are only 11 which have a single and fairly invariant meaning."[4] Obviously the other fifty-seven prefixes have more than one meaning each.

For example, the prefix *de-* means "of" or "from"; yet the dictionary lists four different meanings for it:

1. It means "down" as in *descend,* which means to pass from a higher to a lower place.
2. It indicates separation as in *dehumidify,* which means to separate moisture from air, or in *decapitate,* which means to behead—that is, to separate the head from the rest of the body.
3. It indicates reversal as in *decode,* which means to convert from code into ordinary language, or in *depreciate,* which means to lessen in value.

Figure 16.2 A Constellation of Words from One Root

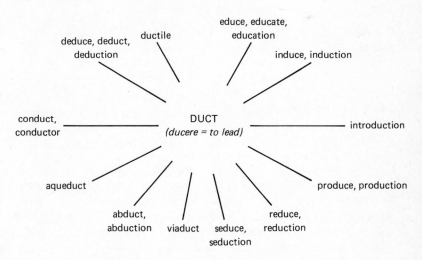

[4]Deighton, *Vocabulary Development in the Classroom,* p. 26.

Table 16.1 Examples of Common Prefixes

Prefix	Meaning	Example	Definition
ante-	before	antebellum	*Before* the war; especially in the U.S., before the Civil War
anti-	against	antitank	Weapons used *against* tanks
auto-	self	automatic	*Self*-acting or self-regulating
bene-	good	benefit	An act of *kindness*; a gift
circum-	around	circumscribe	To draw a line *around*; to encircle
contra-	against	contradict	To speak *against*
ecto-	outside	ectoparasite	Parasite living on the *exterior* of animals
endo-	within	endogamy	Marriage *within* the tribe
hyper-	over	hypertension	*High* blood pressure
hypo-	under	hypotension	*Low* blood pressure
inter-	between	intervene	Come *between*
intro-	within	introspect	To look *within*, as one's own mind
macro-	large	macroscopic	*Large* enough to be observed by the naked eye
mal-	bad	maladjusted	*Badly* adjusted
micro-	small	microscopic	So *small* that one needs a microscope to observe
multi-	many	multimillionaire	One having *two* or *more* million dollars
neo-	new	neolithic	*New* stone age
pan-	all	pantheon	A temple dedicated to *all* gods
poly-	many	polygamy	Having *many* wives
post-	after	post bellum	*After* the war
pre-	before	precede	To go *before*
proto-	first	prototype	*First* or original model
pseudo-	false	pseudonym	*False* name; esp., an author's pen-name
retro-	backward	retrospect	A looking *back* on things
semi-	half	semiannual	*Half* a year
sub-	under	submerge	To put *under* water
super-	above	superfine	*Extra* fine
tele-	far	telescope	Seeing or viewing *afar*
trans-	across	transalpine	*Across* the Alps

4. It may be used to intensify as in *demonstrate,* which means to show or prove publicly, or in *declare,* which means to announce. In both these examples, the root already has the indicated meaning.

So learn as many of the common prefixes and roots as you can, but not to replace the dictionary. Learn them for better and more precise understanding of words you already know and words that you have yet to look up in the dictionary. And when you go to the dictionary, make sure that you spend some time on the prefixes and roots that make up each word. You will soon become convinced that a word is not simply an assemblage of letters put together like an anagram, but the true and natural outcome of evolution.

Table 16.2 Examples of Common Roots

Root	Meaning	Example	Definition
agri-	field	agronomy	*Field*—crop production and soil management
anthropo-	man	anthropology	The study of *man*
astro-	star	astronaut	One who travels in interplanetary space (*stars*)
bios-	life	biology	The study of *life*
cardio-	heart	cardiac	Pertaining to the *heart*
chromo-	color	chromatology	The science of *colors*
demos-	people	democracy	Government by the *people*
derma-	skin	epidermis	The outer layer of *skin*
dyna-	power	dynamic	Characterized by *power* and energy
geo-	earth	geology	The study of the *earth*
helio-	sun	heliotrope	Any plant that turns toward the *sun*
hydro-	water	hydroponics	Growing of plants in *water* reinforced with nutrients
hypno-	sleep	hypnosis	A state of *sleep* induced by suggestion
magni-	great, big	magnify	To enlarge, to make *bigger*
man(u)-	hand	manuscript	Written by *hand*
mono-	one	monoplane	Airplane with *one* wing
ortho-	straight	orthodox	Right, true, *straight* opinion
-pod	foot	pseudopod	False *foot*
psycho-	mind	psychology	Study of the *mind* in any of its aspects
pyro-	fire	pyrometer	An instrument for measuring temperatures
terra-	earth	terrace	A raised platform of *earth*
thermo-	heat	thermo-electricity	Electricity produced by *heat*
zoo-	animal	zoology	The study of *animals*

SUMMARY

Why is becoming interested in words so important?

Interest means motivation. Interest will drive you to the dictionary to find the meanings of words. In addition, interest is the first step in helping you to remember words and their definitions.

How does reading books on word origins help?

When you find out, say, that *daisy* comes from the Anglo-Saxon words "day's eye," and *spider* from the Anglo-Saxon verb *spin*, you begin to realize that words got their meanings not by chance, but by design; that is, words have a past, an ancestry like a living thing. Once you realize that, words become like people—interesting.

Does learning prefixes and roots help vocabulary?

Yes, but not in advance. It helps you "see" and remember meanings only after you read the dictionary entry. Prefixes and roots have changed so much over the centuries that they are no longer precise clues to definitions. Only a good dictionary can give you that.

HAVE YOU MISSED SOMETHING?

1. **SENTENCE-COMPLETION.** Complete the following sentences with one of the three words listed below each sentence.

   a. An unabridged dictionary or a good-sized college dictionary provides a word's definition as well as its _____.

   homonym   history   antonym

   b. Fewer than one-sixth of all common prefixes have only one _____.

   root   meaning   vowel

2. **MATCHING.** In each blank space in the left column, write the number preceding the phrase in the right column that matches the left item best.

   _____ a. Interest

   _____ b. Context

   _____ c. Textbook

   _____ d. Pocket dictionary

   _____ e. Word root

   1. Less complete than other types
   2. Best source for technical definitions
   3. Gives rise to a "constellation" of words
   4. Not a great way to learn meanings
   5. The driving force for vocabulary building

3. **TRUE-FALSE.** Write *T* beside the *true* statements and *F* beside the *false* statements that follow.

   _____ a. Words by themselves are easy to remember.

   _____ b. Sometimes, when you obtain a meaning from context, you can be very wrong.

   _____ c. Over the years, many prefixes have changed in meaning and spelling.

_____ d. Knowing a word's definition is enough to keep it in your vocabulary.

4. **MULTIPLE-CHOICE.** Choose the phrase that completes the following sentence most accurately, and circle the letter that precedes it.

To learn words genuinely and well, you need a

a. complete encyclopedia.
b. box of 3×5 cards.
c. knowledge of prefixes and roots.
d. sense of interest in words.

> *All words are pegs to hang ideas on.*
> —HENRY WARD BEECHER

17

Learning Words with the Frontier System

Would you like to build up your vocabulary? You can, with the Frontier System. Learning lasts longer with the Frontier System because you blaze your own trail instead of going over somebody else's territory. This chapter explains . . .

- Why some vocabulary systems don't work
- Why the Frontier System does work
- How to find frontier words
- How to make the Frontier System work for you

and

- What to do with technical terms

MOST VOCABULARY IMPROVEMENT SYSTEMS are based either on chance or on learning standard lists of words that have been compiled by experts. But a person's vocabulary is too important an asset to leave to chance, and people are too different from each other (in interests, ability, personality, and intellect) to learn the same words in the same way and at the same pace. As examples, here are four vocabulary systems of these types—systems that don't work.

1. *Natural growth.* The idea in this system is that your vocabulary will grow with experience and age. Actually, your vocabulary will grow with time only if (a) you are exposed to words that you have an interest in learning and (b) you expend the effort to learn them. Otherwise, your vocabulary is liable to shrink in time.

2. *Reading books.* Here the notion is that your vocabulary will automatically grow if you read the right books. This system might work if (a) you and the recommended books are perfectly suited for each other, and (b) you stop to consult your dictionary whenever you come across a word whose meaning you don't know precisely. Otherwise, it can lead to extreme frustration.

3. *Memorizing lists of words.* In this system you memorize several words and their definitions each day, from a standard list. In theory, memorizing five words a day adds up to over 1,800 words learned in a year. In practice, however, no such learning takes place. Word lists have too many strikes against them. First, memorizing is a chore. Second, forgetting is rapid. Third, learning someone else's list is nonmotivating. And fourth, word lists are artificial since words do not exist in isolation, except in crossword puzzles and quizzes.

4. *Learning prefixes, roots, and combining forms.* The idea here is that you will recognize the meaning of a new word if you have learned the meanings of its parts. At first thought, it would seem that this system has great potential because an estimated 60 percent of the English words in common use are made up partly or entirely of prefixes and roots derived from Latin and Greek. Unfortunately, the system does not work well except for those who already have a strong vocabulary. Here are the reasons. First, memorizing lists of prefixes and roots is not much different from memorizing lists of words—it is boring and nonmotivating. Second, forgetting is rapid because these word parts are not learned in a meaningful context.

Rather than force the learner to conform to some standard, it seems more logical to base a vocabulary-building system on the individual— his or her needs, abilities, present vocabulary, and interests. "Fine," you might say, "but can anyone develop such a system?" The answer is yes; it has been done.

THE FRONTIER
VOCABULARY SYSTEM WORKS

The Frontier Vocabulary System, developed by Johnson O'Connor, is based on natural learning processes.[1] We know that before a child can run, he or she must learn to walk; and before walking, he or she must learn to crawl. We know, too, that a child can pronounce the letter *P* at about age three and one-half, but the letter *R* is usually not pronounced clearly until age seven and one-half. Many other skills develop along with physical growth and general maturation. In all these processes, we find four characteristics:

1. Skills progress from the simple to the complex.
2. Each skill is developed in an orderly sequence of steps.
3. Each step is at a different level of difficulty.
4. No significant step may be skipped. It seems that each step develops the muscle or brain pattern that makes the next step possible.

From his analytical research over the past thirty years, O'Connor has concluded that learning new words is much like any other skill. We progress from simple words to more difficult ones in an orderly sequence. The difficulty or ease of learning a word does not depend on its length, its frequency of use, its geographic origin, or its pronunciation, or on teachers, books, or parents. Instead, difficulty in learning a word depends on the complexity of the *idea* that it stands for. Defining words with simple synonyms does not provide the learner with a background sufficient to think with the words. Since words stand for ideas, the ideas behind them should also be learned.

S. I. Hayakawa, the noted semanticist, agrees with this view. He questions the old-fashioned notion that the way to study words is to concentrate one's attention exclusively on words. Hayakawa suggests that words should be understood in relationship to other words—not only other words on the same level, but also words at a higher (more abstract) level and words at a lower (more concrete) level.

PRINCIPLES GOVERNING
THE LEARNING OF WORDS

The following specific findings by O'Connor form the basis for the Frontier Vocabulary System:

---

[1]Much of this discussion is based on an article by Dean Trembly, "Intellectual Abilities as Motivating Factors," *Japanese Psychological Research* 10, No. 2 (July 1968), 104–108.

The easier words are learned first; then the harder ones are learned.

At the forward edge of the mass of all the words that have been mastered is the individual's *frontier*. Only a very few words *beyond the frontier* have already been mastered.

The greatest learning takes place in the *frontier area* (Edgar Dale calls it the "twilight zone"), which lies between all the words mastered and the words unknown. (See Figure 17.1.)

The most significant characteristic of the words in the twilight zone is that they are, to some extent, *familiar*. The maximum advancement in a person's mastery of words takes place in the twilight zone, where hundreds of almost-known words need only a slight straightening out to make them familiar.

Learning becomes extremely inefficient, and actually breaks down, whenever a person skips the twilight zone and tries first to learn totally unknown words.

Familiarity with a word in the frontier area means that you already know something about the word or its definition. You may, for example, know how to pronounce the word and know its general meaning. Or you may know only one of its several meanings. The important point is this: By singling out such a frontier word and learning its specific meaning, or

Figure 17.1 The Concept of Frontier Words

ZONE OF KNOWN WORDS

These are the words already mastered. They are used in reading, writing, listening, and thinking.

The Edge of the Frontier

TWILIGHT ZONE

The words in this zone are the frontier words. They are somewhat familiar.

ZONE OF TOTALLY UNKNOWN WORDS

An occasional word, like an island in an unknown sea, might have been discovered and made one's own because of necessity.

its several definitions, you can master the word with a minimum of time and effort.

By working continually in the frontier area, you can make rapid progress in mastering words, thus extending the edge of your frontier into the twilight zone. At the same time, you will continually be creating new frontier words to conquer. As the process continues, the frontier area will enter into the area that was formerly the zone of totally unknown words.

Remember that your frontier words are always the easiest and the most natural ones to master. Best of all, you will never run out of frontier words.

EXAMPLES OF FRONTIER WORDS

Frontier words tend to fall into several groups or categories, which are listed in this section. (Of course, the specific examples may not be your own personal frontier words, but they are typical of the categories.) From the examples you will readily see why a frontier word is the easiest to master. It already provides a "handle"—a meaning or an association. A person may already have brought a great deal of interest and imagination to the word. All that is needed is to straighten out some of the irregularities and the person will have a precise, full-blown word-concept of his or her own.

Words That Sound Somewhat Alike

In the following pairs of words, a person may mistake one word for the other. For example, students have written, "The man was arrested for the *elicit* use of drugs." (*Elicit* is incorrect here.)

illicit	= not permitted; improper; unlawful
elicit	= to draw out (as, to *elicit* truth by discussion)
bizarre	= odd, extravagant, or eccentric in style or mode
bazaar	= a fair for the sale of fancy wares, toys, etc.
magnet	= an iron bar having the power to attract iron
magnate	= a person prominent in the management of a large industry (as, an oil *magnate*)
criterion	= a standard of judging
centurion	= a captain in the Roman army

Words That Look Somewhat Alike

The following pairs of words are frequently confused because they look so much alike.

posterity = all future generations
prosperity = success, good fortune

psychic = a person apparently sensitive to nonphysical forces
physique = one's body or a type of body

derelict = given up by the owner; abandoned
dialect = a local or provincial form of a language

marital = pertaining to marriage
martial = pertaining to war (as, *martial* music)

Words That Are Used Together

Like a chameleon, one of a pair of words can take on the color of the other. These are words that are so strongly associated as pairs that many people attribute to one word (the ones in italics below) the meaning of the pair—even when the pair is separated.

Pair	Incorrect Meaning of Italic Word	Correct Meaning
prodigal son	Wandering	Wasteful; a spendthrift (as a noun)
anonymous donor	Generous	Nameless; with name kept secret
exotic flower	Beautiful	Introduced from a foreign country
capital crime	Important	Punishable by death

Words That Suggest an Embedded Word

Some new words often incorporate a smaller, more common word which, in itself, has a definite meaning. So it is quite natural to attribute (incorrectly) to the new word the meaning of the embedded common word.

Word	Incorrect Meaning	Correct Meaning
succulent	To suck up like a vacuum cleaner	Juicy; having juicy tissues (as most cacti)
ramify	To butt, as with a long log	To divide or spread out into branches, or ramifications
longevity	Tall	Length of life; long life
strident	Having a long stride	Harsh-sounding; shrill
archaic	Having arches	Old-fashioned; antiquated

Words That Set a Prefix-Root Trap

If only a prefix or root is known, one can occasionally infer the wrong meaning for an unfamiliar word.

Word	Incorrect Meaning	Correct Meaning
sublime	Underneath the ground	Elevated or exalted; noble
biweekly	Twice a week	Occurring every two weeks
ingenious	Not a genius; not very bright ("in" equals not)	Having high mental powers, clever
preponderance	To ponder, to think beforehand	Superiority of weight or influence
expound	To flatten out	To set forth (as, to *expound* a theory)

Right Church, Wrong Pew

Some words are one-directional. For example, *infer* means "to draw out," whereas *imply* means "to put in." Also, some words are used with the correct meaning but in the wrong context.

Word	Correct Definition	Wrong Use
dwindle	To diminish; decrease	The money *dwindled* in slowly.
senility	Old age (usually of people)	The chair is antique because of its *senility*.
affable	Pleasant; gracious; courteous (people)	We had an *affable* trip.
prolific	Multiplying fast	Ralph gets A's in arithmetic because he's *prolific*.

Slightly More than a Case of Spelling

These pairs of look-alikes and sound-alikes can lead to humorous consequences if mixed up:

> The town's *hysterical* society held its regular meeting in the museum.
> *historical:* based on history; former events and people
> *hysterical:* wildly emotional

The bride and groom were happy and *contentious.*
  content: happy and satisfied
  contentious: quarrelsome

They found the mountain air clean and *accelerating.*
  exhilarating: enlivening
  accelerating: gathering speed

The prize was awarded *posthumorously.*
  posthumously: occurring after one's death
  posthumorously: no such word

The *pastoral* colors made the room bright and gay.
  pastel: a soft, delicate hue
  pastoral: relating to rural life and scenes

Many stories have come out of Tibet about the *Abdominal* Snowman.
  abominable: hateful or horrible
  abdominal: relating to the belly

THE FRONTIER SYSTEM

Finding Your Frontier Words

Here's how to find your own frontier words:

First, become aware of your daily speech, and make a list of the more unusual words you use. These are words for which you have a head start.

Second, be on the lookout for words that you recognize in reading, but that you do not use in speaking and writing. From this source choose *only* the words that appeal to you, that is, the words which fit your personality. These are your type of words.

Third, listen attentively while other people speak. The chances are great that you will recognize and know the general meaning of all the words you hear. Choose from this stream of speech the words that appeal to you—words that you could easily incorporate into your own speech.

Fourth, later, after writing out the definition for each of your frontier words, look for its opposite. If it interests you, learn that word too. Learning pairs of contrasting words creates the strong force of spontaneous suggestion—either word suggests the other.

Making the Frontier Vocabulary System Work

Use 3 × 5 cards as follows:

1. Write each of your frontier words on a separate 3 × 5 card, preferably in the sentence in which you encountered it. Underline the word so that it stands out.

2. When you have accumulated a small number of these cards, look up the words in an unabridged dictionary.

3. On the same side of the card that bears the excerpted sentence, print the word with its syllables and diacritical markings, so that you'll be able to pronounce it accurately. You will find it much easier to use the word in conversation if you practice saying it out loud. Nothing else should be placed on the front of the card, unless you wish to footnote the source of your sentence or word.

4. Now use the reverse side of the card. If the word is made up of a prefix and a root, record this information on the card. Knowing the derivation of the word and some of its ancestry will help you learn the word with greater precision.

5. Write the several definitions, or variations of the definitions, on the reverse side. Place an asterisk beside the definition that best fits the word as it was used in your original sentence. (Figure 17.2 shows two typical cards.)

6. Carry about a dozen of these filled-out cards in your shirt pocket or

Figure 17.2 Frontier System Cards. These two cards happen to show a pair of words that are opposite, or complementary. Such words, studied side-by-side, are bound to take on more precise meaning. Notice that the front of each card shows the new word underlined in a complete sentence. It also shows how to pronounce the word and its variations. The reverse of each card defines prefixes and roots and gives important dictionary definitions of the word. An asterisk is placed beside the definition that most nearly matches the use of the word on the front of the card. Brief synonyms are also given.

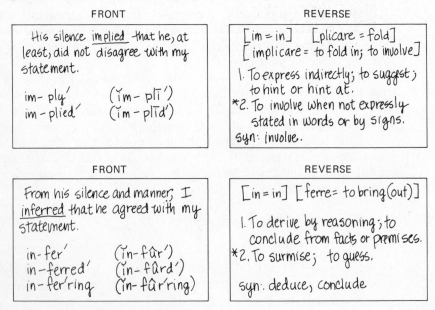

handbag, so that they will be handy to review whenever there is a spare moment. You can look at them while standing in a cafeteria line, waiting for a bus, sitting in someone's outer office, and so on.

7. Always look at the front side of the card. Pronounce the word correctly, read the sentence completely, and then define the word, not necessarily in dictionary language but meaningfully in your own words. All this should be done before you look at the definition on the back.

8. After you have defined the word to the best of your ability, turn the card over to check on the accuracy of your definition.

9. If you are not satisfied with your definition, place a dot on the front of the card, in the upper right-hand corner. The next time you go through your cards, the dot will remind you that you missed on a previous try. When a card has three or more dots, it is time to give that word some special attention.

10. After the small stack of cards has been mastered, place them in a file and pick up additional ones for mastering.

11. Review the words that you have mastered from time to time.

As you master the precise meaning of each frontier word, there will be more than a corresponding advance in your reading, writing, speaking, and thinking.

WORDS AND TERMS IN LECTURES AND TEXTBOOKS

Words and terms encountered in your lectures and textbooks have to be learned cold, whether you like it or not. Not knowing the precise meanings of such words will leave a gap in your understanding and keep you from learning the subject. It can also be devastating on examinations.

Throughout your college years, you'll be exposed to a flood of technical words, and each is likely to be the key to a new idea or concept. Some may be words that you have never heard before. Others, like *base* in chemistry and *accommodation* in psychology, may be familiar but will have new, specific, technical meanings that must be learned as if they were new words. These words are not just nice to know; rather, they are absolutely necessary if you are to grasp fundamental ideas and facts.

Work with these words as if they were your frontier words. Use the 3×5 card system. Do a first-class job in researching each word or term, and put plenty of vigor into understanding, reciting, and memorizing them. Use them whenever you can: in discussions with other students, during class discussions, and in your writing. In other words, be very professional in mastering the words and terms that are basic to your subjects.

SUMMARY

Why aren't the "chance" and "word-list" systems effective?

In the "chance" systems, you have to happen on words that are right for your personal vocabulary, either in your reading or in other everyday pursuits; if you don't, then you don't learn. In the "word-list" systems, you work with other people's words or word parts, so there really is little motivation to learn—and little context to help you learn. And neither type of system promotes real interest in learning words.

Why is the Frontier Vocabulary System effective?

Because it allows you to follow a natural sequence of steps. You, as an individual, are at a stage of vocabulary development that is different from the stages of other individuals; you need a system that recognizes this individuality. You begin learning words at *your* frontier; that is, words that you have heard or have seen before, but whose meanings you have not fully grasped as yet. These slightly familiar words are the easiest to learn. Once they are learned, they establish the foundation and set the stage for learning other words at the front edge of your frontier. The front edge thus continually advances, so you never run out of frontier words. The system's a natural!

Why use 3×5 cards?

Using 3×5 cards is effective for these reasons. First, they define a system for you. Second, they provide a place where you can write all the information about the word accurately from the start. Third, you can look at the face of the card and recite without looking at the definition. Fourth, they are portable, so you can learn wherever you go, whenever you have a few minutes. And fifth, they provide proof of progress, which is highly motivating.

HAVE YOU MISSED SOMETHING?

1. **SENTENCE-COMPLETION.** Complete the following sentences with one of the three words listed below each sentence.

a. Words in lists are harder to remember than words which appear in

_____.

context   tables   syllables

b. Technical words must be learned _____.

precisely   occasionally   approximately

2. **MATCHING.** In each blank space in the left column, write the number preceding the phrase in the right column that matches the left item best.

_____ a. Antonyms

_____ b. Frontier System

_____ c. 3 × 5 cards

_____ d. Twilight Zone

_____ e. Definition

_____ f. Frontier edge

1. Help provide a system for vocabulary building
2. Appears on the back of a Frontier System card
3. Tailored to the individual
4. Best source of new words
5. Will advance into unknown-words zone
6. Create a strong force of spontaneous suggestion

3. **TRUE-FALSE.** Write *T* beside the *true* statements and *F* beside the *false* statements that follow.

_____ a. It is easier just to skip the twilight zone when using the Frontier System.

_____ b. Only a few English words are derived from Latin or Greek.

_____ c. We all have the same vocabulary frontier.

_____ d. The Frontier System parallels natural development.

_____ e. All your Frontier System cards should be kept close at hand for a quick review.

4. **MULTIPLE-CHOICE.** Choose the phrase that completes the following sentence most accurately, and circle the letter that precedes it.

Of the following, the one that is *not* a good source for your frontier words is

a. your speech and that of others.
b. your reading materials.
c. the reading materials of your classmates.
d. the opposites of your frontier words.

PART VI

YOUR READING

When we read too fast or too slowly we understand nothing.

—PASCAL

18
Improving Your Reading Speed

Almost anyone who reads can read faster. But the way to do so is to strengthen your natural way of reading and thinking—not to use some artificial method. This chapter includes information and expert research on . . .

- Eye movements during reading
- How much the mind can see
- Vocalization and reading

as well as

- A method for reading faster naturally

*T*HE SIMPLE QUESTION, "How can I improve my reading?" does not have a simple answer. There are many different purposes in reading, many different reading techniques that can be used, and many ways in which reading can be "improved." However, when this question is asked by a student, it usually means, "How can I *speed up* my reading so I can finish my homework in half the time with high comprehension and almost complete retention?" There is no easy way to do so, despite the numerous brochures, newspaper and magazine articles, and television programs that extol the marvels of "speed reading." Many students, as well as the general public, are convinced that speed reading is a technique that is easy to learn and that can be used with any page of print. Unfortunately, speed reading is virtually useless to anyone who desires to learn from the printed page.

If you desire high comprehension and almost complete retention, then you must use systematic study techniques. There is no other way to master your courses. This entire book is devoted to making learning a reality through the use of efficient study skills. This chapter and Chapter 19 focus on specific skills you can use in reading. Before examining them, however, we must take a little time to discuss two aspects of reading: eye movements and vocalization. In doing so, we shall emphasize some negative aspects of speed reading, for two reasons. First, academic improvement through speed reading is just not in the cards, so you should not spend your time, money, and energy on this dead end. Second, by clearing the decks of so-called easy ways to read and study, we shall set the stage for some reading and studying systems that work.

EYE MOVEMENTS DURING READING

Facts about Eye Movements and Speed Reading

Newspapers have carried sensational stories about high-school students reading at astronomical speeds. One student, as the story put it, was clocked at the rate of 40,000 words per minute. Another student was timed at 50,000 words per minute! A peculiar characteristic of all such stories is that they include the statement, "with nearly 100 percent comprehension."

How fast is 40,000 words per minute? There are about 300 words on an average paperback book page. By dividing 300 into 40,000, we find that to read 40,000 words per minute, a person would have to read 133 pages per minute! The reader (or, more accurately, the page turner) would have less than one-half second to spend on a page. Some students find it difficult to *turn* 133 pages in a minute, let alone see any words on those pages. Readers who are fast page turners might be able to see a word or two on each page as it flutters by, but this would hardly lead to "almost 100 percent comprehension." Such readers could not possibly reconstruct the ideas contained in the 133 pages.

The basic premise of speed-reading advocates is this: The eye is able to see a vast number of words in one fixation. (A *fixation* is a focusing of the eyes on an object. The eyes must pause—they must be still—to fix on the object.) Some advocates say the eye can see phrases at a glance; others say entire lines; still others say paragraphs at a time; and a few say the eye can see an entire page at a glance. But let's look at the facts.

First, eye-movement photography clearly shows that the average college student makes about four eye fixations per second. Second, eye-movement photography shows that the eye sees an average of only 1.1 words during each fixation. It is seldom that any person, trained or untrained, has a usable span of recognition of over 2.5 words.[1] Recent research, using computers, shows that good readers take in an average of about ten usable *letters* per fixation: four letters to the left of the center of fixation and about five or six letters to the right of the center of fixation.[2] Thus, a reader may take in less than one long word, such as *informational*; or one complete word, such as *basketball*; or more than one word, such as *high grade*.

These facts indicate that only a most unusual person can see 10 words per second (2.5 words per fixation × 4 fixations per second). So, in sixty seconds it is arithmetically possible for the eye to take in 600 words. (And this calculation does not include the time needed to return the eyes to the beginning of each line and to turn pages.)

There is no evidence that anyone's eyes can see a whole line of type "at a glance." So any advice to run your eyes down the middle of a page or column, to speed-read the page, is nonsense. All you'll get is a word or two from each line—a handful of scrambled words.

Dr. Richard Feinberg[3] reported that when a reader focuses on a word, "only four to five letters immediately around the fixation point are seen with 100 percent acuity" (sharpness). The letters of words half an inch from the point of fixation are seen with only 40 percent acuity, and those one inch from the point of fixation are seen with only 26 percent acuity. If the reader has less than normal vision, the fall-off in acuity is even more pronounced.

[1]Stanford E. Taylor, "Eye Movement in Reading: Facts and Fallacies," *American Educational Research Journal* 2, No. 4 (November 1965), 187–202.

[2]Keith Rayner, "The Perceptual Span and Peripheral Cues in Reading," *Cognitive Psychology* 7 (1975), 65–81.

[3]Richard Feinberg, "A Study of Some Aspects of Peripheral Visual Acuity," *American Journal of Optometry and Archives of American Academy of Optometry*, 26 (February-March 1949), 1–23.

An Experiment with Eye Movements

Here's how to find out how the eyes work (move) during reading. Use any page of print. (I often use the text shown in Figure 18.1, mimeographed on a half sheet of paper.) Punch a hole near the center of the page, as at the dot in Figure 18.1. Hold the page close to your own eye, with the printed side facing toward another person (the reader). As the reader silently reads the printed matter, watch his or her eyes through the peephole. You will immediately notice that the reader's eyes *do not* flow over the lines of print in a smooth, gliding motion. Instead, the eyes seem to jerk their way across the page, alternating fast forward movements with momentary pauses, much like a typewriter carriage. The pauses are absolutely necessary, for they allow the eyes to focus upon the type, to get a clear image of it. When the eyes are in motion, they record nothing but a blur on the retinas.

INSTRUCTIONS TO THE READER.   When you read the material, actually slow down your rate so that your partner will be able to count, as well as carefully observe, your eye movements. Don't try to manipulate your eyes in some unnatural way, such as trying to focus on an entire line in one fixation; it won't work.

CALCULATIONS.   You can make a rough calculation of the number of words perceived by the eye by dividing the number of eye pauses into the total

Figure 18.1 The Peep-Sight Experiment. See the text discussion on this page for instructions.

A knowledge of words, what they are and how they function, is the first and last essential of all liberal education. As Carlyle says, "If we but think of it, all that a University or final highest school can do for us is still but what the first school began doing — teach us to *read.*" When a student has been trained to make the words of any page of general writing yield their full meaning, he has in his possession the primary instrument of all higher education.

●

In these days when the nation is asking that its schools produce good citizens first and specialists second, there is a marked need for a rich and wide "universal" training of the mind. This book on reading is designed to forward the process by which the whole mind, intellectual and emotional, becomes a more accurate instrument for the reception and transmission of thoughts and sensations. If our system of education does not so train the minds of its students, if it does not teach them to recognize differences, to distinguish shades of meaning, to feel as by intuition not only the hypocrisy of the demagogue and the flattery of the bootlicker but also the depth of a statesman like Lincoln and the insight of a poet like Shakespeare, it fails of its purpose.

Source: From E. A. Tenney and R. C. Wardle, *Intelligent Reading* (New York: Crofts, 1943), preface.

number of words on a line. For example, if the first line contains twelve words and the reader pauses eight times, he or she is taking in roughly one and one-half words per fixation.

HOW MUCH CAN THE MIND SEE?

Our emphasis has been on the question, "How many words can the eye see in one fixation?" A more basic question is, "How does the mind process the words that are imprinted on the retina of the eye?"

Suppose the eye takes in two words at a single fixation. Does the mind impose a meaning upon both words instantly and simultaneously, or must it consider each word in sequence, one at a time, to get at the meaning of each word? If the mind can handle only one word at a time, however swiftly, wouldn't it be easier for the eye to deliver to the mind one word at a time in the first place?

The Limitation of the Mind

Research done at the Massachusetts Institute of Technology, using M.I.T. undergraduates, gives scientific evidence that the mind can attend to only one word at a time. In one part of the study, as reported in *Scientific American*, "The letters of two different six-letter words were presented simultaneously in pairs for brief intervals of time. If the words were *canvas* and *dollar*, for example, *c* and *d* would appear in the first frame, *a* and *o* in the second frame and so on to the end of the words."[4]

You can see how this test was presented by imagining that you yourself were shown the following frames one at a time:

When the subjects were asked to identify either one of the two words, they scored correctly on 57 percent of the trials; but when they were asked to identify both words, the score was only 0.2 percent (one correct report in 420 trials). The researchers concluded that "even the skilled reader has considerable difficulty forming a perception of more than one word at a time."[5]

[4]Paul A. Kolers, "Experiments in Reading," *Scientific American* 227, No. 1 (July 1972), 84–91.

[5]Kolers, "Experiments in Reading."

A reader often has the impression that he or she is seeing more than one word at a fixation because the eye is moving rapidly from left to right, taking in words in rapid sequence. It is almost like watching a movie. Although each film frame is a still picture, we "see" motion and action when the film is projected at a rate of twenty-four frames per second. Similarly, words projected on the brain at the rate of seven or eight words per second give us the impression of living, moving ideas. Nevertheless, the brain is "viewing" only one word at a time.

Speed Reading and Remembering

A final objection to speed reading is that it does not give the mind time to consolidate new information.[6] Even if the eye were able to take in several thousand words a minute (impossible) and the brain were able to comprehend the meaning of them all (impossible), the mind still would not have time to consolidate the meaning before it was assaulted by the next batch of several thousand words. As you saw in Chapter 5, the brain requires a certain period of time in which to convert a temporary idea to a permanent one.

VOCALIZATION WHILE READING

For many years it has been thought that vocalizing while reading is a bad habit that should be eliminated. There are four types of vocalizers: the person who *whispers* each word aloud; the one who pronounces each word with *lip movements*; the one who moves only the *vocal cords*; and the one who *thinks* the sound of each word. Those who want to eliminate vocalization claim that vocalizing slows down reading speed. This claim is probably true. However, the assumption that vocalization can and should be eliminated is highly questionable because there is no research to support it. On the contrary, there is strong evidence that vocalization of one kind or another is an essential part of all reading.

A Practical Experiment

Perhaps you don't believe that subvocalization (silent pronunciation) takes place in all readers to some extent, and are not sure what it means. Silent pronunciation is not necessarily the syllable-by-syllable pronunci-

---

[6]R. S. Woodworth and H. Schlosberg, *Experimental Psychology* (New York: Holt, 1954), p. 773.

ation of oral reading. Rather, when subvocalization takes place, the sound of the word is heard by the "inner ear" instantly and whole.

Here are two two-line bits of poetry; see if you can read them by sight alone:

> *Beside the lake, beneath the trees*
> *Fluttering and dancing in the breeze.*

> *'Twas too much heart to hide behind a cough*
> *All heard the icy snap of the wintered bough.*

Did both rhyme for you? The first two lines are a voice rhyme from Wordsworth's "The Daffodils." They will rhyme only if the words are vocalized, because *trees* and *breeze* do not rhyme for the eye. The second bit of poetry will not rhyme if the words are vocalized, because then the mind recognizes the different sounds of *cough* and *bough*. (The second two lines are an example of an eye rhyme; it rhymes only to the eye, and only because the rhyming words have the same ending.) Thus, if the first two lines rhymed for you but the second two lines didn't, then you subvocalized as you read them. Actually, we all subvocalize as we read; we must, in order to comprehend.

What Does Research Say?

Robert A. Hall, Jr., an internationally known linguist, has this to say about vocalization, or inner speech:

> *It is commonly thought that we can read and write in complete silence, without any speech taking place. True, many people learn to suppress the movements of their organs of speech when they read, so that no sound comes forth; but nevertheless, inside the brain, the impulses for speech are still being sent forth through the nerves, and only the actualization of these impulses is being inhibited on the muscular level, as has been shown by numerous experiments. No act of reading takes place without a certain amount of subvocalization, as this kind of "silent speech" is called, and we normally subvocalize, when we write, also. Many slow readers retain the habit of reading out loud, or at least partially moving their lips as they read; fast readers learn to skip from one key point to another, and to guess at what must lie in between. The good rapid reader knows the subject-matter well enough to guess intelligently; the poor reader does not know how to choose the high spots or guess what lies between them. As the rate of reading increases, the actual muscular movements of pronunciation are reduced; but, just as soon as the going gets difficult, the rate of reading slows down and the muscular movements of pronunciation increase again, even with skilled rapid readers.*
>
> *From these considerations, it is evident that the activities of speak-*

ing and reading cannot be separated. Curiously enough, literary scholars are especially under the delusion that it is possible to study "written language" in isolation, without regard to the language as it is spoken; this is because they do not realize the extent to which, as we have just pointed out, all reading and writing necessarily involve an act of speech on the part of both writer and reader.[7]

Ake Edfeldt, of the University of Stockholm Institute of Reading Research, has studied vocalization with a team of medical doctors who used electrodes to detect movement in the lips, tongues, and vocal cords of volunteer readers. After exhaustive medical tests, Edfeldt concluded:

> *On the basis of the present experimental results, earlier theories concerning silent speech in reading may be judged. These theories often appear to have been constructed afterwards, in order to justify some already adopted form of remedial reading. In opposition to most of these theories, we wish to claim that silent speech occurs in the reading of all persons.*
>
> *In any case, it seems quite clear that all kinds of training aimed at removing silent speech should be discarded.*[8]

Decades ago, E. L. Thorndike said that "reading is thinking." And psychologists agree that thinking is silent speech. So if reading is thinking, and thinking is silent speech, then reading must also be silent speech. It seems that if we spend our time and energy trying to knock out vocalization, we are in fact trying to knock out comprehension. Vocalization cannot and should not be eliminated, because it is part of the reading process.

READING FASTER— THE NATURAL WAY

Speed-reading methods cannot be effective if they interfere with natural processes, or if they require that we read in a way that isn't natural to us. For example, vocalization is a natural and necessary function; methods that attempt to eliminate vocalization so as to increase reading speed cannot succeed. Methods that impose an artificial eye-fixation scheme must likewise fail.

The only effective way to increase your reading speed is to do so naturally—to do exactly what you are doing but do more of it or do it faster. The method described in this section will help you read faster naturally.

[7]Robert A. Hall, Jr., *New Ways to Learn a Foreign Language* (New York: Bantam, 1966), pp. 28–29.

[8]Åke W. Edfeldt, *Silent Speed and Silent Reading* (Chicago: The University of Chicago Press, 1960), p. 154.

However, you must realize that it is *not* meant for textbook reading, where you must read (and often re-read) slowly, to get the full meaning of each sentence and paragraph. Use the method to increase the speed at which you read novels, magazines, journals, and newspapers. To read these materials at the slow textbook rate is a waste of your time; in such cases, the mind is eager to sprint, but the textbook reading habit limits it to a plodding pace.

Setting the Stage for Faster Reading

Here are five things to do or to keep in mind as you practice faster reading. They are fairly general in nature, but they are important to the method. In the next subsection you will see, step by step, how to practice faster reading to increase your reading speed.

ESTABLISH A BASE. Before you begin to read a new book, take a few minutes to think about its title and to look through the table of contents. Extract as much meaning as possible from both. For example, if your book were *The Adventures of Sherlock Holmes,* you would know that you had a handful of absorbing detective stories to read. Knowing the nature of the book will create a *mental set* highly favorable to reading; it will be derived from the two powerful forces of anticipation and concentration.

As you looked through the table of contents, your eyes might stop at "The Five Orange Pips." You would wonder to yourself, "Pips? I guess that's the British word for seeds. What else could it mean relative to oranges? Not the skin, of course. It must be the seeds." With pips and seeds on your mind, you would already be concentrating without having read a single word of the story. You would be working up a natural and powerful head of steam—a solid base from which to begin your reading.

BE FLEXIBLE. Match your reading speed to the material you are reading. If the book begins with introductory, "warm-up" material, move through it fast. But slow down a bit when you come to the first solid paragraph. You need to grab and hold in mind such items as names, places, and circumstances, for these are the magnetic centers around which ideas and details will cluster as you sprint through the pages. When the going gets easier, speed up again. As you read, be continually alert to slow down at paragraphs that are full of ideas and to speed up when you can. There is no reason to expect—or try—to read at a constant rate.

FOLLOW IDEAS, NOT WORDS. Don't try to remember words. Simply use the words to visualize the ideas, facts, and actions that the author is presenting. And once you have done so, let the words drop out of your mind.

Retain only the development of the story, or the important ideas and facts.

IGNORE YOUR EYE FIXATIONS.   Don't think about what your eyes are doing, for that will break both your reading rhythm and your concentration. The eye fixations will take care of themselves easily and naturally as you move along at your own pace. You don't need to think about eye fixations any more than you need to think about moving your feet while you walk. The feet take care of themselves, and so do the eyes.

ENJOY THE CONCLUDING PARAGRAPH.   Slow down for the last paragraph, and savor it. You will enjoy seeing how the author connects the various facts or events in an article, or the various parts of a short story or novel.

   This whole process—of establishing a base, being flexible in reading speed, following ideas, ignoring eye movements, and enjoying the conclusion—you see, not only leads to faster reading, but to intelligent reading as well.

How to Practice Faster Reading

For your first book, choose some novel that you've wanted to read but never had time for. The novel you use to practice reading faster should be on the light side; it is difficult enough to increase your reading speed without struggling at the same time with a tough book.

   When you first begin practicing, don't push yourself too fast. Otherwise, you'll find that your mind is unable to follow the story and tends to wander; this can create the bad habit of not concentrating. Read faster than you usually do, but slow enough so you can follow and *enjoy* the story. Remember, you want to build a good habit that has a future.

   Do not, at any time, attempt to calculate your words-per-minute reading speed. If you do, speed for speed's sake will become your goal, rather than speed for efficient comprehension. You must avoid this misplaced emphasis.

THE FIRST BOOK.   Push yourself to read the first book much faster than you've read before (but, again, at a pace at which you can follow the development of the story). Read at this fast pace for ten full minutes. Then read for ten minutes at a slightly slower pace—just to catch your breath, so to speak. Finally, read for another ten minutes at your fast pace.

   This program will give you thirty minutes of practice, and that's enough for one day. Put the book aside, to be used only to practice faster reading. Practice every other day in this way, until you have finished the book.

THE SECOND THROUGH FIFTH BOOKS. As with your first book, practice faster reading every other day with your second through fifth books. Begin with a fast-reading session, follow that with a moderate-reading session, and end the practice with another fast-reading session. Figure 18.2 shows how long each of these sessions should be, for each book. In the fast-reading sessions, remember to read as fast as you can without losing your grasp of the story.

THE SIXTH BOOK AND BEYOND. After your fifth practice book, you've served your apprenticeship. Henceforth, read as fast as you can with comprehension, remembering to be flexible in these ways. First, when you begin to lose track of the development of a story, slow down until you pick up the track; then continue at high speed. Second, if you get tired but want to continue reading, slow down slightly for a while; later, if you feel like speeding up, do so gradually.

You must never continue to push for speed when you feel even a bit tired; if you do, you will begin to destroy the skill that you have developed through patient practice. And, if you start losing interest in a book, don't feel obliged to read it to the end. Put it aside, and pick up another book that seems more interesting.

Figure 18.2 Durations of Reading Sessions for Practice Books One Through Five

Book 1	Reading speed	No. of minutes
	Fast	10
	Moderate	10
	Fast	10
Book 2	Reading speed	No. of minutes
	Fast	15
	Moderate	10
	Fast	15
Book 3	Reading speed	No. of minutes
	Fast	20
	Moderate	10
	Fast	20
Book 4	Reading speed	No. of minutes
	Fast	25
	Moderate	10
	Fast	25
Book 5	Reading speed	No. of minutes
	Fast	30
	Moderate	10
	Fast	30

CARNEGIE LIBRARY
LIVINGSTONE COLLEGE
SALISBURY, NC 28144

SUMMARY

How does purpose affect reading?	Purpose determines how much time you'll spend in reading almost anything. For example, looking over a textbook chapter to gain familiarity before listening to a classroom lecture might take no more than half an hour; but to read the same chapter in preparation for a quiz, three or four hours might be necessary.
If 600-words-per-minute is the maximum possible reading rate, how have claims for rates of thousands of words per minute persisted?	Claims is all they are. No so-called speed reader has yet submitted to an impartial test. Any claim of over 600 words per minute would necessitate the skipping of many words. You, too, could make about four or five fixations on a page, turn it, and repeat this on page after page. After a minute of glancing and turning, you'd end up with a count of thousands of words per minute, but you would have understood nothing.
Are eye pauses and subvocalization really necessary during reading?	According to all the research and researchers, they are absolutely necessary. The pauses allow your eyes to focus on the words, and the subvocalization is required for comprehension.
Should we use your faster reading method on textbooks?	No, never! Textbooks are packed too full of ideas and facts for fast reading with complete comprehension. It would be a waste of time, for you would understand little and remember almost nothing. Use the method on the easier novels that you read for pleasure, as well as for magazines, newspapers, and journals.
What do you mean by the "natural way" to read faster?	I mean that you practice reading faster using the same techniques that you use naturally, but push yourself to higher and higher speeds. This method includes none of the artificial techniques advocated for so-called "speed-reading systems," for such techniques will only interfere with your natural development.

HAVE YOU MISSED SOMETHING?

1. **SENTENCE-COMPLETION.** Complete the following sentences with one of the three words listed below each sentence.

   a. For most students, improved reading means improved _____.

   comprehension   vision   speed

   b. The best way to read faster is _____.

   technically   naturally   artificially

2. **MATCHING.** In each blank space in the left column, write the number preceding the phrase in the right column that matches the left item best.

   _____ a. Eye movement   1. Processes words one at a time
                                   2. Blurs words on a page
   _____ b. Fixations   3. Always accompanies reading
   _____ c. Subvocalization   4. Should not be applied to textbooks
                                   5. Allow the eyes to focus
   _____ d. The mind

   _____ e. Faster reading

3. **TRUE-FALSE.** Write *T* beside the *true* statements and *F* beside the *false* statements that follow.

   _____ a. Moving your lips when you read indicates a lack of intelligence.

   _____ b. You need not read for comprehension when you practice faster reading.

   _____ c. Your eyes can see only about ten printed letters at one time.

   _____ d. Your eyes can see clearly only when they are not moving.

   _____ e. You should practice faster reading every day.

   _____ f. You should slow your reading down when you get tired.

4. **MULTIPLE-CHOICE.** Choose the word that completes the following sentence most accurately, and circle the letter that precedes it.

   Reading for understanding does not require

   a. speed.
   b. fixations.
   c. thinking.
   d. subvocalization.

There is an art of reading.
—ISAAC D'ISRAELI

19

Ten More Techniques for Improving Your Reading

Just as there's more than one way to skin a cat, there's more than one way to improve your reading. This chapter features ten of the best . . .

- The intonation way
- The vocabulary way
- The background way
- Gibbon's way
- The paragraph way
- The organizational-pattern way
- The page-at-a-time way
- Daniel Webster's way
- The pivotal-words way

and

- The skimming way

R EADING CANNOT BE IMPROVED through mechanical techniques like turning pages faster or moving the eyes in some artificial pattern. There is no magic in such concoctions. The magic comes only when you work at your reading skills.

Most methods for improvement suggested in this chapter require hard work, but the rewards are great. A few of them require only the willingness to try a new way of using old knowledge, and here, too, the rewards can be great. But it's up to you to try them.

THE INTONATION WAY

As you saw in Chapter 18, vocalization is part of the process of reading and comprehending. You can use it to read faster with a high degree of understanding.

The most efficient use of vocalization is through *intonation*, which is the rise and fall of the voice in pronouncing a sentence. In other words, reading with intonation means reading with expression. Intonation provides a natural means for combining individual words into meaningful mental "bites."

To use this system, let your eyes move rapidly across the page as usual. You need not make any sound, but let your mind swing along each line with an intonational rhythm that can be heard by the "inner ear." That is, read with expression. In doing so, you will be replacing the important *rhythm, stress, emphasis,* and *pauses* that were taken out when the words were put into written form.

The passage in Figure 19.1 has been divided into thought units according to my own intonation. The clusters of words, as I would group them, are separated by slash marks. (Of course, different readers would group these words into different clusters, depending on their individual intonation.) Read the passage silently, letting your eyes move rapidly over the lines and permitting your "inner voice" to cluster the words

Figure 19.1 Reading by Word Clusters: The Intonation Way

Athens and Sparta / were both Greek cities / and their people / spoke a common language. / In every other respect / they were different. / Athens rose high from the plain. / It was a city / exposed to the fresh breezes / from the sea, / willing to look / at the world / with the eyes / of a happy child. / Sparta, / on the other hand, / was built / at the bottom / of a deep valley, / and used the surrounding mountains / as a barrier / against foreign thought. / Athens / was a city of busy trade. / Sparta / was an armed camp. /

Source: From *The Story of Mankind* by Henry B. van Loon and Gerard W. van Loon. Reprinted by permission of Liveright. Copyright © 1972 by Henry B. van Loon and Gerard W. van Loon.

through intonation. You will probably notice how rapidly your eyes move and how easy it is to comprehend the meaning when you read with intonation.

To make silent intonation a regular habit, start by reading aloud in the privacy of your room. Spend ten or fifteen minutes on one chapter from a novel. Read it with exaggerated expression, as if you were reading a part in a dramatic play. This will establish your own speech patterns in your mind, so that you will "hear" them more readily when you read silently.

THE VOCABULARY WAY

There is probably no surer or sounder way to improve your reading permanently than by building a strong, precise vocabulary. In a precise vocabulary, every word is learned as a concept. You know its ancestry, its principal definition as well as several secondary ones, its synonyms and the subtle differences among them, and its antonyms. Then, when you encounter it in your reading, this vast store of knowledge will flash before you, illuminating the sentence, the paragraph, and the idea the author is trying to convey. If you have not yet read Part V on building a precise vocabulary, this would be a good time to do so.

THE BACKGROUND WAY

You can improve your reading tremendously by reading good books. The first reason for this is that you'll be getting a lot of practice. Even more important, you'll be storing up a stock of concepts, ideas, events, and names that will lend meaning to your later reading. This kind of information is used surprisingly often.

David Ausubel, an outstanding psychologist, says that the most crucial prerequisite for learning is your already established *background of knowledge.* Ausubel means that if you are to understand what you read, then you must interpret it in light of knowledge (the background) you already have. A background is not something you are born with. You accumulate one through both direct and vicarious experiences. The vicarious experiences, of course, are those you acquire by listening, seeing films, and reading books.

Authors often make allusions to famous books, famous people, or well-known events. In many cases you can miss these references and still understand the story. In some instances, however, an allusion will be crucial, and you will have to search for its meaning if it is not in your background. To make my point, here's a short passage by Robert Louis Stevenson:

> *And not long ago I was able to lay by my lantern in content, for I found the honest man.*

This sentence is composed of twenty simple words, many consisting of only two and three letters. It contains one word that is crucial to the understanding of the sentence. As an experiment, go back and see if you can pick it out before you read on.

The two words that are most often chosen from this sentence are *honest* and *content*. Admittedly, both are fine words and qualities, but neither is the crucial word. That word is *lantern*. It is, however, no ordinary lantern to which Stevenson refers, but one that is associated with a real person in history. Whose lantern? The lantern of Diogenes. Diogenes was a fourth century B.C. Greek cynic and critic who walked the streets of Athens during the daytime, holding a lighted lantern, peering into the faces of passersby, and saying that he was looking for the honest man. He was dramatizing the idea that it was difficult to find an honest man, even with a lighted lantern in the daytime.

Obviously, without knowing the story of Diogenes you cannot fully understand Stevenson's line. And that is only one example from millions. You cannot take every fact, myth, story, and poem into your background. But you can, through your reading, increase the size of your background and, thus, the effectiveness of your reading. In other words, you can improve your reading by reading.

Read the *great* books, for it is in these books that the wisdom of the ages is passed on to posterity. These books will give you the chance to "talk" with princes, kings, philosophers, travelers, playwrights, scientists, artists, and novelists. Begin with the books and subjects that interest you, and don't worry about having only narrow interests. Once you begin reading, your interests will widen naturally.

Here are some books that will guide you in selecting books to read. They not only tell you about books but also suggest titles, lists, and plans.

Dickinson, Asa D., *The World's Best Books* (Bronx, N.Y.: Wilson, 1953).

Downs, Robert B., *Books That Changed America* (New York: Macmillan, 1970). A paperback edition is published by New American Library.

Downs, Robert B., *Books That Changed The World* (New York: New American Library, 1971). Paperback.

Downs, Robert B., *Famous American Books* (New York: McGraw-Hill, 1971). Paperback.

Downs, Robert B., *Famous Books: Great Writings in the History of Civilization* (Totowa, N.J.: Littlefield, Adams, 1975).

Downs, Robert B., *Books That Changed The South* (Totowa, N.J.: Littlefield, Adams, 1977). Paperback.

Fadiman, Clifton, *Reading I've Liked* (New York: Simon and Schuster, 1958). Paperback.

Fadiman, Clifton, *The Lifetime Reading Plan* (New York: Crowell, 1978). Distributed by Harper & Row.

Pauk, Walter, *Reading for Success in College, a Student's Guide to Recommended Books for College Background Reading and a Practical Handbook for Developing College Study Skills* (Clearwater, Fla.: Campbell Publishers, 1968). Paperback.

Weber, J. Sherwood, *Good Reading: A Guide for Serious Readers* (New York: New American Library, 1980). Paperback. A guide to the world's best books, prepared by the Committee on College Reading.

GIBBON'S WAY: GREAT RECALL

The great English historian Edward Gibbon (1737–1794), author of *Decline and Fall of the Roman Empire*, made constant use of the "great recall" technique. This is simply an organized and rather intense use of one's general background.

Before starting to read a new book, or before starting to write on any subject, Gibbon would spend hours alone in his study, or take a long walk alone to recall everything that he knew about the subject. As he pondered some major idea, he was continually surprised how many other ideas and fragments of ideas he would dredge up.

Gibbon's system was highly successful because he had some natural learning principles on his side:

1. His old ideas were brought to the forefront of his mind, ready for use.
2. His old ideas could act as magnetic centers for new ideas and new information.
3. This type of great recall promotes concentration.

THE PARAGRAPH WAY

You can improve your comprehension by stopping at the end of each textbook paragraph, to summarize and condense it to a single sentence. To summarize and condense, you must understand the functions of the three main types of sentences: the *topic* or controlling-idea sentence, the *supporting* sentence, and the *concluding* sentence.

The *topic* sentence obviously announces the topic (or the portion of the topic) to be dealt with in the paragraph. Although the topic sentence may appear anywhere in the paragraph, it is usually first—and for a very good reason. This sentence provides the focus for the writer while writing and for the reader in reading. When you find the topic sentence, be sure to underline it so that it will stand out not only *now*, but also *later* when you review.

The bulk of an expository paragraph is made up of *supporting* sentences, which help to explain or prove the main topic. These sentences present facts, reasons, examples, definitions, comparisons, contrasts, and other pertinent details. They are most important, because it's the supporting sentences that sell the ideas.

The last sentence of a textbook paragraph is likely to be a *concluding* sentence. It is used to sum up a discussion, to emphasize a point, or to restate all or part of the topic sentence so as to bring the paragraph to a close.

Figure 19.2 shows these three types of sentences in an actual paragraph.

Of course, the paragraphs you'll be reading will be part of some longer piece of writing—a textbook chapter, a section of a chapter, or a newspaper or magazine article. Besides the expository paragraphs, in which new information is presented and discussed, these longer writings contain three types of paragraphs:

1. *Introductory paragraphs.* These paragraphs tell you, in advance, such things as (1) the main idea of the chapter or section; (2) the extent or limits of the coverage; (3) how the topic is developed; and (4) the writer's attitude toward the topic.

Figure 19.2 The Three Elements of an Expository Paragraph

Topic sentence ⟶ Henry Ford was probably the first man to have his car stolen. Ford, as you may know, developed the automobile in the United States. Back when his motorcar was still being perfected, he would often take it out for a spin. The "horseless carriage" was sure to attract a lot of attention. This was fine with Ford, as long as he was driving. But if he parked the car he was taking a risk. As soon as the inventor was out of sight, some curious person would try to escape with his vehicle. Luckily, the car caused such a commotion that it was easy to locate the thief. Even so, Henry Ford was annoyed. Finally, he got into the habit of linking his parked car to a lamp post with a chain.

Supporting sentences {

Concluding ⟶ sentence

2. *Transitional paragraphs.* Such paragraphs are usually short; their sole function is to tie together what you have read so far and what is to come—to set the stage for succeeding paragraphs.

3. *Summarizing paragraphs.* These paragraphs are used to restate briefly the main ideas of the chapter or section. The writer may also draw some conclusion from these ideas, based on the evidence in the chapter, or speculate on the basis of that evidence.

All three types should *alert* you: the introductory paragraph of things to come; the transitional paragraph of a new topic; and the summarizing paragraph of main ideas that you should have gotten.

THE ORGANIZATIONAL-PATTERN WAY

The secret of good reading is *thinking.* You must think the words you see, and give thought to the ideas they generate. This sounds simple, but it isn't. The problem is that our thoughts tend to wander as we read. When we are thinking about something else, we cannot think about what we are reading.

One way to keep your mind on your reading is to recognize and keep yourself aware of the *organizational pattern* that the author is using. Then you will *think with the author* as you read. For example, suppose you recognize that a paragraph you're reading is organized according to a chronological pattern. Then you would say to yourself, "Yes, I see what she's doing. She's describing the major events of the Great Depression as they happened, year by year." As you followed the pattern, your mind would stay on your reading and you would be thinking about it.

Here are brief descriptions of the most commonly used organizational patterns. You should have no trouble recognizing them when you encounter them in your reading.

1. *The time or chronological pattern.* Events are presented in the chronological order in which they happened. This pattern can be recognized quickly from the author's use of dates and of such phrases as, *in previous years, the next day,* and *two years later,* which denote the passage of time.

2. *The process pattern.* Steps or events are presented in an orderly sequence that leads to a desired situation or product. A recipe and the instructions for assembling a bicycle provide examples of process patterns. They often include such words as, *first, after this, then, next,* and *finally.*

3. *The place or spatial pattern.* Items are presented or discussed on the basis of their locations or their arrangement relative to each other. For example, an author might use this pattern to describe the geographical features of the United States, say from the West Coast to the East

Coast. (In such a case, this pattern is often called the *geographical pattern*. It is also called the *topical pattern* when it is used to describe the organization of a corporation along the lines of purchasing, manufacturing, sales, and so forth.) The progression from item to item is usually orderly and easy to follow: from left to right, from high to low, from north to south, or whatever.

4. *The increasing-importance pattern.* In this pattern, the most important or most dramatic item in a series is placed at the end. Each succeeding item is more important than the previous one, so a crescendo effect is created. (Thus, this pattern is often called the *climactic-order pattern.*)

5. *The decreasing-importance pattern.* In this pattern, the most important or most dramatic item in a series is placed at the very beginning. Such an organization grabs the reader's interest immediately, so there is a good chance he or she will stay with the writing all the way through.

6. *The cause-effect pattern.* This exceedingly important general pattern has such variations as the *problem-cause-solution* pattern and the *problem-effect-solution* pattern. Whatever the combination, you should be able to identify the various parts of the pattern—the problem, cause, effects, and solution—and think along with the author as you both move from one part to the next.

7. *The compare or contrast pattern.* Writers usually *compare* things, events, or people when they emphasize similarities, but *contrast* them when differences are emphasized. Either individual characteristics may be compared or contrasted, one at a time, or lists of characteristics may be discussed as a group. In either case, the pattern can be recognized from the various similarities or differences and from such words used as *similarly, likewise, conversely,* and *on the other hand.*

THE PAGE-AT-A-TIME WAY

Thomas Babington Macaulay (1800–1859) was an English statesman, historian, essayist, and poet. At the time it was published, his greatest work, *The History of England,* outsold all other books except the Bible.

Macaulay began reading adult books at the age of three. But after consuming shelf after shelf of books, he suddenly realized that he wasn't gaining much knowledge for all his effort. He understood every word of what he read and seemed to comprehend what the writer was saying, but later he could *not* summarize the ideas presented or even describe, in general terms, what the writer had written.

He described his solution to this problem as follows:

> At the foot of every page I read I stopped and obliged myself to give an account of what I had read on that page. At first I had to read it three

or four times before I got my mind firmly fixed. But I compelled myself to comply with the plan, until now, after I have read a book through once, I can almost recite it from the beginning to the end.

There's something very basic, honest, and refreshing in the Macaulay way. There are no complicated formulas to follow. You simply stop at the bottom of a page and ask yourself, "In brief, what did the writer say on this page?"

This technique will do for you what it did for Lord Macaulay. It will make you concentrate. It will also teach you to think continually while you read. And every time you pause for a brief recall, your memory will be getting stronger.

DANIEL WEBSTER'S WAY

Daniel Webster had his own special technique for building concentration: Before reading a book, he would look at the table of contents, read the preface, and turn some of the pages. Then he would make lists of (1) questions that he expected would be answered in the book; (2) the knowledge he expected to gain from his reading; and (3) where it would take him. These three lists guided him through the book; his attention and concentration were intense.

THE PIVOTAL-WORDS WAY

No words are so helpful while you read as the prepositions and conjunctions that guide your mind to and through the author's ideas. A word like *furthermore* says, "Keep going!" *However* says, "Easy!" Master the words and phrases listed below, and you will almost immediately become a better reader.

> *Additive words.* These say, "Here's more of the same coming up. It's just as important as what we have already said."

also	further	moreover
and	furthermore	too
besides	in addition	

> *Equivalent words.* These say, "Both what I have just said and this too."

as well as	equally important	similarly
at the same time	likewise	

Amplification words. With these, the author is saying, "I want to be sure that you understand my idea; so here's a specific instance."

as	in fact	such as
for example (e.g.)	like	that is
for instance	specifically	to illustrate

Alternative words. These point up, "Sometimes there is a choice; at other times there isn't."

either/or	other than	otherwise
neither/nor		

Repetitive words. These say, "I said it once, but I'm going to say it again in case you missed it the first time."

again	in other words	that is (i.e.)
to repeat		

Contrast and change words. "So far I've given you only one side of the story; now let's take a look at the other side."

but	instead of	regardless
conversely	on the contrary	still
despite	on the other hand	though
even though	nevertheless	whereas
however	notwithstanding	yet
in spite of	rather than	

Cause-and-effect words. "All this has happened; now I'll tell you why."

accordingly	for this reason	then
as a result	hence	therefore
because	since	thus
consequently	so	

Qualifying words. These say, "Here is what we can expect; these are the conditions we are working under."

although	providing	whenever
if	unless	

Concession words. These say, "Okay! We agree on this much."

accepting the data	granted that	of course
even though		

Emphasizing words. These say, "Wake up and take notice!"

above all   indeed   more important

Order words. With these, the author is saying, "You keep your mind
on reading; I'll keep the numbers straight."

finally	last	second
first	next	then

Time words. "Let's keep the record straight on who said what and
especially when."

afterwards	meanwhile	subsequently
at the same time	next	then
before	now	ultimately
formerly	presently	until
later	previously	while

Summarizing words. These say, "We've said many things so far. Let's
stop here and pull them together."

briefly	in brief	to summarize
for these reasons	in conclusion	to sum up

THE SKIMMING WAY

Both students and business executives report that the workhorse of reading is skimming. Covering many speeds and uses, skimming can range
from just fast reading to *searching,* which could hardly be classified as
reading. So, whether to use rapid reading or searching—or anything in
between—depends on your *purpose.* Tailor skimming to your purpose,
otherwise you'll waste time.

Here are five purposes for skimming and the techniques for each.

Searching for a Needle in a Haystack

If you want to find specific information (name, date, word, or phrase) in
a textbook or article, the *searching* method of skimming may be used because recognition, not comprehension, will give you the answer. To ensure that your eyes do not overlook the word or fact you seek, concentrate on it, keeping it in mind as your eyes run over the pages. This
concentration will trigger your mind to recognize it out of the sea of
words.

Once the specific word or fact is located, it is wise to pause and read at a normal rate the sentence or paragraph surrounding it to make sure, through context, that you have found what you were looking for.

When using the searching technique, if your time is short, resist the temptation to read the whole article. What you may really be doing, subconsciously, is putting off studying. But, if you do have time, follow your curiosity and finish that article. It may not help you on the next exam, but the knowledge gained will give you an edge and contribute to your general wisdom.

Looking for Clues

When you are seeking specific information but do not know in what words the information may appear, you must use a slower searching method. In this case, you won't be able to anticipate the exact words, so you must be alert for *clues*, which can appear in various forms.

In this kind of searching, you will have to infer the answer. For example, I remember a question regarding the birthplace of Paul Bunyan. The answer is Canada, yet nowhere in the article did the word *Canada* appear. The answer had to be inferred from a sentence which stated that Paul Bunyan was born at the headwaters of the St. Lawrence River. Since I knew—or could check on a map—that the headwaters are in Canada, I had found the answer. When you are looking for clues, try to guess the form in which the information might appear. In the above example, I looked for a place name in connection with Bunyan's name.

When you believe you have found the information you want, go back and read the paragraph to make sure, from context, that this is exactly what you seek.

Getting the Gist

Sometimes skimming may be used to *get the gist* of a book or article. You can use this technique to find out whether a book pertains to the topic you are working on. To get the gist, read both introduction and summary rapidly, as well as those paragraphs with topic sentences indicating that they contain important data.

This skimming method can help when you have a term paper to write. After you have looked through the card catalogue, and made a list of books that seem related to your topic, get the books and look through them to eliminate those that are not pertinent and to keep those that are. Obviously, you would waste time and energy if you attempted to read all the books on your list. To get the main idea of each book, look at the table of contents, or select a chapter with a title related to your topic and skim it for its outstanding ideas.

Because this method of skimming involves reading paragraphs, avoid the temptation to forget your purpose—surveying the book. Your primary goal is writing that term paper.

Overviewing a Textbook Chapter

One important use of skimming has been discussed in Chapter 7: surveying or getting an *overview of a textbook chapter* before reading it thoroughly. Overviewing may be done to attain various degrees of comprehension. In most cases this type of skimming calls for understanding captions, headings, subheadings, and portions of paragraphs well enough to locate key concepts in the chapter. Such skimming puts you in a position to see the relative importance of each part to the whole.

Skimming to Review

Skimming also can be used *to review* for an examination or for a recitation. After skimming chapters that you have previously read, studied, and noted, for effective study you should pause from time to time and try to recite the main concepts in each chapter, or to summarize the chapter.

After having finished a textbook chapter, always overview to understand the chapter as a whole, like a finished jig-saw puzzle.

For skimming to become an efficient tool, you need practice, remembering to use the method best suited to your purpose. Skimming can save you time with your academic work as well as in your future professional work.

SUMMARY

How can anyone use intonation silently?

Intonation in reading means saying the words silently—but saying them with expression or rhythm, not in a monotone. Just a little practice reading aloud will show you how it works. Reading with intonation requires close attention that will get you to concentrate. The end result will be high comprehension plus speed.

Why is a background of information important in reading?

Many words have meanings beyond their definitions, meanings that are derived from their use in various writings. Unless you are aware of these meanings, you will fail to understand them when you encounter such words. Moreover, even dictionary meanings are expanded and extended through use. The larger your background of information, the more of these meanings you will understand as you read.

Won't pausing to summarize each paragraph slow us down?

Of course it will; but what's the sense in moving through a whole chapter without learning or remembering anything? Reading a textbook chapter straight through will yield almost no long-term remembering, so you'll have to go back and read it again anyway. Overall, you'll save time by pausing to summarize—to make sure you understand each paragraph.

How does recognizing the organizational pattern help comprehension?

Once you recognize a familiar pattern, you know what's going on. You become part of the process. You therefore concentrate better, comprehending and absorbing the facts and ideas because you know exactly how they are related and why the author has presented them in a particular sequence.

How does the paragraph way differ from the page-at-a-time way?

The idea in both systems is to pause, think, and summarize what you have read. Do so paragraph by paragraph when the writing is packed with facts; page by page, when the material is written in a more leisurely narrative style.

How does knowing pivotal words help reading?

These words direct your reading and your thinking. They also point to ideas, modify or connect ideas, and even reverse ideas in midsentence. If you truly know the meanings of the pivotal words, you will understand almost anything you read.

Why are there various methods of skimming?

The varied methods and speeds in skimming let you tailor the method to fit the job.

What is the one rule for using skimming?

Use skimming as a tool. Determine what the main purpose of your assignment is, and then judge whether skimming can help your purpose.

HAVE YOU MISSED SOMETHING?

1. **SENTENCE-COMPLETION.** Complete the following sentences with one of the three words listed below each sentence.

   a. Edward Gibbon learned new ideas by letting his old ones act as

   _____.

       magnets   examples   summaries

   b. A summary paragraph or sentence usually restates _____.

       references   information   transitions

2. **MATCHING.** In each blank space in the left column, write the number preceding the phrase in the right column that matches the left item best.

   _____ a. Intonation way

   _____ b. Paragraph way

   _____ c. Macaulay

   _____ d. Pivotal words

   _____ e. Webster

   _____ f. Background

   _____ g. Overviewing

   1. Advocate of a "list before you read" technique
   2. Most crucial prerequisite for learning
   3. Involves efficient use of vocalization
   4. Advocate of the "page-at-a-time" way
   5. Involves pauses for summarization
   6. Helps you to understand the chapter as a whole
   7. Direct your thinking as you read

3. **TRUE-FALSE.** Write *T* beside the *true* statements and *F* beside the *false* statements that follow.

   _____ a. You should do all your reading out loud in the intonation method.

   _____ b. A good vocabulary is one of the best tools for effective reading.

   _____ c. Transitional paragraphs help you to follow the writer's train of thought.

   _____ d. Supporting sentences are usually placed in the middle of a paragraph.

_____ e. You will read more effectively if you read great books.

_____ f. You should skim a chapter after you read it.

4. **MULTIPLE-CHOICE.** Choose the phrase that completes the following sentence most accurately, and circle the letter that precedes it.

A description of the events leading up to World War I would probably be organized in the

a. process pattern.
b. compare pattern.
c. increasing-importance pattern.
d. chronological pattern.

PART VII

SPECIAL SKILLS

Nothing has such power to broaden the mind as the ability to investigate systematically.
—MARCUS AURELIUS

20

Researching and Writing Papers

At worst, writing a paper can be a tedious ordeal. At best, it may be an adventure in learning. The difference lies in knowing how to approach your writing assignment—whether you have been asked to write a report, a theme, or a research paper. This chapter tells you how to . . .

- Choose a topic
- Do the research
- Record your information
- Organize the paper
- Do the writing
- Edit your work

and
- Make the final copy

W RITING EVEN A SHORT PAPER can seem to be a tremendous under-
taking. From the time the paper is assigned until the day it is due
(or overdue), it can occupy your mind like no other type of assignment.
But the truth is that writing a paper isn't much more difficult than reading about a subject in detail, taking notes on your reading, organizing
your notes, and reciting them. You should already be doing these things
when you study. The only added step is putting your recitation down on
paper, to communicate it to others. If you take it one step at a time, you
may even find—as many other students have found—that writing papers
can be a most absorbing way to learn about a subject in depth.

WRITING GOOD PAPERS IN COLLEGE

You may be asked to write any of several kinds of papers, depending on
the subject and the instructor's approach.

Theme. Usually fairly short, and based on your own conclusions,
your experience, or your reading.

Report. A factual discussion (usually in one of the sciences) of the
results of a piece of research. The format is usually supplied to you
by the instructor.

Critical essay. Your opinion on a book or other piece of writing, usually assigned in an English or other language course.

Research paper. Of any specific length, but usually at least four
double-spaced typed pages. Based on extensive research of published material on a subject. The topic may be left up to you,
within fairly broad guidelines, or you may be given a specific
assignment.

The most extensive type is the research paper. The other kinds of papers will require less library work and may be handled a little differently.
However, the techniques for writing a research paper, as discussed below,
are applicable to any paper you write.

Most papers are assigned well in advance of the date they're due. If
the assignment is given at the beginning of the term, set up a schedule
on your calendar that allows plenty of time for your research, time to
write several drafts or versions—at least three—and time to make the final copy before the paper is due. *Don't* start the night before.

The length of the paper is given in number of words or number of
double-spaced pages required. The assigned length of the paper is chosen
by the instructor to indicate how deeply you can get into the subject. A
five-hundred-word paper must focus on one specific aspect of a topic,

while two thousand words or ten pages gives you room to cover the topic more broadly. For example, you might use five hundred words to discuss one presidential candidate's stand on the issue of price controls, but ten or more pages to discuss his whole platform and its implications. Try to stay within the given limits, but don't think of them as exact length requirements.

Assignments may be very clearly written and well organized—so that you know precisely what you're expected to write on—or they may be phrased very generally. If you have any doubt about what your instructor expects you to cover in the paper, by all means make an appointment to discuss it with him or her. Feel free to ask for suggestions as to approach and sources of information.

CHOOSING A TOPIC

Finding a topic is often the biggest stumbling block in writing a paper, so it's essential that you know how to choose one easily and efficiently. There are actually three steps in the process of selecting a topic for a research paper. Some or all of them may also apply to other types of papers, depending upon the particular assignment:

1. Choose a subject that interests you.
2. Narrow your subject.
3. Find a focus.

Choose Your Subject

If you are writing a research paper, you will most likely be able to choose a topic from a broad subject area. In that case, choose a subject that you are interested in, or that you can develop an interest in. If it isn't a subject that everyone else is writing on, all the better. If you're not sure about your choice of a subject, do a little preliminary research—in the library—to see what's involved in several subjects before you make your decision. (The use of the library is discussed in the next section.)

Suppose that you are very interested in the medical profession and have decided to write about that. But "medical profession" includes the training of doctors, their career patterns, their patient relations, the best way to build up a practice, foreign-born doctors, the shortage of doctors, and scores of other topics. How can you do justice to all of them? Obviously you cannot. You will have to narrow your subject.

Narrow Your Subject

The most common criticism of research papers is that the topic is too broad. However, the problem lies in knowing when you have narrowed your topic enough. A Cornell professor of English suggests this sure-fire method: Put your subject through three or four significant narrowings, moving from a given category to a class within that category each time. As an example, here is a sample narrowing for a paper of ten to fifteen pages:

General topic:	*The Civil War*
1st narrowing:	The Crucial Battles of the Civil War
2nd narrowing:	The Crucial Battle of Chancellorsville
3rd narrowing:	Lee's Tactics at Chancellorsville
4th narrowing:	"Stonewall" Jackson's Attack at Chancellorsville

Or suppose that after considering many different aspects of the medical profession, you feel that you are most interested in the shortage of doctors. The subject seems to be a natural one, because you immediately begin to speculate about it: Why don't the medical schools accept more medical students? But more students would mean more professors and enlarged facilities. Then why not shorten the number of years of training? All these ideas springing into your mind show that you have a natural interest in the topic; in fact, any of these ideas could be the focus for your paper.

Let us pause at this point to sum up the topics you have considered, and the amount of narrowing that has been done. Here is what the summing up looks like:

General topic:	*The medical profession*
1st narrowing:	The Shortage of Doctors in the U.S.
2nd narrowing:	Overcoming the Doctor Shortage
3rd narrowing: (Alternative)	Overcoming the Doctor Shortage by Accepting More Medical Students
3rd narrowing: (Alternative)	Overcoming the Doctor Shortage by Shortening the Term of Training
3rd narrowing: (Alternative)	Overcoming the Doctor Shortage by Government Subsidies

Since the shortage of medical doctors is a subject of current concern, many articles have been written about it in newspapers, magazines, and journals. Now it is time to go to the library and dig for more ideas in the *Readers' Guide to Periodical Literature.*

You look in the *Readers' Guide* under the caption, *Physicians,* and you find a long list of titles of articles. But there is not even one article on any of the three topics of the third narrowing. After looking through several more volumes of the *Readers' Guide* and finding only one or two titles on each topic, you decide to abandon the three topics because of the lack of material.

Going back to the current volume of the *Readers' Guide,* you begin looking for another topic with an emphasis on the shortage of doctors. The list of titles on the page looks somewhat like this:

Physicians

1. Family doctor: Medicine's newest specialty
2. Dilemma in Dyersville: doctors needed
3. Let's give foreign doctors a fair shake
4. Curing the doctor shortage: apprenticeships
5. Never marry a doctor
6. Medical assistant; the health team approach
7. Who is the doctor's doc?
8. Medical shortages abroad, too

Your eyes stop at title 4, "Curing the doctor shortage: apprenticeships." You sense that this topic could lead to an exciting paper. You imagine this article might take the approach that the doctor shortage could be cured by having select students learn how to become doctors by working under the supervision of practicing physicians. Your thesis could be on the side of apprenticeship. Of course, you need to find other articles that would support your view.

But there are no other articles on apprenticeship training. You must drop what seemed to be a promising and exciting topic, and begin searching for another.

After perhaps one or two more false starts, suppose you finally find a category with a list of articles like this:

Electronics in medicine

1. Expensive machines save lives
2. The electronystagmograph
3. A 200-mph surgical drill
4. Measuring blood pressures—a new machine
5. Relieving pain electronically
6. An electronic nurse (for 2¢ a day)
7. Electronics: a solution to the doctor shortage?
8. Engineers design medical devices
9. Medical devices: an unhealthy situation
10. Electronics aid the busy doctor

As your eyes move down the list of titles, you know that you have found enough material to support both a topic and a point of view. You are particularly interested in number 9, "Medical devices: an unhealthy situation." It indicates that there may be both positive and negative aspects to the use of medical devices. You may find that volumes of the *Readers' Guide* for other years reveal that there are more articles under the heading *Electronics in medicine.* You have finally narrowed your subject effectively.

Provide a Focus

To avoid making your paper a mere accumulation of facts, you must develop a genuine question, and your facts must then be used to answer this question. Whether it can be *definitely* answered or not is unimportant. The important thing is to focus all your research on answering the broad question, so that your paper will have direction and purpose.

Once you have narrowed your topic to medical electronics, your focus might be expressed with the question

> In what ways do electronic machines help a doctor in the practice of medicine?

or, more pointedly,

> Do electronic machines help or hinder a doctor in the practice of medicine?

The answer to the second question could make extremely interesting reading. You may even discover, after you have done all your research, that you are willing to take a stand on the question. Then your facts could be organized around your point of view.

A word of caution about taking a stand on your subject: Don't become so biased that you consciously or unconsciously pick out the strongest arguments for the side that you want to win, and ignore or minimize the evidence for the other side. Remember, you are not writing the research paper to win an argument. Your task is to inform both yourself and your readers. This does not mean that your guiding idea or point of view cannot be the essence of your organization. But be fair. Present both sides of the argument.

At this point, you have finally found a manageable topic, and you have found a focus by asking a good question about it. You do not yet know the answer to your question, but you are ready to start your research.

DOING THE RESEARCH
FOR YOUR PAPER

If you're writing a theme or a critical essay, you will be assigned the book or books to read. If you're writing a report, you will be reading about others' research or doing an experiment yourself and then writing the report. For these short papers, the assigned reading material will be quite specific. For a research paper, you need to do the kind of library research discussed in this section and the next section.

Start your research on the subject early. Books may be in great demand when the deadline for a paper is approaching. If you are going to choose one view and support it, don't decide definitely which one it's going to be until you've had a chance to do some preliminary research. Once you see what's available to support the different viewpoints, then you can decide which one you'll choose.

Your research will consist mainly in finding and reading published material that is relevant to your topic. For this, you will need to make full use of your school and neighborhood libraries. Libraries vary in resources, but the major sources you'll be concerned with are the *card catalog,* the *reference section,* and the *periodical section.* Find out where each of the sections is. Get a map or a friendly librarian to help you at first.

The *reference section* is the place where reference books are kept—everything from encyclopedias to telephone directories. More important for your research are the current indexes (lists) of articles in various magazines and journals. One index that I have already mentioned is the *Readers' Guide to Periodical Literature.* Other useful indexes are the *New York Times Index,* the *Business Periodicals Index,* and the *Education Index.* They can all help you find pertinent articles.

The publications themselves will probably be located in the *periodical section.* There you will find magazines, newspapers, and other publications that come out periodically (weekly, monthly, etc.). Some libraries have microfilms of newspapers in a special location that is not part of the main periodical section. If you need them, a librarian will show you how to use the microfilm readers.

The *card catalog* is your guide to the books and other materials in the library. It is usually, but not always, located near the entrance. If you don't see it, ask. If you don't know how to use it, ask or read about it. This one resource is the indispensable key for finding all that the library has to offer you.

In the card catalog, books are listed in two ways—under the author's name and under the subject (sometimes under the title, too). They're cross-referenced, and you'll find some helpful duplication in subject areas. If you should draw a complete blank, a librarian may be able to suggest some other categories that you can check. (If you have the names of authors of books that deal with your subject, look them up first to see if they're available in the library.) Look up your specific topic in the card catalog; then try a more general subject area, to be sure you've found all that the library contains on the subject. For example, here are successive steps you could take to find information on the American winemaker James Smith:

1. Look up "James Smith" in the card catalog.
2. Then look under "American winemakers"—information on Smith may be included in a book about a number of people in the field.
3. Then look under "wine."
4. Then look under "grape growing"—most winemakers grow their own grapes.

Once you have located all the available sources of information, you can begin taking notes for your paper. (Don't forget that you can sometimes derive a wealth of information from experts on your campus or in your town, through personal interviews.)

RECORDING YOUR INFORMATION

Take *two* sets of notes. The first set of notes will be your bibliography: one card for each book, magazine, or other source of information. The second set of notes should contain the detailed information that you gather from each of your sources.

This system may sound time-consuming. "Why bother to write all that information down twice?" you may ask. But you won't be writing the same information twice. You'll be gathering *more* information with *less* writing. Here's how the system works.

Start with a Working Bibliography

A working bibliography is a list of the books and articles you are going to consult. Not all of them will prove to be useful, but you have to check them all anyway. Be generous with your list. It's better to check out several references that do not help than to miss a good one because its title isn't appealing.

Instead of listing all these references on a large sheet of paper, use one 3×5 slip or card for each reference. Then, if a particular reference doesn't help you, you can simply throw away its slip.

An efficient method for making a 3×5 working bibliography is shown in Figure 20.1. The different parts of each slip are used as follows:

A. On the front of the slip, record the name of the library where the reference is located. Later, if you should need the reference for additional material, you will be able to find it directly, without going back to the card catalog. (If your college has only one library, you can omit this.)

B. Record the short title of your subject. This will be important when you are working on current and subsequent papers.

C. Record the library call number, so you will not have to refer to the card catalog whenever you want to use the same book again.

D. Accurately record all the reference information, in exactly the form that you plan to use in the bibliographical portion of your paper. This ensures that you will include all the essential parts of the reference; also, using the correct form now will make typing your paper much easier.

E. On the back of the 3×5 slip, briefly record your opinion of the reference. You may write such comments as "Not useful—does not discuss principles," or "Excellent case studies of poor readers at the secondary-school level."

Take Detailed Notes

This stage is time-consuming. However, if you take notes with painstaking care, you will be well repaid for your effort, because your paper will

Figure 20.1 Working Bibliography: 3×5 Slip Method

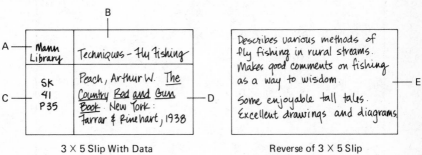

3 X 5 Slip With Data   Reverse of 3 X 5 Slip With Comments

be half written. Here are eleven suggestions that will help you take better notes and produce a better final paper.

1. Use note paper of uniform size. I suggest you use 3×5 paper slips because they are uniform and are less bulky and less expensive than cards. Never make a running list of notes on large paper; such notes are almost impossible to organize.
2. Use only one side of the slip, and record only one topic on each slip.
3. Identify the reference on each slip by writing the author's last name or the title in the top left corner. Write the page number or numbers in parentheses at the end of each item of information. Then you can quickly find the exact page again if further information is needed, and you have all the information you may need for a footnote (see Figure 20.2).
4. Just as in taking notes on a textbook, always skim the article or chapter you are reading before writing the notes.
5. Write notes in your own words. This will help you understand what you are reading. Furthermore, you will be putting the information into a form that can be used in your paper. Always distinguish clearly between your words and the author's. Failure to do so might lead you unwittingly into plagiarism.
6. Make your notes concise, yet sufficiently detailed to provide accurate meaning.
7. Take the time to write neatly, to avoid the frustration of having to decipher the notes later.

Figure 20.2 Detailed Note Written on One Side of a 3×5 Slip

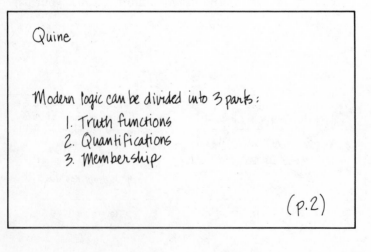

Quine

Modern logic can be divided into 3 parts:
1. Truth functions
2. Quantifications
3. Membership

(p.2)

8. Use ink. Notes written in pencil will become blurred through handling and sorting.
9. If you need direct quotations, use only a few of the outstanding phrases or sentences. Most students tend to quote too much and too often.
10. Abbreviate only the common words; otherwise you will lose time figuring out an unfamiliar shorthand.
11. When ideas and insights occur, write them on separate slips under the caption "my own."

Record all the pertinent information. If you find something you're not sure you'll need (remember that I suggested that you not decide exactly what approach your paper will defend or take until you've done the research), put it on a card anyway. It's easier to do this when you're in the library than to decide later that you need it. Then you may make a special trip to the library only to discover that the book isn't available because someone else is using it.

Be sure you have enough information. Too much is easier to work with than too little. If you haven't enough, you'll have to stop writing later, to look up other references. Or, you'll be tempted to pad skimpy information with words that mean little.

Copy Quotations Carefully

When you quote exactly from a book or an article, place quotation marks on your slip, around the exact words copied from the reference. Then you'll know what is a direct quote and what you have put into your own words. To be sure you have copied it exactly, go back to the beginning and compare your quotation with the original. Be sure you have spelled all words exactly as they are in the original. If you note what seems to be an error or misspelling—some English spellings are different from those we use—retain the exact spelling, but use *(sic)* after the word. Here is an example:

> "They did research on the properties of chemical fertilisers (sic), and valuable research on animal nutrition."

If you leave a section or even one word out of the quoted material, use an ellipsis (a series of three periods . . .) to indicate that you omitted something. If the omitted material comes at the end of the sentence, add a period after the ellipses. (Usually what's omitted is left out because it doesn't relate to the point you're using the quote to support.)

Original quote: *"Now that we know what has been the causative factor in this area of disaster we can, without further concern, move on to eliminate that cause."*

Quote with ellipsis: *"Now that we know what has been the causative factor . . . we can . . . move on to eliminate that cause."*

When you want to use the essence of what an author says but do not want to quote the exact words, you may paraphrase. This also allows you to condense the major thought. Even though you use mostly your own words, however, the material must be attributed to its source. In other words, in your paper you must give the author credit for having supplied the idea.

ORGANIZING YOUR PAPER

Choose Your Basic Premise

Look over the information in your notes, and then ask yourself some hard questions. If there's a choice of viewpoint—for or against a question, for example—which view has the most evidence to support it? Or what should the basic theme or focus of your paper be? If you've done a good job of research, you should be able to decide now what you want to say in your paper; and you should have the evidence to support the view, right at hand on your slips.

Organize Your Paper Around the Basic Premise

Now comes a very important step. *Before* you start to write, organize your material. You could use any of the organizational patterns listed under "The Organizational-Pattern Way" in Chapter 19. However, most college papers seem to work best with the *time* pattern or the *process* pattern.

Another organizational pattern that might work for you is that of *development of an argument.* You state a premise, and then set out to support it with logical examples that build to a conclusion. More flexibility may be possible with this kind of organization than with the others.

The important thing is to decide what kind of organization is best for your basic premise. If you don't know how you want to proceed in your writing, the paper will probably appear haphazard and purposeless to the instructor.

Draw up a Detailed Outline

Once you've decided what kind of organization fits the material you have, write down the points you want to cover in your paper—in any order. Don't worry at this time whether the points are major ones or less important. Just write them down briefly. Then go through them and decide which are the major points and which come under or support each major point (see Table 20.1). At this time you may decide that some point isn't important to your argument at all. Maybe it's interesting, but it won't help support any of the major points. Set the slip with this information aside.

You should now have your major points listed, with minor points under each major point. It is time to decide in which order you want to use the major points. Here's where your decision regarding the organizational pattern comes into play. Arrange the major points in the order that best fits the pattern you've chosen; then organize the slips with the information on them in the order of this organized outline. Number the slips in order from one to whatever, and you're ready to start writing. Note that you will already have spent some time thinking through, or "digesting," your information.

Table 20.1 How to Set up an Outline

    I. Introduction: Pertinent quote or striking statement if available
      a. Your purpose
      b. How you will accomplish it
    II. (Major Point 1) State this point concisely.
      a. Example of incident and supporting evidence
      b. Another example
   III. (Major Point 2) State it as above.
      a. Support for major point 2
   IV. (Major Point 3) Again, state it clearly.
      a. Facts or quotes to support major point 3
      b. More examples to support major point 3
    V. (Major Point 4) State the major point.
      a. Supporting evidence for major point 4
      b. More examples
      c. Other supporting evidence
   VI. Conclusion

WRITING THE RESEARCH PAPER

How Do You Start?

You start by writing. If you're typing or writing in longhand, just start. Once your hands are going through the physical motions of writing, your brain will follow, and then you can get into the meat of the paper. You already have most of it worked out—information, sources, organization. So now all you have to do is put it into sentences and paragraphs. Remember that you are planning to leave time for three drafts, so what you write on this first draft need not be perfect. You can always discard or rewrite the first part if you don't like it.

On your first draft, write as rapidly and spontaneously as possible. Record your thoughts on paper as they go through your mind, to help ensure continuity. Don't stop to ponder alternatives. Although this manner of writing often results in too much material, don't be concerned, because it is easier to cut than to add.

If your first sentence doesn't sound just as you would like it to, don't worry about it. No writer ever comes out with the perfect beginning sentence. What you read in books and magazines is always the result of revision and rewriting.

Writing the Main Body of the Paper

Begin with the introduction, which may end up as one or two paragraphs that state your purpose and perhaps catch the reader's interest. For now, just write out a general sentence of introduction, stating simply what you want to do in the paper. This can be in very rough form right now. Forget it, and go into the main body of the paper.

Take each slip in order, and write. Start with major point one, state what it is, and then use the supporting evidence to show why it is so, or what happened. As you use a reference from the slip, note the slip number on your paper. You can put in the footnotes later, taking the exact information from the slip. Continue to write, following your organized and numbered slips.

BE SURE TO DEVELOP AND SUPPORT THE IMPORTANT POINTS.   Students often state a main point, and then go on to something else without supporting it. The kinds of evidence you need to support a major point are statistics, quotations from other published works, facts, examples, comparisons and contrasts in views, expert opinion, and description. These are the specifics that will support your points. If you make statements and follow them up with generalities, you will not convince your reader that your main point is true. Use what you have collected on your slips to support your points. Here, with examples, are the steps you can take to develop a major point:

1. State your point clearly.

   Gardening is an enjoyable avocation.

2. Develop the point beyond a brief statement.

   Faced with the pressures of modern living, many people turn to working with plants to relax themselves and become absorbed in the living world around them. For some people gardening may absorb every spare moment.

3. Support with quotes from authorities, statistics.

   Organizations that serve gardeners are growing rapidly. In the past two years garden clubs and other horticultural organizations report significant numbers of new members. An estimate of gardeners actively affiliated with these organizations numbers in the millions, according to James Jones, executive director of Gardeners, Inc.

4. Illustrate with examples.

   One organization, the American Horticultural Society, has purchased an estate for its new headquarters to serve a membership that has tripled in the last 18 months.

5. Interrelate with other main points.

   In addition to joining general gardening organizations, gardeners who specialize can join societies for those interested in growing irises, primroses, daylilies, African violets, orchids, and other garden favorites. Most of these groups have grown, too, as a result of the increased general interest in growing plants.

Be sure that all the main points are supported about equally with this kind of evidence. If you can't find enough evidence to support one point, perhaps it's not a major one. Then you need to reorganize the structure to include it under one of the other major points.

Avoid padding. You may be tempted to add extra words or rephrase a point in several ways to make the paper seem longer. This sort of padding is very obvious to the reader, who's looking for logical arguments and good sense in your paper. It will not improve your grade. If you haven't enough evidence to support a statement, leave it out or get some more information to use.

MAKE A CLEAR COPY.   The first draft is usually rough—full of deletions, additions, and directions that are understandable only to the writer (see Figure 20.3). If you leave it in this state for even a day, you may lose a lot of time trying to recall exactly what you meant by some of your notes. If you retype or rewrite the material while it is still very fresh, you may do some spontaneous revision. The result will be a clear copy that will be ready for revision after a "cooling off" period of a day or so.

PUT IT ASIDE FOR A WHILE.   What you now have is a first draft, organized in the order it will appear in the final paper, without a completed introduction and without a conclusion. You'll need both of these as well as a title. But they can come later, after you've set the paper aside for a day or so. (Start early!)

A "cooling off" period is important. During the writing stage your mind is so full of associations with the words you have written that you are likely to see clarity and step-by-step sequences where these do not, in fact, exist; that is, your mind will fill in and bridge gaps that you have left in the writing.

When you read your manuscript after your mind has dropped some of these associations, you will have to read the words themselves to gain the meaning. You will then easily spot glaring errors.

EDITING YOUR WORK

Editing your written work is one of the most important skills you can learn in college. It requires the ability to view your own production with enough courage to anticipate (and be concerned about) the potential reader's reaction. This means polishing and boiling down ideas; struggling to say things more clearly; tearing down and rebuilding sentences and paragraphs; and even, if necessary, writing three or four drafts.

Technical Details

Here are some technical details that you must have under control if your paper is to make a good impression on the reader.

Figure 20.3 Page from a First Draft

Even if you ~~have~~ make a false start and have to discard
and begin over, you will have made the plunge and will

Intro sometimes a stumbling block

be mentally set to write. ʌ

If you have constructed a careful outline, ~~and have~~
thought about your topic, and done a conscientious job
(if research is necessary for the kind of paper you are doing),
of research ʌ you should be able to produce a first draft
that ⟨is reasonably close⟩ in substance + general organization
to what you want to say ~~write as rapidly and spontaneously~~
~~as you can. Don't try this first time round to shape~~
~~perfect sentences.~~ *with your outline before you,*
  ʌ Write as rapidly and spontaneously as you can. Don't
strive, on this first draft, for gemlike perfection of
sentences and paragraphs. ~~the~~ Your aim at this point is
to get your ideas and information down on paper. ʌTrue,
it is likely to be a very rough draft — ~~full of~~ *messy with* deletions,
additions, and ~~jotted notations.~~ *scribbled afterthoughts.* But now you have
something tangible to work with. ⌗ When you have finished
your first draft, read it through. ~~and then, while the~~
~~whole thing is fresh in your mind.~~ Make notes of any
points you *have* left out, any new thoughts that come to
you as you read, or any places where you would like
to make changes or improvements. Now, ⟨make a clean copy⟩
while all these matters are fresh in your mind, ↓ incorporating

TRANSITIONS.   In writing your paper you need to consider how to help your readers move easily from one main point to the next. If they feel that there's no connection—that you simply jump from one point to another—they will find it hard to follow the logical sequence that you have so clearly established in your own mind. You must, therefore, use transitional words and phrases to make your paper easier to follow. Check carefully for transitions, and insert them where they are needed (see "The Pivotal-Words Way" in Chapter 19).

GRAMMAR.   Students who use the English language correctly get their ideas across to other people more clearly and forcibly than those who fumble on every sentence. Moreover, students who apply the rules of grammar in their papers get better grades. If you are unsure about these rules or careless with them, your meaning may get lost. If you feel that you could use a review of grammar, there are good texts that give you the elements of English grammar by a programmed method. Some of them are even fun to read.

SPELLING.   If your spelling problems are not severe, you will find a dictionary helpful. If your spelling is very bad, look for one of the paper-backed books that list the most commonly misspelled words. If you cannot recognize that you are spelling words incorrectly, have someone who is good at spelling read your paper and mark the words that are wrong. Have the person mark them, *not* correct them. Then you can look up the words and write them in correctly. If you do this conscientiously over a period of time, you will improve your spelling.

Plagiarism

Plagiarism is stealing other peoples' words and ideas and making them appear to be your own. It need not be as blatant as copying whole passages without giving credit. If you paraphrase something from already published material and do not give the reference, you're guilty of plagiarism even though you have no intention of stealing! Simply rearranging sentences or rephrasing a little without crediting is still plagiarism.

Those who grade papers are quick to note a change in writing style from one of your papers to another or from one part of your paper to another part. Your writing is like your fingerprints—individual. This is your style. If you try to use another's work, his or her style will not match the rest of your paper, and the difference will be obvious. Instructors may give you the benefit of the doubt if they cannot prove where you got plagiarized material. But if they can—and it's usually not difficult—

it's grounds for expulsion from college. In a world where the written word is a major product, stealing it from someone else is a serious offense.

ADDING THE MISSING ELEMENTS

Footnotes and Bibliography

Quoted or paraphrased material from other sources must be credited. You may include a credit right after the quoted material, within the body of the paper, in a format like *(Jones, 1965, page 264)*. This citation refers to page 264 of the work by Jones that was published in 1965 and is listed in your bibliography. (More about that later). Or you can use a superscript [1] and cite the full source at the bottom of the page or in a complete listing at the end of the paper. Credits that appear at the bottom of the page are called footnotes. Figure 20.4 shows a format for listing credits at the end of the paper. Both forms are numbered in the order in which they appear in your paper. Other forms are given in handbooks on English usage.

The *bibliography* includes the sources you used in your credits and may include other books or published material you read as background for the paper but did not quote in the paper.

A bibliography is just that—not "notes," "endnotes," "sources," or any other title. It's a listing of books you used in preparing the paper, and you should use the correct title for this listing. When you write the bibliography, use the slips you prepared earlier. Each entry should include enough information so that a reader could identify the work and find it in a library.

Entries should be listed alphabetically by author. Different bibliographic forms are used in different fields. Either select a standard form from a handbook on English usage, or follow the form used in one of the journals that pertains to the subject you are writing about. No matter

Figure 20.4 One Way to List Footnotes

```
1. Hunter Shirley, Your Mind May Be Programmed
   Against You! (Lafayette, La.: 21st Century
   Books, 1982), pp. 112-115.

2. Frank H. Winter, Prelude to the Space Age
   (Washington, D.C.: Smithsonian Institution
   Press, 1983), p. 18.
```

what form you use, it is most important to follow it consistently in every single entry in your bibliography (see Figure 20.5).

The Title

It's often a good idea to wait until you've written the paper before you decide on a final title. The title should reflect the content of the paper, but it can have an interesting twist, or perhaps make use of part of a quote that you think is especially appropriate to the paper. A straightforward title is also fine. In some cases a straightforward title, telling what the paper is about, is best.

The Introduction

You already have a general statement of the purpose of the paper—this is the basis of your introduction. Now, in revising the paper, you can write the introduction in its final form. It should briefly state your purpose in writing the paper and how you are going to carry out that purpose. It might include a quotation that is particularly suitable or an interesting example or anecdote. Choose any of these devices carefully; they must be right on target. If you're not sure they will add to the paper, then settle for a straightforward statement of purpose and general method.

Figure 20.5 Useful Format for a Bibliography

```
                        Bibliography


Boyer, Ernest L., and Hechinger, Fred M. Higher Learning
   in the National Interest. Washington, D.C.: Carnegie
   Foundation, 1981.

Chaplin, James P., and Krawiec, T.S. Systems and Theo-
   ries of Psychology. 4th ed. New York: Holt, Rinehart,
   and Winston, 1979.

Kleppner, Paul. Who Voted?  New York: Praeger Publishers,
   1982.

Shirley, Hunter. Your Mind May Be Programmed Against You!
   Lafayette, La.: 21st Century Books, 1982.

Uhler, Harry B. "Semicentennial: Baltimore-to-Venus At-
   tempt," Science News, 114 (July 1978): 78-79.

Winter, Frank H. Prelude to the Space Age. Washington,
   D.C.: Smithsonian Institution Press, 1983.
```

The introduction, the title, and the conclusion should, however, have some continuity, something in common.

The Conclusion

Don't leave the paper without a concluding passage. If you do, your readers will be left dangling, wondering what happened to you and the rest of the paper. Let them know they have come to the end.

Usually the conclusion summarizes or restates the purpose described in the introduction. It can also draw a conclusion or state your opinion that something should be done about a situation. Or, it can predict what is in store for the future, drawing on what you've written in the paper. The kind of conclusion you draw will depend on the kind of paper and the subject. It need not be long or involved; just be sure you do have one.

MAKING THE FINAL COPY

All the time and energy you have spent on your research paper should be reflected in the appearance of the final copy. Make it neat, clean, and attractive.

1. Use only one side of white paper. Although few instructors will specify precisely what size paper to use, the most commonly used paper measures $8\frac{1}{2} \times 11$ inches.
2. Type your paper or have it typed. Handwritten papers are difficult to read, and they may not be accepted in some courses.
3. Leave a generous margin at the top and bottom of each page and a margin of one and one-half inches on both sides, to provide room for the instructor's comments.
4. Type your paper without any strikeovers (erase errors thoroughly and neatly), and be sure to double-space.
5. Set up long direct quotations (five or more lines) in "block" style; that is, single-space and indent the lines from both sides about a half-inch or five typewriter spaces. You omit the quotation marks when you block a quotation in this way, because the block setup shows that you are quoting.
6. Proofread your final copy. Go over it carefully to catch spelling errors, typing errors, and other minor flaws. This is a very important step that is too often neglected.
7. Hand in the paper on time. It is not uncommon for instructors to deduct points for late papers.

Figure 20.6 shows a typical format for a title page. The format for identifying and numbering an inside page is shown in Figure 20.7.

Figure 20.6 Title Page of a Research Paper

THE COMPULSIVE READER

Linda Logan

Special Problems in Education

Education 207

January 18, 1984

Charles Fay,
Associate Professor of Education

Figure 20.7 Format for Inside Pages of a Research Paper. Each inside page is identified and numbered at the top.

L. Logan   -1-
The Compulsive Reader
Education 207
January 18, 1984

Among the persons who people this planet there are
some who have a yen for the printed word. They are the
ones who watch television with a book in their laps.
They are the visitors who riffle your magazines while
pretending to converse. Their eyes have an unquenchable
thirst for printer's ink which they devour whenever it
is poured out in words. This addiction may vary in
degree, and with age "matters of consequence" may allevi-
ate it, but generally they remain a close friend of books
for life.

From a fairly intensive search through the literature on "Reading" no mention of this type of reader could
be found. Hildreth[1] has a section entitled "The Bookworm
Problem" in which she states that "life in the modern
school" which encourages many activities "will counteract
the tendency toward excessive bookishness." Many articles deal with the "gifted" and the "able" reader. The
gifted, and even the able reader, however, read with
discrimination and purpose which is foreign to the wanton
habits of the compulsive reader. An article in *Time*

---

[1]Hildreth, Gertrude. *Teaching Reading* (New York: Holt,
   Rinehart, and Winston, 1961), pp. 596-597.

SUMMARY

What one thing is most important in writing a paper?

Actually, there are two things, which I believe are equally important. First, give yourself plenty of time; don't put off the assignment until the night before it's due. Second, write about something that interests you; you'll work with enthusiasm, and your paper will show it.

What's the toughest part of writing a research paper?

Finding a topic. You'll need one that interests you, that suits the requirements of your instructor, and for which there are sufficient research sources. You can find out about research sources by checking the *Readers' Guide* and the library's card catalog. To make sure the topic is not too broad, you'll have to narrow it down three or four times.

Once I've chosen my topic, can I start doing research?

Not yet. First give your topic a focus. Come up with an important question concerning your topic. This will give your paper direction and purpose. Then you can start.

What comes next?

Begin by accumulating references. Use listings in the card catalog as well as in the *Readers' Guide*.

Why do I have to take research notes twice?

You don't. However, you should list your information in two different places. Use one set of 3 × 5 cards or slips for the detailed information from each article or book. Use a separate set as your working bibliography, or list of references.

Do I have to credit authors even when I paraphrase them?

Yes! Whether you use their exact words or not, the ideas are still those of the authors—not yours.

When all the notes are taken, what comes next?

Choose your paper's organizational pattern. (You will most likely use the time, process, or argument-development pattern.) Then list (in any order) all the points that you want to cover. Next, pick out the major points, and arrange the minor and supporting points below each major point. Finally, organize your major points into an outline, according to your premise. Then organize your note slips in the same order, and number them.

Can't I skip the detailed outline?

No! The outline is the only control you have over your data. And outlining helps you to think through your paper, so that the writing will come naturally.

Now that the organizing is over, how do I begin writing?

Just start writing, as rapidly and spontaneously as possible. Begin with a sentence or two of introduction to set the mood, and then go straight to the body of the paper. Write from your slips, one at a time and in order—first a main point, and then the supporting points. Then go on to the next main point, and so on.

Can I leave out the support for some of the main ideas?

No! All main points need support. If you can't find support for one of your main points, it shouldn't be a main point.

Would this be a good time to take a break?

Not quite. You've finished your first draft, but it's probably in very rough form. Make a clean copy of your paper by rewriting or retyping it. Then set it aside for at least a day before you edit or rewrite it.

What does editing my paper require?

A pen or pencil and lots of courage! To edit your own paper well, you need the guts to tear down, rebuild, and rearrange sentences and paragraphs until they're just right. This can sometimes take three or four drafts. By the way, a good time to expand your purpose sentence into an introduction is while you're editing. The introduction should explain your purpose and method in writing the paper. Try to start it with a "grabber" like an anecdote or quotation.

Should I determine my paper title right from the start?

You can, but it's better to wait until you've finished writing. That way you have a better feel for the paper's overall content and tone.

Can I skip the conclusion? I never know what to write.

Definitely not, although many students do. A paper without a conclusion will leave the reader dangling. You should be able to draw some conclusion from your information, or state an opinion or prediction based on your information, or even summarize your main points. Whatever it contains, you should have a conclusion.

Why is a good final copy so important?

This is really the only draft that your instructor will see. It should reflect the time and energy that you have put into your paper. A sloppy final copy will give the impression that your paper contains sloppy work.

HAVE YOU MISSED SOMETHING?

1. **SENTENCE-COMPLETION.** Complete the following sentences with one of the three words listed below each sentence.

   a. Writing notes in your own words helps to avoid _____.

   plagiarism   understanding   confusion

   b. A paper without a conclusion is apt to leave the reader _____.

   interested   dangling   alone

2. **MATCHING.** In each blank space in the left column, write the number preceding the phrase in the right column that matches the left item best.

   _____ a. Librarian

   _____ b. Theme

   _____ c. Editing

   _____ d. Outline

   _____ e. Choosing a topic

   _____ f. Interviews

   1. Orders and controls your information
   2. The "smoothing and improving" step in writing
   3. Helpful source for locating references
   4. Perhaps the most difficult writing task
   5. An often-overlooked reference source
   6. Often based on personal experience

3. **TRUE-FALSE.** Write *T* beside the *true* statements and *F* beside the *false* statements that follow.

   _____ a. Ellipses are used to indicate left-out words and sentences in a quotation.

      b. You should use many quotations in a research paper.

      c. It's usually best to choose a title after the paper is written.

      d. Promising information sources should be included in your working bibliography.

      e. You should never take a stand in a research paper.

4. **MULTIPLE-CHOICE.** Choose the phrase that completes the following sentence most accurately, and circle the letter that precedes it.

In most libraries, you will find the *Readers' Guide to Periodical Literature* in the

a. reference section.
b. card catalog.
c. periodical section.
d. circulation area.

The whole of science is nothing more than a refinement of everyday thinking.

—ALBERT EINSTEIN

21

Studying Science

Science has been called the "endless frontier," but for some students it seems just plain endless. There are endless lectures, endless textbooks, endless problems, and worst of all, endless labs. This chapter presents some techniques to help make science a little less intimidating and a little more exciting. It provides effective methods for . . .

- Learning from Lectures
- Reading a Science Textbook
- Working Scientific Problems

and

- Working in the Laboratory

*I*N EVERY SUBJECT THAT YOU STUDY, including science, you must learn new terminology, facts, and ideas; then you must develop the ability to apply them to solve various types of problems. But studying science is different from studying other subjects. First, the terminology, facts, laws, and principles must be learned with extreme precision. And second, the problems are almost always quantitative; in fact, most ideas are stated in quantitative (mathematical) terms.

A good example is the definition of *work*, which is learned early in the study of physics:

> The *work W* done by a force of magnitude *F* in moving a body through a distance *d* in the direction of the force is $W = F \times d$.

Such a definition can cause several kinds of headache for a student who isn't accustomed to precise and quantitative terms:

1. The definition is precise, and it must be learned and used precisely. What might seem like a minor rewording could change it to an incorrect (and thus useless) definition.
2. The definition contains several parts, and the reason for each part must be understood if the definition is to be understood.
3. The definition is quantitative. It makes use of a formula to define *work*, and that formula may be used to calculate work under certain conditions.
4. The student must learn what these conditions are, and how to take them into account when using the formula.
5. The word *work* is used in a different sense from the one we're used to. Some common words are given special meanings in the sciences, and the usual definition can get in the way of remembering the scientific definition.

The reason for all this precision is simple. The sciences deal with actual, measurable things. If these things are not described or computed precisely, then they are described or computed incorrectly.

So you need to learn the precise terminology, facts, and ideas when you study a science. But you *should not* try to learn a science as a collection of isolated facts. That would be an almost impossible task, and the isolated facts would have little meaning for you.

The way to learn science is to fit facts and principles together into groups, or *clusters*, in your memory. Within each science, the facts and principles are related to each other, to a much greater extent than in nonscientific subjects; so clustering should be easier. Actually, much of science is concerned with finding and explaining the relationships among various facts, concepts, and theories. Even our precise definition of *work* is really a relationship; it is given as a formula because the relation is a precise one. Your textbook and teachers will be pointing out many more. Your job is to use these relationships to cluster the facts and ideas in your mind.

As you learn in this way, your knowledge of a few facts in a cluster will easily extend to new facts and ideas that you want to include in the same cluster. You will find yourself becoming more and more comfortable with science and its precision. You may begin to ask yourself questions about how new ideas fit in with old ones; about the patterns that you find in both old and new facts; or about why a principle that you learned in one science course seems so much like a principle you learned in some other science course. Then you will *really* be learning science.

LEARNING FROM LECTURES

Remember that your objective is to learn (1) the facts and (2) their interrelationships, and your ears and eyes must be alert to both. Take full, legible notes at lectures, paying particular attention to explanatory diagrams. And don't hesitate to ask questions if you cannot grasp a point after reviewing your lecture notes and reading your text.

Taking Lecture Notes

You should take science lecture notes as described in Chapter 6, and study them using the method of Chapter 11.

1. *Take notes on ideas, not words.* Do not try to get the lecture word for word. If you do, the words will get in the way of the ideas. The objective of taking notes is to have a record of the main ideas, so you can study them later in the privacy of your own room, for deeper understanding, for review, and in preparation for examinations.

2. *Be systematic.* Use the Cornell System for taking notes, as illustrated in Figure 21.1. Write your notes in the large right-hand column. Then, as soon as possible after each lecture, put your notes in order by filling in missing steps in the arguments, by detecting and correcting any errors, and by relating these new notes with the previous lecture's notes. Label each idea on the right with a key word, placed in the left-hand column.

3. *Make master summary sheets.* Periodically (to prepare for tests or at spaced intervals), reorganize your notes on separate sheets of paper, by clustering the ideas and details under main topics and categories. By constructing such summary sheets, you will be relating facts and ideas to each other and fixing them in your memory.

Figure 21.1 Cornell Format for Taking Lecture Notes (and Notes Based on Textbook Reading)

	February 26 (MON.) - Physics 101
ends stronger	I. Polarity of Magnets 　1. Magnetism is stronger at ends than middle
like = repel	2. Like poles repel each other 　　Ex. Two N poles when brought together, fly apart when released. Same for "S" poles.
unlike = attract Earth - magnet 　poles 　compass Experiment 　iron filings	3. Unlike poles attract each other 　4. Earth is one big magnet 　　a. Magnetism strongest at poles 　　b. Compass needle aligns N to S 　5. Experiment to show stronger ends 　　a. Place bar magnet under glass 　　b. Pour small iron filings on glass 　　c. Tap glass & filings arrange selves showing lines of force
Theory: 　not sure 　molecule 　　arrangement	II. Theory of Magnetism 　1. Not sure what causes it 　2. Believe: way molecules are arranged

Asking Questions

If you have difficulties in relating concepts, in solving assigned problems, or in completing lab experiments satisfactorily, there may be gaps in your understanding. In such cases, you should start asking questions.

ASKING THE TEACHER AT THE START OF THE CLASS.　This is usually the best time to ask questions, because they probably have been considered carefully. Well-phrased questions about the previous lecture or the reading assignment can often be cleared up quickly. Moreover, something that presented difficulty for you probably did the same for other members of the class; your teacher may want to discuss it during the lecture.

Never worry about being the only student who doesn't understand, or about showing that you didn't grasp a particular idea. If you do, you will only be underestimating the teacher and yourself, misjudging the purpose of the course, and making it harder for the teacher to keep in touch with the class.

But don't ask questions like "How do you do this problem?" Such a question may get you the answer to the problem, but it will be of little help to your understanding. Much better questions are, "Did I use the right strategy in attacking this problem? Are there other strategies that I could have used?" This type of question will get you useful information—ideas that you can apply to a broad range of material.

INTERRUPTING A LECTURE.   Don't be bashful; interrupt a lecture with a question if you need to. Often it is helpful for the whole class to have a lecture slowed down or brought to a halt for a while—especially if some point is obscure. But don't interrupt too often, and make sure your question is an important one to you.

ASKING THE TEACHER BETWEEN CLASSES.   A good teacher's interest in his or her subject and students continues between classes in spite of many other duties. Most teachers enjoy a discussion with an individual student, because that is the most favorable teaching situation. But remember one thing: You must have done (or tried) the assignment and thought about the problems for yourself, before you ask for assistance. Private sessions between teacher and student should only supplement your own work. The major part of learning must be done by you alone.

ASKING OTHER STUDENTS.   Discussions with other students can be a great help. Friends learning a subject together share the same difficulties, and they need not hesitate to contradict each other. They can enlighten each other very effectively.

READING A TEXTBOOK IN SCIENCE

In some ways, studying a science textbook is like studying any other textbook. You should take notes using the Cornell format, review them using the recitation method, and from time to time make master summary sheets. However, there are also some special techniques that you should use to get the most out of a science textbook. For example, you should keep in mind the fact that science texts are packed with information. You must read them sentence by sentence, making sure you understand each sentence before going on to the next.

Here are four more techniques.

Using Mental Visualization

James Clerk Maxwell, a British mathematical physicist, recognized that different people, as they read and study science, mentally visualize or reconstruct concepts and ideas in their own personal ways. He believed that (1) the concepts and ideas of science can be lifted out of a textbook and placed in one's mind only by the process of mental visualization, and (2) different people have different ways and abilities to visualize, but, they all visualize to varying degrees.

Fortunately, most textbooks and articles in science are heavily illustrated with diagrams to aid the process of visualization. Learn to use the illustrations and text to complement one another. When there is no diagram to illustrate a process or idea, or if a given diagram doesn't work for you, then make your own. The technique is discussed and illustrated in Chapter 5, under "The Principle of Imagery."

Learning New Terms

A second important technique is learning new terms. You will find that your science textbooks are crowded with terms that are new to you. Since these terms stand for essential concepts, you must know precisely what they mean if you are to understand the subject matter. To help you pick them out, these important new terms are usually emphasized by italic or heavy type when they first occur and are specifically defined there or in a glossary at the end of the book. Give extra time and attention to the task of memorizing these terms and learning what they mean. Put them on 3 × 5 cards, and master them as you would any new vocabulary word.

An Important Tool:
The Language of Measurement

Learn the language of scientific measurement. Most commonly used are the metric system and the Celsius and Fahrenheit temperature scales. Learn to think meaningfully in these quantities and measures, so that you will not be reading mere words and symbols.

For example, you should know that the word *metric* comes from *meter*, which is the principal unit of length in this system. The metric system was developed by French scientists in 1799 and is now used everywhere in the world for scientific work. Table 21.1 (page 370) compares some metric units with English units of measurement.

You will want to know about the Celsius and Fahrenheit temperature scales, too. The thermometers for both look alike and have the same size tubes; both are filled with mercury; and the mercury rises and falls to the same levels. They differ in the way the scale is graduated. On the Celsius thermometer, the point at which water freezes is marked 0 (zero), while on the Fahrenheit thermometer it is marked 32. On the Celsius scale the boiling point is 100, while on the Fahrenheit it is 212.

Table 21.1 Comparison of Certain Metric and English Units of Measurement

Metric System		English System	
Length			
Meter	=1.093 yards	Yard	=0.9144 meter
	=3.281 feet	Foot	=0.3048 meter
	=39.370 inches	Inch	=0.0254 meter
Kilometer	=0.621 mile	Mile	=1.609 kilometers
Weight			
Gram	=15.432 grains	Grain	=0.0648 gram
	=0.032 troy ounce	Troy ounce	=31.1 grams
	=0.0352 avoirdupois ounce	Avoirdupois ounce	=28.35 grams
Kilogram	=2.2046 pounds avoirdupois		
Metric ton	=2204.62 pounds avoirdupois	Pound	=453.6 gram
Carat	=3.08 grains avoirdupois	Short ton	=0.907 metric ton

On the Celsius thermometer, then, there are 100 equal spaces or degrees between the freezing and boiling points of water. On the Fahrenheit thermometer, there are 180 degrees between the freezing and boiling points. Thus,

> To change Celsius readings to Fahrenheit readings, multiply by 180/100, or 9/5, and then add 32.

> To change Fahrenheit readings to Celsius, subtract 32 and then multiply by 5/9.

Using Study Guides

Study guides accompany the textbooks for many science courses. These guides can be very valuable in mastering scientific subject matter.

One type of guide uses what is called a *programmed* approach. In this approach, a section of the guide containing sentence-completion questions corresponds to each section of the textbook. The questions help you evaluate what you've learned and what you still need to review. They also help you rehearse for real examinations on which you'll be graded. In addition, there is a brief summary of each chapter and a list of chapter objectives. The value of the summary is self-evident. The objectives are a ready-made self-test that you can use to make sure you've learned the important concepts in the chapter.

A second type of study guide contains the following, for each text-

book chapter: an overview, chapter objectives, an expanded chapter outline, student study objectives, a vocabulary checklist, and self-tests.
When you are using this type of guide, you should read the text chapter
before attending the lecture on that chapter. Then, after the lecture, read
the overview, objectives, and outline in the guide, and summarize the
chapter in your own words. Check through the student study objectives,
and write out any answers that are called for. Next, make sure you can
define all the terms in the vocabulary checklist. Finally, take the self-
tests to check that you have mastered the chapter. And don't forget to
use the study guide along with your notes when you review for an
examination.

A Final Word

Different sciences call for different attacks and emphases in your reading.
Generally, biology and geology place relatively heavy emphasis on key
terms and definitions; physics and astronomy, on measurement and
mathematics; biology and chemistry, on manipulation; and physics and
chemistry, on visualization. Make sure you adapt your study methods
accordingly.

WORKING SCIENTIFIC PROBLEMS

The Value of Practice

You should never skip an assigned practice problem. The most successful
way to solve a problem on a test is to remember how you solved a similar
problem previously. When you first attempt a new kind of problem, it is
natural to be hesitant, to make false starts, to be temporarily stumped—
to waste time. But as you work more problems of the same kind, you
learn to do them more quickly and surely. Besides, each problem usually
has some feature that is not present in previous ones. So you gradually
build up the ability to attack a wider and wider range of problem types.

Complex problems are usually solved in many simple steps. If these
steps are so familiar that they are automatic, you can concentrate on how
they fit together in the problem. Then you can proceed from start to finish without confusion. But if each step presents a difficulty, you'll get so
involved in the details that you won't find the right path to the solution.

In studying a science, therefore, you should really do more than only
the assigned problems. If your own textbook does not have many extras,

look for problems in other books on the same subject. Use a study guide. Or, best of all, try to *make up appropriate problems for yourself.* Making up good ones is harder than solving them, but it is an excellent exercise—particularly for two students who are studying together. If you do this, try to imagine the problems your teacher will make up for your tests.

Doing New Types of Problems

If you do your assignments faithfully, you should come across new and unfamiliar problems only in your homework. A recommended approach to such problems is as follows:

1. Don't start doing problems until you have studied your lecture and textbook notes.
2. Make a list of what is given in the problem, and what is to be found.
3. Try to develop a chain of logical steps leading either forward from the known quantities to the one you have to find, or backward from the unknown to the given quantities. If necessary, work from both ends to the middle, until you find a logical connection.
4. Express these logical steps in the form of equations.
5. Combine the equations and solve them for the unknown.
6. Check your answer by determining whether it is reasonable in magnitude. If you are unsure, substitute the answer into the original relations, and see whether it fits consistently.

Answering Discussion Questions

Discussion questions appear occasionally in quizzes and examinations. Before you answer one, try to understand the purpose and point of view of the person asking the question. Learn to put yourself mentally in his or her place. Ask yourself how the question is related to subjects that were recently discussed in class or in your reading assignments, and what principles it is intended to bring out. If you can visualize the question within your clusters of facts and ideas, you should know how you want to answer it. All that remains is to express your answer in clear language, using the technical words accurately.

Practice is needed to become skillful in answering discussion questions. This skill can be developed by taking part in discussions with your friends; by participating in classroom discussions; and by paying careful attention to your *writing* skills. Usually, the problems are not in grammar, but in vocabulary, in logic, and in ordering the steps in an argument.

WORKING IN THE LABORATORY

Here are some hints on good attitudes and habits for laboratory work:

1. *Do not trust your memory.* Write down everything you think may be pertinent. Some things that you observe in the laboratory may seem to be so clear at the time that there is no point in writing them down. But memory fades; if an experiment is not completely written up when it is performed, you may not be able to recall important items. Figures 21.2 and 21.3 (pages 374 and 375) show some of the items that should be noted immediately.

2. *Make a permanent record of your observations.* Keep a full record of your calculations, observations, and results in a special notebook; don't ever write anything down on separate scraps of paper—not even your arithmetical calculations. If you make mistakes, cross them out and go on from there, but keep everything as part of your complete record. Start your record of each experiment or laboratory session on a new page, headed with the date. This will give you a permanent log of all your data and your thinking, regarding every problem on which you have worked— the raw materials for your final report.

3. *Organize the recorded data.* Arrange the data so that they will be clear and fully labeled for later reference. The few extra minutes you spend to make neat and orderly records during the lab period will save you time that you might later have to spend in deciphering sloppy notes. (See Figure 21.3.)

4. *Do not trust yourself or the apparatus too much.* It is unwise to record a lot of untested numbers, dismantle the apparatus, and leave the laboratory before knowing whether your data are of any use. It is much better to do at least an approximate analysis (including rough graphs) of the data while they are being taken. Such a check will give you a chance to detect anything that is going wrong, in time to do something about it—such as readjusting the apparatus, checking or repeating an observation, or asking your instructor for assistance.

5. *Baby the apparatus.* Poor performance in a laboratory is often due to carelessness, but it may also be the result of an uncooperative attitude: being too ready to say the apparatus doesn't work, or to believe it is limited in capability. The trick is to regard the apparatus as your friend, not your opponent. Treat it tenderly, and coax out of it all the accuracy it is capable of. Make notes of its limitations. And watch the apparatus like a hawk for signs of strange behavior. No real equipment is quite like the ideal version pictured in a textbook or laboratory manual; each piece of apparatus has an individual personality.

6. *Keep the purpose of the experiment in mind.* This can save you much wasted effort, and keep you from overlooking the main point of the lab work.

7. *Write up your reports clearly, legibly, and concisely, in the proper*

Figure 21.2 Diagram of a Loading-Jig Apparatus, as Part of a Laboratory Report

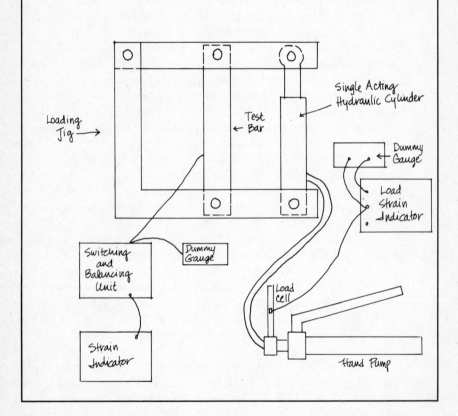

```
Experiment #3053 - Strain Measurements
October 27th

    The purpose of this experiment is to determine stress
sustained by a rectangular bar by means of wire resistance
strain gauges. Six of these gauges are taped onto different
positions on the bar, then strain readings taken, during
both loading and unloading processes, and the results con-
verted to stress by using appropriate equations.
```

form. The writing style should be impersonal; in technical reports it is customary to use the passive voice. The usual laboratory report contains as many of the following items as apply (see also Figure 21.4, p. 376):

Purpose (object): A statement explaining what the problem is.

Theory: The background for the problem and the justification for your method of attack.

Apparatus (equipment, materials): A listing and brief description of the essential apparatus, often including a sketch of the apparatus.

Figure 21.3 Page from a Student's Record Book, Showing Raw Data Gathered Directly from Measurements Made by Instruments

Experiment 3057 - October 27

Measurement of displacement, velocity and acceleration
EQUIPMENT: (a) Linear Variable Differential Transformer;
(b) an Oscilloscope ; (c) an accelerometer; (d) an
Analyzer-Recorder; (e) a Vibrating Table.

- -

Raw Data

FREQ (CPS)	DISPLACEMENT	VELOCITY	ACCELERATION
40	Micro (mm) 1.6176 } Δ=101.9 mils 1.358 } VIB. MTR. 97 mils	VIB. MTR. 29.2 $\frac{in}{sec}$	V.M. 9300 (in/sec²)
30	Micro (mm) 1.621 } Δ= 96.8 mils 1.375 } VIB. MTR. 98 mils	VIB. MTR. 21.9 $\frac{in}{sec}$	V.M. 5100 (in/sec²)
20	Micro (mm) 1.609 } Δ= 94.7 mils 1.369 }	VIB. MTR. 14.9 $\frac{in}{sec}$	V.M. 2950 (in/sec²)
10	Micro (mm) 1.607 } Δ= 96.3 mils 1.363 } VIB. MTR. 102 mils	VIB. MTR. 6.9 $\frac{in}{sec}$	V.M. 1020 (in/sec²)

Procedure: A step-by-step report of what you did.

Results: A step-by-step record of your observations.

Conclusion: A summary of your findings and an assessment of their accuracy, showing how your results succeed or fail in resolving the problem.

Figure 21.4 A Student's Abbreviated Work-Type Lab Report

Experiment 34

A. PURPOSE: To observe the increase in birefringence of
nylon by increasing the orientation of fibers through
stretching, despite the thinning of the nylon by necking.

B. PROCEDURE
   (a) A narrow strip of thin transparent nylon sheet,
   stretched in some spots and not stretched in others,
   was observed between crossed polarizers with low
   magnification.
   (b) About 1 mm diameter as-extruded nylon monofilament was stretched and the necking observed.
   (c) Textile-grade nylon fiber was observed as-
   extruded and stretched. The diameters and polarization colors of each region of the fiber were noted.

C. RESULTS
   (a)

unstretched nylon;
polarization colors:
1st order white.

stretched nylon;
polarization colors:
3rd order red and
green.

   (b) Nylon monofilament necked abruptly, rather than
   breaking, when pulled:

   (c) 16 mm objective, 1 eyepiece micrometer division =
   16.0 μ

	Diameter	Converted diameter	Retardation
Unstretched	4.3 div.	68.8 μ	200 μ
Stretched	1.9 div.	30.4 μ	1850 μ

	Birefringence
Unstretched	0.003
Stretched	0.059

D. CONCLUSIONS
   Unstretched nylon fiber exhibited a 1st order white
   polarization color, i.e., showed very low birefringence. The birefringence was calculated to be
   about 0.003.
      When pulled in tension, the nylon fiber necked
   abruptly. The stretched portion of the sample showed
   3rd order and higher polarization colors, despite
   decreased thickness. This was due to a marked increase
   in birefringence, to about 0.059, resulting from the
   parallel orientation of fibers effected by stretching.
      Without polarizers, the nylon fiber appeared
   slightly greyed or opaqued where stretched. Orienting
   the polymer fibers leads to a decrease in clarity. Also,
   the stretching results in mechanical discontinuities
   which would tend to scatter the light.

Above all in writing a report, remember that your purpose is to make your findings understandable to a reader. Make full use of your writing skills (see Chapter 20).

SUMMARY

How is learning science different from learning other subjects?	There are two differences. First, the terms, facts, and principles must be learned precisely. Second, the facts and problems are quantitative in nature.
What is "learning in clusters"?	Briefly, it is finding the relations among various pieces of information and then grouping the information in your mind according to those relations. It makes remembering much easier.
How can we improve our notetaking in science lectures?	There are three ways. First, concentrate on the ideas that are being presented, rather than on the words themselves. Second, use the Cornell System, which allows you to take, review, recite, and consolidate your notes more easily. Convert your notes into master summary sheets as a part of your studying.
What's the best time to ask a question in class?	At the beginning of the lecture. Questions asked at this time are usually well thought out. And the instructor may want to make use of them in the class discussion.
What is mental visualization?	This is the way most of us understand abstract concepts, whether we realize it or not. With mental visualization you create a picture in your mind's eye. As soon as you do, the concept becomes easier to see and remember.
What's the best way to solve a test problem?	Remember how you solved it before. This recall requires experience, and the only way you can get experience is with plenty of practice. Work out all the assigned problems, and then look for some more to work on.
How should I handle a type of problem that I've never faced?	Be logical and systematic about it. First, figure out just what you need to find. Then try to plot a logical course from the given quantities to the unknown quantities, or

vice versa. Once you have plotted this course, convert it into one or more equations and solve them.

What's the key to answering discussion questions?

Figure out just what sort of answer the question requires. Then try to connect it with your clusters of learned facts and principles. Once you've made the connection, write out your answer in clear, precise language.

What is the object of the seven hints for doing lab work?

It's the same objective you have in writing lab reports: to make sure you have all the information or data you need, in a logical and legible form, to communicate your lab results clearly and precisely.

HAVE YOU MISSED SOMETHING?

1. **SENTENCE-COMPLETION.** Complete the following sentences with one of the three words listed below each sentence.

   a. The secret of solving science problems is _____.

   practice   genius   questioning

   b. In science lectures, it's best to take notes on ideas, not _____.

   words   facts   principles

2. **MATCHING.** In each blank space in the left column, write the number preceding the phrase in the right column that matches the left item best.

   _____ a. Clustering

   _____ b. Precision

   _____ c. Questioning

   _____ d. Metric system

   _____ e. Writing skill

   _____ f. Maxwell

   1. Used for scientific measurement
   2. Realized that people mentally visualize abstract concepts
   3. Characteristic of the sciences
   4. Needed to do good lab reports
   5. Helps to fill gaps in understanding
   6. Placing facts and ideas into groups and categories

3. **TRUE-FALSE.** Write *T* beside the *true* statements and *F* beside the *false* statements that follow.

   _____ a. Complex problems are often made up of simple parts.

_____ b. No real practice is needed in order to answer a discussion question.

_____ c. A science should be studied as if it consists of isolated facts.

_____ d. A quantitative principle is one that is stated in mathematical terms.

_____ e. Your lab equipment is almost always right and should be trusted.

4. **MULTIPLE-CHOICE.** Choose the word that completes the following sentence most accurately, and circle the letter that precedes it.

A standard lab report need *not* include the

a. purpose.
b. argument.
c. procedure.
d. apparatus.

Genuine good taste consists in saying much in few words, in choosing among our thoughts, in having order and arrangement in what we say, and in speaking with composure.

—FENELON

22

Speaking Effectively

Friends, Romans, countrymen: All these people—and many more—could use some pointers about making a good speech. Could you? This chapter discusses . . .

- The outline for a speech
- How to plan your own speech
- How to rehearse a speech
- How to give a speech

as well as

- How to present a written report orally

*I*N COLLEGE YOU WILL ALMOST CERTAINLY be called on to give speeches or other oral presentations from time to time. If that doesn't exactly make you jump with joy, you are not alone. Yet the ability to speak effectively before a group is not difficult to develop, and it is a skill that you can use all your life.

Even experienced and successful speakers may feel apprehensive before giving a speech. But they have learned to convert nervous tension into constructive energy that actually makes them alert, vigorous, and effective in speaking. To make nervous energy work for you, rather than against you, you must be (1) fully prepared to do your job, and (2) motivated by a strong and sincere desire to communicate to your audience. This means knowing your subject well; taking ample time to think about and plan what you will say; evaluating your topic in terms of your intended listeners; and concentrating on giving them something of interest and value. In a word, it means that you must be audience-minded instead of self-centered. This mental attitude will affect every stage of your speech, from the planning through the delivery.

THE PLAN FOR A SPEECH

The ideal plan for a speech or oral report is a very detailed outline that contains 30 to 50 percent of the number of words in the actual speech. It is thus much fuller than an outline for a written paper, but is far from the word-for-word speech. From it, you can see the order and relationship of ideas, distinguish main ideas from supporting materials, and note where the major transitions come. The plan helps you learn the speech as a complete, organized pattern of ideas, so that you avoid the rote memorization, which often results in a parrot-like delivery.

Basic Parts of the Outline

The outline consists of four parts: the introduction, purpose statement, body, and conclusion.

1. *Introduction.* In the introduction you try to win the *good will, attention,* and *interest* of your listeners. You may use such devices as a striking example, statistic, or quotation, an interesting but relevant anecdote, or material relating the topic to something the audience is already interested in. The introduction should also provide any *background information* the audience is likely to need, such as definitions of important terms, or the historical or social context.

2. *Purpose statement.* Your statement of purpose tells your audience just what you intend to cover. You should state your topic and either list

the main points you intend to cover or explain your basic strategy in the speech. This will give your audience a chance to follow along as the speech unfolds.

The purpose statement usually comes at or near the end of the introduction. You should write it out completely in your outline, in clear, direct language that you will use in your speech. As an example, suppose your introduction reminds the audience that they have studied the way various film directors prepare to shoot films. Then you might state your purpose as follows:

> Today, I will explain how Ingmar Bergman prepares to make a film. I will consider three main points: how he gets his initial ideas, how he plans the scenario, and how he selects the cast and locations. On each of these three points I will contrast his methods with those of other major directors we have studied.

3. *Body.* The body or main part of the speech should take up between 65 and 90 percent of the speech. In this part you develop the topic stated in your purpose statement. The main points listed in your purpose statement now become the main headings in the body.

4. *Conclusion.* The conclusion is essentially a summary of the main points given in the body of the speech. It also allows you an opportunity to round off the speech smoothly by referring to something mentioned in the introduction, by extending the ideas of the speech, or by specifically relating the speech to the audience.

Components of the Speech

A speech may be thought of as consisting of main ideas, supporting materials, and transitions. A good speaker gives close attention to each of these components, separately and in combination.

MAIN OR KEY IDEAS.   Shrewd speakers do not expect an audience to remember hundreds of details. Instead, they try to convey only a few key ideas (for example, the four main stages in building a house, or five characteristics of Hemingway's prose style), and they construct the speech so as to help the audience grasp and remember these ideas. Some of the audience may remember subordinate points also, but these are used primarily to make the key ideas clearer and more memorable.

Thus, when you outline your speech, you must have a precise idea of the main points you wish to put across, and the best order in which to present them. You must then build your outline on these points, ensuring that every item in the body of the speech contributes to a main idea. In this way you make sure you will not digress or backtrack, and thereby confuse your audience.

SUPPORTING MATERIALS. Supporting materials help your listeners understand, accept, and remember your main ideas. They provide evidence for the main points, relate the subject to the knowledge and experience of the audience, and maintain interest. They are used more in speaking than in writing, to give the audience a chance to absorb and accept the main points—because a listener cannot stop to think about or look back at a main point.

Supporting materials should be specific. They may include *factual data*, such as names, dates, places and events; *examples*, which can be either real occurrences or ones you make up to illustrate your point; *descriptions* of how things look, feel, sound, smell, or taste; *comparisons* and *contrasts* with things familiar to the audience; *expert testimony* or *opinion*, cited or quoted; or *literary quotations*, when they are apt. *Statistics* can be useful, but must be handled with care since they are harder to take in by ear than by eye. If they can be translated into concrete or pictorial terms, so much the better. For example, suppose you stated the estimated number of gallons of water wasted by leaky plumbing over a period of time. You might also state the number of homes that could be fully supplied by this wasted water in the same time period.

A special type of supporting material is *visual aids*, which include blackboard or chartboard drawings, poster-type materials displayed on an easel, three-dimensional models, specimens, and films. Visual aids are useful in holding the audience's attention, presenting statistical data (as in graphs), and explaining complicated structures or processes. You should prepare your visual aids in advance and practice with them, to avoid having to think about them when you give your speech.

TRANSITIONS. Transitions help emphasize your main ideas and enable your audience to move with you from one point to the next. If your transitions are not clear, your listeners will become confused. An oral presentation requires far more transitional material than writing, and the transitions must be more obvious and repetitive than those used in writing.

There is a variety of oral transitions. You may emphasize a main idea by *restatement*, saying it twice in different words. This gives your listeners a better chance—a little more time—to grasp the idea and see that it is relatively important.

Another transitional device is *pre-outlining*. Near the beginning of your speech, perhaps within the purpose statement, you may outline the main points you intend to take up. Similarly, at the beginning of each major section, after stating the main idea, you may outline the ground you intend to cover.

If your speech has several sections that are parallel in nature and importance, you may make use of *listing:* You can use either *enumeration* ("First, . . . , " "Second, . . . ," etc.), or a *key phrase* repeated for each main idea, or a combination of both ("The first type of jet engine is . . . ," "The second type of jet engine is . . .").

Connective transitions tell your audience that you are moving on to a new section of your speech and indicate how it is related to the previous section. Here's an example: "Now that we understand the problem that faced the engineer, let's see how he solved it."

Finally, in *internal summaries* you can condense and restate some or all of the points you have presented so far.

MAKING YOUR OWN SPEECH PLAN

Choosing a Topic

Many speakers get off to a bad start by selecting a topic that is too broad. In ten minutes of speaking, you can cover the equivalent of only five to seven typewritten pages. You should not try to get more than three or four main points across in such a short speech. Concentrate on getting these few points across clearly, rather than on packing your speech with information.

If you have a choice, pick a topic you are really interested in. Your interest, or lack of it, will be sensed by your listeners and will influence their reaction to your speech. Also, you will find the preparation of the speech more enjoyable if you are really interested in the topic.

State your topic in one simple sentence that will serve as a tentative purpose statement. Make sure it is clearly focused. Avoid such vague wording as, "I am going to talk about speech preparation and how it makes things easier"; instead, rephrase this as, "This morning, I will explain the five steps in the efficient preparation of a speech."

The Preliminary Overview

Search your mind for information, ideas, opinions, and bits of supporting material on the topic and for ideas about further sources of information. List them all, so that you can use the list as a guide in gathering additional information. If you start from what *you* know and think, your own personality will emerge in the speech. This will provide some originality and perhaps even a fresh outlook on the topic.

At this stage you may also want to discuss your topic with friends or experts, and check the library to see how much material is available on your topic.

Break your subject down into the main areas or ideas you want to cover. Your topic statements for these areas will become the tentative main headings in the body of your speech.

Doing the Research

Use the list you made in your preliminary overview to decide what material you must obtain from the library or other sources of information. If you have already checked to see what library sources are available, you can select the most promising ones to try first. Don't overlook your own experience and imagination as a resource, especially for supporting materials such as analogies, comparisons, and actual or hypothetical examples. But keep the needs of both your topic and your audience in mind as you do your research.

Preparing the Final Outline

At this point, you should have a good idea as to what your purpose statement will be, since it is the focus of your speech. The introduction and conclusion are usually planned after the body of the speech—unless you get an inspired idea while you are doing research or working on the body.

The outline for the body of the speech should be taking shape around your main headings while you are doing your research. When you have all your material together, plan the exact phrasing of your statements of main ideas, sub-ideas, and transitions. Write these down in oral style, just as you intend to say them in the speech. For example, say, "As my last point, I will explain the great care Bergman uses in selecting his cast and locations," rather than, "Bergman takes great care in selecting his cast and locations."

Now write in your supporting materials, as sub-entries under the proper main headings; but don't write them out in full as you did the main statements and transitions. A few words to remind you are enough. If you mess up a main idea or a transition, your whole structure may come crashing down. But if you slip up on a supporting detail or two, the consequences are not serious. Moreover, your delivery will be more spontaneous if you develop supporting details from notes rather than from pre-planned sentences.

At least two days before you are to give your speech, go over your outline to put it in final form. Make sure that you have sufficient supporting materials and that they are relevant to the main ideas; that irrelevant material is deleted; that you have sufficient, clear transitions; and that your key ideas are clearly and forcefully phrased.

PREPARING TO DELIVER THE SPEECH

Learn Your Ideas Thoroughly

First, read your outline through several times, both silently and aloud. Your aim should be to learn the sequence of ideas, not to memorize words and sentences. To fix the sequence in your memory, test yourself with such questions as, "What are my main points?" and "How do I explain my third main idea?" or "What transition do I use after the section on . . . ?"

Next, say your speech aloud a few times, referring to your outline when necessary. Time yourself to be sure you meet the required time limit. Keep thinking in terms of ideas, not phrases and sentences. Remember that oral speech patterns are more conversational and less formal than written ones.

To maintain contact with the audience when you give your speech, you may want to use conventional speaking notes—an abbreviated outline of words and phrases, typed or written on 4 × 6 cards. These notes will help you keep to your plan but will not tempt you into reading, as your full outline might.

Practice Your Delivery

With your speech plan well in mind and your notes in hand, you are ready to practice delivering your speech. Try to duplicate the actual speaking situation as closely as possible. If possible, practice your speech in the room or hall where you are to give it, with a few friends serving as the audience. At least rehearse the speech standing up and aloud. This is your chance to experience the physical "feel" of speechmaking. Pay attention to your gestures and your voice, and decide what you are going to do with your hands. Use your speaking notes so you will be accustomed to them. Speak loudly enough to be heard at the back of the room, and try to look alert and confident. Practice sessions are the time to take care of the mechanics of your delivery; when you actually present the speech, you will want to concentrate on getting your ideas across to your listeners.

Go through the speech from beginning to end. Keep right on going even if you make mistakes—you can give special attention to troublesome parts later. Some students can get by with one or two trial runs; others need ten or a dozen. In either case, practice is more valuable if it is spread over two or three days. Even for a simple class report, you should avoid the temptation to practice only at the last minute, or not at all. Remember that practice is what produces confident and effective delivery.

FACING THE AUDIENCE

No matter how much you practice, some things can be worked out only in the actual speaking situation. Effective speakers are sensitive to the response of their listeners and will make minor adjustments as necessary. For example, they will slow down and insert internal summaries if listeners seem confused, or omit some supporting material and get on to the next point if they seem restless.

An important element in speaking is good eye contact with the audience. You should be in a genuine two-way relationship with your listeners, and this is impossible if you are looking at the ceiling or the floor, or staring at your notes or your hands. When you talk with individuals, you look directly at them; do the same with your audience. You should have some eye contact with all the audience, but your confidence will be increased if your eye contact is mainly with the more attentive listeners.

Don't let yourself sag or lean against a desk or speaking stand, and keep from fiddling with a pencil or a ring or your note cards. Stand erect, but be free to gesture and move naturally. (Remember that the time to develop effective gestures, movement, and posture is during your practice sessions.)

Speak loudly and clearly enough to be heard and understood. Vary your rate and pitch to hold the attention and interest of your listeners. As a rule, you should speak more slowly and formally when you are giving main ideas or difficult material, and more rapidly and conversationally when you are citing examples or narrating anecdotes. And don't be afraid to pause. Good speakers often use pauses to emphasize important points or to recapture an audience's wandering attention. If you forget what comes next, take time for an unhurried look at your notes. Don't fill the time with uh's or um's or other vocal fillers.

AN ORAL PRESENTATION
OF A WRITTEN REPORT

In some classes you may be asked to make an oral presentation of a paper that you must also hand in as a written report. This can present a problem, for two reasons. Oral and written presentations differ in several significant ways, and the written report may be too long to be given orally in the allotted time. There are three ways of solving the problem:

1. You can write your paper and then use it as source material for your oral report. This solution can produce an effective oral presentation, but it requires that you prepare two reports—one written and one oral.

2. You can write the paper with the idea of oral presentation primarily in mind. But this has disadvantages too. For one thing, *writing* a speech is a specialized skill. Moreover, the things that help make an oral presentation a success—the restatement and repetition, the numerous transitions, the many supporting materials, the personal and conversational tone—may be criticized as flaws in a written report. (See Figure 22.1.)

3. Probably the best plan is to write the report as you normally would, and then *adapt* it to oral presentation. On a clean copy of the written report, note (but do not write out in full) the supplementary supporting materials and transitions you intend to add when you give the report orally. By only noting these items, allow yourself the chance to work in some conversational spontaneity. Practice reading the paper

Figure 22.1 Contrasting Written and Oral Presentations. Notice how the lecturer restates and repeats the points and uses obvious transitions to help the audience move from point to point.

	Writer	Speaker
Beginning	Nothing in English history contains such tragic overtones as the Battle of Hastings.	Last hour we discussed the political events that led to the Battle of Hastings. Let us turn now to the tragedy itself.
Thesis	But a divided England was less the cause of downfall than Norman lances vs. English axes.	Thus the English had to fight without the army that was still in the north. More important the Normans wore armor and fought on horseback, while the English had no armor and fought on foot.
Transition	The Normans fought with propaganda too; the Pope was on their side.	Third, it is important to remember that the Pope favored William, and his standard on the field frightened many English from the battle.
Conclusion	Everything lent William power and conspired to change the fate of England.	To sum up, then, a divided England, superior weapons, and the favor of the Church gave William the advantage in every area of the conflict.

aloud until you can look up from it frequently to establish eye contact with your audience. Know exactly where the supplementary oral materials come in, and practice moving smoothly from reading to speaking and back to reading again.

SUMMARY

What's the key to a good speech?

A detailed, well-thought-out outline. A good outline contains 30 to 50 percent of the actual speech. It provides the most important sentences, written as they should be delivered. At the same time it allows you to be spontaneous. If you bring the whole speech with you, you'll be reading, not speaking. Your audience will become restless when they see that your eyes are glued to your notes.

What sort of things go into a good introduction?

Your introduction should give the audience a reason to listen. It may provide some particularly interesting examples, statistics (not too many!), quotations, or anecdotes relative to your subject. It may also include the background that your audience may need before they can understand the main ideas in the body.

Must all speeches have a purpose statement?

Almost without exception. The purpose statement is the first big clue that the audience will get. It tells them where your speech will be heading and just what sort of topics you're going to cover. That allows the audience to follow the development of your explanation or argument.

How much of a speech should be devoted to the body?

That depends on the nature of your subject and how well you plan to develop it. The main points of the purpose statement are the main headings of your body. Each heading must be reinforced by enough supporting material to effectively explain it. With this much material, the body can take up anywhere from 60 to 90 percent of your speech.

How does a speech's conclusion come to the rescue?

The conclusion is your chance to tie things together. It gives you the opportunity to save yourself and your speech if, for some reason, it left your audience confused.

Won't just a few main ideas make for a very short speech?

No! You'd be surprised at just how much time it takes to explain and support a few main ideas so the audience will remember them. If you try and pack too much into your speech, your listeners may leave remembering next to nothing.

What is the purpose of transitions?

Transitions move the audience from one point to another. They are more than the links in writing. Spoken transitions have the extra job of emphasizing the main ideas. They can also give listeners the time they need to reflect on what's been said.

What should I look for when I'm choosing a topic?

Your topic should be specific and interesting to you. If it is too broad, you won't be able to cover it well. If it doesn't interest you, then you'll have a hard time getting your audience interested in it.

Can I write out my entire speech?

No, don't! Write out your purpose statement, main ideas, sub-ideas, and transitions, but outline your supporting materials. Also plan your introduction and conclusion carefully.

Is rehearsing necessary? I feel silly.

You'll feel sillier when you stumble over your main ideas before a real audience. Rehearsal is essential to a good speech; and the closer the rehearsal situation is to the actual speaking situation, the better.

What can I do to help improve audience response?

Do three things. Look at your audience, not at the floor or the ceiling; stand up straight when you're speaking; and vary the pitch of your voice and your talking speed.

What's the best way to give an oral report on a written paper?

On a copy of your written report, note down some supporting materials and transitions—but don't write them out completely. When you give your oral report, read the main points from your paper, but present the supporting materials and transitions conversationally, as in a speech.

HAVE YOU MISSED SOMETHING?

1. **SENTENCE-COMPLETION.** Complete the following sentences with one of the three words listed below each sentence.

   a. In the introduction of a speech, you seek your listeners' good will, attention, and _____.

   interest   questions   advantage

   b. Inexperienced speakers often choose a topic that's too _____.

   broad   narrow   boring

2. **MATCHING.** In each blank space in the left column, write the number preceding the phrase in the right column that matches the left item best.

   _____ a. Purpose statement

   _____ b. Conclusion

   _____ c. Transition

   _____ d. 30 to 50%

   _____ e. 60 to 90%

   _____ f. Pausing

   1. Percentage of speech that should be contained in the outline
   2. Moves the audience from one point to another
   3. Tells the audience what you will cover
   4. Can recapture the audience's wandering attention
   5. Can effect a last-minute rescue of a vague speech
   6. Percentage of a speech that is devoted to the body

3. **TRUE-FALSE.** Write *T* beside the *true* statements and *F* beside the *false* statements that follow.

   _____ a. A good speech contains many main ideas.

   _____ b. Supporting materials are used more often in speaking than in writing.

   _____ c. The purpose statement comes near, or at the end of, the introduction.

   _____ d. Supporting materials should be written out precisely as they are going to be read.

   _____ e. It's best to start again if you make a mistake while rehearsing your speech.

4. **MULTIPLE-CHOICE.** Choose the phrase that completes the following sentence most accurately, and circle the letter that precedes it.

In outlining a speech, you should not write out the exact wording of the

a. main points.
b. introduction.
c. supporting points.
d. all of the above.

Appendix A

Chapter 1   Mastering Study Skills

1. a. flexibility   b. systematically
2. a. 4   b. 6   c. 1   d. 5   e. 2.   f. 3
3. a. F   b. T   c. F   d. T
4. c.

Chapter 2   Understanding Your Emotional and Physical Needs

1. a. procrastination   b. channeled
2. a. 3   b. 6   c. 1   d. 2   e. 4   f. 8   g. 9   h. 7   i. 5
3. a. T   b. T   c. T   d. T   e. T
4. a. Yes   c. Yes   f. Yes   g. Yes
5. c.

Chapter 3   Controlling Your Time

1. time
2. a. 4   b. 1   c. 2   d. 3   e. 6   f. 5
3. a. T   b. F   c. F   d. T   e. T
4. b. Yes   d. Yes   e. Yes   g. Yes
5. b.

Chapter 4   Concentrating to Learn

1. a. by-product   b. exercise
2. a. 3   b. 1   c. 4   d. 5   e. 6   f. 2
3. a. F   b. F   c. T   d. T
4. c.

Chapter 5   Forgetting and Remembering

1. a. regularity   b. sub-topic   c. organization
2. a. 2   b. 1   c. 3   d. 7   e. 5   f. 4   g. 6   h. 10   i. 9   j. 11   k. 8   1. 12
3. a. F   b. T   c. F   d. T   e. T   f. T
4. b. No   f. No
5. d.

Chapter 6   Listening and Notetaking

1. a. 80%   b. memorize
2. a. 4   b. 2   c. 5   d. 1   e. 3
3. a. T   b. T   c. F   d. F   e. T   f. F
4. a.

Chapter 7   Surveying Your Textbook

1. system
2. a. 3   b. 5   c. 1   d. 4   e. 2
3. a. T   b. F   c. T   d. T   e. F
4. a.

Chapter 8   Learning from Your Textbook

1. a. written   b. questions
2. a. 4   b. 5   c. 2   d. 6   e. 3   f. 1
3. a. T   b. T   c. F   d. F   e. T   f. F   g. F   h. T
4. c.
5. a. Yes   b. Yes   d. Yes

Chapter 9   Understanding Visual Materials

1. a. systematically   b. survey
2. a. 4   b. 3   c. 5   d. 2   e. 1   f. 6
3. a. T   b. F   c. T   d. T   e. F
4. c.
5. b. Yes   c. Yes   e. Yes   f. Yes

Chapter 10   Making Notes On (and From) Your Textbook

1. a. paragraph   b. meaningful   c. sketch
2. a. 3   b. 5   c. 2   d. 1   e. 4
3. a. T   b. F   c. T   d. T   e. F   f. F
4. b.

Chapter 11   Preparing for Tests

1. a. notes   b. panic
2. a. 3   b. 6   c. 4   d. 2   e. 1   f. 5
3. a. F   b. T   c. F   d. T   e. F   f. T
4. b.

Chapter 12   Answering True-False, Multiple-Choice, and Matching Questions

1. a. circled   b. correct
2. a. 3   b. 5   c. 6   d. 1   e. 4   f. 2
3. a. F   b. T   c. F   d. F   e. T   f. F
4. d.

Chapter 13   Answering Sentence-Completion and Short-Answer Questions

1. a. context   b. telegraphic
2. a. 4   b. 1   c. 5   d. 3   e. 6   f. 2
3. a. T   b. F   c. T   d. T   e. F   f. T
4. b.

Chapter 14   Answering Essay Questions

1. a. reasoning   b. question
2. a. 3   b. 6   c. 2   d. 5   e. 1   f. 4
3. a. F   b. T   c. T   d. T   e. F
4. b.

Chapter 15   Assessing Your Vocabulary

1. a. reading   b. definitions
2. a. 5   b. 6   c. 1   d. 2   e. 4   f. 3
3. a. T   b. T   c. F   d. F   e. T
4. d.

Chapter 16   Exploring and Analyzing Words

1. a. history   b. meaning
2. a. 5   b. 4   c. 2   d. 1   e. 3
3. a. F   b. T   c. T   d. F
4. d.

Chapter 17   Learning Words with the Frontier System

1. a. context   b. precisely
2. a. 6   b. 3   c. 1   d. 4   e. 2   f. 5
3. a. F   b. F   c. F   d. T   e. T
4. c.

Chapter 18   Improving Your Reading Speed

1. a. speed   b. naturally
2. a. 2   b. 5   c. 3   d. 1   e. 4
3. a. F   b. F   c. T   d. T   e. F   f. T
4. a.

Chapter 19   Ten More Techniques for Improving Your Reading

1. a. magnets   b. information
2. a. 3   b. 5   c. 4   d. 7   e. 1   f. 2   g. 6
3. a. F   b. T   c. T   d. T   e. T   f. F
4. d.

Chapter 20   Researching and Writing Papers

1. a. plagiarism   b. dangling
2. a. 3   b. 6   c. 2   d. 1   e. 4   f. 5
3. a. T   b. F   c. T   d. T   e. F
4. a.

Chapter 21   Studying Science

1. a. practice   b. words
2. a. 6   b. 3   c. 5   d. 1   e. 4   f. 2

3. a. T b. F c. F d. T e. F
4. b.

Chapter 22   Speaking Effectively

1. a. interest b. broad
2. a. 3 b. 5 c. 2 d. 1 e. 6 f. 4
3. a. F b. T c. T d. F e. F
4. c.

Appendix B

ANSWERS TO PSAT AND SAT TESTS

Table 15.1 Answers to PSAT Vocabulary Test

Question Number	Correct Answer	Grade Level*	Percentage of Students Answering the Question Correctly†
1	D	6	68%
2	B	12	30
3	E	8	87
4	C	6	69
5	E	6	73
6	A	10	70
7	B	10	72
8	D	12	79
9	B	13	64
10	E	16	63
11	E	10	75
12	C	16	79
13	A	16	79
14	D	16	23
15	E	12	47
16	D	16	40
17	A	16	50
18	D	16	71
19	B	16	59
20	A	16	59

*Grade levels of students who attained the listed percentages.

†Percentage scores of students in specified grade levels as determined by Edgar Dale and Joseph O'Rourke in *The Living Word Vocabulary* (Chicago: Field Enterprises Educational Corporation, 1976).

Table 15.2 Answers to SAT Vocabulary Test

Question Number	Correct Answer	Percentage of Students Answering the Question Correctly
1	E	96%
2	C	95
3	B	90
4	B	87
5	A	85
6	D	80
7	E	80
8	A	71
9	B	75
10	C	69
11	C	66
12	B	68
13	D	55
14	D	35
15	E	32
16	A	24
17	A	22
18	A	20
19	B	19
20	A	18
21	A	16
22	E	15
23	C	13
24	A	18
25	B	10

Index